MW01025553

CHASIA BORNSTEIN-BIELICKA
ONE OF THE FEW
A Resistance Fighter and Educator, 1939–1947

Neomi Izhar

CHASIA BORNSTEIN-BIELICKA
ONE OF THE FEW
A Resistance Fighter and Educator, 1939–1947

Yad Vashem ★ Jerusalem ★ 2009

Neomi Izhar
Chasia Bornstein-Bielicka
One of the Few
A Resistance Fighter and Educator, 1939–1947

Translated from the Hebrew by Naftali Greenwood

Language Editor: Leah Goldstein
Managing Editor: Daniella Zaidman-Mauer

This book may not be reproduced, in whole or part, in any form,
without written permission from the publisher.

Responsibility for the opinions expressed in this publication
is solely that of the author.

© 2009 All rights of the English edition are reserved to Yad Vashem
P.O. Box 3477, Jerusalem 91034, Israel
publications.marketing@yadvashem.org.il
First published in Hebrew by Moreshet – Mordechai Anielevich Memorial and
Research Center, Tel Aviv
www.moreshet.org

ISBN 978-965-308-352-3

Typesetting: Judith Sternberg
Produced by: Artplus

Printed in Israel

DEDICATION

Lovingly dedicated to Heini, my daughters Yehudit, Racheli, Dorit, my sons-in-law Yehiam, Stanley, Tsur, my grandchildren Sharon, Matti, Idan, Hadas, Keren, Yaniv, Liat, Eilon, Ofri, Ortal, Ya'ala, my great-granddaughters Adi, Maja, Yali, Gali, Lotan, and great-grandson Ziv

To the memory of my beloved family
and of those valorous fighting women and men

For almost sixty years I have been living with a sense of squandered opportunity, transgression and injustice, for not having visited our Polish benefactors after the war in order to thank them personally for their assistance and support in those tough times, when the whole world around us was hostile.

Allow me, then, to summon the memory of a few of those who stood
at our side:
Olla of Poleska Street, who helped us at the entrance to the ghetto during the resistance period; The geography teacher; Bronja Zynmuch, the dear woman who lived at the edge of town and whose home was our inn as we headed toward the forest.

And others whose names I do not know.

ACKNOWLEDGEMENTS

I would foremost like to thank Rutha and Felix Zandman, my dear friends, to whom I am especially grateful for their significant support of the publication of this book, and for the encouragement they gave me.

I am very grateful to Gabi Hadar, Director of Yad Vashem Publications, for her time and efforts in bringing this book to publication; to Naftali Greenwood, for his careful and fluid translation; to Leah Goldstein for her fine editing; and to Daniella Zaidman-Mauer, for her devotion and sensitive understanding of the proposals I offered, and for seeing this book to fruition.

I wish to express special gratitude to Amira Hagani, the former director of Moreshet, The Mordechai Anielevich Memorial for convincing me that I should write my memoirs of the war years, and for persistently assuring me and providing the necessary conditions for the publication of the original Hebrew edition of this book. I am so appreciative of her sensitive and topical approach to the project. The relations of understanding we created were very important to me; to Mario Rapaport, Director of the Publications Department at Moreshet, who devoted much thought to the design of the book so it would be aesthetic, unique and contextually accurate; to Neomi Izhar, for her devotion and willingness to sit with me day and night in order to interview me and craft my remarks into a permanent record; to Prof. Dr. Heiko Haumann, head of the Historical Seminar at the University of Basel, for his important historical advice regarding the original text of the book.

Last but not least, I would like to thank Heini, my beloved husband, who entreated me for years to write my memoirs. He stood by me, encouraged me, and offered useful and important advice as this book was being written; To my daughters, sons-in-law and grandchildren, who kept an alert and curious eye on me as this book was being written. Their interest in the project strengthened and encouraged me, by communicating the immense value that the publication of the book would have for them, the second- and third-generation survivors of my family.

Chasia Bornstein-Bielicka

CONTENTS

PROLOGUE

This book contains the memories of my life, recorded and written more than fifty years since the events described. As I performed the reconstruction, I could not base myself on written words or on a personal diary or indeed on writings of any kind. All I had was a small fraction of the documents I had used during the resistance era. They were of little use to me in preparing the book.

Just the same, the events in my life have never slipped my mind and were never consigned to a bygone past. I have lived and experienced them day after day, night after night. My three daughters knew what I had been up to. I told them how, as a young girl, I had been one of the women who fought the Germans, and I dwelled with particular emphasis on the history of the group of children I had helped raise immediately after the war and whom I led to the Land of Israel. Nevertheless, I did not envelop my family in a cloud of melancholy and allow the memory of the Holocaust to overshadow our lives.

As I said, more than fifty years passed until I was willing to allow my story to enter the public domain. For long hours, Naomi Yitzhar of Kibbutz Gan Shmuel interviewed me, took notes, and recorded what she had heard. As the book was being prepared, my family worked up a plan to go to Poland and visit the places that are meaningful for me. For years I had refused to set foot on Polish soil ever again. However, my daughters and my husband, Heini, entreated me to undertake the journey. At the age of eighty, I overcame my hesitations and became ready for the experience of encountering what remained of my past.

I made the trip to Poland with Heini, the three girls — Yehudit, Racheli and Dorit — and Naomi Yitzhar. I returned to my house in Grodno, the area where the ghetto had been, the school I had attended, and the Movement House of my Hashomer Hatzair cell. To my amazement, the sites and buildings remained intact. Thus I returned, as it were, to a family that no longer existed, and to the Jewishness of my town, which had been destroyed in the war. We also visited Białystok. We stepped into the house I had lived in as a Polish girl, and from where I had set forth on all the resistance operations. We stood across from the office of Otto Busse, my German civilian boss who became an assistant and collaborator with the resistance. We toured the ghetto area, where the uprising took place. We stood facing the monuments to the resistance fighters, where I communed with many of my fallen fighting comrades. We drove along the road to the forest, where I and others had walked tens of kilometers at night, laden with gear, to the partisans' camps. We stood at the foot of the monument to the Grodno Jewish community at Treblinka, where in a moving ceremony prepared by the girls we honored the memories of my family members murdered there. In Warsaw, we stood in silence at Miła 18 and other memorial sites to the Jews of Warsaw and the heroism of the uprising.

I spent six days immersed in my past. My family members returned amazed and agitated after palpably experiencing the meaning of the Holocaust and the valor of the resistance members in combat. The experience of the journey left me firmly convinced that it was imperative to create a written account of my actions during the Holocaust.

When the war ended, I began a new chapter in my life. I opened the first children's home of the Zionist Coordination for the Redemption of Children. Some of the children in the home had been claimed from convents and the homes of non-Jewish Poles; others had been found in railroad stations after they had returned from the Soviet Union or emerged from various places of hiding. Our task was to return them to the bosom of their people. After counseling these children at the home in Łódź, I found creative ways to move them to Germany and France, from where we sailed to Mandatory Palestine on the clandestine immigrants' vessel *Theodor Herzl*. These children are my "present," in the sense of my here and now. We still stay in touch. Today they are happy grandparents. My activities in the resistance during the war have altogether receded into the past and the domain of memory. However, I do have partners — some men but mostly women, my few surviving friends from the resistance period — in the commemoration of those bygone days. Today they are my sisters, partners in the ineradicable intensity of the personal relations we formed in combat together.

I started life anew. Wishing to build a home from the ground up, I joined Lehavot Habashan, then a new kibbutz near the Syrian border. I lived in a tent and endured all of Israel's wars. I established a large, warm and devoted family: a husband whom I cherish, three charming daughters, and their life partners, three delightful sons-in-law. Today I have eleven grandchildren and six great-grandchildren.

The pages of this book are a personal testimony. They recall my murdered family. They also reflect an era in Jewish history and the steadfastness of a movement. I was one of a few, a young girl from Grodno. Most of my comrades in arms fell or were murdered. Their images have accompanied me throughout my life with growing impact, and their memory has accompanied me in the writing of this book.

CHAPTER 1

Home

My paternal grandfather, Avraham Weiss, had a large farm in Grandzice, a village not far from Grodno. I don't know if his name was really Avraham and whether the family name was really Weiss, but that's what my memory tells me. Antisemitic laws passed under Poland's new state constitution dispossessed the Jews of their estates. At the counsel of his Polish neighbors, Avraham polonized his Jewish surname to Bielicki, a coinage that preserved the "whiteness" of Weiss.

My family's house stood in a spacious courtyard bordered by three other houses, a factory that belonged to us, and a spacious garden with a hillock at its far end. It was known as "Lilac Hill," because it was covered by a profusion of lilac bushes in pink, white and purple — a sea of colors and fragrances.

A fence of slats stood at the top of Lilac Hill. Beyond it was the Pravoslav cemetery. We children would pull out some nails, push a few slats aside, and sneak in to see the lovely tombstones, flowers, gilded crosses, and the funerals.

Our garden sprawled from the base of the hill to the courtyard demarcated by the houses. Fruits and berries grew there: plums, cherries, apples, red and yellow mulberries, red raspberries, gooseberries and black *samarodiny*. The bushes were drowned in a thick overgrowth of thorny nettles. To reach the fruit, we girls would put on Mother's long dresses for protection, and only then cross the stinging nettle fields on the way to the coveted fruit. The fruit that attracted me was almost always green and raw, but I loved it and ate it even when it was sour. The resulting bellyache caused me to double over, but I made sure not to tell Mother our secret.

My favorite object in the whole garden was the pear tree, a monster of a tree that we loved to climb, my brother Avramele and me, and afterwards Rocheleh and Zipporka, too. We older kids hoisted our little sisters into the tree, lowered them back to earth, picked the fruit and hid in the branches.

One spring, as the tree wore a jacket of white and green flowers, we woke up one morning after a stormy night and found the tree completely blackened. It had been struck by lightning. What a frightening thing it was to see all of a sudden: a black tree in the heart of the green garden. The tree I had loved so much had become a charred effigy, silent and sooty. For years afterwards I dreamed at night about black monsters emerging from its burnt branches.

My paternal grandfather, Avraham Weiss, had a large farm in Grandzice, a village not far from Grodno. I don't know if his name was really Avraham and whether the family name was really Weiss, but that's what my memory tells me and there's no one left to ask.

The peace treaties that followed World War I had made Poland an independent state. Antisemitic laws passed under Poland's new state constitution dispossessed the Jews of their estates. At the counsel of his Polish neighbors, Avraham polonized his Jewish surname to Bielicki, a coinage that preserved the "whiteness" of Weiss. However, the name change brought Grandpa no real benefit. He was known as a Jewish farm owner who had managed to sell his farm before he lost it. He used the proceeds to buy the large courtyard and the huge garden in Grodno. Such courtyards existed only in the suburbs, the Polish areas. Few Jews lived there, but Grandpa refused to part from his land.

I was born in one of the buildings that abutted the courtyard. I spent a significant part of my life there, at 72 Podolna Street, a.k.a. Rabelees Gasse or (as the Jews called it) Rebbe Eliyahu Street, on the way to the Grodno railroad bridge.

My grandparents had four children: Aunt Manya, my father Yehuda, Uncle Chaim and Aunt Rosa. Grandpa Bielicki had died before I was born. Grandma had died before they'd left the estate.

My maternal grandparents, Velvel and Sarah-Chaya Jablonski, lived in the Forstat, a suburb of Grodno at the western approach to town, on the slope across the Niemen River. Grandpa Velvel was a tinsmith — a small, slender man with grey hair and a mustache, a good Jew, quiet, taciturn and diffident. He would break his silence to tell jokes and parables and quote sayings and adages that have long since dissipated, along with the world in which he told them.

Velvel and Sarah-Chaya bore five daughters and two sons: Shifra, Pesia, Ita, Devorah (my mother), Sonya, Zeidel and Jakob.

After Grandpa Velvel died, Grandma Sarah-Chaya moved to our side of town, next to Aunt Sonya on Mostawa Street, across from the bridge to the Forstat. I was still a little girl then.

For years afterward, Grandma Sarah-Chaya kept her husband's felt cap and some of his working tools among the objects in her dowry trunk.

Grandma Sarah-Chaya was a woman of noble bearing, delicate, tiny, plumpish, and with an apron perpetually around her waist. She was warm, embracing, pampering. I loved her to the depths of my soul. She was an astounding raconteur, a consoler and a protector. Always wearing a dark skirt and a blouse with an embroidered collar. Coiffured, meticulous, clean.

Grandma always had something to warn about. When you go to school, don't cross the street if you see a black cat crossing it. Wait for some *goy* (gentile) to cross in front of you. Another object of bad luck in Grandma's eyes was an empty bucket. You had to hold it at arm's length, a slightly problematic thing to do in a town where distant neighborhoods obtained their drinking water from public wells and lots of people walked the streets with empty buckets in hand.

Once, when a dog bit me, Grandma hadn't provided me with a warning but did deliver commiseration. When I came in frightened from the encounter, my good Grandma said, "Come, let's do something." She lifted a pot of hot water off the gas jets, tossed a hunk of wax into it and, lo and behold, the wax melted before my very eyes. In the shapes that formed, Grandma and I saw a girl running and a dog chasing her.

Some time later, Grandma moved in with us. She brought along a dowry trunk containing the vestiges of her wedding gifts: a string of pearls kept in an old dark wooden case with black clips and hinges; a few pieces of china wrapped in paper and shreds of old sheets; a round, gold pin with a gem; and some embroidered tablecloths. It was a huge wooden trunk with protruding metal pieces and two locks. Grandma never locked it, but we respected her too much ever to open it without her permission. Instead, we asked her to play show-and-tell with her treasures.

She related stories folklore-style — flowing, chromatic and clever. She recounted her wedding to Grandpa, whom she met for the very first time under the wedding canopy. She told us about the string of pearls she had received, and wound around her neck seven times. She recalled her good neighbors, who sat at the entrance to the house at the end of the day, gossiping as women do. And she recounted that when her five daughters had reached maturity she wasn't concerned at all, because after she'd married off the first one, the boys in the neighborhood pounded on her window shutters and asked for *noch fun di zelbe*, more of the same.

Avramele was too old to eavesdrop by this time, but we girls seated ourselves around Grandma on the wooden floor and listened to her tales, always beginning with a promise: *Kinderlach, hot nisht moyre; der shrekt zikh nisht vayl der sof iz a guter. Shtendik endikt es gut.* Girls, don't be scared; the story isn't frightening. It all ends well. Then came the tales of Hans Christian Andersen, the fables of the Grimm Brothers and others of their genre — *Czerwony kapturek* (Little Red Riding Hood), *Yan i malgoshye* (Hansel and Gretel), and the Ugly Duckling, too, somewhere in there.

Father joked around and taunted her good-naturedly. Grandma, in turn, knocked him every day for the newspapers he read: *Vos iz haynt nayes in tzaytung?* What's new in the paper?!

Grandma died shortly before the war. They moved the table into a corner of the large room. Her body, wrapped in a sheet, was laid on the floor with white candles at its head, flickering in their lovely silver candlesticks. Mother baked little round rolls and served them, hot and fragrant, on a large tray. We arrayed ourselves around Grandma, seated on the floor or on low stools. I stared at the silhouette created by the sheet and the body, and pondered: there lies my Grandma, my Grandma who's dead. With all my strength I tried to force the fact of her death into my consciousness. Our consolation over Grandma's death came belatedly, when the war broke out. Whenever we mentioned her, we said, "Thank goodness she died before the war, before the atrocities and the hell it has brought."

Four houses abutted our courtyard. Ours was a two-story brick residence; the others were built of heavy logs and crowned with red clay shingle roofs.

After she married, my Aunt Rosa moved into the house across from ours. Uncle Chaim and his family inhabited the third house. And at the edge of the courtyard, in front of the garden, stood the house of the Mikhailoviches — a Belarusian family, Pravoslav Christians.

Aunt Rosa was like a big sister to me. We spent our childhood growing up together, and for many years I didn't realize she was my aunt, Father's little sister, whom he had taken her into our home after her parents' death. Even after I'd figured out the kinship, I thought of her as an older sister for the rest of her life. We shared the same bedroom until she got married. Her bridegroom was Uncle Yehoshua.

My aunt was a practicing Communist. Lots of comrades, the young Turks of the Communist Party, the whole *Aktiv,* the Executive Committee, came to her wedding. It was the same bunch that was tossed into jail for a few days every year before May Day so they would be prevented from organizing workers' demonstrations. After May Day, they were always released.

Mother arranged a modest wedding for Rosa and Yehoshua, and the guests sang all evening — Yiddish songs, proletarian songs, prisoners' songs, and songs of the oppressed and the downtrodden, followed by happy songs and dancing. They tugged us into the circle — Rosa, Rocheleh and me — and hoisted Zipporka in their arms. I still remember the sense of warmth and togetherness, the tempo of the pounding feet, and Zipporka being passed from arm to arm, shouting with joy and excitement.

They stayed with us in the courtyard. Aunt Rosa, a marvelous seamstress, worked from home; Uncle Yehoshua labored at a bakery. Their children, Yehuditkeh and Avrahamek, were born in that house.

The courtyard and the garden buzzed with life. We had a lot of everything there: the children of our family; the Mikhailoviches' kids; the huge German shepherd, Mars, who was tethered because he was really, really aggressive; the neighbors who visited Mother; Mitzi the cat; lots of fruit that ripened in the summer and tasted better and better until the end of the autumn; Gutman's kids; members of our Hashomer Hatzair groups and Gdudim (Battalions, age groups); and sometimes chickens that Mother raised to ensure the supply of fresh eggs.

Behind the houses, at the entrance to the garden, Mother kept a vegetable patch where she grew carrots, tomatoes, strawberries, green onions, cabbages and beets — each in its own season — to meet the household's needs. Economic necessity could not have been the only reason for this; she also must have loved to work in the garden. Our windowsills facing the street were also lined with flowerpots she tended.

Our house was a two-story red brick place crowned with a roof of clay shingles. The floor was made of wood, and its windows were large. It had a kitchen, three bedrooms and a *lebns-tsimer* — spacious living room — the core of the house. Affixed to the main door was a metal *mezuzah*, a simple, long, narrow object embellished with relief designs. Three steps descended from the door to the yard. The threshold, including its little rooflet and the wooden bench next to it, was Mother's. Mother would sit on the bench in the yellow afternoon sunlight, embroidering, knitting or mending socks. Neighbors came over and sat next to her on the bench, conversing and telling stories — sometimes in a barely audible tenor due to sheer fatigue, but sometimes rolling with laughter. I would come home from school, set my briefcase on the stoop, and run off to my friends.

The entrance to the house opened onto a corridor equipped with two doors. The door on the right led to Mother and Father's bedroom and was always shut. The other one, at the end of the hall, opened onto a large kitchen with a floor of simple planks. Its window faced the yard and was bracketed by an icebox and a sink with a cold-water faucet. Next to the sink stood a low wooden cupboard where pots and kettles were kept; Mother used the top of the cupboard as a working table. A large mirror stood on the other side of the kitchen; at its base was a white porcelain bathtub, the Shabbat tub. A basin for daily face washing sat on a wooden chair; a three-winged curtain separated the two fixtures.

A wide, squat, brick oven rested in one corner, stoked with wood or coal. Its metal top had four round apertures adjusted to the size of the implement stationed on them by means of metal rings that Mother positioned or removed with a thick metal hook. On the porcelain surface between the oven and the wall, a white pitcher of oil sat on a wide, shallow saucer that caught any drips. The daily eating utensils were a mishmash of leftovers: white china dishes with a blue stripe at their edges, glasses for milk, delicate glasses with silver holders for tea and *kubels* — large mugs — for the ersatz coffee made from the chicory plant. At the crack of dawn, before going to school, we used simple earthenware bowls from the market to sip our winter soup: hot water with a little goose fat in which we dipped *podla*, a flat bread Mother brought us from the Littman family's bakery one alley over. A large brass samovar stood on the kitchen table, and atop it rested a little kettle containing tea extract. The samovar was always filled with hot water with which you could offer an overnight guest, or members of your own household, the hospitality of the cold countries: a glass of tea.

We did our food shopping at the two grocery stores on our street. At the conclusion of every purchase, the shopkeeper recorded the bill in a thick, dog-eared ledger stained with grease and speckled with crumbs of food. He ran the tip of his finger over his tongue, moistened it with a little saliva to make the pages separate, and thumbed through the ledger until he came to our page. We bought on credit and paid at the end of every month. We were totally confident that the shopkeeper would not cheat us, and he felt the same way about us.

Mother didn't go to the market much. Instead, peasants brought their merchandise to our house. They came by foot, shoes tossed over their shoulders so they would not get dirty in the dust or the mud. (The peasants put on their shoes only at the entrance to the church, at the conclusion of their work in the market.) Carrying fresh eggs and butter wrapped in cabbage leaves, they hauled their large baskets among the houses, hawking their goods.

Autumn was potato time. A peasant would unload a cartful of potatoes at the entrance to the cellar of our factory, which we had upholstered with straw. There they were stored until spring. Milk was delivered to the gate of the house in large jugs, where it was poured into our glass bottles with two funnels that allowed the standard measures of milk, a liter and a liter and a half, to enter. Fish was also delivered to our home. Fishermen stood along the banks of the Niemen with their rods, and sold their hauls of carp at the market. Mother, however, would order live fish, leaving them in a tub of water until she got around to cooking them.

Let me suspend this voyage into memory for a moment in order to spend a little time in that house. I have not visited the place in years. It's been ages since I was in Mother's kitchen, but look: her hands are stretching toward the pitcher of oil on top of the oven, and the saltshaker. There's the glint of her knife as it chops celery on the cutting board. There's the breadbox and its roll-up door. Look how the jars on the windowsill break up the light. See how Mother takes off her apron and hangs it on the hook next to the icebox. Inhale the aroma of the cakes as they bake, the fragrance of cinnamon and raisins, the fresh Shabbat *challas*, the warmth in your palms as you clutch the little soup bowl, the clinking of the fork on the chinaware plate.

I venture to the stoop for a moment. Mother is getting chickens ready. Shabbat or a festival must be near. She sits on the stool, a towel on her knees and lots of old newspapers strewn about. The chicken sits on the towel and she plucks its feathers with swift motions. The cloud of white plumes float over her until they settle like snowflakes on the newspapers spread at her feet. Then Mother holds the chicken with her legs, dunks it in a pot of boiling water next to her, pauses a bit, and takes another run at some feathers that survived the first attack. Now she starts a fire in the yard and brushes off a few tiny feathers for a last cleaning. I can still see the flames, smell the charred feathers, and contemplate Mother's face, reddened by the fire and the effort.

As I said, at the center of the house was the spacious *lebns-tsimer*, the living room. Everything there was big: the rug, the table, the chairs, the windows, the potted fig tree in the flowerpot that grew to the ceiling, the fire-

Chasia's house, where she was born and was raised until 1941.
The photo was taken in 2001, sixty years later.

place, the window sills (each serving as a garden for plants and cacti tended by Mother), and the home winemaking industry she never quit.

The *lebns-tsimer* had two windows: one facing north, onto the courtyard, and the other west, toward the street. Long, bright mesh curtains covered the windows, keeping the outdoor sights from invading the interior of the house. The curtains, in turn, were covered by dark wooden shutters that opened sideways and were supported by a long iron hook. The sills were wide and the panes doubled to keep out the winter chill. In late autumn, Mother and Father would caulk the windows against the cold, leaving them that way until spring. This made the interior windowsill, behind the double windows, a greenhouse for potted plants. To assure external insulation, sawdust was strewn in the space between the double windows and covered with lots of colorful paper flowers we made as decorations. White flowers of frost lined the outer panes like patterns on cloth.

Each window had a little porthole. Every morning after we left for school, Mother opened the portholes to air out the house.

The room also had a big bookcase: a wooden cupboard with glass doors in which lots of literature was arrayed: Jewish history, Graetz's monthly journal on the history of the Jewish People, Sholem Asch and Sholem Aleichem, C.N. Bialik, I.L. Peretz, the poetry books of Leyb Naydus (a Jewish poet from Grodno), the Russian literature that Mother and Father loved, festival prayer books and holy books, all in a jumble of Yiddish, Hebrew and Russian. Across from the bookcase stood a large wooden bar with relief designs on its doors. Its shelves and drawers contained lovely tableware for Shabbat and festivals, festive silverware, tablecloths, napkins and crystal glasses. The bar supported a huge silver samovar with landscapes suspended from its sides: horizons and trees, in wide wooden frames.

When I was seven, Father bought a radio: a big four-legged wooden cabinet adorned with wooden protrusions, behind which cloth netting and big tuning dials lurked. We also had a gramophone with an enormous ear, and records of songs in Yiddish. A large clock punctuated one of the walls. Before I went to bed at night, Father wound it up by pulling its heavy weighted chain.

Khap a plats, grab a seat, next to the white-tiled oven. That was the most urgent thing to do whenever we came home from the cold. For hours we stood at the crackling fireplace, reading books and newspapers with our backs pressed to it. Avramele and I always fought over the closest place to the hot wall. At adult eye level, in the room nearest the kitchen, was a *dochovka* — a niche in the oven where we placed pots of cooked food to keep them warm. The fireplace was not connected to the ceiling. As children, we were sure that the only reason for this was that a space should remain for our baby teeth to go when they fell out. Whenever we lost a tooth, we gathered around it and, in a ritual whose progression was foreknown, Father threw the tooth into the space between the oven and the ceiling and then handed us some coins.

Until I was six, the house was illuminated with kerosene lamps. Then electricity was installed and the silhouettes on the walls stopped trembling. One day at dinner, Father said, "Children, electricity's precious. Don't leave a light on when there's no one in the room." Three-year-old Rocheleh leaped from her chair. The rest of us followed, calling, "Rocheleh, *vos iz geshen?* What happened?" "I'm going to be with the electricity," she replied, "so it won't be lonely."

Avramele shared a children's bedroom with Zipporka and Rocheleh, and I slept in the second room. This arrangement, however, worked only some of the time. Whenever Aunt Rosa stayed with us, I shared a room with Avramele. I remember the pillow fights we had at night. It was before Grandma moved in with us; after that Rosa stayed with my little sister and we three older ones shared one room. When Rosa got married, cousin Yankeleh moved in with us — at first because his mother had died and his father remarried, but then because my uncle moved to Indury. When the Russians invaded, two officers moved into our home. They took Mother and Father's room and we older girls slept in the large room. Grandma had died a short time earlier; Zipporka and Avramele slept in the small room. Afterwards, the wife of one of the Russian officers arrived, and he left. The second officer, however, continued to occupy my parents' room. At that time, Avramele married Bella and they lived in our house, in the large room. Then the three of us girls moved into the small room and Mother and Father used the room with the window facing the street.

The door to Mother and Father's room was always closed, but not locked. We girls would sneak in and play hide and seek on the large bed, sinking into the depths of the comforter and the large, plush, down pillows.

Two little stools sat next to the bed. So did a large clothes closet, with a mirror on the door and an enormous chest of drawers that held towels and linen. The bottom drawer contained the real treasures: Mother's old dresses and some hats, shoes and purses. They served as playthings throughout our childhood.

The house was always open during the day. A huge metal key with three teeth dangled over the interior of the lintel on an oval-shaped ring with relief designs at the top. Sometimes, when Mother went out and no one was at home, she locked the door and left the key under the doormat. All the neighbors did the same. Locking strangers out was one thing, but not neighbors.

I don't remember being afraid at night, but I must have been. We closed the shutters that faced the street. When my parents went to the theater, to a movie or to friends, we locked ourselves in, the thrill of being alone surmounting the fear. As young children, we caroused naughtily. As we got older, we read or played chess, checkers or Lotto.

One place was truly enchanted: the factory cellar with its wealth of treasures, accessible by steps that had been dug into the ground — wide, low steps that we loved to run along. The walls of the staircase were propped up by boards and strengthened by stakes. In the winter it was cold down there, but not as cold as outside. Therefore, the place was used for the storage of food that had to be preserved but not allowed to freeze. Heaps of apples, pears and potatoes lay on an upholstery of straw, separated by wooden barriers. The bottles of wine Mother had prepared were also kept there, alongside jars of homemade jam and vegetables she had pickled all summer long.

But the real prizes, the realms of our imagination and the tools of our games, were the furniture and implements our parents were no longer using and had stationed in faraway and poorly lit corners of the cellar. The only light that broke through did so by means of itsy-bitsy windows at ceiling height inside and sidewalk height outside. Amid this gloomy scene of forsaken objects and forgotten tools — wooden crates that contained copper, tin and iron implements, old chairs and tables, unwanted pots, pails and bowls — we girls created worlds populated by little demons and hideous witches, declared the cellar the home of *Swientego Antonjo* (a.k.a. Santa Claus), the saint of the *Boze Narodzenie,* Jesus' birthday, as we scared and delighted each other at the same time.

The garden and the yard were encased in a fence of slats spaced so that you could see through them. It wasn't a fence that kept people from entering; no one thought of coming through. It was there to mark the boundaries of the property, the limits of the location. All the courtyards outside the center of town were demarcated in the same way.

I remember winter, white winter: you go out and take a right turn at the gate and walk ten houses down. At the railroad bridge you take another right turn, and climb to the top of the hill on the main road to the Pravoslav cemetery, towing the sled behind you. At the summit, by the cemetery gate, you sit down on the sled and race all the way home, the cold and wind in your face, the frozen snow gleaming, the street slippery. Flying down the hill, losing control, flipping over, getting bruised, standing up, and continuing. Often I did this alone. Sometimes we carefully loaded our little sisters aboard and slid down with them.

Snowballs, snowfights. Mittened hands launch the ball into the air. Then it explodes and shatters against the body, filling the mouth, eyes and hair with icy shrapnel. The warmth of burning, reddened cheeks causes the flakes to melt. Sometimes you press a clod of snow against your mouth. Your breath runs dry and your throat becomes hoarse from shouting, from straining. You melt snow on your tongue and swallow the freezing water. A moment of quiet in the commotion of childhood.

How transparent the scene becomes with the passage of years. When we didn't turn right, we would cross the street, pass the sidewalk and go down the steep slope through the vacant lot to the Niemen, a mighty river that froze over in the winter, from which blocks of ice were carved out for the town's use.

The holes in the ice were truly dangerous to life and limb, especially to youngsters like us who went there to skate. Grodno had several skating rinks, but they charged admission and we, being frugal, sneaked to the river without our parents' knowledge. We affixed blades to our winter boots with a special wrench that fit them into their allotted place by means of two hooks, front and back, that gripped the shoe.

The sense of freedom in skating. The blades slashing the ice. The shards that shattered against them in a spectrum of colors, glinting in the sunbeams. The blue sky, the dark pines, the workers quarrying the ice.

We crossed to the opposite bank of the river through the ice expanses of our youth. When spring began, the river thawed and overflowed the banks, washing away poor people's homes. The album of my memory contains a horrifying picture: terrified families screaming as the churning current sweeps them away. I cannot recall anyone trying to rescue them.

Tarbut: that's what they called the Zionist Jewish school system — kindergartens, primary schools, *gymnasia* (high schools), teachers' colleges, and a school of agriculture — all taught in Hebrew. The Tarbut system was established in 1917 in Russia, but most of its operations took place in pre-WWII Poland.

It was in the autumn of 1928. Mother and Father wanted me to attend the Tarbut elementary school with my brother Avramele, so we could then go to the Hebrew *gymnasium*. But then an economic crisis broke out and my parents fell behind on the tuition. The school did not yield and sent me, the youngest, a first-grader, home to bring the money.

It was a snowy winter day. I'd never gone that way before. I'd always been escorted by Avramele, a fourth-grader who knew the way and protected and watched over me. They had placed a note in my hand and added a verbal directive: Tell your parents that once they've paid you can return to class.

Snow had fallen, melted and frozen over. I slung my heavy briefcase over my shoulder and took to the slippery streets. I skidded and fell. I made my way home and burst into tears, not from the indignity of it — I didn't realize there was something about the affair to be indignant about — but from the stress, fear and crossing town alone for the first time. Mother was at home. She hugged and caressed me, took off my wet clothing, and gave me a kiss. Then she removed my soggy shoes and changed my socks, rubbed my frozen hands with her warm hands, commiserated, wiped away my tears, and sat me down for a bowl of hot soup. When Father came home from work, he and Mother conversed in whispers in a corner of the kitchen.

The second time I was sent home from school, there was only one possible response. My parents removed me from Tarbut and transferred me to the municipal Jewish school, which was closed on Shabbat and open on Sundays and did not charge tuition. All the kids there were Jewish. Some of the teachers were Poles. They taught in Polish and I was miserable. All my friends and Avramele attended Tarbut. I wanted so badly to go to school with them and be with them. I envied them so much that until I finished school years later I remained upset about having been torn away from them. Only afterwards, while on the Aryan side of Bialystok where my life depended on speaking Polish correctly, did I make my peace with my school years.

My new school was a huge building next to the home of the author Eliza Orzeszkowa. The street was named for her, too. The building stood on the slope of a little hill, three stories on the street side and four facing the courtyard. The classrooms were enormous — each accommodating very large classes — and the yard was spacious, as we found when we poured down the stairs during recesses. Classes began and ended when a janitor passed through the halls ringing a bell.

An elderly woman with silver hair sat in the schoolyard. She was short and squat, with a lovely, radiant face in which her blue eyes took in everything with a tender smile. A large apron, tied to her waist, covered her floor-length skirt. During recesses, she walked around carrying two large plaited baskets full of hot, fresh *taygelakh*, a sweet honey-dipped pastry that she would sell us for five *grosh*. Whenever we were short on coins, she would say, "Pay tomorrow," and never wrote it down. I trust you, her response hinted; you're already a grown-up — a demonstration of trust that was so important for young children. We all loved her dearly and made sure to pay our debts. Years later, it turned out that she was Sarka Shewachowicz's grandmother.

My Sarka, my clever, wise, determined, loving friend. When we were shoved into the sequestered ghetto in a matter of hours, Sarka and her grand-mother vacated a room in their little apartment for us. We spent our entire stay in the ghetto living with them and Sarka's paralyzed grandfather. They shared their poor abode in their typically unruffled, kind-hearted and affable way. But do not allow me to put the cart before the horse. Important details may get lost: scenes, sounds and people, feelings, associations and places. The cart will surely come, I know. I'll definitely reach those venues of terror and pain, of weeping, helplessness and incomprehension. So let me spend one more mo-ment in my digression of childhood, youth, youth movement and family, when our world was still intact, beautiful and good.

When Mother took me to school on the first day, we faced two first-grade teachers: Mrs. Fenster — pretty, tall, robust, round and jovial of face — and Mrs. Dym — older, short, dark-complexioned, skinny and desiccated. Mother was eager to assign me to Mrs. Fenster but they sent me to Mrs. Dym and I came out ahead. She loved children as no one else did. Tender, warm, attentive and humane, she was both teacher and educator in one package. In her geography classes, I dreamed of voyages to the unknown countries and faraway places whose weird names were written in gaudy letters on the maps and in the books. When Lilac Hill blossomed, I brought a wreath to Mrs. Dym's desk every week. I loved lilacs and I loved Mrs. Dym.

Uniforms were compulsory at all times, from first grade on, summer and winter: a fleece skirt and a dark blue blouse, a narrow purple stripe around the collar, and a beret. Only on Trzeci Maj, the Polish national holiday that began on May 3, did we report to school in white blouses and embark on a parade along the city streets.

The classroom was large and well lit. It had a whole wall of windows without shutters and curtains. Lots of things were installed on the opposite wall: a blackboard, a map of Europe, a map of Poland, a relief of the white eagle (Poland's national emblem) and a photograph of the president, Marshal Pilsudski. A round coal-burning stove with protruding chimney pipes stood in one corner. On the harshest winter days, it was unable to defeat the cold, so we sat in coats and gloves to keep ourselves warm. The other corner was the humiliation corner, where pupils were punished for being late, talking in class, failing to do homework or furtively slipping notes to their classmates. For long minutes one had to stand in the corner, facing the wall, one's back to the rest of the class. Throughout my years in school, I wrote with a fountain pen that I dipped into a little pot of black ink.

Bassia Brawer. Bassia from the Forstat. Dark-haired Bassia, a really pretty girl, my classmate and, later on, my comrade in the youth movement's Carmel Gdud (Battalion). We spent most of my school years sharing a wooden bench with an armrest attached to the desk. The top of the desk opened up and revealed a cavity where we placed our notebooks and textbooks. Together we spent our recesses playing hopscotch and jumping rope.

Bassia Brawer became a member of the resistance in the Grodno ghetto. All trace of her vanished in the February 1943 *Aktion.*

Every day Father wore *tefillin* and recited the prayers at home. On Fridays and Shabbat, he went to synagogue and we waited for him in the house.

Shabbat Eve. I picture Mother's hands moving as she prayed and blessed the candles. Tall, silver candlesticks resting on four legs, flattened orbs rising all the way to the cup. They stand on a silver tray. The flames of the Shabbat candles cast yellow light into Mother's cupped palms. We gather around her, standing. We're shorter than her so our heads and eyes angle upward. She presses her fingers over her eyes.

She recites a prayer that is much longer than the blessing over the candles. She's with herself at this moment of silence, bathed, clean, at ease after her lengthy week, wearing a Shabbat dress, her hair wet from the shampoo. She makes the transition from bothersome mundane life, abounding with concerns about livelihood, health and responsibility for the family, to Shabbat, which descends like a curtain and creates a buffer between us and the world. At this exact place, where the profane and the sacred are separated, and at precisely this moment, she is like the creator of the passion of exaltation.

She never whispered her requests and entreaties. She said them aloud so we children would hear them, so we, too, would gather around and enwrap ourselves in an abstract sense of sanctity. With perfect faith she addressed the *Riboyno shel Oylam*, the Master of the Universe, in a jumble of requests, prayers and pleas. She combined issues related to Shabbat, livelihood and health with the virtue of honesty and trust that is the special possession of those of pure faith. We stood silently until she finished — looking, listening, not daring to utter a sound — not only due to the sanctity of the moment, but also so as not to disturb God as He listened to Mother's words.

Mother baked her *challas*, Sabbath loaves, by twisting braids made of four ropes of dough, speckled with poppy seeds. Father came home from the synagogue after what seemed to us an eternity, an eternity that dragged on anew each Friday. He uncovered the *challas* by pulling aside the embroidered cover that Mother had made, recited the blessing, and with his fingers broke off a piece of bread for everyone. Like an old movie I see his hand clutching the plait of bread, the torn crust of the loaf, the poppy seeds, and the crumbs scampering helter-skelter across the white tablecloth.

Shabbat afternoon: the cast-iron pot, huge, round and black that contained the thick *cholent*. Mother had made the ingredients herself. She'd cleaned out the intestines and filled them with a mixture of flour, goose fat and green beans. Then she'd sliced the meat, peeled the potatoes, and laid everything in the pot. I loved to stand and watch the painstaking order of ingredients, followed by the spices and the water. Rocheleh and I carried the pot to the bakery, walking slowly so as not to spill the water. Carefully we went down the stairs and presented it to the baker, who stood at the bottom of the pit and slid the pot into the sizzling oven. We saw the glowing embers that remained after the baking of the *challah*, the masses of pots — great and small, round and oval, narrow and wide — and the baker with his long apron and tall hat. Excitedly we peered into the oven to see exactly where he'd put our pot. Afterwards, on the afternoon of Shabbat, we walked all the way back, clutching the handles of the sizzling pot with mittens or heavy rags and bringing it to the Shabbat table.

The Shabbat midday meal: a memory of an aroma, a memory of a flavor. Around the festive table sat Mother and Father, Grandma and Avramele, Rocheleh and Zipporka, and me. In the middle rested Mother's wonderful *cholent*, frugally appointed because we children did not like green beans and eggs. Now the heavy lid comes off, the vapors rise like a cloud, their color like that of potatoes.

Afterwards came the tea — the silver Shabbat-and-festival samovar, the delicate glasses with their silver holders, and the tiny silver kettle that held the extract, followed by the water and the bowl of sugar cubes. And the denouement: the sense of sugar melting in the mouth and the sipping of the hot tea.

Mother took the silver candlesticks and utensils to the ghetto and eventually sold them for food. The glasses, the huge samovar, the white tablecloths and the embroidered napkins were lost in the frantic rush to leave our homes.

Father wanted to leave Poland. He'd wanted to leave Poland all his life but couldn't afford to fulfill his dream of "making *aliya*" — emigrating to Palestine, *Eretz Israel* — or leaving for some other destination overseas.

To obtain a family "certificate" (immigration visa) for Palestine, you had to prove you had a lot of money. You couldn't even dream about an ordinary certificate. *Halutzim* (Zionist pioneers) spent years waiting in training farms before their turn for *aliya* came. Emigration to America was exorbitantly expensive. However, when the great economic crisis began in late 1928, Father decided to take action. In counsel with Mother, he went to Argentina to find work that would provide an honorable livelihood, and to hunt for a suitable emigration setup. His uncles had gone there several years earlier and promised to help. I don't remember saying goodbye to Father, but I do remember that lengthy year very strongly. Mother spent it alone with four children: ten-year-old Avramele, five-year-old Rocheleh, little Zipporka, three-and-a-half, and me, all of seven. For the first time we didn't get new winter clothes. Every Friday afternoon, Mother cried when Aunt Etka came over with baskets of food for Shabbat and the rest of the coming week.

Mother toiled alone at the plant, turning out seltzer, lemonade and *kvas* (a beverage made of barley or rye malt) for which there was hardly a market during the long winter. She prepared them in huge tubs, mixing water with fruit concentrate that came in enormous bottles. I have no clear recollection of how the juice made its way from the tubs to the bottles, but I can imagine a channel that carried the fluid to the filling station, where it was funneled into the bottles. It was all done by hand and foot: picking up the bottle, pressing the filling pedal, pressing the carbonation pedal, sealing the bottle with a cork, gluing the labels on. The corks were made of real cork or porcelain, with a rubber strip and a metal clasp. The labels — brown and yellow for *kvas*, green for lemonade — were affixed to the bottles with a wide brush dipped into glue.

Soda siphons were also filled at the plant. They were clear, white, glass bottles with a fixture at the top made of a metal seal, a handle to squeeze, and a little tube through which the soda flowed. For delivery to large shops, wooden crates and huge copper containers of soda were loaded onto a horse-drawn cart. Two or three workers escorted the wagon driver, who hauled the goods to town.

Father sent us letters. He was working somewhere and staying with the uncles for Shabbat. He said nothing about the grueling labor he was performing — hauling sacks at the port — nor his wretched living quarters between the piers. Mother replied with lengthy letters written at night. When I asked what she was writing about, she said, "Only the good things. You don't have to tell everything." Father shouldn't think that we are having a hard time, that we are not getting by. Mother sheltered Father from life. Always.

There was also the matter of money. For the first few months, we received an envelope each month with money from Father. Then, all of a sudden, the envelopes stopped coming. For two months Mother refused to write to him about this. She didn't want him to worry. Only in the third month did she write about the missing money. It turned out that his good friend, a neighbor of ours, had offered to send the money himself instead having both of them do it. It was a shame, his friend said, for both of them to waste work time going to the post office and standing in line. Father agreed gladly. The man sent all the money to his wife. To this day I don't know whether it was she who failed to forward it to us or whether he had not told her that the money was not only his. Either way, the friendship ended.

Father came home. He was poorly suited to the brutal life of the lone migrant. The economic crisis had not eluded Argentina. The work had worn him out. I've always thought that had Mother gone instead of him, she surely would have done well. She had that amazing ability to survive.

Mother went to the train station to greet him, using the cart they used to distribute the beverages, and we waited at home. Suddenly Father came to the door, smiling from ear to ear, pale and skinnier than ever. As we pounced on him, he gathered us into one cloying embrace and emptied his suitcase of its contents of clothing and sweets. The main items there were big bags of candies in flavors and quantities we had never known. That's what remained of his journey to Argentina — the memory of the hard winter and the taste of candies from a distant land.

Years later, during the war, when I was already alone, I would daydream in anguish about the possibility of having been together in Argentina, all of us alive, if Father's attempt to settle there had ended well.

Father belonged to no political party and did not attend rallies or meetings. However, he was a "Weizmannist," sympathetic to the views of Chaim Weizmann and very close with the General Zionists. A blue box for the Jewish National Fund stood in the kitchen with other charity boxes into which Mother emptied the coins left over from a shopping trip.

Father was a modest, humble, nose-to-the-grindstone person. At the synagogue, he was a cantor with an impressive voice and a stage presence, chanting prayers and entreaties, performing the public Torah reading and leading the services. On festivals and family gatherings he told stories and spun jokes that made us laugh our heads off. A refined man with a dry sense of humor, keen vision, and sayings that were always on target.

Years after I left home, after the war, I left Łódź by train to visit some friends from the youth movement. Facing us in the train were several Jews who stared at me incessantly. I neither recognized them nor understood why they were contemplating me that way, until one of them mustered his courage and asked, "Are you the daughter of Yehuda Bielicki?" Astonished, I answered in the affirmative and asked him whether he had known my father. "Your father," he replied, "was one of the most honest and decent men in Grodno. A good man who was good to others. A quiet man who never raised his voice. Whenever anyone needed serious help, he was the one they turned to." It was the first time I'd run into someone who had known my father. And, although I did not know it then, it would also be the last.

My father. Always dressed in a three-piece suit and a hat, always clutching an elegant cane. At the end of a silver chain attached to one of the buttons of his vest dangled a round object, flat and ornate: a *tsibele*, an onion-shaped

My mother, Devorah Bielicka-
Jablonska, aged 19,
September 4, 1917

My father, Yehuda Bielecki,
aged 19, October 20, 1916

Right to left, seated: Father, Rocheleh, Avramele, Mother; standing: Chasia,
Aunt Rosa, Zipporka

My paternal grandmother, Chasia

Zipporka with Yehudit,
Aunt Rosa's daughter

Vova, son of my cousin who fled to
Asiatic Russia, April 18, 1945

Avramele aged 6, Rocheleh aged 2,
Chasia aged 4

Right to left: Father, Aunt
Manya, and her husband Eizik
Epstein, December 13, 1916

Avramele aged 8,
Rocheleh aged 4,
Zipporka aged 2,
Chasia aged 6

Avramele and Bella, October 1, 1937

Aunt Rosa with her husband,
Yehoshua Nowogrodski

Zipporka aged 14

Rocheleh

My cousin, Yaakov Bielicki

watch that lived in a special pouch. A pack of Avanti cigarettes sat in the other pocket. We sang "Avanti Popolo," the song of the Italian revolutionaries, to him. He didn't smoke much: three cigarettes a day, one after each meal. He concluded each day by sitting down and reading the newspaper. Not one but two Yiddish papers, *Haynt* and *Moment*, which he bought on the way home from work. Mother, still occupied with housework at that time of day, asked him to tell her what was new. She spent most of her little spare time reading books.

After he returned from Argentina, Father realized that the soft-drink plant was not providing a real livelihood. Trained as an accountant, he went to work for a rival company, a decision that said something both about him and about them. Rivals or not, they were on excellent terms. The situation at home improved; Rocheleh and Zipporka could now attend Tarbut.

Mother and Father were very much in love. They had a good, strong friendship and gave each other unreserved support and much appreciation. However, they fought life's hardships in very different ways. Every day when Father came home from work, he kissed Mother on the cheek and asked her how she was. Then they discussed matters related to the house and the children's education. Father never raised his voice at us; Mother rebuked us whenever we had it coming. They were similar in their attitudes toward people; both were willing to offer help and support, to listen and to ease distress. The house was an easy-going, warm and very friendly place, accessible to people in need who could stay there for days, if not years.

My parents attended the theater, heard speeches by big shots from *Eretz Israel*, and visited comrades, friends and acquaintances. Their theater of choice was the traveling Yiddish theater that occasionally visited Grodno. We saw the Vilna Yiddish Theater perform *The Golem* and *The Eternal Jew* even before the war.

My parents trusted us immensely, and cultivated an atmosphere of freedom of thought and choice and an open-minded view of people and the world. We may have learned social theories from the writings of Socialist and Communist intellectuals at the Hashomer Hatzair Movement House, but our social outlooks, our attitude toward mankind, and our patience and tolerance for strangers and those who were different from us were shaped in our parents' home.

In 1938, to help support the household, Mother opened a little grocery store of sorts. One night she hired some workers to turn a window into a door that would open onto Podolna Street. The process of obtaining official permission to change the building façade was lengthy and not assured. It was simpler to punch a hole through the façade at night, when the streets of the remote suburb were empty of people, not to mention city police. Thus, the morning after the workers did their labor, the door opened onto the street and anyone who peeped in discovered a tiny space furnished with a lovely wooden counter (installed a few days before the entrance was pushed through), shelves along two walls, and a row of little bags that contained mainly lentils and rice. Packets of chocolate, bags of sugar and clods of halva and marmalade occupied a shelf behind the counter. In the evening, before going to sleep, we were privileged with a piece of marmalade that Mother had cut over a little dish into gleaming chromatic little cubes.

Among the memories of fragrances and flavors that have remained with me to this day, one belongs to Aunt Etka, Mother's older sister: the aroma of smoked fish. Aunt Etka's home was the playground of our youth and our rule of thumb there was "anything goes." My cousin Oka and I fantasized about a dense forest, hidden caves and faraway mountains amid the spacious courtyard, hallways, chimneys, burning oak logs and fish.

On Shabbat afternoon, after the *cholent*, the tea and the nap, we would walk over to Aunt Etka's. Across the bridge, the stairs continued from the bank of the Niemen to the top of the hill. Alongside the stairs was a path of trodden soil. Mother and Father took the stairs; we children ran along the path.

How we loved going there. Auntie Etka was the spitting image of Grandma Sarah-Chaya — short, plump and bursting with warmth, love and kindness. During Father's year in Argentina, she brought us baskets of food every week so that we would not run short.

When all is said and done, not a trace of the Forstat remains. The neighborhood of wooden homes, the old sixteenth-century synagogue, Aunt Etka's house, the place where they smoked the fish — they all went up in flames, gone forever, in the conflagration kindled by the Germans.

My family let birthdays glide by unnoticed. Only the boys celebrated bar mitzvahs. Avramele celebrated his twice. His class from the Tarbut Gymnasium was invited to celebrate on the first Shabbat. All the students came, as well as his teachers. One of his teachers, Zvi Belko, gave a speech in Hebrew. I didn't understand a word. Father spoke in Yiddish so that everyone there would understand, and concluded his remarks with a few sentences in Hebrew. Belko shook his hand and everyone was moved by the honor this signified. The second celebration took place the next Shabbat. The whole Nahshon Gdud of the Hashomer Hatzair Movement came over in the morning and the whole family gathered in the afternoon — my uncles from the Forstat, those from Mostowa, the ones from the courtyard, cousins, relatives and acquaintances. Everyone brought presents, mainly books and some photo albums. Avramele liked to read; he craved books and totally consumed them. Mother and Father gave him a watch. I don't know who gave him the silver Passover goblet, the cup of the Prophet Elijah.

Avramele, my first-born brother, our first-born brother, the big kid, the one who preceded the three sisters. In our childhood, before Rocheleh grew up and Zipporka was born, he was a companion for games, amusements and entertainment. He was a little boy, short, skinny and pallid. Mother fretted over him throughout the years and made him special food. Since he didn't care for dairy items, she removed the butter from the cakes and potatoes for him. He was this itsy-bitsy thing. That's why they called him Avramele, a diminutive of Avraham. Later on, after the bar mitzvah, he experienced a growth spurt and became big and strong. By then, however, the nickname Avramele had stuck. Even when, as a young man, he became head of the Hashomer Hatzair Movement in Grodno, he remained Avramele.

I envied him for his ability to speak Hebrew with Father. He had acquired the language at Tarbut; I had missed out. I envied him for the bar mitzvah they threw for him and, especially, for the tons of books he received. I was furious at him for not having made the effort to get me into Hashomer Hatzair as a special candidate, forcing me to wait in line for half a year like everyone else. Afterwards, however, we became very good friends, me and my handsome, smart, big brother, the leader. We had little time left for this adult friendship and love, which was composed of being partners in the movement and in our choice of way of life. Back then we did not know how little that time would be. Maybe it was for the best.

The festivals did more for us than separate the sacred from the profane. They also afforded us a marvelous voyage, on the wings of our spirit, to *Eretz Israel*, the Land of Canaan, the provinces of the Bible and Scripture, the spectacle of the matriarchs and patriarchs, the humble heroes who, in their eyes or in our dreaming eyes, fought and were vanquished. The festival periods extended to the days before and after the festivals themselves; they marked the times and the seasons of the whole year.

We'll begin with Shavuot. Everything is white: the cheese, the table-cloth, the candles, the eating implements. On the festival table, also white, are cheese dumplings in soup, a huge bowl filled with *kluskii,* balls of cooked cheese filled with dried fruit and coated with breadcrumbs soaked in butter. Next to them are blintzes and cheesecakes. Everything sizzles and steams, ejecting vapors — tiny bubbles of sweet fragrance — into the void of the room.

The signs of Rosh Hashanah became visible in stages. First, the wine: in late autumn, Mother made *czarnej guzi*, a wine produced from dark red apples that were almost black when we picked them. Mother shredded the apples, lots of them, with a grater and placed the mash in special cloth bags. She stationed two wood fetters on the floor next to the living room window and positioned a long rod atop them. Then she tethered the cloth bags to the pole, allowing the juice to drip from the bags into a wide chinaware bowl. After a few days, she dispensed the juice into large glass bottles. Patiently and very painstak-ingly she let the product ferment, filtered it and strained it until it became wine.

The second sign of the approaching New Year was the greeting cards. The preparations began in mid-summer, when Mother and Father went to the printer's and ordered cards adorned with colorful flowers, streaming ribbons or birds carrying in their beaks a Hebrew inscription for a good year, and our family name festooned across the top. Then, they procured paper and enve-lopes to write felicitations and, sometimes, letters, first to members of the fam-ily and then to all the friends — Auntie Shifra in Kovno, Sonia-Rivka, daughter of the aunt in Białystok, Uncle Chaim in Indory, relatives in Skidel, Father's distant cousins in Argentina, and Aunt Manya in America. A third indication of the coming festival was shopping for winter clothes and shoes. Shoes first of all!

On Rosh Hashanah we performed the *tashlich* ritual on the bank of the Niemen River. The Jews of Grodno stood at the very edge of the water, emptied their pockets, and tossed all their sins into the flow. Every year until I reached adulthood, I raced down the path to the Niemen in order to have enough time to watch the sins drown in the surging current.

Avramele always said about us children that we fasted on the evening of

Yom Kippur. Mother and Father spent the whole day in synagogue. We young ones gathered in the synagogue courtyard with lots of other children, played games, shouted and made noise. Occasionally a worshiper would come out and growl until we fell silent. Sometimes we went inside to visit Mother and Father.

Once we grew up, we spent Yom Kippur at home. I remember the solemn quietude of the day. For hours we read books in bed. In the afternoon, we went to the Movement House, where we played ping-pong, walked around, talked to each other and had some food (but only at the Movement House, out of respect for Father and Mother).

For the closing *Neilah* service, we always went to the synagogue, all of us, even when we grew up. It was then that Father took over as cantor — at the end of the day, in the last of the services. And when Father's voice fell silent, one final blast of the *shofar* was heard.

Afterwards, at home, we sat down with our parents for a fast-breaking repast — a huge spread from which no one really ate. A piece of fish, a slice of *challah*, and Mother and Father recounting their experiences in *shul*. Lots of talking and not much eating, discussing men and women and friends and acquaintances and news and regards and, only afterwards, dinner.

The family *sukkah* was built along the wall of Aunt Rosa's house. Five construction workers — Uncle Chaim and Uncle Yehoshua, Father, Avramele and cousin Yankel — erected three wooden walls crowned with thatching made of enormous fir branches brought by the peasants from the forests.

The *sukkah* was lit with kerosene lanterns kept in terrariums with metal carrying handles. Their illumination flickered across the thatching, the paper decorations, the *reyzelakh* and the paper *mizrach* design. The interplay of light and shadow also danced around the dates, carobs, figs and construction-paper chains. And all of it against the background of chilly summer nights and the fragrance of the first rain.

"Maybe you don't want Hanukkah *gelt* this year?" That's how Father greeted the next festival. Each year he tested us jokingly and scared us for real. "I can see on your faces that you don't want it," he taunted us again and again.

Father loved to play the storyteller and was good at it. Every evening during Hanukkah we sat down and listened. Spellbound, we were borne on the wings of his words and our imagination to *Eretz Israel*, to Modi'in and the

Maccabis, to the Greeks and the hills of Jerusalem, to wicked Antiochus, the uprising, the war, the frightening defeat and the consoling victory.

The menorah stood on the table; a lovely menorah perched on a tall stand. Next to it were dishes of aromatic, crisp, hot, potato *latkes* that melted with every bite. And there were Hanukkah songs of course, lots of Yiddish songs about spinning tops and *latkes*, the flask of oil, and solid lead.

The four Hebrew initials of the expression **N**es **g**adol **h**aya **s**ham, "a great miracle happened there," were engraved on the sides of the solid lead tops that we spun endlessly. I concealed the Hanukkah *gelt* in my mitten, deep inside, in a secure and safe place where I couldn't lose it. My fingertips touched the coins, reassuring me that they were there and they were mine. Each year I amassed my Hanukkah *gelt* to buy something I really wanted. I don't remember what I bought as a little girl, but when I grew up I used some of the money to buy books, and kept the rest for summer camps with the movement. Once I bought a purple kerchief that had woven fringes with alternating dull and shiny stripes, a soft, caressing kerchief that you could look through and see the whole world in purple.

Tu Bishvat — *chamshuser,* we called it, the *hamisha-'asar* (fifteenth) day of the month of Shvat — was the festival of the fruits of *Eretz Israel*. A bowl with fruit from *Eretz Israel* was set on the table, including a special shipment of Jaffa oranges that arrived ahead of the holiday. Each of us got half an orange. Next to the bowl were almonds and figs, dates, raisins and carobs, which exuded the aroma of sunshine and the flavor of dreams and yearnings. A gleaming white tablecloth adorned the festive table and snowflakes peppered the window.

And then, in mid-winter, came Purim. For years I was Queen Esther, costumed in a long dress of Mother's and high-heeled shoes. Several days before the festival, Mother labored over the baking of *hamantaschen*. She bought large bags of tiny poppy seeds that she cooked with milk and sugar. Then she spread the dough across the wooden kitchen table. When the baking was over, the molds emerged from the oven sizzling, the pastries arrayed atop them in precise rows. The traditional sending of foods for our large family was engineered on porcelain dishes draped with white cloth napkins. Mother also prepared special and large portions of food for poor families living nearby, beefing up the normal portions with festival goodies. I delivered them each year.

The first sign of Pesach appeared at the end of the summer: making *med*. I could smell its honeyed fragrance at the courtyard gate, even before the threshold. Each year when it happened, I raced home and shouted, "Mom, you're cooking *med*!"

Med was a Passover wine for children. It was cooked in a *mednice*, a huge copper pot that Mother positioned on the gas jets. A sea of gold bubbled slowly, thickening more and more over a period of hours. Mother stirred it now and then with a large wooden ladle that I licked after each stir. Eventually the kitchen window sill filled up with bottles of *med*, translucent as amber. After they cooled off, Mother stashed them in the cellar for the entire lengthy winter.

We rendered our eating and kitchen implements "kosher for Pesach" by immersing them in boiling water. Rocheleh and I sat down and made a chain. We tied all the Pesach silverware to a long rope and Mother boiled water in a large tank over the gas. Then, using long wooden pincers, we dunked into the water teacups and wine glasses, pots and pans, and our chain of silverware.

Who joined us at the Seder table? Grandma Sarah-Chaya; Aunt Rosa and Uncle Yehoshua; the children Yehuditkhe and Avrahameleh; Grandma Menuha, Uncle Yehoshua's mother; Uncle Chaim, his first wife, Rachel, and their children, Yankeleh and Yente; and Auntie Sonya, the widow, with her sons, Ephraim and Aharon, the redhead *yeshiva bocher*. They celebrated the festival with us one year, with Aunt Etka the next year, and so on.

Despite concern about the possibility of antisemitic pogroms on Pesach night, we opened our door wide in the expectation of greeting the Prophet Elijah. One Seder, when Rocheleh was little, she suddenly leaped out of her chair and ran into the hall. She did this so abruptly, and with such a serious look on her face, that everyone ran after her in fright. Rocheleh, *vos iz geshen?* What happened? "I wanted to see whether Elijah is already waiting outside," she said. After that, at each Seder we sent her out early to see whether Elijah was already waiting outside.

Father buries the *afikoman* somewhere and dares us to find it. Then come the *afikoman* gifts: a ball, table games, a new chess set. Once Zipporka asked for a donkey. Go find a donkey in Poland. I made her a donkey, a weird, long-eared donkey, by sewing some old rags together. She was delighted with it; it was exactly the kind of donkey she had been dreaming of.

Afterwards we sang. Father, Aunt Sonya and Avramele led the singing with their strong, lovely, clear voices. Rocheleh and I sang in a whisper because we got lots of things wrong. I loved to sing, but only when no one was at home. I also sang in the family choir — *sotto voce.*

To this day, Pesach is the only Jewish festival I cannot endure. I spend every Pesach back there, in that house. Physically I'm here in Israel, but my soul and being remain at the Seder table at home. I listen to the kibbutz retelling the Hagadah, but the voice I hear is Father's. I listen to the little ones asking the Four Questions, but hear the voices of Rocheleh and Zipporka. Through a haze of tears I see the long tables, the white tablecloths, the flowers, the utensils and glasses, enveloped in the tones of the festival songs and hymns rendered in Israeli Hebrew, using the Sephardi pronunciation. They are drowned out by the voices of my family back there, pronouncing the words in the Ashkenazi manner. Surrounded by my large family, I yearn for the family that has slipped from my grasp. To this day, every Pesach is a maelstrom that sweeps me away and squeezes me dry, a cause of bitter pain spattered with the sweetness of the home I once had. The touch of Mother's hands and Father's voice. Lots of uncles and cousins and all my siblings. To this day, Pesach for me is not the festival of freedom and spring. It is everything that these are not.

I say names. I say them again and again: Rocheleh and Zipporka and Aunt Rosa and Aunt Etka and Father and Grandma. I say names several times in each sentence. I repeat them in an unbroken flow of couplets and trios. Maybe the more I say them, the less gone they will be, the less they will sink into the abyss of forgetfulness. That way, they won't disappear on me. They won't disappear with me. As long as I say them, they exist inside me. They exist within the circle of the living and they do not fade into oblivion.

CHAPTER 2

Teen Years

The movement was a world unto itself — a school-away-from-school, a home-away-from-home. After I reached adolescence, I spent more time at the Movement House than at home. The movement gave all its members tools for thinking, learning, criticizing and understanding. It taught us not only to see and hear, but also to observe and listen. We learned prodigiously — by ourselves, from each other, and from the counselors. Our intellectual curiosity was boundless.

There were four *gymnasia* (high schools) in Grodno: Tarbut, which I couldn't even dream about because the tuition was so high; Realni, a Jewish *gymnasium* that taught in Polish and also charged steep tuition; and two Polish *gymnasia* that didn't charge much tuition but demanded excellence in all subjects and used the *numerus clausus* system to limit Jewish enrollment.

Father knew how badly I wanted to attend a *gymnasium* and I knew how assuredly the tuition was beyond our reach. Even when I finished elementary school, the situation did not improve. In a lengthy talk moistened with tears, Father made it clear that I would have to attend a vocational school, but promised he would make up the last two years of *gymnasium* for me. He didn't know how, but he promised to find a way.

So I went to the ORT school. "You never know what's going to happen

in life," Father said, "but you can always study. A trade is a source of livelihood and economic power."

Years later, in the ghetto, on the Aryan side, and on the long journey
with the children, I realized how right he had been.

By the time I enrolled in ORT, the branch in Grodno had become part
of a global network, a good school that taught at a high level. Boys had lots
of electives to choose from; girls had only two, sewing or fashion design.
The school also taught all the regular subjects. However, I was fourteen years
old and really angry. ORT was not for me! I kept my classmates at arm's
length. Reluctantly I set out from home each morning, sat in class, counted
the seconds until the day ended, and consoled myself in the evenings at the
Hashomer Hatzair Movement House. My friend Cyla Szachnes said, "Chasia,
don't make a big deal of it. The school's okay and the kids who go there are
okay. It'll be all right."

Slowly I got caught up in the action: design, cutting, sewing, working
with dyed fabric, transparent silk papers and yarn, exploring the possibilities
of creative knits.

By making peace with the school, I also acquired friends and status.
Although I refused to take part in the social events and festival parties that
took place at school — after all, they clashed with activities at the Movement
House — I became the chief decorator of the school's party room. As soon as
I finished decorating the place, I slipped away to the Movement House. The
parties at ORT involved everything that we at Hashomer Hatzair detested:
salon balls with the boys' classes, fancy dresses, silk stockings, face powder,
and doing the tango, the foxtrot and the waltz.

ORT students were not allowed to belong to youth movements. I had to
sneak out to avoid discovery. I'm almost positive that the teachers knew what
I was up to and turned a blind eye. The girls in my class definitely knew. After
all, they saw me in the street in my movement getup.

We spent Shabbat mornings on outings with the movement and evenings at ORT parties. I had duties to perform on both ends: choosing the destination of the outing, and preparing the party decorations. Early in the morning
I slipped plain clothes over my movement uniform and headed for school.
I was much the hybrid, wearing two blouses, two skirts, high-heeled shoes
and a backpack. As soon as I had finished decorating the hall, I stepped into
the restroom, stripped away the layer of regular clothing, donned a Hashom-

er Hatzair tie, and headed out in full movement attire, crossing the entire school.

Amid the mass of faces, names, dates and places I have accumulated over the years, various details slip away. I can't say what "method" I use to remember or forget. Whatever it is, it definitely does not correspond to the importance of these people in my life. Thus, I cannot explain how the name of my second- and third-grade teacher at ORT eludes me. She was an authoritarian, a tall, pretty woman with hair drawn back into a bun, always wearing stiff dresses with a special collar. She was my homeroom teacher for those two years, too. She taught the whole class, but gave each of us plenty of personal attention, too. It was she who steered us to the legacy of knit and garment design, the clothing of Louis XIV and Marie Antoinette, the history of crinoline (the stuff of Victorian petticoats), and the costumes used in Shakespeare's plays. She introduced us to books, pictures and paintings, taught us how to dye textiles, and acquainted us with textile and weaving technologies.

The school covered part of its tuition by charging for students' works. Townswomen of the *hoi polloi* ordered hand-made dresses for balls and festive events. The most difficult and complicated projects were given to me. Once I was asked to sew a very special dress for the wife of a Jewish doctor — a lovely, elegant woman who kept her black hair in a ponytail. She pored over the newspapers and chose something she liked. I took her measurements and she brought me the fabric the next day.

I remember the day the dress was measured. Tension gripped the whole class. My classmates tried to sneak a glance into the teachers' room. After the measuring was done, my teacher said, "Bielicka, the customer is very satisfied." A few days later, the customer expressed her gratitude by sending me a huge chocolate bonbonier, my first ever. She was pleased; I was happy and proud. I shared the chocolate with the whole class.

Aunt Rosa had a Singer sewing machine, a large, handsome appliance with metal legs embellished with relief designs, supporting a dark, smooth board that was varnished to a shine. Whenever I had projects to prepare for ORT, I did my sewing at her house. Now and then I asked Father when he'd buy me a machine, but added in the same breath, "It's not all that important, I don't have to have one, I'm not going to be a seamstress anyway…."

But Father wanted to make me happy. One day during my second year at ORT, I came home from school and found a wooden crate at the entrance of the house.

"What's that?" I asked Father.

"I don't know," he answered. "It must be a mistake; they delivered something that isn't ours...."

Father approached the crate to open it by himself. I wanted to help him but Avramele, the big hero, pushed me aside. They opened the crate. Its interior was lined with thick brown paper coated with black tar, and atop the padding rested a new sewing machine, gleaming and beautiful. In my excitement I pounced on Father and kissed him.

When we went to the ghetto, we took the machine with us. It provided us with a dining table and a source of livelihood.

Much later, Mother told me that Father smashed the machine when I left the ghetto, not wanting it to fall into German hands.

The teacher who had brought me my first dress project was also the one who prepared us for the final internal exams at ORT as well as the external ones given by the Polish Ministry of Education for the conferring of an official diploma. The test included a practical phase, in which the candidate had two days, eight hours each day, to make a dress. It had to be done from scratch: the model, the drafting, tracing the outline onto the fabric, the cutting and sewing the final product. We practiced for the external test by taking an identical internal one.

Almost fifty years afterwards, Bronja Klebanski, who attended the Realni Gymnasium, told me how jealous she had been when she first saw me wearing a dress I had sewn myself.

The graduation ceremony took place in a roomy hall. Students sat without their parents; the teachers occupied a lengthy table on which rested the government diplomas, each written on thick paper and inserted into a cardboard cylinder bound with a ribbon. Polish and Jewish students sat on opposite sides. After a profusion of speeches, we were invited to come up and receive our diplomas.

I was proud of the diploma. After we came home, Mother said, "You see, it was all for the best. You got your diploma, you have a trade, and you passed the practical exam with flying colors." She was proud of me, too — for earning the diploma, attending the commencement, producing the dresses, and, perhaps above all, having made peace with necessity and finishing the ORT program that I had not wanted in the first place.

Hashomer Hatzair was an outgrowth of two other Jewish youth movements. One of them, Tze'irei Tzion, came about as part of an effort to establish study groups for national awareness in the late nineteenth century, when the initial Zionist awakening took place. The second movement, Hashomer (the Jewish Scouts Association) was founded by the Dror societies in Galicia in 1913. The two movements officially merged in 1916. By the eve of WWII, there were Hashomer Hatzair branches all over the world. Half of the members were teenagers from Poland and Galicia, some 30,000 of them in Poland alone. Because the Polish government prohibited all organizing related to socialism, the Grodno branch was registered not as a member of the Hashomer Hatzair Federation but rather as part of Shomriya, which was then nothing but a sports club.

The turbulence of that era stimulated us and added depth to our Zionist and socialist worldview. We prepared for *aliya* — emigration to *Eretz Israel*, Palestine — and Zionist fulfillment. We conducted heated debates on literary themes, and put historical figures and literary heroes "on trial." We immersed ourselves in scouting activities, sports and cultural endeavors at the Zionist Organization center in Grodno. We celebrated Jewish festivals and events occurring in Palestine. We went to regional conferences and seminars. Counselors attended regular in-service activities on education, and enhanced their knowledge in all fields. We held evening sing-alongs until midnight, yearning for our faraway homeland.

Reading was a value. We read and read and read. We read everything in print about *Eretz Israel*, the new Jewish villages, and agriculture. As we matured, we also read Marx, Engels and other socialist and communist thinkers. We read Makarenko's "Pedagogic Poem" and "Flags on the Battlements," and the writings of Freud, Thomas Mann and Ibsen.

The Movement House was a warm home where we also acquired an education. We studied Palestinography; we heard stories about the country — a wilderness the pioneers were conquering, a place of swamps they were draining, a land where kibbutzim and moshavim ("colonies") were making gardens and fields blossom and where warriors stood fast against rioters and attackers. We celebrated whenever a new settlement was founded. We established movement *moshavas* in the hills, imagining we were building kibbutzim amidst

Carmel Gdud, 1937. Bottom row, from right: Cyla Szachnes, Miriam Poupko, Hinda Kokhun, Bassia Brawer, Sarka Shewachowicz, Lolek. Second row, from right: second — Chasia Bielicka, Yisrael Rubinczyk, Lizke Lewin, Eliahu Tankus, Hillel Kantor; third row, from right: Pinke (Pinchas) Zilberblat, fourth — Fania Lipkies, Miriam Wiszniewski, Elimelech Hurwitz (Gdud commander), last — Naomi Chasid. Fourth row, top, from right: third — Sonia Hurwitz (counselor), Gedalyahu Loubitz (counselor), eighth — Eliahu Jerzierski, Yisrael, Miriam Gorbulska, Moni Burla, Sonia Altshuler, last — Dodik Rozowski

the conifers, and draining spring marshes along the banks of the Niemen. In 1936, we fretted over every report from Palestine about the "disturbances." Newspaper articles and letters from movement alumni who had made *aliya* were posted on the walls; we read and memorized them. Our entire age group attended collective sessions in which we learned Hebrew songs — songs of pioneers and defenders, dreamers and shepherds, songs of longing, songs of Zion. We learned to dance the *hora* and the *debka*, the *Kazachok* and the

Krakowiac — in couples, in rows, and in endless circles — into the night. And there was the "blue box," the Jewish National Fund fundraising receptacle. Every member of the movement was responsible for weekly collection of the haul from these boxes on a certain street. Special appeals took place for tower-and-stockade (emergency settlement building) and defense operations in *Eretz Israel*.

When I joined the movement in 1933, it was one of the largest and grandest branches in all of Poland, with some 500 members. Adult members who deferred their *aliya* worked at headquarters in Warsaw, or stayed on training farms all over the country while waiting for their immigration visas to come through. Comrades who had already made *aliya* stayed in touch. And letters arrived from Ein Hahoresh, Ein Shemer and Kefar Menahem, with stories and reports about happenings in Palestine and on the kibbutzim. When someone from one of these places came to visit their parents, their stay became a festival. The groups and Gdudim stopped what they were doing and held special meetings so that we, the members, could listen, ask and feel. These visiting comrades wore halos of promise, of the fulfillment of the dream. They came to us tanned, the palms of their hands coarsened like those of peasants, and their dress different from what we had known. Even when they returned to *Eretz Israel*, we continued to speak of them. Their repute stayed behind with us.

The Sneh Gdud (*sneh* means "bush," as in The Burning Bush) was the older members' Gdud when I joined the movement. Elimelech Hurwitz headed the movement. Our district capital was Białystok, a much larger city than Grodno. There the district leadership held periodic meetings attended by delegates from all the local branches. The bond this created was very strong.

Lots of *shtetlach* were arrayed around Grodno. Not all of them had branches but most at least offered Jewish education. Therefore, members in these places joined us for activities such as brief weekend seminars. We put them up in open houses that were also open-hearted. Members of the movement leadership or emissaries from *Eretz Israel* also attended most of the seminars.

Polish was not spoken at the Grodno branch. We spoke Yiddish, and did our roll calls in Hebrew. The order of the day was read out in Hebrew and then translated into Yiddish. In some groups at the Movement House, all members attended Tarbut. They used Hebrew not only for the internal discourse, but also for activities and discussions. Visiting members from Warsaw spoke Polish. We found this disgusting; it smacked of assimilation.

The movement was a world unto itself. It was a school-away-from-school, a home-away-from-home. Once I reached adolescence, I spent more time at the Movement House than at home. So did all the members. They became our only social group. We went to plays and films together and held lengthy discussions about them, if only to practice the "culture of debate." We discussed Russian literature. The romantic heroes of French literature melted our young hearts. Jean Christof's enchanted soul; Pierre and Elise of Roland's novel, Tolstoy's Anna Karenina — they all lived inside us in the passion of our youth and our craving for grand romance. We were indefatigable philosophers, debating this or that for hours with immense self-importance and ultimately laughing at ourselves until we doubled over.

Hashomer Hatzair gave all its members tools for thinking, learning, criticizing and understanding. It taught us not only to see and hear but also to observe and listen. We learned prodigiously — by ourselves, from each other, and from the counselors, who were bigger bookworms than we. Our intellectual curiosity was boundless. Positioned between the Tarbut teachers (whom we all met) and the Hashomer Hatzair counselors, no young girl or boy had a choice, it seemed, but to grow up to be a humanist, an inquisitive and thinking person, and a great believer in Zionism.

We read newspapers in Yiddish and Polish. We were up to date on everything. Maps of the world and Europe were posted on the walls of the branch secretariat on the second floor. When people spoke about the fighting in Spain and the international brigade in which our comrade David Koren fought, they always accompanied their rhetoric with a map.

In 1933, a new topic of discussion came up: Hitler's accession to power. I was too young to understand it then, but by 1938 I was quite old enough. After *Kristallnacht*, the Nazis embarked on a prewar purge that included the deportation of the *Ostjuden*, Polish Jews who had migrated to Germany, back to Poland. Overnight they were loaded onto trains and dumped over the border in Zbąszyń, a town teeming with Jews. We mobilized to raise donations of money, clothing and equipment for them. The world's day-to-day political life was our lives, inseparably intertwined with class and national aspects.

We talked a great deal at home, especially when we ate together. Avramele, the first-born and already a leader of our branch, was the main speaker, along with Father. But I too, and afterwards Rocheleh, managed to join in. Mother definitely did.

The Movement House had been put together from a series of Polish apartments no longer habitable. Several interior walls had been torn down to create one cavernous space. Some large rooms and a few smaller rooms were reserved for individual groups. In the summer, we tugged benches into the courtyard in the back and sat outside, removed from the street and its noise, our voices not carrying to the neighbors' apartments.

Group of comrades from the Bitsaron ("Bastion") Gdud. Below left, reclining: Feivel Zilberblat, who was shot in the ghetto by Otto Streblow. Middle row, from left: Chancia Jerzierski (murdered in Białystok), my brother Avramele, head of the branch. Behind them: Miriam Milachowski (counselor), Josef Dworecki (counselor), and Shula Rubinczyk. Top row, first from left: my sister Rocheleh Bielicka, who leaped to her death from a train to Treblinka. Second from right, standing: Keyla Cheszes

Until I was fourteen, we visited the Movement House on activity days only. As we matured and turned into the Carmel Gdud, we really made the Movement House a home-away-from-home. We counted the hours and days on the basis of activity there. We met every day after school and did our homework there. We used the Hebrew names our parents had given us. Most of us had been named for deceased grandparents — Naomi and Elimelech, Pinchas and Miriam. We made sure to pronounce these names right, without errors or Polish inflections. As the years passed, our friendships deepened. After movement activities or something for leisure time, our group sometimes pampered itself by going to the Kapulski café. Pampering is a relative matter. We were all *shleppers,* chronically broke. The few of us who had a little money bought three cakes and divided them into fifteen pieces. Each of us took a nibble and passed the pastry on.

We knew how to share, to work together, to defer one to another, to surmount obstacles, to outdo ourselves. These are prime essentials of the human spirit; we did not realize then how badly we would need them in the years to come. And we learned to be responsible for each other. When the girls left the Movement House, they did so in groups that split up and were escorted by male comrades as far as the boys' homes; only from there did they continue by themselves. Naomi Chasid and I were the exceptions: we lived at the edge of town but we never went home alone in the evenings. We were always escorted.

Moshava — that's what we called the two- or three-week movement camps, twice a year, summer and winter. Each year we collected food and money for *moshavas*, half for the winter and half for the summer. Every Shabbat, each member delivered two sugar cubes and some flour and rice to the storeroom of the Movement House, and tossed 10 or 15 groshy into a kitty for comrades who were really destitute. This educated us in helping each other, being friends, and sharing the little we had.

Moshavas were always held out of town, in the villages surrounding Grodno. The peasants hosted them willingly. We paid them for lodgings and caused no damage. We didn't have a vandalistic streak in us. We tried to hold each *moshava* in a different location, in different surroundings. Getting to know new places was part of the deal. We were to bond with whatever we found: fauna and flora, geography and topography, opportunities and challenges. But we always camped close to some little town where we could buy food.

The winter *moshava* was for study. We went on outings in the mornings and sat down at dusk for talks, conversations, lectures and studies. It was a whole self-administering world of adolescence, a learning society that also educated, a formative experience that toughened its participants. It was bitingly cold at night; windburns, cold blisters and pulmonary infections were our regular chaperones. Food was scant. We prepared porridge in huge metal pots on primus stoves, under a metal awning we installed next to the building. Exposed to the wind and snow, we had porridge for breakfast, lunch and dinner, chased down with a little sour milk and butter on the bread we bought from some peasant. Sometimes we also had potatoes or rice.

The summer *moshava* was devoted mainly to scouting activities, field craft and nature studies. The first thing we did there, as kids do in summer camps, was put up a flagpole — the taller the better — and run a flag to its top. The flag grounds were in the middle of the *moshava*. This is where we had morning and evening roll call, gathered before heading into the field, set up meetings and heard heart-rending lectures. The letters of fire kindled at the first and last roll calls provided an appropriate backdrop for dreams and aspirations, ideas and yearnings.

At the summer *moshavas* it was standard practice for different movements' encampments to try to steal each other's flags. Both the thieves and the guards had to obey clear rules about what they could and could not do. It was thrilling and challenging to steal a flag: walking through the forest, sneaking into the enemy camp, trying not to be discovered as you felt your pulse racing, your heartbeat echoing in your head, the twigs breaking under your feet. You went into hiding, thrilled by the sense of invisibility, bracing yourself for the moment when you'd burst into the circle!

In one of our summer *moshavas* we were joined by our comrade Khalif, none other than Moshe Chizik from the Warsaw headquarters. He had come to run the *moshava*. One night that summer, we were awakened by the shriek of the counselors' reveille whistle. We found our flag sentry unconscious, hands and feet bound, a kerosene-soaked rag stuffed in her mouth. And the flag was gone — torn down and stolen. As our comrade came to, vomiting repeatedly from the kerosene vapors she had inhaled, she managed to tell us what had happened. Members of Betar (the right-wing Jewish youth movement) from the *moshava* next door had attacked her, bound her and gagged her, and made off with the flag.

Khalif decided to send a three-person posse — two boys and me — to the Betar camp. I was so proud to have been chosen for the mission. We set out confident and guileless, marching through the forest, kicking up sprays of mist from the soil, illuminated by diagonal sunbeams that penetrated the thicket of needles. We headed east, toward the rising sun, and Khalif said over and over that we ought to subject the perpetrators to a *berur*. Well, *berur* means a sorting or winnowing out — a ferocious term for a "comrades' trial."

Our defeat was immediate, brief and painful. The "Betarniks" barred us from their camp, ridiculed our Hashomer Hatzair outfits, and laughed at Khalif when he spoke about the existence of rules and practices. They recognized no rules and were bound to no practices. Khalif said that he'd write to *Eretz Israel* and summon them to a *berur* at the joint institutions. This only touched off a wave of booing and more laughter and ridicule.

Disgraced, we retraced our steps — flagless, wounded, furious and unable to grasp the notion of the rule of no rule. Khalif called the whole *moshava* into session and said that a lawless society could not endure and that we should have no dealings with such people. We were neither to settle scores nor exact revenge. And that's how it ended.

Then we found a piece of purple cloth somewhere and embellished it with the words "Grodno Branch" in black ink and the movement emblem. We pulled the flagpole down, tethered the improvised flag to it, and erected it again.

About a year later, Betar members unleashed a nocturnal pogrom against our Hashomer Hatzair center on Witoldowa Street. They shattered windows, broke furniture, tore maps off the walls, burned documents, pamphlets and books, and hurled benches into the yard. An awesome tide of fury, rage and sense of helplessness swelled inside me and reminded me of Khalif's remark about a lawless society.

During my tenure as a Scout, I was chosen to be a counselor. I gathered some members and formed a group. I did this after school hours, waiting at the gates of the Jewish schools because they didn't let youth movements in. We had to wait outside the fence.

At home, the desk next to my bed was piled up with counseling pamphlets, books and movement publications from headquarters in Warsaw. It was at the desk that I did my homework, and that's where I began to organize movement activities. I put up two bulletin activity boards over the desk, one with the school schedules and the other with the movement's weekly schedule. Activities took place with clockwork regularity.

The first activity I prepared and conducted was the Ten Commandments of Hashomer Hatzair. It took nearly a full year of activity to discuss them. They were more than the imperatives of Hashomer Hatzair; they were a world unto themselves, including their sources and purposes. We spoke about education and worldview, human dignity, building of society, appreciation of nature and self-discipline, all in simple terms that young people would understand and assimilate as values for life. I valued nature and man above all. I loved children and cherished counseling.

My first memory of antisemitism is the 1935 pogrom.

When we were young, mainly Rocheleh and I would ask Mother why people didn't love us, why they shouted *zhid parchati* (lousy Jews) or dirty Jews or stinkier-than-onions Jews as we passed by in the street. In response, Mother tried to explain the inexplicable.

We were obviously different. We went about life differently. We lived among Poles, they were our neighbors; the laundry woman entered our house and peasants came by to deliver goods. But we didn't really befriend them, even though they were there, the same people, for years. It wasn't the Poles' custom to visit neighbors. Their houses and gardens were their private domains on the other side of the fence. Encounters always took place in the street. When neighbors spoke with each other, they leaned on fences or stood on opposite sides of gates. Even our neighbor Narbut — a widow with a daughter who lived in the house across the courtyard and with whom I played a lot — I visited only on Christmas.

As a girl, I wasn't afraid of the *shkotzim* (a nasty word for gentile boys) as I went to and from school or walked at the edge of the neighborhood. Whenever they provoked me, I paid them back in kind, especially when I became older and joined Hashomer Hatzair. In the movement, we spoke about antisemitism and debated it back and forth. By then we realized there was more to antisemitism than unpleasant personal encounters. Poles considered Jews economic rivals, the Church fomented hatred of the Jews on religious grounds, and various public figures and parties exploited antisemitism for political gain. Antisemitism existed even in eras when Polish Jewry obtained privileges from various rulers — kings or governments. It was persistent, latent and absorbed by babies with their mothers' milk.

Ours was a time when Polish Jewry blossomed and flourished as it never had during its 600-year presence in the country. For almost twenty years between the world wars, Jews figured significantly not only in Poland's demographic growth, but also in its schooling, creative arts and culture. Still, we always felt foreign and unwanted. The older we got, the more we circulated in town, and the more we read newspapers, the more we felt this way. At the movies and on the street, in the institutions of state, the laws and the wording of newspaper articles, it was inescapable. It was this above all, I think, that led us to Zionism and the Zionist youth movements.

This generalization, like any other, does an injustice to the exceptions. There were other Poles, though too few, who considered Jews their equals. I do not mean only during the war — I'll talk about that separately — but specifically in my "ordinary life" in Poland from the time I was born until the autumn of 1939.

I do not remember being afraid of gentiles as a little girl. Our suburb was Polish; few Jewish families — maybe ten — lived there. We were on friendly terms with the Mikhailoviches, Mother's Polish friends, and Father did business with Poles. But after the death of the President of Poland, Marshal Josef Pilsudski, on May 12, 1935, a wave of pogroms — riots against Jews, their property and their lives — swept the country.

The pogrom in Grodno took place almost a month later, on Shavuot, June 6, 1935. It began with a tussle between two young men over the affections of a girl in a nightclub. The scuffle ended when the Jew stabbed the Pole, who died several days later. On Friday afternoon, at the end of the funeral, the murdered man's mourners — some 1,000 people — set out from the cemetery armed with hatchets, clubs and butchers' knives, and rioted in the center of town. Up and down Dominikanska Street, the main thoroughfare of Grodno, display windows of Jewish-owned shops were shattered and merchandise looted. The mob then headed into the side streets and parallel streets off Dominikanska and attacked Jewish-owned houses in the vicinity.

Adult members of the Grodno community convened at the Hashomer Hatzair House on Witoldowa Street and elected a self-defense committee. Aharon Jerzierski, who carried a licensed handgun, and other similarly armed young men headed for the Jewish quarter and recruited associates: freight haulers who were known for their immense strength, a few butchers, and some people from the market. Together, they organized the Jewish defense.

Father came home from work at dusk and described the pogrom that was raging in town. My parents weren't fazed. In our Polish neighborhood, everyone knew us and there was nothing to worry about. In the middle of the night, we heard a threatening drumbeat of vile, hateful shouting. Mother raced to Mrs. Mikhailowa and asked her what to do. "Come to us, all of you," she and her husband answered.

We went home the next morning after silence had fallen and we could trust that none of the rioters remained in the area. My strongest memory of our return was the fragments, shreds and shrapnel of shutters, windows, glass, furniture, books, utensils and stones they had left behind.

Our Polish neighbors gathered around and said, "It wasn't us. It was the drunken painter!"

A painter did live at the end of the street; a short, hunchbacked man who had fortified himself with booze and recruited a gang of pogromists. It was they who had marched down the street, shouted into the night, halted and hurled stones through the windows of Jewish-owned homes, but did not dare to enter.

By midday, we found out that the rioters had crossed the bridge during the previous night and kept on going into the Forstat. When the mayhem petered out several days later, two Jews had been murdered and more than forty injured. The *status quo* never recovered. We moved back into our house and remained on speaking terms with our Polish neighbors, but the rupture could never be healed.

The summer of 1939 was the last summer of my youth, of my previous life, and I didn't know it. No one knew it.

After Chamberlain betrayed Czechoslovakia by signing the Munich Accord, after Germany invaded Czechoslovakia and perpetrated the mass "repatriation" of its Polish-Jewish immigrants, after *Kristallnacht* and after the seizure of the *pomorze* — the corridor of Polish territory that Hitler demanded in order to link Germany with Eastern Prussia — even then, no one imagined that war was drawing closer. Even we members of Hashomer Hatzair, so involved and well-informed, able to read European and global maps and interested in everything happening around us, could not conceive of the way that summer would end.

That summer, my Gdud, the Carmel Gdud, took over the movement leadership from the Nahshon Gdud, most of whom had moved to a training farm in Rowno ahead of *aliya*. My brother Avramele wound up his duties as movement leader and was about to join his comrades at the farm. Since I was already a counselor, I did not head out with the first members of my Gdud for pioneer training at a farm near Slonim. The counselors and activists stayed behind to run the movement.

Every summer after the local *moshavas*, the main leadership of Hashomer Hatzair held a central *moshava* for its executives, a national seminar for educators and movement leaders. Representatives of all movement centers in Poland and all the Gdudim, the administrators of the movement and the national leadership's reserve forces took part. The seminar was always held in some central location large enough to accommodate everyone. The locale chosen for the summer of 1939 was Olegsowski, a town in the Carpathian Mountains. Cyla Szachnes and I were chosen to represent the Grodno Branch. Cyla, my beautiful, amazing, brave friend. What a strong friendship we developed. It sprouted in the Carmel Gdud and lasted all our lives — her short life, my long.

Mother and Father were proud of me for having been chosen for the seminar in which Avramele had taken part three years earlier. They knew how important it was for me. Nor did I have to pay for it. Since the movement had chosen me, it covered the entire cost of the trip (the train ride cost a fortune) and the seminar. All Mother had to do was prepare some food for the trip and stuff the camp backpack with my personal gear.

Olegsowski was a small town in the heart of a valley, surrounded by mountains and so remote it didn't even have a post office. At its edge stood a few wooden buildings ringing a spacious plaza. We gathered in a huge empty granary for activities on the rainy summer mornings. More than 100 comrades were there; every branch sent at least one delegate, and some posted two or three. On the agenda: three solid weeks of academic and applied study. Nahum Streichmann ran the seminar. Tossia Altmann, Yosef Kaplan, Yosef Shamir and Zameret Fogel were among the counselors in attendance.

Each morning began with academic study. I wrote the whole thing: theories of education and counseling, methods of administration and organization, followed by ideas and conclusions about the political state of the world. We talked a lot — about Germany and Hitler, the menace of Fascism, Spain and Franco, Italy and Mussolini.

We devoted our evenings to reports and surveys from the branches. Delegates described the places they had come from, their branches and members, ongoing activities, and special features. It was more than an annual summation of everything the movement was doing; it was an encounter that established latitudinal relations among members of our age group everywhere and conveyed a sense of unity and identity, empathy and friendship. Here, as in the winter and summer *moshavas*, we created a safety net we would need badly — we didn't know how badly — in the years to come.

I found two weeks of pure happiness at that seminar. Cyla and I spent lots of time drawing up plans — how to share the vast knowledge we accumulated with our friends, how to organize the Movement House the following year, how to build up the membership, and how to conduct a training seminar for new counselors.

One evening, a week before the seminar ended, two guests suddenly appeared: Kuba Riftin and Avramek Lipsker, emissaries from *Eretz Israel* who had been active in the movement in Poland and were on their way back from the Zionist Congress in Geneva. That very day, Radio Poland broadcast a government order concerning general mobilization. Every man aged eighteen or over had to report for military service. It was the kind of order that governments gave at the last minute before war. Only then did we begin to comprehend what was happening. All the emissaries from *Eretz Israel* were ordered to leave Poland at once.

It was decided to dismantle the camp right away. We packed up our belongings and the camp equipment and donned our full Hashomer Hatzair regalia, including ties, whistles, badges and medals. We set our camp alumnus emblems against a background of black cloth to show that we were administrators and counselors. Then we reported for the last roll call.

The movement camps in Poland had the custom of burning the flag at the end of every camp — not the Gdud flag, the age-group flag or the movement flag, just the camp flag. We all stood up for a brief and moving impromptu roll call. Then, to the strains of *Tehezakna* and *Hatikva*, the camp flag was set ablaze. Nahum Streichmann, director of the seminar, said, "May it only be that this flag will flutter again over Polish soil."

All of a sudden everything became bleak and sorrowful, like the odor of an impending rainfall or the approach of a stormy bank of clouds. An atmosphere of finality, of something over and done with, engulfed us. Even before it faded away, yearnings and longings took shape. We sensed, more strongly than we could know, that what had been would never be again.

We sat up all that night, embracing and weeping. Even the boys. The new acquaintances, the friendships that had taken shape among all of us, the plans we had concocted — for joint camps, regional seminars and encounters at the province level — did not seem possible anymore. Our world was lurching toward its doom. We felt something horrific and terrible was about to happen. We heard the radio announcements. In our wildest fantasies, however, we could not imagine how immense the devastation would be.

We went to the train station at the crack of dawn. We traveled together as far as Kraków; then we split up. Cyla and I stayed together, two Polish-looking Jewish girls in Scout uniforms. Our misleading appearance was our salvation. As a day and a night and another day passed, we waited at the Warsaw station until evening for a train to Grodno. Among us were masses of people: soldiers and enlistees, people in civilian clothes and uniforms, mothers and wives, children and lovers, making noises, weeping, and calling "Come back!" in all directions. The radio announcer drowned everyone out, his voice booming from loudspeakers affixed to the pillars of the platform, as he declared the general mobilization, the patriotic duty of every Pole to pit himself against the enemy, over and over.

The train pulled into the station. Along with the crowd we pushed our way toward the cars. A group of uniformed Polish Scouts watched us trying to file through the sea of people with our huge camp backpacks, unable to move with them and unable to hoist them overhead in the terrible congestion. They made their way to us through the wall of humanity, surrounded and protected as, carried our backpacks as far as the steps of the car, lifted us aboard, and then boarded the train themselves, separating us from the other shoving people.

After we boarded, we found places to sit, clutched our backpacks, linked our arms, and pressed against each other as we sat down. The train moved. We whispered to each other in Yiddish, mouths to ears, not allowing our words to enter the void of the car. The Polish Scouts were probably sure we had come from some other city; it would've explained why our Scout uniforms were gray while theirs were khaki-colored. We sensed that had they known we were Jewish, they might not have come to our aid. We were lucky, we told each other.

I do not know how many days and nights that trip took. It had been a nine-hour trip to the *moshava*. Now the train stopped at every little village and every remote station where trains did not usually stop. Men who had just been drafted climbed aboard. The sights, the sounds, the crowding and the sobbing recurred each time anew.

Tired, hungry and thirsty, hair unkempt and clothes wrinkled, clutching each other's hands in addition to our heavy backpacks, we stepped onto the platform in Grodno and passed through the crowd that surged toward the train, amid tears of parting, blaring loudspeakers and military marches. We pushed our way to the station exit, headed toward the street, and fell into the arms of two mothers, Cyla's and mine, Rocheleh and Zipporka. Ever since the general mobilization had been declared, all four had been spending their days at the railroad station, waiting for us to return.

We came home. I fell into bed and slept for hours. I woke up to a home in the throes of a spasm of hoarding and bustle. Mother was making all the fruit in the garden into jam. Father, Avramele, Rocheleh and Zipporka gathered the fruit and wrapped it in straw in the cellar to preserve it. Then they went to shops all over town to stock up on potatoes, sugar, salt and lentils. Mother sewed bedding into huge sacks that she packed with noodles, peas and lima beans. She stored them in the kitchen and atop the bedroom cupboard.

The scariest part of it was that we knew nothing and understood nothing. I asked Father what it was like to live in a war, what did one feel? My parents, however, had known a different war, World War One. Mother told me how to know whether the front is approaching: you put your head to the ground and listen for the sound of the wheels of the artillery pieces.

Amidst all the commotion, the activity and the fears that filled the house during those days, I spent hours sprawled on Mother and Father's huge bed, reading Tolstoy's *Anna Karenina*. I laughed at myself. How, at this moment of almost-war, could I plunge into this book instead of reading something more serious, like Dostoyevsky's *Crime and Punishment,* which also sat near the bed? I remained in my parents' bed anyway, as if detached from the world, lying on my stomach, flipping my legs up and down, and living Anna Karenina, far away from the encroaching war.

Pinke came over and we went to the garden together. They'd announced on the radio that the Polish Army was ready, he said. He was sure that war would erupt in another day or two.

Pinke was Pinchas Zilberblat, the love of my youth, the love of his youth. Five years of going steady. It began at the Movement House in a low-key way. He sat next to me at the movement activities, danced with me in the *hora* circles, asked me out to a movie, and walked me home. We spent our teen years together, immersed in the platonic love that members of Hashomer Hatzair allowed themselves. After all, the tenth commandment of the movement forbade sexual relations, but sanctified love.

He was the eldest of four brothers; Feivel was the second oldest. A well-to-do family of textile merchants, the Zilberblats had a spacious apartment and shop in the center of town, on Zamkowa Street next to King Stephan Báthory's palace. Pinke attended the prestigious Polish *gymnasium*, the Macierz Szkolna. An excellent student, he thought it important to be top among the gentiles.

Pinchas Zilberblat

We didn't celebrate birthdays, but they did. Pinke was born on New Year's Eve. The first time I visited his house it was with the entire Carmel Gdud, which had come to celebrate his twelfth birthday. From then until the end of our adolescence, we would gather in his home on December 31 each year and celebrate until midnight. Then we would go out, rent *sanki* (horse-drawn sleighs), and race around town, from church to church, to hear the bells proclaim the New Year.

Both sets of parents treated us wonderfully. We were beloved in both homes. At our house we spent hours in the garden, mostly during vacations from school. Pinke came in the morning and we headed out, spread a blanket at the edge of the garden and read books, ate fruit, talked, hugged and kissed, came home to eat and went out again, almost until evening. Sometimes we dozed off on the blanket.

Pinke's house had so many rooms that he had his own bedroom. To enter it, one had to cross his parents' room. While we were growing up, 11pm was our Cinderella hour. When it came, we tiptoed out in order not to wake his parents. Pinke walked me home and then retraced the entire way by himself.

Although we strode late at night across a city that did not like Jews, we were not afraid. Pinke was tall, rugged, blue-eyed and golden-haired. He looked like the epitome of a *goy* and spoke Polish amazingly well. It was a custom at the Polish *gymnasium* that students in the two uppermost grades were allowed to embroider their uniform caps, and I did this honor for Pinke. Patterning my work after a specimen of a multi-chrome chain, I filled the top of his cap with embroidery. Pinke was so proud of the embroidered cap that he wore it all the time.

When the Germans invaded Grodno in the summer of 1941, Pinke was out of town, working as a counselor at a summer camp organized by the Soviets. German aircraft buzzed at the level of people's heads, gunning down fleeing fugitives and dropping bombs on convoys heading east. The shoulders of the roads were lined with corpses.

People who returned to Grodno told Pinke's mother that they had seen him prostrate, dead, on the side of the road. "I don't believe it," I told her again and again. "No one would murder Pinke. I'm sure he's alive somewhere."

Long after those events, in a different city, on the life-bestowing Aryan side, I walked up and down the Polish streets, certain that I would encounter him with his embroidered cap — just like that, in the middle of the day and in the middle of town. Once in a while, I saw in the distance a person of similar height, blond hair and blue eyes. Sometimes I mustered the courage to approach him and check him out. That's how certain I was that Pinke was alive.

CHAPTER 3

The Germans Invade Grodno

*Fear. That's the strongest memory I have of the German occupa-
tion. We had no premonition about it. We didn't imagine how
scared we should have been, especially since the Poles had joined
forces with the Germans and did not hesitate to assault Jews.*

On August 31, we gathered at the Movement House. We wanted to be
together. We dismissed all thoughts of the school year, which would
not begin the next day in any case. We were all there: young Scouts
and older Scouts, members of the Sneh Gdud, my Carmel Gdud and the Nahshon Gdud, which had been at a training farm, Avramele and his girlfriend
Bella Bielicka-Petrushka, Rocheleh, Pinke and me.

When we set out from the Movement House at 44 Witoldowa Street,
we locked the doors in the customary manner and stashed the key under the
shutter along the window sill. We broke into groups, each heading toward its
own neighborhood, in order to escort each other. We parted, as we did every
evening, with the Biblical sendoff *chazak ve-ematz* — be strong and brave
— and added, "See you tomorrow at Witoldowa." No one imagined that we
had locked the doors of the Grodno Movement House for good.

Amidst the turmoil of uncertainty and fear, we found out that evening
that the Poles had opened the gates of the central prison on Listowski Street,
near the *Farni Kościół*, the great church. It was an enormous prison, its towering walls looming over the heart of a densely populated area that was home

to many Jews. Thus the Poles, aware that the Germans would be entering Grodno within a few hours, allowed themselves free rein to murder Jews on this particular night, on the seam between orderly governance and the chaos of war.

An antisemitic Polish mob poured into the streets and invaded Jews' homes in an orgy of murder and looting. The reports reached us in the suburbs, the Forstat, and the fringes of town. My parents' faces reflected the horrifying, terrifying fear of helplessness. The defensive barrier our home had represented collapsed in one stroke. Who knew what had become of our uncles on Pocztowa Street, in the center of town? And what about our family in the Forstat? The atrocities became known only days later.

September 1, 1939. The first bombs fell before sunrise. Windows trembled and shutters rattled from the blasts. We mistook the first booms for rounds of thunder. It was late autumn, after all. But as they drew closer and rose in volume, we slowly came to the chilling realization that they were not thunder. A terrible panic gripped us. We raced to our parents' room, seeking a place to hide, to swaddle ourselves in the protected space that Mother and Father had created, the domain of soft pillows and the warmth of bed. Father dashed the illusion of the moment right way: "Get dressed right now!" he snapped. "Before you do anything else, get dressed!"

Baskets packed with bread and other foodstuffs stood in the hallway. Since I had returned, Mother prepared them every day, just in case someone set the house ablaze, just in case we had to run away. Everybody knew which basket was his.

Daybreak. In the inferno of the shelling, I saw a wounded person for the first time in my life: a man who lived down the street from us, a short, slightly hunchbacked, and very lonely Jewish man. He was the first casualty on our street. He must have gone out to see what the terrible noise was all about and been hit by bomb fragments. He had spent the entire night lying in the road. Only in the morning, when people came out of their homes, did they bring him into our courtyard. We went to our doorway and suddenly saw a man lying in front of us — his abdomen perforated, his clothing torn, his intestines visible, and everything covered with blood. I raced back into the house and burst into tears. It was my first view of atrocity, my first hands-on experience with terror.

It was only a short distance from the German territory of Eastern Prussia to Grodno. The bombardment of Grodno began before daybreak, and the Germans were upon us by morning.

The morning of Friday, September 1. It is a worldwide custom for the school year to begin on this date. I looked out the window and saw Germans for the first time in my life. Poles were pouring into the streets, showering them with wreaths of flowers.

Announcements and edicts were strewn in the city streets, pasted to electricity pylons, and posted on wooden fences in the suburbs. One of them, in big black letters in Polish and German, said, "*Achtung!* Attention! A total curfew will be in effect from 20:00 on." Another announcement had to do with bread: henceforth it would be rationed and sold by coupon only. Immediately, queues formed at the entrances to the bakeries. When Jews joined them, Poles waylaid them with cries of *Zhid* and shoved them to the back until they were forced out altogether.

After her first experience of coming home without bread, Mother said, "Chasia, you look like a *shiksa,* a genuine Polish girl. Go to Jeruzolimska [Jerusalem] Street. It's a Polish area, no one knows you, they won't kick you out of line." And that's what happened. Every other day I gathered our bread coupons and walked to a different bakery in a Polish part of town and come home with the rations. For two weeks we were stuck in our homes. Apart from me, no one set out for town. No one went to work. To be precise, Jews did not go to work. Our Pravoslav neighbor went to his factory job every morning.

The movement leadership sent out a message: don't try to go to the Hashomer Hatzair House. The girls forwarded the instruction like a baton in a relay race — from house to house, area to area — until almost all the comrades received it. Consumed by yearnings for my friends, I stood all day at the gate of the wooden fence on Podolna Street that faced the path to the railroad bridge. There, I searched the street until my beseeching eyes could no longer distinguish between people, homes and trees. Might one of my movement comrades be out there, walking toward our house?

We endured two weeks of fear. The Poles enjoyed *carte blanche* under the Nazi occupation to assail Jews openly, in broad daylight: to rob and loot, to destroy and devastate, to invade houses, threaten, demand property, valuables and clothing, and to receive them.

When I became a counselor at Hashomer Hatzair, I bought myself a Finnish steel knife with a bone handle, a standard piece of scouting equipment, for use in camps, *moshavas* and outings. When rumors about rapes began to arrive from town, I decided to remove myself from the list of potential victims. Hero stories from history and literature were my immediate inspiration. So I carried that knife, its leather belt threaded through its pouch, day and night — under my skirt, under my nightgown.

One day, two Germans entered our house with rifles on their shoulders. I went into hiding, afraid of being raped. They spoke with Mother and asked for fur coats. We are poor, she replied; we have no furs. They accepted this and went away. It was late autumn; our fur coats were hanging in the wardrobe. As soon as the Germans disappeared from view behind the gate, Mother called me over. The situation is not good, she said. We have to begin hiding things. If these two came, others will surely follow.

Fear. That's the strongest memory I have of the German occupation. We had no premonition about it. We didn't imagine how scared we should have been. We were afraid because we knew about *Kristallnacht*, because we had collected clothing and money for the Jews who'd been deported to Zbonszyn and circulated as refugees among the Jewish communities, and maybe, in the main, because the Poles had joined forces with the Germans and did not hesitate to assault Jews.

Sometimes we took "time out" from being afraid of the Poles and the Germans to read and play games. We had a few isolated, brief moments, like when we went into the yard with Zipporka, like when we picked the last fruit in the garden. Mother always said, "Take something, keep yourselves busy with something." So badly did she want to keep us within the contours of a sane world.

This war was very different. Mother and Father had prepared us for the previous war, the one that they had experienced, World War One. No one knew then that the second one was already brewing. Their memories of the earlier war were fires, starvation, the depredations of the Russian invaders and the enlightened nature of the German occupation.

After the first frightful days, life seemed to fall into some sort of pattern — an unfamiliar, incomprehensible and very threatening pattern, but not a relentless one. At night, we went back to sleeping in our beds and in pajamas. Mother stopped preparing baskets every evening, even though she and Father were certainly more on their toes than before. But just as regularity seemed to return, the Soviet attack began. As the Germans retreated, vestiges of the

Polish Army fought the Soviets. There was nowhere to hide. At night, we sat in the hallway, fully dressed and wrapped in blankets. The nights were already cold. Fear augmented the chill and the trembling.

How I remember the moment when, as we sat in the darkened hallway, we heard gunfire over our house: from the Soviets in the Forstat and the Polish stragglers at the Pravoslav cemetery on the hill at the edge of our garden. The battle lasted several days. The Soviets dropped pamphlets from aircraft, urging the Polish masses not to fight on the side of the Fascist capitalists.

Then the shooting stopped. In a moment, a sudden silence descended. It was daylight by then. Father went over to the little peephole at the large gate that opened onto Podolna Street, exited through the gate, and looked right and left. No living soul was in sight. No Germans, no Poles, no motor vehicles, no war machines. In the distance he saw two people in uniform carrying a stretcher with someone aboard. He ran back home and shouted, *Di Rusn, di Rusn! Ikh ze di Rusishe soldatn!* The Russians, the Russians! I saw Russian soldiers! We're saved!"

We didn't believe him. We sat in place, frozen in a block of fear that had not thawed. Father repeated: We're saved! We're saved! Then we moved toward the window, our steps creaking on the wooden floor. It was the morning of September 17, 1939. In the gray light of autumn, they came, a few at first but more with each passing moment. Red Army soldiers advanced along the road to town after having occupied the Forstat and crossed the Niemen. Through courtyards and fences we saw Polish soldiers and officers fleeing from the banks of the Niemen toward the Pravoslav cemetery at the top of the hill. The radio began to broadcast soothing announcements from the Red Army: We have come to liberate you; obey orders and you will come to no harm!

The announcements were broadcast in Russian and then in Polish — soothing words coupled with slogans about the liberation of the proletariat and the new world that would be built. In our innocence, we really believed them. We stepped into the street to greet the Soviet forces, delighted that they had won and that we were free. The Poles who had thrown flowers at the German soldiers two weeks earlier now hurled them at the Soviet tanks.

The delight and the sense of freedom lasted two days. Mother and Father spoke Russian with soldiers in the street. Then, on the morning of the third day, two officers suddenly knocked on our door and asked whether this was the home of the bourgeois Bielicki. Father said he was indeed Bielicki but was anything but bourgeois. They ordered him to raise his hands, step outside, and stand with his face to the wall of the little cabin in the middle of the yard, in front of the garden that spread up the hill. The rest of the family went outside with him.

The officers turned to Avramele and asked, "Who are you?"

"I'm his son." With that, they ordered him to stand next to Father, hands up.

"You fired at the Red Army," one of the officers said.

"That's not so," Father answered. "We waited for you eagerly. We were happy when you came."

"But your neighbor said that you fired," the second officer said. Our Polish neighbor.

Just then, Uncle Chaim heard the commotion and the voices in the yard and came over. The officers stood him against the wall with his hands up, too.

Mother burst into tears; Rocheleh, Zipporka and I followed in kind. Amid her weeping, she turned to the officer and said, "After everything that the Poles and the Germans did to us, how can you even think that we would harm you?"

A moment that lasted an eternity followed. It must have been the blink of an eye, because as Mother continued to speak, plead and champion the cause of her men folk, Avramele shouted, "Look, there are the Poles, the Polish officers who fired at you!"

Through the fence of the neighboring house, which also bordered the Pravoslav cemetery, we saw uniformed Polish soldiers and officers running away with their weapons. There was no mistake about it. The Soviet rifles that had been trained at Father, Avramele and Uncle Chaim changed direction instantly, toward the neighboring courtyard. Then, running, firing, shouting and summoning additional soldiers in the area, the Soviets set out after the Poles.

We went home, Mother tugging Father, who had gone pale and was trembling all over. Uncle Chaim, Aunt Rosa and Uncle Yehoshua joined us. We stood in the living room, sobbing, embracing and caressing each other. Zipporka held Mother's hand and refused to let go. Mother hugged Father with one hand and in the other gathered up Zipporka, the most frightened of all.

Several days later, two Soviet officers knocked on our door and walked in. My siblings and I were in the living room, playing with our uncles' young children on the sofa. The adults were sitting around the table, conversing about what might be coming up, trying to understand the inexplicable, the improbable. It was evening. The officers' sudden entry brought on a spasm of fear, anxiety and terror that took our breath away. The terrible silence was violated only by the tea glasses that clattered to the table and the crackling of the logs in the fireplace. All eyes focused on the officers as their boots creaked across the wooden floor.

"Izbinichye," they said. "We have come to apologize. We captured the fleeing officers who had shot at us. We captured the Polish neighbor who denounced you. We have come to beg your pardon."

Father invited them to the table. Mother poured tea from the boiler, served the sugar cubes that remained in the pantry, and described the two weeks of the German occupation and the Poles. Her fluent Russian poured forth. Father joined the conversation, also in fluent Russian, and my uncles did the same. For them, they said, there was no difference between Jews and Christians; the only differences were between the working class and its exploiters, the capitalists. We were soothed and began to believe. After that evening, they continued to come over now and then for a glass of tea and a friendly chat, even after the sugar ran out.

CHAPTER 4

The Soviet Occupation

Everything was different: on the one hand, our Jewish and Zion-ist lives were over. On the other, we received schooling, free edu-cation, and equality before the authorities. New horizons opened up.

The first winter under Soviet occupation was not too bad. We had been hoarding firewood all summer in the cabin in the yard. We stocked up on potatoes in the early autumn, when the peasants brought them from the countryside. Piles of food from the garden rested on their upholstery of straw in the cellar. Salt, sugar, lentils, rice, flour and groats were cached inside the house. Vegetables from the garden — cabbages, carrots and cauliflowers — lasted into the early winter. I obtained bread using ration cards. Then the peasants stopped coming into town and we were afraid to visit them in the countryside. Things were in short supply, but we were not hungry.

The Soviet occupation was absolute, not only militarily but ideologi-cally as well. Sovietization embraced all areas of life. The occupiers imported their entire governing apparatus: the army, the regular police, the secret police (NKVD), government ministries, the education system, cultural institutions and bureaucracies. Grodno teemed with government and military people — men, women and their families. Officers arrived in complete units and went to work right away. The Soviets did not leave the area ungoverned for even a moment.

They declared Grodno a border town. Military guard posts were set up at all government offices. You were not allowed to pass near them; you had to cross the street.

The Soviets distrusted everyone, including long-time Communists. They accused the Alexandrovich brothers, well-known Jewish Communists, of Trotskyism — the sin of believing in the teachings of Lev (Leon) Trotsky, who had lost favor in Stalin's eyes. For this they were tossed into prison. The Soviets deported anyone whom they deemed a capitalist. They also deported Zionists. Noah Bass, chairman of the Zionist Organization office in Grodno, was exiled for the misdeed of his public activity. This wonderful, charming human being, a picturesque character with his thick white hair and heavy eyebrows, was packed aboard a deportation train with his wife. Both were killed when the Germans bombed the train from the air. They didn't even make it to Siberia.

The Soviets imposed a reign of terror. People didn't fear for their lives, but that they might do something prohibited, unusual, wrong. Jewish and Zionist activities were halted instantly. The regime usurped the Jewish functions of *tzedaka* (charity), mutual aid, kindness and compassion, the Jewish institutions — hospital and orphanage, schools and synagogues — and the Jewish word (press and literature). Youth movements were forbidden, as were Zionist entities.

For generations, the Jews of Grodno had gone about their lives in a tightly organized community web. Jewish religious and social institutions were a structured part of the individual's world. The community saw to its members' psychological, religious and living needs. Celebrations and funerals, welfare and philanthropy, charity and free loans, mutual responsibility and social commitment, education in solidarity and giving, concern for the other, partnership in fate — all of these vanished at once and were replaced by civil rule that drew on Communist beliefs about how to create a better world.

There were no antisemitic incidents during the Soviets' stay in Grodno. The Poles didn't dare. When the Germans returned, however, they got their revenge.

The officials and their families who had come from the USSR had to be housed. Buildings were nationalized and their inhabitants evicted to make room for the newcomers. Families with plenty of rooms were required to accommodate officers and bureaucrats who had arrived without their families.

We were ordered to make one room available — not right away, but at some later time — for two Soviet officers. They ate in the army camp and bathed at the municipal bathhouse opened at the onset of the occupation. They came back clutching gray towels in which they had wrapped a large square chunk of soap, shaving accessories and clothing. The vapors of the bathhouse still wafted from their bodies, steaming in the chilly winter air.

Education for socialism was part of the upheaval. Huge numbers of courses opened up. They embraced every vocation imaginable: nursing, shoe-making, teaching, metalwork, needlework, smithing, and so on. A frenzy of study broke out. Even simple factory workers had to study. Anyone who wanted to increase his earnings studied. Petty artisans countered the menace of nationalization and confiscation by forming groups and establishing coop-eratives in every field — tailors, shoemakers, what have you. Establishing a productive cooperative was a process under law.

Enterprises and factories were seized and nationalized. Father went to work for Marasz, a manufacturer of beverages similar to ours. The two of them may even have formed a cooperative, for all I know. Avramele learned accounting, and went to work with Father. The records were kept in large, thick and very long notebooks. They figured out everything in advance.

Education for socialism was another hallmark of the time. Children, teens and adults — everyone had to work. Study was considered work, too. Shaikele Matus came late to studies one morning and was placed on trial in front of a crowd, in order to create a public spectacle and, above all, to frighten the masses. Fear was an important factor in imposing order in life. The punish-ment for Shaikele's tardiness was a month of "reeducation," i.e., a compulsory course.

Life in the town stabilized within a few weeks. The value of money, however, plummeted. The Soviets replaced 100 zloty with 100 rubles, which were worth much less. Shops were nationalized and reopened under govern-ment management. Trade in everything — bread, sugar, flour, you name it — took place by means of coupons and queues. You could buy nothing without queuing. The shortages made people yearn for the ordinary shops of the old days, the sort where you walked in and found everything — soap, shoes, hand-bags and clothes. Now the shops were desolate. Display windows had emp-tied; one could look through them and see the barren shelves inside. Wretch-edness, want and poverty became the norm.

The only surviving shops worthy of the name were canteens, special dispensaries for soldiers and bureaucrats, who used scrip to make their purchases. I don't remember by whose merit I once entered such a canteen with Sarahle Braude. What a delightful and surprising thing to behold: a real shop!

Commercial practices were wholly irregular. Uncertainty was their main component. Anything delivered was taken to the shops and sold until it ran out. This happened very quickly, and you couldn't tell when new merchandise might show up. People circulated in the streets near the shops with no apparent ulterior motive, but the moment goods showed up they formed a queue. *Shto dayut?* What are they handing out? Sometimes people joined a queue without even knowing what lay in store for them at its end. Defending your place in line was immensely important; you might be the last one to get something. As a prank on the way home from school, we formed fake queues. By lining up at the door of a closed shop, we immediately attracted a train of people that got longer and longer as time passed. Then we ran away. This delighted the people who stood behind us; they now moved to the front of the line. We fled as far as we could before the practical joke was discovered.

Food was the immediate concern; clothing, footwear and home accessories of lesser importance. Meat and fish disappeared from the shops in a moment. Some was sold to the people in line; the rest accrued to employees of the shops, who sold the goods on the illegal but lucrative black market. Personal belongings and valuables were bartered for flour, butter and milk smuggled from the countryside. The punishment for *spekulantii,* black-market traders, was a lengthy prison term or death. The market persisted anyway.

The Soviets did lots of shopping from the moment they arrived. We found it bizarre. They immediately snatched up all inventories of watches, jewelry, houseware, furniture, fabrics and, especially, clothing. Within a week, the officers' wives emptied one opulent haberdashery of anything they thought looked like ballroom dresses. The items at issue were silk and satin dresses with lace and embroidery, long and narrow cut, with generous cleavage. One evening as we attended a performance at the municipal theater, we observed a row of Soviet officers whose wives had dressed up in magnificent nightgowns. We laughed our heads off all night long.

Shop owners began to conceal goods and commodities right away. Pinke's parents had a large fabric shop in the center of town. They distributed their rolls of fabric among friends, relatives and acquaintances. Pinke delivered a few of them to us; some time later, he reclaimed them to sell and barter for food.

Grodno was transformed. Not only the winter drained the color from the homes, rooftops, people's faces and the sights reflected in the orphaned display windows; poverty, want and emptiness played their part, too.

Soviet rule also had its benign and beneficent side — the attitude toward education and culture. It was this that allowed me to finish my last two years at *gymnasium* and complete high school as all my friends did. Culture was accessible to all. Films were shown on giant screens. Outdoor plays and performances were put on, choirs gave concerts, and *garmoshka* (harmonica) players and *kazachok* dancers entertained the masses. There were May Day and Revolution Day parades, as well as mass gymnastics performances in which we schoolchildren took part. The whole city — parents, friends, students from the other schools — turned out to watch in a huge, packed stadium.

Life was good in the sense that work, security, education and food were available. Simple folk such as laborers and even poor Jews had jobs, made a living, belonged to the proletariat, and were better off than ever before.

We were appreciative of these benefits, not only after having experienced two weeks of German occupation, but also because of what we had heard from refugees who had fled from German-occupied western Poland. Their ordeal preceded the establishment of ghettos and concentration camps, but even so, every refugee opened our eyes to the terror of the occupation: the draconian edicts, the discriminatory laws, the disappearance of people, the executions of Jews.

Life flowed on. We learned to live with the fear of denunciations and false accusations, arrests and investigations. Although we had no telephones in our homes, word spread with stunning speed. Members of the intelligentsia, activists and anyone who owned any property whatsoever lived in dread. Most members of the Jewish Communist Party were suspect. Accused of Trotskyism, they were arrested, tried, and sent or exiled to the Soviet interior. Some Jews enlisted in the governing institutions, the police and the NKVD apparatus; some denounced other Jews — "squealers." There is no other way to explain how the authorities knew that my brother Avramele had been the head of the Hashomer Hatzair branch, or why all activists of the Zionist movement were sent to Siberia.

Our parents were scared. People in the immediate vicinity were scared.

Since the Soviet officers had moved in with us, we had stopped talking and begun whispering, even though we spoke Yiddish at home. Walls had ears. People who had something to say about the deactivated youth movement and other matters said them outdoors only — in the garden, in the street, in public squares. The presence of Soviet officers in our house gave us no added security. Maybe it did the opposite: we were increasingly afraid of being evicted. You never knew what topic would become a pretext for an accusation, imprisonment, interrogation, trial and exile.

The winter of 1939/40 was very difficult: 30 degrees below zero if not colder, unendurably cold. Schools were closed for weeks. Children could not be allowed out of the house. When we went out, Mother stuffed newspapers between the soles of our shoes and our woolen socks and tucked newspapers into the socks to keep our knees warm. We girls went about in skirts and suffered terribly despite long woolen socks. Women and girls in Poland did not customarily wear pants; we did so only at camp and at the summer *moshava*. We joked that the Russians had opened the Siberian border and allowed the cold to enter.

Everything was different. On the one hand, our Jewish and Zionist lives were over. On the other, we received schooling, free education, and equality before the authorities. New horizons opened up — all of which in a world engulfed in war. On the other side of Poland, Jews were being torn away from their homes, condemned to ghettos, made to disappear in camps, or executed. We expected the Soviets to win, and were sure the Germans would settle for the border they worked out with Moscow.

We were not hungry. Meat and dairy products were unavailable that winter and afterwards, but Mother continued to make jam from the fruit in the garden as long as the sugar lasted. We ate bread with jam and lots of potatoes. Mother was unable to plant her vegetables that year; she depended on the peasants to sell her seeds and sprigs, and they did not come to town.

Mother and Father, drawing on their experience in life, were sure that the war would blow over and the *status quo ante* would return, as had happened after the First World War. Seldom did we ask them to buy us anything. When we asked anyway, they would say, "After the war. When the good times really come back." They believed that it would all go away, that no war lasted forever.

During the Soviet occupation, Father put on *tefillin* every morning. He recited the Shabbat and festival prayers at home, but I cannot recall celebrating any festival. Maybe my memory is tricking me. I have a vague recollection of a Pesach during that time that was nothing but potatoes — no getting the house ready, no matzah, no festival tableware. For years I remembered nothing at all, and now that I want to remember, I can't.

Our last family celebration took place during the Soviet occupation. Oka, Aunt Ita's daughter, married a Jewish high-ranking officer in the Soviet Army. The official wedding took place at ZAKS, the civilian registration office. The party took place at the spacious house of Bluma, Aunt Ita's oldest daughter, in the Forstat. Oka wore a pretty dress — not a bridal gown, just a pretty dress. Aunt Ita wore a black dress and festooned herself with all the jewelry she owned: necklaces, rings and bracelets. Mother bought her a gold chain. I don't know where she found it and how she got her hands on it; the shops had long been shut down. Now that I think about it, she must have bought it from a Jewish silversmith.

The entire family gathered for the celebration. From the yard near the Niemen River, we walked uphill to the Forstat with Aunt Rosa, Uncle Yehoshua and their children, Uncle Chaim, his second wife and their children, and all of Aunt Ita's grown children and their families. The refreshments were modest and so were the gifts, but the coming together, the encounter, the family togetherness, the warmth and the love gave us a physical rush of joy. It was the last time the whole family got together. What a kindness it was that we didn't know that. Our joy was unmitigated.

The Movement House never reopened. As soon as the Soviets moved in, they posted notices in the city streets outlawing all political parties. The paper they used was gray. All the paper during the Soviet occupation, even that of school notebooks, was gray. Huge black letters in Russian and Polish forbade teenagers to organize. In lieu of the banned movements, branches of two Soviet-sponsored movements were established: "Pioneers" for youngsters and "Komsomol" for teenagers. Just the same, Shaikele Matus and Gedalyahu Browarski organized an encounter session in the first days of the Soviet occupation.

They were neighbors; they lived at the beginning of my street on the side facing town, at the end of Mostowa Street and the beginning of Polodna. We passed the word from house to house and met at a bench in the municipal park. It was our one and only get-together. Afterwards, they let you circulate in town only in couples. If we had been more than two, we might have been suspected of the punishable offense of illegal assembly.

So from then on we met only in our garden. But we met often. It was a cold autumn; the trees in the garden were shedding their leaves. However, we found the wooden bench and picnic table comfortable, mainly because the courtyard provided us with a place to hide, far from the eyes of the secret police. It is there that the underground Gdud, my Carmel Gdud, was founded. The *Aktiv* (executive leadership) we formed there functioned well into the war. When we went into action, it occurred to us that we should co-opt some friends from the older Nahshon Gdud. After Avramele was arrested and interrogated, however, we decided to distance all older members from the activist core; activity was too risky for them. The only friend whom we added was Yocheved Taub, who had reached the Grodno branch from Wroclawek before the war as an emissary from headquarters to coordinate the province-level leadership. When the war had broken out, she was unable to go home, so she stayed with us.

We were not exactly a resistance movement, let alone a fighting one. However, we decided not to disperse, but instead to stay together as a group and see how life unfolded in order to make our *aliya* a reality. We didn't know then about the center of Zionist pioneering movements, the *Rikuz*, taking shape in Vilna. We merely organized in small groups that liaised with each other in order to stay in touch and ease the loneliness.

Father said it again and again: be careful. There are ears everywhere. Don't speak out and don't say a word against the Soviets. He addressed this especially to Avramele, who was working with him. Even if somebody standing next to you says anything negative, tell him that it isn't so, that the Soviet regime is good and correct. It could always be a trap.

One evening, there was a knock on the door. Usually this meant strangers, not family members. We stiffened in fear and dread. Two uniformed Russians walked in and asked for Avraham Bielicki. Avramele stepped forward soundlessly. We arrayed ourselves around him, motionless. A terrible silence tore at our ears. Then Mother burst into tears: "He's done nothing wrong.... What do you want of him? He's a good boy.... He's just a kid." She extended her arms. They remained outstretched and empty, because Avramele and the intruders had already left.

It happened so quickly. Avramele had been snatched. He was gone; he

had disappeared. The door slammed. Outside was darkness and inside a mute-
ness disrupted only by Mother's weeping, now as subdued as a dirge. My
uncles came over right away to be with us and to offer solace. Mother's only
son, the apple of her eye whom she loved so. For two nights and two days she
was distraught beyond relief. When Avramele failed to return that night and
the next day, she went to the NKVD to inquire about him. What courage it
took to knock on the doors of the secret police. What determination it took to
enter the lions' den and interrogate the lions, the agents of fear and arbitrary
rule, about the whereabouts of her boy and what they intended to do with him.
Don't worry, they told her laconically, he's OK. Mother came home sobbing,
her tears blurring and befogging her vision all the way home. She didn't even
bother to wipe them. She walked and wept, marching from the police station down Mieszezanska Street, then down Mostowa Street, past the railroad
bridge, and along Podolna Street, the long cobblestone road, to our home. Her
fear, anxiety and worry had the power to paralyze, if not kill. Another night
and day passed. Then, in the evening, the door suddenly opened and there was
Avramele. He had returned, but he wasn't himself anymore. He was wounded,
frightened, trembling, pale and spent. Mother wrapped him in her arms, caressing, kissing and caressing him again in order to confirm by her touch what
her eyes beheld. Father and the rest of us stayed in the background.

　　Avramele never said a thing. I do not know if he was afraid to tell us
how grievous and brutal the tortures had been, or whether he did not want
to remember. He said only that they had asked him about the movement, the
activities, the books we read, our ideological activities, and the members of
the head leadership, Yosef Kaplan, Yosef Shamir and others. He told them we
had studied and memorized the *Communist Manifesto,* that we were fulfillers
of Socialist Zionism and Soviet sympathizers. They laughed in his face when
he said that.

　　Members of Hashomer Hatzair who had escaped the German occupation
had received several addresses from headquarters in Warsaw: Yocheved's, my
brother's, and that of the *hachshara* (training center) in the Forstat, across the
Niemen. There, down the Forstat hill, in a grove of trees on Zbozowa Street,
the Street of the Wheat, stood the home of Leib Jaffe. The large two-story
residence with its abundance of rooms became a *hachshara* because Jaffe had
donated it to Hashomer Hatzair for this purpose.

　　Groups and Gdudim of movement seniors visited the *hachshara* from all over Poland. For the most part, they worked at a lumber mill and board factory, supporting themselves and learning to live together in preparation for *aliya* and the establishment of a kibbutz. After a year or two of training, their turn for *aliya* came. The Hashomer Hatzair of Grodno, especially the older groups, was like a sorority of comrades and role models for them. We visited them often, and they visited us at the Movement House, either while in transit or on purpose.

When the Soviet occupation began, the *hachshara* continued to exist for a while. The first refugees among the movement members who had fled from the Germans in western Poland joined it, too. After the first arrests, imprisonments and deportations of Jewish community leaders and Zionist activists, however, anyone could see that its days were numbered. Even before the closure order was issued, nearly eighty members of the *hachshara* moved to the Vilna *Rikuz* via Lida. Leib Jaffe's house was nationalized.

We mobilized to help our comrades. Every home inhabited by a member of the Carmel Gdud took in refugee members. Our parents knew that these were members of the movement and opened their warm hearts without even being asked.

Sometimes nearly thirty people waited to slip across the border. No refugee in our movement was left to fend for him/herself. If the living room was full, Mother let comrades sleep on the kitchen floor. The house was packed with refugees even while the Russian officers were living with us. To be a refugee was a reasonable and ordinary state of affairs amid the reality of war.

The Soviets did not object to the act of helping refugees. They needed working hands and encouraged people to migrate to the east. Thus, the masses of Jewish refugees who thronged from the German-occupied Polish territories at the beginning of the war were put up in synagogues and Jewish public institutions that had been deactivated by law. No refugee retraced his/her steps because of the harsh conditions and the families they had left behind, but some agreed to be mobilized for mining work in the Soviet interior. There they encountered starvation, poverty and unfit housing; a few managed to escape and return to us after a period of such labor. At a later time, the authorities began to register the refugees and give them ration cards. They constituted a crucial labor force migrating among Grodno, other towns and various villages, returning every few weeks and then heading out again.

Most of the Hashomer Hatzair members who headed eastward via

Grodno reached the Vilna *Rikuz*. Some managed to make *aliya* via Teheran or Romania; others continued eastward into the Soviet interior. They worked, got by and survived the war. Others stayed with us; they went to the ghetto and were deported in the transports.

Between October 1939 and July 1941, 700–800 members of Hashomer Hatzair and several hundred members of other Zionist movements — mainly seniors and members of *hachsharas* who had managed to escape from the German-occupied areas — gathered in Vilna. By June 1940, they had organized under the movement umbrella and in general settings that had established a joint leadership, *hachsharas*, an agricultural farm, workplaces and ways of making a living. As long as the *Rikuz* existed, it exchanged messengers with the movement in Poland.

Some of the refugees were relatives. Aunt Pesia, Mother's sister, came from Suwalki for a short time and then moved on to Białystok, where all her children lived. Henjek Dudkevitch of Kielce had been with me at the "executives' *moshava*" in Olegsowski. The night we broke up so hastily we had exchanged addresses in order to stay in touch during the few weeks that we'd be separated. No one imagined the possibility of five years of war. I received one letter from Henjek before the German invasion. Judging by the address, I believe he came to us as a refugee. Blond, blue-eyed and totally gentile in appearance, he was too impatient to wait for an opportunity to cross into Lithuania and join the Vilna *Rikuz*. Instead, he decided to head south via Lwów to Romania. An energetic, focused, organized person, he must have made his way to Palestine, I was sure.

Years later, I met his brother, Moshe Dudkevitch, who had survived Auschwitz and joined Kibbutz Lehavot Habashan after the war. He did not know what had become of Henjek after he left home. When I told him, it was as though I was conveying a final message of regards that had been delayed for so many years.

The members pledged themselves to becoming tough and strong. We matured overnight. We lost some of our innocence. The clandestine activities, the starvation, the deprivation, the fear of the Soviets, and the totality and totalitarianism of the regime, which promulgated a one-size-fits-all ideological line that you had to identify with — they were new and hard for us. Hashomer Hatzair had habituated us to thinking, arguing and using judgment. We did have a guiding worldview: Zionist, Socialist, favorably disposed to the Communist revolution and the Soviet Union. Under this umbrella, however, one could challenge, query and judge everything. Now, all of a sudden, you were not allowed to think independently. Topical debate did not exist. At Hashomer Hatzair, a person who really took issue with the ideology simply left but remained within the Zionist national consensus unless he or she went over to the Bund.

We had been brought up to identify with the Soviet Union, the liberation of the working class, the dictatorship of the proletariat, etc. We were ardent believers in Socialism and Communism. Now, without a moment's forewarning, we faced a threatening, frightening reality, different from anything we had imagined or dreamed about. Comrades who had returned from their hasty voyage to the east told us that the Soviet reign of terror had been imposed not only due to the occupation and the foreign population that had arrived. The authorities behaved this way within the Soviet Union, too. Avramele told us that he was closely tailed whenever he left work to go home. We knew that there were provocateurs and denouncers. We learned to be furtive, to look for ways to throw them off our tracks. We did nothing against the Russians, but the very act of getting together was risky. We learned how to communicate among ourselves, to walk whole blocks as if in idle conversation, as if waiting for someone, carrying clothing and food as though we weren't carrying them. Most of us had attended the Soviet *gymnasium* together; this made our lot easier. At times, when something urgent came up, we crossed the entire city to notify someone about something or to consult together, leaving the house unattended. A world without telephones was a world with lots of walking. I didn't know how useful what we learned would be in saving each other's lives.

The Carmel Gdud. We'd grown up together in Hashomer Hatzair for five years. At the beginning of our sixth year, when the war broke out, our comradeship evolved into sisterly love. The connection was formed of thousands of dreams, experiences and activities together. From age fourteen we had been getting together every day after school. The movement, the comrades and the unity had been the core, the focus and the essence of our adolescence.

Applying the skill and understanding I have acquired over the years, I think that the foundation and basis for what we created during those years gave us the strength, power and commitment to do everything we did, collectively and singly, from the Soviet occupation until the end of the war. We met immediately after school, arriving one by one with intervals of time in between, following a predetermined order. In the lengthy autumn of 1939, we met at the wooden bench in our garden. When the days got shorter and colder, we moved to Tankus' bakery, hid out in the warm cellar, listened to the commotion of the work being done, inhaled the aroma of the nardine loaves, and soaked up the warmth of the oven. If something urgent was up, we sometimes met in small groups of two or three at Cyla's in the Forstat, or at Miriam Poupko's. Eliahu was the liaison; he determined who would be responsible and who would do what. We established our communication protocol anew each time we met. Many of our meetings concerned refugees and arrangements for them. Since the *hachshara* had been dispersed, we were responsible for the movement refugees in every sense: food, board, clothing, coordination with the peasant border-runners and paying the liaisons. However, we also spoke about other matters, any old thing — ourselves, the future and *Eretz Israel* and how we would get there. We wondered when the war would end, and discussed how the Russians must be rearming and regrouping due to the Ribbentrop-Molotov pact, which gave them a respite almost two years long. We really believed they would defeat Hitler and that what used to be would be once more.

We shared the secret of the underground with no one. Even those at home and our extended families were excluded. Our parents, however, noticed it. I have no doubt about that. The friends who came and went, the bustle, the refugees we put up for the night, the food for the road we packed up for them — they unwittingly divulged all the details.

We were very purposeful. Reality had made us that way. Our first decision concerned the continuation of our activities. We were the senior members of the movement, the stratum of counselors. We believed we had to keep Hashomer Hatzair going so that it would not disappear by the time the storm blew over, so that when the war ended someone would be there to reopen the Movement House.

Despite everything — the fear, distress, hunger and deprivation — the young people flourished. The world was at war. People were dying of starvation and atrocities, but we were alive. Our immediate world carried the constant menace of deportation and exile. We lived in fear of denunciations and provocations and had been deprived of all prior ingredients of life and its religious and cultural markers. The shops were empty; the shortages of basic commodities worsened. However, we continued to study and to pursue lively social and cultural lives. Our formal studies carried us far beyond what we could have hoped for in Poland. The Soviets saw to this immediately, amazingly. They opened the schools to everyone — working teens, poor families and Jews who inhabited the Polish milieu.

Everybody studied. Were it not for the Soviets, I could never have attended the *gymnasium* or graduated from any school with an academic program. Father had not been able to keep his promise from years back. Now, however, people who finished high school with honors went on to higher studies in the USSR. Everyone could study. Everyone was equally entitled to embrace the value of study and schooling. Russian culture was abundantly available, too. In groups we attended lots of concerts, plays and films — films of the Revolution and about patriots and the Stakhkanoviches, the Soviet heroes of labor. They were lovely films that portrayed an ideal world. We believed and identified with what we saw. It corresponded to the world we dreamed about, the world we wanted to build.

The Jewish schools opened that year but not as Jewish schools. CYSHO (the Bund school), Tarbut Gymnasium, Realni Gymnasium, ORT and the Jewish schools that taught in Polish all became Russian. Within a few weeks, posters all over town, radio broadcasts and newspaper advertisements announced the beginning of the school year and gave instructions on how to enroll. I enrolled in Realni Gymnasium, along with Lisa Czapnik and Bronja Winicka (I use their maiden name here).

Father thought it important for us to know Russian, and wasted no time in preparing us for it. A few days after the occupation began, he wrote out the Russian alphabet and sat us down at home to memorize it. I thought the Cyrillic characters were just fantastic, an enchanting set of paintings. Immediately I developed a penchant for Cyrillic calligraphy and began to read and write in Russian. I combed *Izvestia* and *Pravda,* Soviet newspapers we had at home, for combinations of letters and words I knew. When the Russian-language school opened, it made the bond easier to create.

The institution that had been the Jewish Realni Gymnasium before the war was now School 9. It offered a long school day and taught all conventional subjects plus two new languages — Russian and Belarusian. All the students were Jews. The classes were co-ed, just like before the war.

Math and chemistry were my favorite subjects by far. They pitched me into a wonderful world of numbers, substances, quantities and ratios. My math teacher, Pinczanski, turned every class into an amazing story that abounded with mathematical allegories. I had always loved arithmetic, and now became addicted to the magic that each lesson brought anew. My chemistry teacher was Aharon Zandman, Felix's father. Years later, after all was said and done, Felix and I would get together with his uncle, Sender Friedowicz, in postwar Grodno.

The chemistry lessons were clear, understandable and fluent. They ushered me into a world of substances and elements, mixtures and compounds, bases and processes, reactions and interactions, combinations that each time created something new, different and other. The beauty of their colors, the power of the substances, the magic of change. The reduction of elements and salts, the deciphering of processes and structures into formulas that defined exactly what they did.

In my second year at Realni, they brought in a geography teacher from Białystok, a soft-spoken Polish teacher in his thirties. His classes were fascinating, and we really liked him. He introduced us to the geographical and political world, the world of natural resources and climates. He turned the whole world into a picture on the wall, illustrated with giant maps in shades of brown, green and blue – mountains and crests, rivers and valleys, seas and oceans, gulfs and islands. We mastered the Soviet Union with supreme thoroughness – its republics, borders, inhabitants, natural and topographical resources, and their importance to the republic and to the nation. This young guy was unique among all my teachers. Long after that year, I discovered that he was also unique among the other people I knew.

Our funniest and most ludicrous teacher was the one who taught us nineteenth-century Russian literature – not because of her personality but because of how she taught. As members of Hashomer Hatzair, we were old hands at reading, examining, analyzing and debating literature. Thus, we could not accustom ourselves to dogmatism, the prohibition of independent thinking, the dismissal of any interpretation other than the one handed down by the authorities. We were given a précis that told us what to think about each book and a profile of every literary character as viewed through Soviet lenses.

The very fact that I was strongly pro-Soviet made things difficult for me. How could the USSR, of all places, forbid us to think for ourselves? We were too scared to discuss the matter at school. We did so only among ourselves, with our close friends, on the way to and from school.

The world of Russian literature that I had known in Polish translation — Chekhov, Dostoyevsky, Tolstoy and Gogol — now unfolded before my eyes in the original. It did so on the huge bed in my parents' room, which I shared only with the books, and in the hours of reading together at home around the dining table. Pushkin's and Lermontov's poetry, flights of the imagination and soul into the vastnesses of Russia, to *Uncle Vanya*, *The Three Sisters*, the living and the dead.

Valentina Ivanova Ochanina. Comrade Ochanina, principal of School 9. A woman and a personality. Born in Leningrad, she had been decorated as a Hero of the Soviet Union for her role in the 1938 Soviet-Finnish War. It was our privilege to have this charming, interesting, indefatigable woman as our principal. From the day the school opened, it was equipped with everything: books and notebooks, ink and pens, writing paper and construction paper. The shops carried none of them. Comrade Ochanina hung pictures of Stalin and Lenin, Marx and Engels on every vacant wall in the school, apart from the latrines. A smart, funny woman, unblemished with affectations of importance or a big head, she knew all the students personally. She sat, asked questions, listened and held heart-to-heart conversations about home, hardships and life. We will have more to say about her later, after Grodno, after Białystok, after the forests. Her towering persona and wondrous humanity will illuminate this account like a kind caress in a world gone totally mad. In a place where nothing of our past really existed, she came and searched, investigated and discovered, gathered us up and asked for us as though we were her lost daughters. She was a true Communist in heart and soul.

The school was run in a Stalinistic spirit. Every occasion, and especially every festival, was a pretext for paeans to the patriarchs of Communist theory. Once a month, the *politruk,* the political-education officer, visited our school and gave us a review of world events, the achievements of the Communist Soviet Union, and the situation of the two wars — that of the proletariat against world capitalism, and that of the world against Nazi Germany. On one of his first visits, we asked him questions. Afterwards, we stopped. We learned not to ask. And there was "Kratki," an especially brief course about Stalin, the history of the Communist Party and the October Revolution that had brought the USSR into being.

It was our privilege to attend a school enlisted for the Supreme Soviet elections. This was probably Ochanina's doing. The great auditorium became a polling station, and we students in the upper classes labored all night to get the place ready in an atmosphere of nocturnal bustle and togetherness — playing, talking and decorating. In the morning, after final arrangements, the furnishings were set in place: a long table for the committee, the ballot box and slips of paper next to it. There were only two slips: one with Stalin's name and one that was blank. Voting was compulsory, and we spent the day maintaining order. There were lots of members of the Komsomol, the Soviet youth movement, among us. The movement had a branch in our school. Lisa Czapnik, a Communist even before the war, joined it. You didn't have to join, and I chose not to. In retrospect, Komsomol members were better off, but I don't remember exactly how. Perhaps they had a stronger sense of belonging. After having been persecuted in pre-war Poland, the Communists were riding high. Not only had their dream of a better world and a more just regime come true, they had also become equal partners in it.

I spent the entire summer between my two years at the *Gymnasium* working at the Tsentralnaya Biblioteka, the main municipal library on Plats-Báthory, King Stephan Báthory Square. Ochanina had arranged this, encouraging me to have a job and earn a little money. I loved it. A job like this was a joy for anyone who loved words, pages and books. So all that summer, each and every morning, I set out from home happily for a day of pleasure — lots and lots of books on the shelves, massive reading tables, the blanket of silence that covered the place, and unlimited reading rights for the librarian.

In mid-summer, I received an official visitor: the *politruk*, a woman who had been appointed to censor the books. She didn't know enough Polish to read them in the original; someone had to tell her what they said. She arrived with a list of books that were in official disfavor; they were to be removed from the library and destroyed. After all the books on her list had been taken away, she extended her inspection to the others. One by one they were taken off the shelves and placed on the table. She opened each one randomly and asked me to read it to her. I recited and explained whole chapters. On this basis, she decided what would stay and what would be destroyed. This may have done more than anything else to focus my attention on the restrictions that the Soviet authorities placed on the freedom to think, to know, to ask — the right to be other.

The year wound down. Final exams. A chilly spring gave way to the beginning of summer. The snow and ice melted; the Niemen overflowed its banks. The days grew longer and warmer. A sense of power surged inside us. Adulthood and freedom seemed closer. Ochanina went out of her way to have me enrolled in further studies — an interior architecture program — in Leningrad. I was to go at the end of the summer. My parents were very pleased and supportive. I would never have had such an opportunity had it not been for the Russians.

Our family conversations always took place after meals, especially Sunday afternoon. They were easygoing and lengthy as Father, Mother and the rest of us mulled the world and daily events. We were all members of Hashomer Hatzair apart from Zipporka, who was too young. Avramele had been a branch leader until the war. The main debates were between Father and Avramele. "Don't be militant," Father cautioned. "The world isn't painted in black and white. Life isn't a straight path."

We said nothing at home about the possibility of fleeing to the east, into Russia, to the endless expanses of a country that offered the promise of life far from the threat of German occupation. Sixty years later, I still wonder why this was so. We were educated people, plugged into the world. Three of the four children were Hashomer Hatzair members in their teens. How had we left this possibility off our discussion agenda? How had the children not asked? What about Mother, what about Father?

The way I pose this question is somewhat unjust. The answer may lie in a more profound point of view, a different perspective. It is hard to see through the lenses of that winter, the winter of 1939/40. There were no instant media back then, no handy information in real time. No one realized that something worse than the previous war could happen. My parents, like the entire world — not only that of the Jewish exiles — lived in ignorance, incomprehension and cluelessness. They lacked the tools to examine the overall picture from the vantage point of their own world, to work through the sparse information they had. They couldn't even tell how correct or misleading the existing information was. My parents believed that the Ribbentrop-Molotov pact would hold firm simply because the Soviets and Germans had concluded it. They could not grasp the possibility of the abrogation of an international treaty.

We had a home, a place to sleep, food, work and a livelihood. Life was difficult, but viable. It was unreasonable, at that point in time, to become refugees by choice, displaced and homeless, cringing under bundles and dependent on others' kindnesses, like the hordes of refugees who had fled the German occupation of western Poland. The Russians who had come to Grodno were totally destitute. Their poverty was scary. Within a week they had emptied all the shops in town of their contents.

Packing up a home means no packing whatsoever. You take some provisions for the way and a very few belongings. You divorce yourself from the security of familiar property, place and surroundings. You tear yourself away from your extended family. There was a responsibility for four children who needed food, clothing and a place to lay their heads.

For lack of choice we made peace with the reality around us. Any other option was worse. We could not assume, hypothesize or realize that choosing something that seemed worse at the moment was actually the choice of life. Mother believed in her ability to protect us in any situation. She thought she was strong enough to provide anything we lacked. In the ghetto she woke up in the middle of the night, bought rolls at the bakery, and walked from house to house selling them in order to put bread in our mouths. She did not foresee a situation in which she could not find any way to make a living, did not imagine that her strength would fail her in doing her duty as a mother. She had an immense capacity for suffering, the ability to improvise, and unlimited willingness to be responsible for us. My amazement over these qualities of hers may be stronger today than it was then. In retrospect, I see that it was our home that gave my parents their false sense of security. They judged matters in view of the reality that they had known previously, that of World War One. There would be pogroms, they assumed, but they had survived pogroms. There would be draconian orders, they assumed, but they had experienced draconian orders before. We outlasted the wicked Haman, people said, and we would outlast Hitler.

It took the young people two more years to figure things out. By then, after the onset of German occupation in the summer of 1941, we were in the ghetto. The messengers who circulated among the Jewish ghettos and centers helped us along. Our own movements in the ghettos showed us what was afoot. We received messages from the main leadership. We joined forces with the other youth movements. All of these produced a painfully clear portrait of the Jewish world.

By then, however, it was too late to survive — for all of us to survive together.

Lisa, Bronja and I finished *gymnasium* on June 22, 1941. The Soviet occupation was also completing its second year. The great auditorium of the *gymnasium* was filled with low brown wooden benches arrayed in straight rows and decorated with multichrome chains and paper flowers that slithered among fragrant, bristly fir branches of dark green. All the teachers sat at a long table, facing their students. The graduating class was seated in straight rows. Ochanina, wearing her civilian outfit and festooned with all her military medals, as one should be on a day of festivities, stood up to deliver a speech. Her words, enunciated in her soft, warm and pleasant voice, were enveloped in affection. She was really pleased with us — the path we had taken together, the opportunity we had not had before and suddenly had now, the future that awaited us as students at universities and institutes across the Soviet Union.

We stood up in turn to receive our diploma. The teachers stood and shook our hands. We were happy. Then we celebrated: a great cheery party that lasted well into the night. Each class put on a skit and we all danced and sang, rejoicing over the end of the year, the end of studies, and the beginning of a lengthy vacation.

A warm early summer's night. We dispersed to our homes, group by group from downtown to the suburbs, walking slowly, clutching our diplomas, holding hands, making the most of our last hours together before the adult life destined for us.

I came home quietly and removed my shoes in the hallway. Everyone had gone to sleep long before. I placed my diploma on the kitchen table so that my parents would find it in the morning. I was so proud of that diploma, so pleased that they would see it. A true sense of joy within a world at war.

CHAPTER 5

June 1941–January 1943

Sometimes, on moonlit nights, we peered through the tiny window straight up to the firmament with nothing in between. We could see a little sky and lots of moonlight. It was a small consolation to think that the moon had not abandoned us, that it seemed to be shining with special intensity in our honor, in our window in the loft of the house on Krochmalna Lane.

The inferno erupted in one stroke. The German bombardment began at 2 a.m.

Awakened in terror, we rushed into the hallway, trembling with cold and fear, the horrific fear of a Polish pogrom. We put on our shoes and layers of clothing. Father stood guard at the door and occasionally stepped out to look toward the gate. Mother scurried about, gathering bedding, food, clothing, silverware and jewelry, wrapping them in small bundles that would be easy to carry in case we had to flee.

The whole city was ablaze. The Forstat was ablaze. Our street as far as the railroad bridge was ablaze. A chaos of fire and bombardments, Russian tanks fleeing, motors roaring and steel treads clattering over the cobblestones. Shutters slamming against the walls with each bomb that fell. Windowpanes shattering against eardrums for hours on end.

When dawn broke, the bombardment stopped and the Germans were in town. A terrible sense of dread, helplessness and impotence overtook us. We could not even comfort ourselves by noting our total ignorance. Aunt Rosa and Uncle Yehoshua came over with the children. So did Uncle Chaim and his family. There was nowhere to run, nowhere to hide. The whole city was burning.

People fled for their lives anyway, in horse-drawn carts, on bicycles, and on foot, along the roads heading toward the Soviet Union. In their panic, they and masses of Russian soldiers were trapped by a German flanking ma-neuver and were mowed down by aerial bombardments and machine-gun fire from aircraft that descended almost to the level of their heads. Only those who had left at the beginning of the offensive, in the dark of pre-dawn, managed to survive and continue into Russia. Others who had avoided the Germans' snare and evaded injury returned to Grodno. Some of them were members of Hashomer Hatzair. They recounted the horrific carnage on the roads, including the sight of Pinke dead, sprawled on the side of the road.

Fear, dread and starvation reigned supreme. Even today, the recollection of that terrible distress has not lost its potency. There was nowhere to escape from the fear and the realization — which permeated the consciousness and the senses — that the hardest thing to cope with was our inability to know what to expect. The awareness that nothing of what had existed as people had known it, recognized it, remembered it or experienced it in their lives, their parents' lives or the family, Jewish or human memory that had accumulated over the generations, existed anymore. We had no tools that could decode the events and could not generate any extent of insight that would help us understand, expect and prepare for the next moment, the next morning, the next breath.

First the Jews were ordered to wear a white armband with a blue Star of David. Reports spread as quickly as a wind-driven fire over the "media," i.e., bulletin boards and the grapevine of family members, neighbors passing through the courtyard and gentiles from our street who knew Mother. Using a white sheet and blue ink, I made armbands for each member of the family.

The second edict followed quickly: Jews were not allowed to use the sidewalk. This made us concerned about how physically to cross from the sidewalk to the street. That, however, was only part of the issue. The rest involved the humiliation of not being equal to those who used the sidewalk. Horses and carts made their way in the street. People walked on sidewalks. Jews suddenly stopped being people.

Then came the order to remove one's hat in the presence of any passing German — a palpable, physical manifestation of otherness, differentness and humiliation. Orders about arrangements for the distribution of bread, the curfew and how to behave during the curfew were posted on bulletin boards and on the picket fences of suburban homes in areas far from the city center. Ration slips for bread were issued against a document proving that the family had registered at the German district office. The document noted the family's place of residence, number of members and entitlement to ration slips. Despite terrible fear, I went into town to obtain bread and, *en passant,* to meet up with friends. I started out wearing the armband but when I turned from our street onto Mostowa Street, after making sure that nobody could see me, I stepped into a courtyard, quickly removed the band, stuffed it deep into my pocket, and returned to the street. By encountering my friends, I also boned up on the latest current events before the reports spread to the suburbs. Now, as in the first German occupation, I queued for bread in places that were far enough from home that I would remain incognito. I stood in line with Poles and froze inside as I saw Jews being pushed to the back of the queue. By the time they reached the place of sale, I knew, it was almost certain that no bread would remain.

It had been different in the summer of 1939. Then there had been time to prepare for war. To hoard food. The crisis followed many good years in which life had pursued its seasonal flow and things happened by the measures of man and nature: the garden and its trees, the bountiful fruit harvests, the productive vegetable patch, the shops packed with goods, the market stalls brimming with produce, the peasants who came from the countryside in laden carts or circulated from house to house, peddling their wares in the city and its suburbs.

The late summer of 1941 found us impoverished and depleted. One could not hoard anything during the years of the Soviet occupation. Furthermore, since the German offensive had erupted so suddenly, not only we civilians but also the Soviet army had been caught unprepared. We hadn't been able to put away anything — food, clothing, firewood — for the autumn and lengthy winter that would follow. The kitchen pantry held small quantities of groats and peas. The trees in the garden and their fruit had become public property during the Soviet tenure. Mother could not make jam because the sugar had run out. Once she cooked a little with saccharin but didn't try it again, either because the saccharin also ran out or, perhaps, because the neighbors invaded the garden and made off with the fruit. During the first week, we ate a little of what remained. The pangs of hunger became less horrific and turned into a constant presence. During the second week, I realized that the household would be eating nothing but bread — a wartime kind of bread, served with hot water instead of soup or tea — unless I did something. So I visited our Polish neighbors and asked for sewing jobs in exchange for food. The first men's shirt I'd ever made earned us a huge head of cabbage. I undid the seams of a shirt of Father's and used it as a pattern. Mother made soup that sufficed for ourselves, Aunt Rosa and her young children for a week.

Several days later, Mother realized, as did we all, that the situation was not temporary. We would not be fleeing to any destination. *Vos vet zayn mit kol Yisruel vet zayn mit unz.* The fate of the Jewish people at large would be ours, too, Mother said, unpacking the parcels in the hallway.

It was then that the abductions began. Men were snatched at random on the street, in broad daylight, for forced labor in town — sweeping streets, clearing bombardment rubble, doing factory work and building military camps. There was daytime work and nighttime work. Other abductions were deliberate, aimed at specific individuals. All the teachers at Realni Gymnasium, for example, were taken out and later executed.

A few days later, Avramele and Father joined the corps of forced laborers. Orders instructing all men to report for labor were posted all over town. From then on, as long as we lived at home, my father and brother set out in the morning and came back at night. The days got shorter and shorter, the mornings darker and darker. They returned at night tired and spent, collapsing to a dish of something that tried to be soup in Mother's devoted hands. There was no Shabbat, no festival, no pause in the unending flow of time.

We stayed at home, Mother and the girls. Only I went out when it was necessary, to obtain bread and to do sewing jobs whenever I found them. Rocheleh and Zipporka helped Mother a little with the housework but spent most of their time reading and playing checkers, Lotto, tic-tac-toe and word games. As a math enthusiast, I had a book of mathematical puzzles, *In the Footsteps of Pythagoras,* over which I poured for hours, solving and studying them. When the weather was nice, we sat at the doorway, playing with Aunt Rosa's kids or the Mikhailovich girls, but we spent most of our time in the large living room.

We were totally cut off from the world, having surrendered our radio to the Gestapo in the initial days. There were also raids on homes; German soldiers came in and demanded property. Mother handed the fur coats to a Polish neighbor in the next courtyard. I do not know which neighbors received our candlesticks, silverware and holiday utensils. Avramele and I placed the treasures of our youth in a wooden chest: photo albums of the family and the branch, friends, letters, notes and writings. One morning we labored together to bury it in the garden, inside the small shelter that stood at its edge.

Years later, after the war had ended, I returned to the house, the garden and the shelter, only to find a large, empty pit in the ground. I do not know who had observed us that morning and what treasures they thought they would find in that chest. Had they excavated the location on the evening we went to the ghetto? Had they waited for evening at all? What had they done with all those papers, photos and albums once they realized that the crate contained nothing of value? Did they vent their anger and disappointment by burning everything, or did they just leave the contents as they had found them, allowing the winter, the snow and the passing years to erase it all?

I do not know and never will. Heartache over memories and lost possessions does not compare to heartache over lost people. It rests elsewhere. Sometimes I wonder about the vileness and baseness of the looters, who presumably lived on our street — people whose neighborhood we had shared for years, people who, perhaps, only resembled people.

Father and Mother did not despair. They had unbridled confidence in their ability to overcome. They believed that we would all survive. They had gone through one war, and trusted their insight about what war was all about. But the fear was so intense that the simple day-to-day world in which we had grown up, along with the confidence that ordinary life allows to exist, vanished in a trace. My sister-in-law Bella, Avramele and I were too old to fall for soothing words; we were old enough to read the stress and anxiety on their faces. We couldn't fail to see it. The saddest and most frightened of all was Zipporka. Her tender age was only part of the problem. As a little girl, she had contracted an orthopedic disease that had not been diagnosed. Terrible pains beset her whenever the weather changed. Father had taken her to a specialist in Warsaw who had prescribed a body cast to protect and stabilize her spine. She lay at home for weeks that way. In the summer of 1939, before the war, they had returned to Warsaw to have the cast removed. They came back by train, carrying a special plaster board on which she was to sleep.

Strange. The first time we felt an easing of the stress, the sense that something very threatening had been lifted off our shoulders, was the evening when the rumor spread that all the Jews would be placed in a ghetto the next morning. Father came home and said, "I spoke with a member of the Jewish Committee…. It isn't just a false rumor…. Tomorrow we're going to the ghetto." The news gave us a sense of relief and well-being because we thought it meant we would be protected, separated from the Polish masses and the German soldiers who could invade our homes, empty them out and wreak violence at their pleasure. In an enclosed space, we confidently believed, we could not be harmed.

The paradox is incomprehensible when pondered at a distance of years and time. You had to be a Jew in that place and that time to relate to the feeling. Our distress had sapped our ability to grasp, to understand, to see things clearly. We knew and were aware only of shreds of things, fragments of processes, bits of events.

Instruction sheets came that very evening. There would be two ghettos: a productive ghetto, to which all artisans would be moved, and an unproductive ghetto, which would house merchants and practitioners of the liberal professions. The place reserved for Ghetto A, the productive one, was the most densely populated part of Grodno, the center of town. It contained the Shulhof, where the main synagogue stood, and the Jewish neighborhood around it — a wretched, overcrowded area that had the Jewish market and the great fish market but no garden, park or open space of any kind. Its old houses leaned against each other as if they might topple over. Ghetto B, the non-productive one, would be situated in a Polish suburb that had wooden houses with gardens and open space.

Mother, Father and I mulled it over: which of the ghettos was better for us? I do not know which of us made the decision — Father the realist, Mother the practical one, or I, who knew that in the center of town I would find all my good friends from the movement and might obtain work.

The moment the nighttime curfew ended, we were given twelve hours to move out and relocate to the declared confines of the ghetto. We had that long to decide what to take, calculate what we would need and remember that our backs and our hands would be our wagons and our legs the wheels. On that basis we had to choose what to leave behind. A home, a family, a whole life. To pack each object or leave it unpacked, to take it or leave it behind, to abandon it and move on.

Mother had already begun to pack that evening; only now I realize that she must not have slept all night. Bedding, blankets, pillows, a few pots for cooking, utensils, the little food that still remained, clothing, soap, shoes, coats. Had she emptied out the little medicine chest in the bathroom? What about the contents of the great bedstead? Where was my Grandma's box of treasures? The silver pincers we used to pick up sugar cubes? What would become of the religious and secular books, the little pepper and salt shakers, the long shoehorn that was hanging in the hallway?!

When the curfew lifted at daybreak, I ran toward town wearing a backpack and lugging two baskets, one in each hand. It took me half an hour at a very fast pace to cover the length of Polodna Street as far as the railroad bridge, and then to Mostowa as far as the pedestrian bridge, to the Forstat, from there to Mieszcanska Street, and then to the corner of Zamkowa Street and Ciasna Lane, where the ghetto entrance was marked. Rocheleh, Bella and Zipporka helped Mother. Father and Avramele packed the large things.

I ran the whole way. I went up the creaking wooden steps and knocked on the door. Sarka opened it; her grandmother was standing behind her. As we hugged, I said, "We'd like to move in with you." I had no doubt that Grandma would agree. The consenting smile in her blue eyes was like a momentary caress on the mask that had formed over my psyche due to the stress, the fear, the running and the morning chill.

I set down the bundles on a narrow metal bed at the side of the room and exited with my backpack and the two baskets, now empty. I ran home and delivered the good news that there was a place for us. A momentary sense of relief: a safe haven. "First of all," Mother said, turning to Father, "the sewing machine." The machine had been folded into its desk but its metal legs protruded. Father loaded it onto his back and set out. We followed with bedding, pillows, cushions and clothing. Avramele came next with the pots, the food and the heavy kitchen implements. I do not know — I cannot manage to remember — how many times we retraced that route that day, racing for our lives as time ran out, rushing to do everything possible in an impossible situation.

Mother stayed behind to pack, joining us only on the last trip. She must have taken her jewels by hiding them on her person. I took everything related to Hashomer Hatzair: the branch notebooks, the journals we had kept, the tie and the badges.

Grodno looked like a beehive that had been ripped open. People scurried about, burdened with pots, not knowing where to put them down. Those who lacked our good fortune, who had no acquaintances and could not find housing, placed their parcels in the street, left a child to watch over them, and ran back for more.

By noon, SS police were standing watch, examining every bundle brought in. There was nothing systematic about their inspection. Sometimes they let people pass and import whatever they wanted; other times they broke, ripped, abused and destroyed items and equipment. One of those items was Zipporka's plaster board, which Father had lugged all the way so she could sleep on it.

The ghetto boundaries were drawn in the old Jewish area across three streets: Zamkowa, Dominikanska and Wilenska. The northern edge bordered the old Jewish cemetery. The main entrance was from Zamkowa Street to the narrow Ciasna Lane, where *der toyer,* the ghetto gate, was built. Garbage and dead bodies were removed via another gate on Wilenska Street.

While in second grade I very much wanted to get a cat. Grandma Sarah-Chaya had one. "When she has kittens, I'll give you one," she had promised. After the birthing, Grandma said I'd have to wait another two weeks. Let them grow up a little; let them open their eyes. Every day on the way home from school I stopped in to see how the kittens were doing and ask again when I would get mine. Each time I was sent away with nothing but a paper bag that Grandma had filled with hot cookies from the oven, redolent of butter and cinnamon. They melted in my mouth, leaving grains of sugar that melted last. One day, she said, "Now." I walked all the way home with my schoolbag on my back and the kitten, a female, pressed to my body. I felt her bristly fur and the pounding of her tiny heart. I held her very close until we got home.

From that day on we were inseparable. She shared my bed and ate everything apart from dairy foods: soup with bread and leftover meat, potatoes and noodles. Only after having litters of her own did she lick from the milk bowl. She didn't let just anyone pet her. She was a wild, clawing creature, totally independent. At dinner she sat on my lap under the tablecloth, dozing in pleasure, and I felt her purring, stretching out or curling up on me again. When I was away and she wanted a quiet corner, she lay down on the windowsill, which caught the sunlight all morning long, and pressed her back against the metal funnel that Mother used to water the potted plants.

A pretty, lovely cat, gleaming black with a white abdomen. Passersby in the street saw her lying at the window. The gentile women in the neighborhood tapped on the pane to wake her up. She was amazingly wise. She sat on a corner of Mother's working table in the kitchen, not touching a thing until it was served to her in her dish. She went outside and returned in the evening by tapping on the window shutter with her soft paws, asking to be let in.

One time, when she was in heat, she disappeared. Rocheleh, Zipporka and I searched for her up and down the street, in the neighbors' courtyards, and as far as the railroad bridge. Mother combed all the corners of the garden. I was more than sad: I was bereaved. That's how much I loved her. Two weeks later, she came back. She pawed at the space between the window and the shutter as if she'd just been away for a moment. I couldn't be angry with her. For ten years we lived and grew up together: Mitzi, me and the house. I started out as a little girl and became a big girl, and my Mitzi did the same.

During the hard times at the beginning of the war, the two of us spent hours together. I lay on my parents' big bed, reading, and Mitzi reclined next to me, curled at my feet and rubbing herself against them, providing warmth and solace. When the family made its last trip to the ghetto with the household effects, we walked together. Mother locked the door and handed the key to our neighbor, Mrs. Mikhailowa. I took Mitzi this time, too. When we set out, I swapped luggage with Zipporka: I took a heavy bundle from her and gave her Mitzi. She walked the whole long way with Mitzi in one hand and a kerosene lamp in the other.

We reached the ghetto and went to the small flat. It was evening by then. We plunged into the commotion of getting organized. The population of the apartment ballooned from three to eleven. Objects and bundles, implements and clothing were piled up in the corners until they filled up the small room and left no place to sit or lie down. A veritable mass of people, we tried to find some room, compose ourselves, get organized, take a breath. Amidst the commotion, Mitzi vanished. When things eventually quieted down and it became possible to make out details, I realized that she was gone. Night after night I called for her and spoke aloud of how I missed her. She must have gone home, I thought. Small consolation.

It was November 1, 1941, a cold day. It began to snow as we made our way to the ghetto: the first snow of winter. That evening, twelve hours after our trek had begun, the Germans surrounded the entire ghetto and sealed it with barbed wire.

The house at 4 Krochmalna Lane, the Lane of the Starch. To the left, you headed toward the Great Synagogue. To the right, the market.

Our new home was part of a two-story wooden house set among other houses, each propping up the other. Ponderous walls, rounded logs, windows and shutters made of ornate boards. Stairs with banisters, some outdoors and some indoors, led to the upper story, a loft with walls that climbed diagonally. Our story began at the roof of the house next door. The stairs, made of aged brown-reddish wood, creaked whenever one placed one's weight on them. The doors and windows had not been repainted in years; all that remained of their paint were shards of old layers in a mixture of beige and brown shades. An old, poor, wretched house.

Our cramped apartment came with a tiny storeroom, two-and-a-half meters wide and three meters long. It had hardly any furniture, and what it had was worn with age. When I had arrived that morning, Grandma had said, "If you make do with five people here, it'll be ok." But then the Epsteins came, too: husband, wife and their son, Salek. They were relatives or acquaintances, so the compassionate Grandma allowed them to move in, too. To accommodate them, she strung some blankets across the wall and the ceiling and created a partition in a corner of the main room, the only real room, of the apartment. The Epsteins set a double bed behind the blankets and slept in it, all three of them. The grandparents slept in a bed that stood next to the door of the little storeroom, which became our room, and Sarka slept on the sofa next to the kitchen.

Grandpa was totally paralyzed. He had been bedridden for years, and never went out. We passed his bed whenever we entered or left our room. He stared at the ceiling all the time. Grandma bathed him, fed him and changed his clothes and bedding as he lay there. She did it all alone, in the midst of the congestion in that tiny apartment.

Our room was little, really little. It had just enough room for an old bed with a mattress stuffed with seaweed, a very small table, and the sewing machine. A tiny window with a rickety shutter opened onto the roof of the building next door. I do not know where Father got the material to make a bed for us; we had not brought it to the ghetto. Either way, he lay a few boards atop two crossbeams to create a surface. The bed was assembled anew every evening after dinner. One side of its surface rested on the small dining table; the other side sat on the sewing-machine table with the machine closed and folded up. In the morning, we dismantled the bed and leaned it against the wall. Zipporka, Rocheleh and I shared this bed. Mother and Father slept in the small bed that had been in the roomlet before we had arrived. Bella and Avramele lived with relatives of Bella's a few blocks away. There were no chairs; all of us sat on our parents' bed. In the morning we folded up the blankets and placed them under the bed. We ate our meals at the two tables we owned, the small one and that of the sewing machine. We also had a stool; I sat on it when I did my sewing. We hadn't brought the stool from home; the good grandmother must have given it to us.

We stowed our clothing in crates under the bed. Over my parents' bed was a little nook. Father knocked a few nails into the wall and that was where we hung our clothes. There was one heating stove in the whole house. It stood in the kitchen: a Plikta coated with white porcelain tiles. We had no heating that winter. Firewood had become too expensive. The supplies we had managed to prepare for the winter had been left behind at home. Afterwards, Father and the Epsteins bought some. Only when we cooked did the house warm up a little. The Epsteins were genial, pleasant people. The husband and wife were large and plump; Salek was tall and thin as a stick. They never fought, never got angry, never raised their voices. This was very uncommon in our kind of accommodation, a one-and-a-half room apartment housing three families. It was the noble-mindedness of the three women that made the home warm for us all. Dr. Epstein regularly gave us attention, patted our heads, asked how we were, said a good word. Salek was also a doctor. People said that he was wonderful doctor, but we knew him only as a tenant in the shared apartment: a rather phlegmatic guy who did everything slowly. He invested a whole hour in every meal and afterwards he licked his plate, turned it over, and licked the other side, too. As he got dressed, we watched his legs under the partition of blankets. First he lifted one foot and pulled a sock over it slowly, as if resting between each pull and tug. Then came the other foot. Then came the pants, one leg snaking slowly up the thigh and thence to the hip, followed, finally, by the other leg. It gave us girls something to laugh about, but never to his face and never out loud.

The only water faucet was in the kitchen: a cold-water tap over the enamel-coated metal sink. Mother brought a tub large enough to bathe parts of our bodies, sort of. On very cold days, Mother heated a little water for bathing on what remained of the flame on which a little soup and a few groats had been cooked. We bathed in turns: Grandma, Mrs. Epstein, Mother.

We did our laundry in cold water, one sheet at a time because that's all the tub could hold. Laundered bedding was hung up to dry on the roof of the house next door. Undergarments and small pieces of clothing were suspended on a string that Father stretched across the windowsill, a little at a time, because there was no room to dry more than that.

The conveniences were outside, past the courtyard of the building. You crossed the lane and passed through a little hole in the fence, behind which were two little wooden cubicles over a pit. This outhouse had to suffice for all inhabitants of both stories of the house. Curfew went into effect at dark. You were not allowed to go outside.

Mother insisted on bringing us the pot, the night pot. We were young; that helped us to hold it in and get through the long winter nights. Only now I think about Mother and Father, the Epsteins, and Grandma: how did they endure it?

Sometimes, on moonlit nights, we peered through the tiny window straight up to the firmament with nothing in between. We could see a little sky and lots of moonlight. It was a small consolation to think that the moon had not abandoned us, that it seemed to be shining with special intensity in our honor, in our window in the loft of the house on Krochmalna Lane.

Later on, during one of the three 2,000-person *Aktionen* of December 1942, we heard knocking at the door in the middle of the night. Policemen barged in armed with lists, looking for the Epsteins. We all woke up. Shivering with fear and cold, we stood around them, unable to help. They got dressed; Mother helped Salek. She stuffed a kerchief into his coat pocket and wrapped a warm scarf around his neck. They packed a few parcels, convinced they were going to a labor camp, and headed for the ghetto gate.

Mother cried incessantly. Zipporka cried with her; Rocheleh and I remained seated on our bed of boards, soundless. Father wiped Mother's eyes and whispered, *Genug, Devoyraleh,* that's enough, calm down....

None of them survived. I do not know if they had any extended family, relatives or acquaintances. However, they were the closest family to us in the ghetto and I think it important to retell their death, to remember them, too.

There was not a moment of respite. The day after we entered the ghetto and began to organize our lives in that niche in the loft, all men aged fourteen and over were ordered to report for labor. Father and Avramele went out and found work together.

The abductions, shootings and beatings in the ghetto began that very night, no sooner than the ghetto was sealed with barbed wire.

The commander of our ghetto, the productive ghetto, was Kurt Wiese, a Nazi, a Gestapo man, and a sadist. He visited the ghetto on its first day in the company of Otto Streblow, commander of the second ghetto, and Karl Rinzler, commander of Camp Kielbasin. They vied with each other in shooting people, in the middle of the street and at all hours of the day. Their aim was excellent.

Our former lives were over for good. Everything became gray and gloomy. Shabbat and festivals were no more. Things that were customary routines even during the Soviet occupation ceased. We were deprived of the relative freedom to move around town, the freedom to try to find work so that we could eat, to be the ones who determined how we would spend our time and organize our daily schedule. We entered the ghetto in November. We did not observe Hannukah; candles were too expensive for anything but dark nights. There was a little electricity at first. Afterwards, we had lots of night-time blackouts and used carbide lamps.

Food was scant, hunger a constant companion that never relaxed its grip, the sense of physical deprivation relentless. The *Judenrat*, the German-sponsored Jewish committee, undertook to provide and distribute food. Sometimes it succeeded, but not in any regular or assured way. The menu featured wretched, bitter cornbread concocted from a mixture of grains, stems, seeds and leaves; a few groats, pinches of salt and handfuls of potatoes; and the rarest delicacy of all, meat.

Some food was smuggled in. A black market took shape under the baton of the wagoners, the *shtarke*, the strongmen, who had also been the commercial stratum before the war. They emptied the ghetto latrines into *bechkes,* huge barrels, that they hauled on horse-drawn carts in which they had installed false bottoms. This was the main avenue of commerce, in which valuables and possessions were bartered for food. Thus, furs, silver implements and jewelry flowed out of the ghetto and vegetables, meat, butter, bread, and — for the rich — medicines flowed in. The ghetto market, the wagoners' smuggling market, was located where the old poultry market had been, on Peretz Street not far from Eliahu Tankus' house. This piece of land was also the ghetto children's playground. In the frenzy of leaving home, games and toys had not been deemed necessities, and were not taken to the ghetto.

The children created games of their own: five stones, jumping rope, tag and hopscotch.

Natasha had been a poultry-monger in the market before the war. An uninhibited blabbermouth, she regaled all passersby, including customers, with a mixture of humor, stinging remarks and ridicule. Clever, intelligent and pungent, she sent congratulations and regards to one and all in a mercurial flow of *double entendres,* her tattered clothing flapping in every direction. Her towering height was crowned with long, scattered, unkempt hair. Her teeth alternated: one there, one missing, and so on, until one that stuck out. This is exactly how I imagined a witch to look when I was a little girl. It scared me to pass Natasha on the way to school. I burst into a run whenever I had to do so. Now that I had grown up, in the ghetto, I noticed how many people liked her. She stood in the middle of market square and orated, her derangement giving her a preposterous courage that no one else could match. She expressed all the curses and wishes we dared not voice. A prophet of rage, she foretold the end of the war and Germany's defeat. She eulogized Hitler for anyone who wished to hear. She wished a different form of death on him each time: burning slowly, being stoned interminably, bound and afflicted with the dripping of cold water, and then the water becoming hotter and hotter with each drop until it boiled as he stood under it for hours, enough time to mention and list all his crimes. In particular, Natasha reminded all of us that Haman had ended his life by being hanged. The new Haman would suffer the same, she promised. Her demise? She died in the ghetto because she refused to allow others to help her.

Ghetto life was an exercise in ghastly, inhuman wretchedness, poverty and deprivation. Housing was such that people lived skin-to-skin with strangers. No one could breathe, cough or cry without having an audience. The killing frost defied escape or deflection. Still, despite the cold and the misery, no one froze or starved to death in the Grodno ghetto. The Judenrat made sure to provide everyone with basic shelter and a little food. At the old cemetery, it planted a vegetable patch and used the produce to prepare soup for visitors to the public kitchen.

In the first few months, despite the murders, shootings, abductions and tortures, one could go to work and cross between the ghettos with relative ease by means of crossing permits. We headed out to help friends and relatives. When a typhus epidemic broke out, I visited Frieda, a former schoolmate, every day to care for her. She died in my arms. Although I had inhaled the air of her house for days, I did not contract the illness; I must have acquired a sort of immunity.

Everything aside, there were relatively placid days. Whenever Wiese, the ghetto commander, wasn't around, people circulated in the streets. On sunny days, the main street of the ghetto filled with people. When Edek Boraks and Tossia came to us, they asked to see the ghetto. Thus, we took them for a stroll down Peretz Street, its side streets, and the alleys that branched off from them. There were peddlers there, not many, just a few. They had set up stalls with a little food and some old clothing. Some tried to sell things in their homes; others went from door to door.

The thing we feared most was an encounter with Germans. Whenever we discerned them from afar, we plunged into hiding among courtyards, narrow alleys and building entrances where the tenants had left the doors unlocked. They entered the ghetto as they pleased; you never knew when. We experienced a fear and dread that penetrated and nestled in the veins, allowing not a moment's respite. Not only our eyes but also our very skin sensed the change in the air, the terror, the panic. Gestapo and SS men, their death's head emblem on their caps, came and went through the ghetto gates. Each time they went away, they left a trail of bullet-riddled corpses in the streets.

Midday in the ghetto: Eli and I were on our way from the bakery to the house of one of the movement members. We were on Peretz Street, passing the row of buildings that opened onto the marketplace, when the corner of our eyes suddenly captured a horrific sight. In a split second, we noticed Streblow and his gang standing at the edge of our field of vision, far from us, itching to murder. Then, as in a freeze-frame that lets you observe every fragment of the events separately, we see three boys going down to the square from Ciasna Lane, oblivious to the danger and the lurking men. Then the hand reaching in, the handgun, and the arm jerking from the recoil. The body collapses, his friends freeze in their tracks, and only afterwards do the sounds penetrate the pounding of one's heart.

Streblow and his men turn to walk away. The boys crouch beside the prostrate body and carry it to the Judenrat building, whence it is taken to the Jewish cemetery on Grandzicka Street. From our vantage point, I knew it was Feivel Zilberblat, Pinke's brother. Right away, the witnesses also began to utter his name. Obviously the rumor would spread to the farthest reaches of the ghetto. I told Eli that we should visit his parents and be the ones to break the news. Better that than allowing them to receive it at random. However, by the time we got to their home, three alleys away, the report had beaten us to it.

The relentless existential struggle reduced life to physical existence only, leaving no psychological room for anything else. A slice of bread, a vegetable for your soup, was a cause to celebrate. We stopped dreaming and, at some point, hoping. In the first period of the ghetto, the quiet one, we received reports from the front. They filtered in drop by drop; we grasped at them and hoped that they would smile on us. We neither knew nor understood how false they were, how they merely supplemented the world of lies and lack of information in which we lived. We did not want to die. We wanted so passionately to live. We believed anything that might provide an oblique reason to hope, anything promising, anything that might postpone the imminent end.

The mighty power of the rumor: the Soviets had occupied Stalingrad, the Germans were retreating, the Russians were drawing near. The rumor flashed through the streets, homes and alleys like a bolt of lightning. You could almost feel it as it passed and spread, pounding the crumbling building walls, climbing the rickety steps to the doorways, and penetrating through the cracks in the wood, borne by the voices of men and women until it struck the barbed-wire fences and the white ramparts and shattered against them as though it had never existed. We knew the rumors were not true, but we wanted so badly to hope.

We used the term "JWO" to denote the mill of rumors that spread through the ghetto. Normally, it stood for the Jewish World Office agency, the old Jewish archives of Vilna, and a book publisher. Now we reinterpreted the initials: *Yidn viln ozoy,* "That's what the Jews want." Our humor did not fade; it helped us to overcome.

Mother in the ghetto. She worked so much and so hard: toiling, scrambling, striving and accomplishing. Like an industrious, stubborn ant, she awakened before dawn to visit the bakery for rolls that she could distribute to houses and earn a few coins. She turned lots of water and a few groats into soup so we would not need the soup kitchen. When chicory was unavailable, she gave us hot water in the morning so that we could warm up a little and not set out on totally empty stomachs. She also fed everyone a small slice of bread that she sometimes enlivened with marmalade. On rare occasions, she gave us a little sugar. Mother's pragmatism saved us. One has to eat to live, even if the meat is horseflesh and, later on, maybe even pork. She didn't say a word. She kept it all to herself: concern and anxiety, intransigence and determination. May it only not be worse, she always said. "Worse" meant that we would be needy, that we would have to go to the place where really poor people ate. The ability to care for oneself distinguished the living from the dying.

Only many years later, when I had children of my own, did I understand the maternal terror of not being able to feed a child, to meet his or her existential needs. Every bird looks out for her young, going to sleep and waking up with this in mind, waging a daily struggle for food. We were too young to understand that, and Mother refused to share her grim burden with us. If only I had understood. If only I had known. How badly she needed a caress, an embrace, support, a sharing of the responsibility. But she refused to share. She protected limitlessly. I helped her with technical things: mending clothes that wore out, darning unraveled knits, patching socks on the wooden frame. The vest I knitted for Rocheleh from the unraveled yarn of an old sweater.

I often said, "Oh, Mother, why didn't we take…?" filling in the blank with a piece of clothing or picture, a book, an implement. A child's wishful thinking. Mother never said a thing and never complained. She had the quality of accepting fate, not in a defeatist way but in the pragmatic sense — practical, fighting, surviving.

Only once did Mother reveal her fears and dreads, her terror and her ghastly helplessness. For one moment she allowed the rampart to be breached, the fissure to widen into a crack in the wall she had built. But I do not wish to put the cart before the horse. I am trying to follow the path along which life steered me: the progression of events in the passing years, the happenings that took place, and the memories that accumulated atop them. I go back and search myself for the feelings, the estimates of time and the right degrees of emotion, so that my words and the records will reflect the sights of this life.

Mother was a hugger. When we were in the ghetto, she hugged us much more than before. She may have needed the physical contact. She may have felt that something about her embrace could defend, protect and envelop us. I cannot pin down her exact thoughts — or perhaps I can, but lack the strength to express them, lest I bring horrible physical pain upon myself, a pain that would make it impossible to continue telling this story. I also use defense mechanisms, barriers and a gird of pragmatism and practicality, the tools of struggle and survival. How similar I am to Mother. How similar to me Mother might have been if she had reached my age today, had she been privileged to live as much life as I have.

Father was the embodiment of tranquility, abounding with placidness, serenity and confidence. His humor entertained us at the grimmest of moments. In the darkest of places, at times when the soul melted into tears and helplessness, he was strength personified, the epitome of might, the buffering, protective and defending rampart. We loved him so. Always — and more so in the ghetto. He suffered terribly from sciatica. In the morning, Mother helped him get up and climb out of bed; she dressed him and buttoned his coat. That's how he set out for forced labor. Father and Avramele met every morning and worked in the municipal storerooms, the Magistrat. They loaded and unloaded, cleaned shelves and arranged them, did lots of hauling, and Father never complained. It was his good fortune that they worked together. When Father confronted an especially heavy load to haul, Avramele ran over to him and either did the hauling or helped. Father was paid for his labor in bread, which he brought home. He left it untouched all day. Mother remonstrated with him over this. You've got to eat something during such a long and arduous day of labor, she said, but he refused. We had dinner when he came home.

Some days, Father came home from work wracked with pain. Those were terrible days. He never said a sound. The tears that welled up in the corners of his eyes and, sometimes, the sighs that escaped his efforts to stifle them — only these divulged his plight. We had no medicines, no salves, nothing to ease the pain. I sewed some fabric into a small bag that Mother filled with sand. We warmed the little sandbag in the oven and then placed it on Father's aching body, moving it from place to place to ease the pain a little. Even in the ghetto, Father never stopped displaying his love and immense appreciation for Mother. He did it by telling jokes in an attempt to unburden himself of anxieties and stress, by showering her with kind words. Mother and Father knew that the meat they were giving us was horseflesh. They also knew that if we children found out, we would refuse to eat it. So Mother cooked it and we ate it, reveling in its flavor and the uncommon sense of satiation it provided. Then, as we were still seated around the table, Father neighed like a horse.

Zipporka, my little sister, our little sister. A child of war. Between childhood and the onset of adolescence, she experienced the first German occupation, the two years of Soviet occupation, and the return of the Wehrmacht. She spent the whole time aching, suffering and ill, bedridden for lengthy periods and ensconced in a body cast for much of the time. She learned to be with herself. Sometimes friends came over; sometimes she went out with Mother or me when one of us was available. We would go for a walk with her or enjoy each other's company in the roomlet. But mostly she read books, lots of books, even books that were beyond her age or that she did not understand. She hardly ever stopped reading. Amazingly, her pains desisted in the ghetto. I do not know if this means that she got better. More likely, her body mobilized to fight its distress. The three of us lay on one bed, on a board raised off the floor, one blanket for us all. We rolled over, hugged, giggled and shifted our legs around, chattering and melding into one body and one breath on the long, dark, cold ghetto nights.

Sometimes I escaped to books. It's funny. Freud and Jung had been compulsory reading at Hashomer Hatzair, especially for the seniors. Several members of the movement had lived in the ghetto area before the Germans' decree; they had not had to abandon their homes and their libraries remained intact. This allowed us to swap books. I read for hours — in the summer on the roof of the building next door, and in the winter on my parents' bed in the roomlet.

Avramele had a girlfriend named Bella Petrushka, a quiet, cute, round-faced, curly-haired girl with round, red cheeks. We called her Pepinka, "red apple." A member of Hashomer Hatzair from Avramele's Nachshon Gdud, she was someone we all knew — Rocheleh and I from the movement, and Mother, Father and Zipporka from her years of going out with Avramele. In 1941, during the Russian occupation, they decided to get married. They went to ZAKS, the civilian office where marriages were recorded, and afterwards we threw a party at home. Bella's father had died, but her mother, her sister, comrades from the movement and relatives came. Mother made refreshments, all very sparse and modest, nothing like those at Avramele's bar mitzvah party or Aunt Rosa's wedding. Still, it was an immensely happy occasion. Afterwards, they stayed with us. They were given the living room; the rest of us packed ourselves in a little more. Mother, Father, Rocheleh, Zipporka, the two Russian officers, Bella and Avramele and I — we all shared that dwelling. When we moved to the ghetto, Bella and Avramele lived with relatives of Bella's — her mother and sister — on Szwętiego Trójce Street, the Street of the Holy Trinity.

Aunt Rosa and Uncle Yehoshua, Uncle Chaim and his wife Rachel decided to move to the second ghetto. It was situated at the edge of town, not far from where we had lived, and they had young children. It was a poor Polish suburb branching from the road that circumvented the Pravoslav cemetery atop the hill at the edge of our garden. Its entire population had been evicted; the Jews who came found a neighborhood of empty houses, simple wooden houses in long rows, equipped with yards and gardens. That made things much easier. The Germans surrounded the neighborhood with barbed wire and set up a gate on Skidelska Street. We lost touch with our relatives the night the ghettos were sealed. During that day, as we raced back and forth in the streets, at home and in the courtyard, we saw them for a few minutes only. After that, no more.

Apart from missing them, we were worried and anxious. We had been separated in one stroke. We hadn't had a chance to say goodbye. No one considered the meaning of truly being separated, cut off, no longer together from now on. In the frenzy of packing up and being thrown out of our home, we hadn't had a free moment to ponder the meaning of the choice they had made. We had never experienced dissociation and quarantine. We didn't understand. We could not grasp what was happening to us. We could not estimate where we stood in the midst of a process that — unbeknown to us — was unfolding so systematically, so neatly, under such meticulous planning, its end almost foreknown. We were preoccupied with the distress and the terror that each passing moment was foisting upon us, preoccupied with surviving day by day — no, moment by moment — busy finding ways to get by and marshalling the strength to overcome cold and hunger, poverty and illnesses, pain and anxieties. Threatened by the unknown, the incomprehensible, the inconceivable. Frightened by the power of the weapons, the uniforms and the decrees that closed in on us.

People could still move from one ghetto to the other. In a family consultation, it was decided that I would be the go-between. I received a *Schein,* a special transit permit, at the Judenrat office. I stepped through the ghetto gate. I walked alone, in the middle of the street, not on the sidewalk like everyone else. I wore my blue coat, which was festooned with two glowing yellow Stars of David, front and back. The streets were the same streets. The trees were barren; it was autumn by then, the sky gray and wintry. I shared the scene with Polish civilians, German soldiers and horse-drawn carts. Slush lined the street. I looked no one in the eye. I walked and walked, eyes ahead and clutching the Schein in my right-hand pocket as if it justified my existence outside the ghetto fences, as if it assured my well-being. It was the first trip that I really took by myself, with no one, alone. I reached the gate of the other ghetto and stepped in. I came to Aunt Rosa's house and immediately found myself in a cauldron of amazement, joy and warm embraces. All the relatives were there: Aunt Rosa and Uncle Yehoshua, Yehuditkeh and Avramek, their young children; Uncle Chaim and Rachel, their little daughter Yenta and their older son, Yankele; and Mother's and Father's cousins.

In the ghetto, as before, Uncle Yehoshua worked at a bakery so they always had bread. Aunt Rosa continued to help support the family by taking in sewing jobs. They and Uncle Chaim grew root vegetables — potatoes, carrots and beets — in the garden. I spent several days with them. After my first trip, it was easy; I visited the second ghetto many times. At first I did it only to be with Rosa and the children but later, when we decided to reinstate movement activity with the young children in the ghettos, I visited in order to be the counselor of the group of children I organized. During one of these visits, I fell ill with bronchial asthma and a high fever. I spent several nights sitting upright on the small wooden terrace, unable to breathe inside the house. I felt terrible. Aunt Rosa did not know how to care for me and neither doctors nor medicines were available. One day, my aunt obtained a glass of milk — I don't know how or where — and heated it up and served it to me. I refused to drink it. Give it to young Avramek, I told her. But she insisted: the kids are young but healthy, she reasoned, and you are sick. I was sure I was going to die, away from my parents and struggling violently and uselessly for my last breath.

I cannot estimate how many days I stayed there, but it was many days. Only now, in retrospect, I wonder what my parents must have been thinking when two or three days had passed and I didn't return. There were no telephones. Did they trust my ability to stay out of trouble? Did they think I had chosen to stay on with my aunt and her children? Might they have been afraid that something had happened to me?

Our situation worsened steadily. My parents' work did not suffice to keep us fed. We had no property or valuables that we could barter for food. We vacillated about whether I should find a job outside the ghetto, somewhere where Poles worked. Maybe the Poles would give me sewing jobs and pay me in the coin of food. I contacted the Labor Department of the Judenrat run by Yisrael Lande, formerly a teacher at Tarbut. I came in and signed up.

I was posted to Cegelnia, an underwear factory. Most of the workers were Poles. I reported to the ghetto gate before dawn, in freezing cold and end-of-night darkness, wearing my summer sarafan, navy-blue with a print of densely packed little flowers. Under the dress were a heavy shirt and a sweater; over it was the coat that Aunt Rosa had made for me. My legs were protected by half-height shoes and long woolen socks.

I stand in the middle of a group of people that had gathered and were waiting to go out, stamping our feet and rubbing our palms to defeat the cold. Then German soldiers emerge from the gloom. They order us to line up in ranks of four and surrounded us. The ghetto gate creaks opened and we begin to march. Our feet clatter on the cobblestones of the deserted streets. No one says a word. I take care not to step on the heels of the person in front of me, trying in the darkness to estimate his pace and the length of his strides. I pass through the vapor of his exhalation, the odor of unwashed clothing, and the stench of the overcrowded nighttime homes, all mixed with the pre-dawn air that stings my nostrils with its freezing clarity. I don't think about the work. It is a long way, a long walk. I see my Grodno from a different perspective. We cross neighborhoods and suburbs, surrounded by soldiers all the time. The closer we get to the factory, the more the blackness of night dissipates. It is my first sunrise march to that place, the first of many.

We reached the factory. I spent the entire winter with a sweater as my only overgarment. I pitied my lovely blue coat and refused to allow it to become dirty and worn. After a few days on the job, I struck up a friendship with Polish women workers and told them I was a seamstress. "What do you sew?" they asked. "Everything, of course," I replied, including things that I had never sewn such as caps and bras, men's shirts and women's skirts. It would be easy to smuggle fabric into the ghetto and remove it in the form of ready-made clothing: I would simply wear it. The problem was how to bring home my pay: heads of cabbage, a loaf of bread, noodles, potatoes and groats. I had a small gray rucksack, my coat pockets, and a long, large interior lining that I sewed into one of the pockets. Ultimately, however, everything depended on the German soldiers who guarded the gate. How painstakingly would they search me, and if they found anything, would they confiscate it or let it go through?

The work was hard: loading finished undergarments onto wheelbarrows, hauling the wheelbarrows to storerooms, and unloading them onto towering heaps. At the end of the day, we marched back to the ghetto. Fatigue always

JUNE 1941–JANUARY 1943   121

made the hike seem longer and more exhausting than it had been in the morning. I came home, emptied my pockets and rucksack, and sat down to sew.

How happy and proud I was to have become a breadwinner. Apart from bread, I brought home bags of salt, a small jar of jam, and once, in the spring, a cloth bag of cucumbers for a complete garment that I had sewn. We had not had fresh vegetables since the beginning of the war. When I came home and removed the bag, the roomlet suddenly filled with a fresh, green, intoxicating fragrance. Mother sliced the cucumbers lengthwise and then into long quarters. The dark thin peel, the clear yellowy interior, speckled with seeds arrayed in long rows. The first bite: the surprising gush of juice, the coolness and the freshness. The enjoyment of a flavor that had been forgotten.

I worked at the factory throughout the winter and spring of 1942, setting out in the morning and returning in the evening. Without noticing, without giving thought to it, I acquired new strength and solidity. The wheelbarrow handles and the weight of the garments coarsened my palms. I became accustomed to hard, monotonous physical labor and exposure to cold and snow, wind and rain. It made me tougher.

That summer, friends told me that they were working in carrot fields, uprooting carrots and loading them onto carts all day long. You could eat a carrot in the field after you'd shaken the soil off it, and you could hide a carrot in your bra or in the pockets of your dress and bring it home. I signed up for this field labor. We set out from the ghetto before dawn and crossed the whole town. The fields were far away: past the Forstat, not far from Lusosna forest. They were vast. Only when we reached them did we notice the broad, large green leaves of the crops and realize that they were not carrots but sugar beets, huge white beets that you had to pull out of the heavy ground. German guards on horseback circulated among the rows of beets and the lines of people on all fours. Anyone who stood up to straighten his back received a blow from horseback height from a long, black, leather whip, its straps digging into your body with a sting as horrific as a burn. The beets were heavy and deep in the ground. You spent the whole day bent over as the terrifying guards circulated. I started out not knowing my workmates but immediately we formed a sorority of common fate. We looked out for each other. We used peripheral vision to chart the guards' movements. Whenever we saw them whispering to each other, we could straighten up or wipe off an especially small beet, nibble at it, and hand it on to someone nearby. The beets were hard and covered with soil but provided a ready source of nourishment. The first time I tasted a beet, I immediately buried it in the earth so it should not be discovered. I remember the flavor of the root and the ground and the sense of bits of soil grinding among my teeth. The work was divided among those who uprooted the beets, those who hauled them to the heaps, and the men who loaded them aboard the carts. It was a long day, with no break, no food and no latrines. We needed special permission from the guards to walk to the edge of the field and crouch behind a few miserable, stubby bushes that left you exposed, visible, and with nowhere to hide. Even there the guards loomed over us, nagging us to get back to work. The sense of humiliation and helplessness. The soiled hem of the dress. The exposed organs. The most intimate actions, exposed to everyone. A terrible blow to one's innermost being. But then the psyche steps in by creating defense mechanisms. We learned to entertain the illusion that there was no one nearby. The person standing over us is not a human being whom you have to relate to. He just looks like one, and since he isn't one then what we're doing is like doing it behind a bush or a house or a tree or an animal. They can't see me either. So we turned the tables and endured. In darkness we set out and in darkness we returned. I came home stooped and aching, almost crawling, unable to straighten up and recover, flopping on the bed. Mother brought me my food, beside herself in her inability to help. I didn't dare quit. Those who signed up for work received bread rations, a very significant supplement to the family diet. Even so, I stopped after several months. The members from the movement talked me into it. They watched me exhausting my strength and knew that I wouldn't give up. I don't know if this has anything to do with it, but we decided at that time to work with the children in the two ghettos. It was for that reason that I stopped working in the fields.

Doctors in the ghetto were not allowed to treat Jews or, for that matter, any non-German. So when I came down with a terrible toothache, I writhed in agony for days with no possibility of relief. I don't know how Mother managed to talk one of the doctors into caring for me. I don't know if she gave him a piece of jewelry that she had stashed away for some greater distress or whether he agreed to take the case from the kindness of his heart. He examined me at his clinic, on the second floor of a building that had two entrances, one in the front, facing the street, and one in the back, opening onto the courtyard. Two teeth had to be pulled, he said. Without anesthetic or anything else that might ease the pain, he ripped out the first one. Then someone knocked on the front door. He pressed a piece of cloth over my mouth, held my hand, and hurriedly pushed me out the back door. I went down the steps covered with blood, clutching the wooden banister. Mouth closed and teeth clenched, I walked home through the courtyards, continuing to bleed. Mother seated me on the bed and pressed on the site of the removed tooth with all her strength. She held me that way for a long time, wiping away the blood and tears until the bleeding stopped. As I retell the story, I can feel the pressure of her hand against my mouth, the warmth of her body, my head pressed to it, and the motion of her other hand, wiping the blood with a kerchief and squeezing it into a small bowl of water. Afterwards, she prepared salt water and made sure that I flushed my mouth with it for several days. That's how I recovered.

Crying was something we did only when faced with exceptional physical pain. Insults, humiliation and helplessness didn't warrant tears. We learned to live with psychological hardships that would defeat people in other times. We learned to suffer without griping, and to accept silently anything that could not be changed, opposed, resisted or fought. We found roundabout methods that demonstrated the Jewish ability to share the little we had with others, despite the suffering and the terrible poverty. People donated food, clothing and heating materials. The humiliation we were going through was not only personal. Deliberate acts of public, national humiliation also took place.

A snowy, winter day. The market square was empty of its stalls. Early that morning, Wiese ordered all the members of the *Judenrat* to report to the square with spoons in hand, one spoon per person. They all came. For hours they kneeled and gathered up the snow with the spoons. The square turned into a messy muck of snow, mud, ice and water. We watched the spectacle from a distance in the freezing cold, standing there so that, I think, they would not be alone. The principal of the Tarbut Gymnasium, the teachers and an engineer named Gozanski stood there with us as the *Judenrat* officials crouched on all fours and gathered up the muck with their spoons. The spectacle continued until the afternoon, when Wiese tired of it. It was not a personal humiliation; it was an obvious and deliberate affront to the important members of our community, to the Jews of Grodno, to my people.

I speak about the *Judenrat*, the German-appointed community leaders, with great caution. I say now, with the advantage of retrospect, but I also said immediately after the war, that one has to be careful about applying the term "traitor" to the *Judenrat* members, as some did. I still think this way today, from the historical perspective, after the passage of a generation. The extermination would have gone ahead without their collaboration, but the period preceding the onset of the mass transports certainly would have been more difficult for the inhabitants of the ghetto had the *Judenrat* not seen to their needs. I know of places where the *Judenrat's* collaboration went beyond what was required. At some point in time, the council members should have figured out what we young people had come to realize: that there was nothing to gain by collaborating, that it would not prevent the killing and the annihilation. Until that point, however, the *Judenräte* were the least of all evils for the communities.

The members of the Grodno *Judenrat* were the Germans' handpicked lackeys. There were no volunteers. Thus the Germans "appointed" Dr. Brawer, the principal of the Tarbut Gymnasium; the teachers Yisrael Lande and Tzvi Belko; and the attorney Gozanski. They had been left behind after the systematic and deliberate elimination of the Jewish intelligentsia in the first few weeks of the occupation. Doctors, teachers and lawyers were hauled away, ostensibly for labor but actually to extermination. It is impossible to sustain a community of 30,000 people without an administrative mechanism of some kind that would assure food and labor first of all. Thus the *Judenrat* planted a vegetable patch for the public kitchen that had been set up in the ghetto. Thus it organized the labor that entitled workers to bread rations. Thus it kept the factories that manufactured for the Wehrmacht operating soundly. Thus the trash was removed, the dead were buried and public order was maintained.

The Jewish police, the *Jüdische Polizei*, were also a German product. With their ubiquitous blue uniforms, the volunteers for this force were wagoners, market people and other strong-arm types who came mainly from the fringes of prewar Jewish society. Acting under German commands and orders, they were charged with maintaining order and pledged their best efforts to the cause. Some of them were better; others were worse. Sometimes they attacked people in the street for no reason. It was no fun to run into them. During the *Aktionen,* they collaborated with the Germans. They were the Germans' flunkies.

By the summer of 1942, we knew what had become of the Jews of Vilna, Ponary and the towns around Grodno. The news forced the members of the youth movements to realize that our fate would be no different. However, the

Judenrat did not see things as we did, or may have known what was afoot but did not know how to back down. The Germans had placed them in an impossible, inhuman situation: their own selves and those of their families against those of the public: my life or yours. Only a few managed to understand that the choice was not really a choice, that it was only a temporary situation, and that ultimately the Germans would murder them, too. Few understood the meaning of choosing between "us" and "them" under those conditions, and even fewer found the ability to choose not to make the choice.

The extermination transports began in the winter of 1942 — from the small ghetto in November and the large one in December. It was then that the lists made their appearance. This marked the crossing of a watershed. At that point the *Judenrat* should have understood the true meaning of their jobs: no longer were they managing and maintaining community life; now they were separating the living from the dead. Anyone who had the wherewithal to ransom himself and his family was crossed off the transport lists, although he didn't know how temporary, misleading and illusory this deliverance was. The *Judenrat* believed that if they met all the Germans' demands, the ghetto would remain in existence and at least some of the community would survive. The conviction that the war would end sometime, that the Germans would not stay around forever, was a form of consolation and hope that allowed people to make peace with the given situation. So badly did they fail to understand what was happening until it was too late. By then, the Grodno ghetto had been wiped out and nearly all its Jews sent to death. Wiese murdered Dr. Brawer and had the few stragglers removed to Białystok ghetto. At that point, Efraim Barasz, chair of the Białystok *Judenrat*, told us that we, the resistance fighters, would be the ones who would cause the Germans to obliterate the ghetto and eradicate its entire population. In that place, the *Judenrat* was not our ally. It couldn't be. It belonged to the other side.

One thing is very clear to me: we in the movement had an easier go of it than the others. Our lives had content; our existence had meaning. Each morning we knew what we were waking up to and for. We had work to do. I encountered former classmates, acquaintances and friends, who moved about like shadows. They had nothing to do, no task to perform. They were just trying to hang on: a book, a newspaper, an old newspaper, a moment of conversation. They were so lonely amid the hardships of ghetto life, the troubles at home, their families' isolation, the hostility, the hunger, the fear and the daily existential threat. We in the movement had a large extended family. In the event of any mishap, we knew that someone would be concerned and would ask, offer assistance, provide care and try to offer some relief. The most important thing, however, may have been that we were not constantly occupied with ourselves.

The transience of our unworkable ghetto lives made it impossible to plan anything. There was no systematic order to things. No day was similar to any other. When you set up a meeting, you did it with the lucid realization that it might not take place. We made sure to stay close, together and connected all the time. We spent every available moment together. Unless we were working, performing some task or carrying out some function, we gathered and grouped — not only to do things at some appointed time, but also just to be together. The strength, resolve and warmth that our togetherness created was like a balm for our souls.

The ghetto streets were paved with little cobblestones and the sidewalks with larger ones. We walked arm in arm, *dorfisher parkn,* like a rural picket fence, six or seven comrades spanning the whole width of the street, strolling together at merciful moments when it was possible. In the paper-tiger kingdom of the ghetto, we were allowed to walk on the sidewalks *and* in the middle of the street. We could to do whatever we pleased. We could not possibly have known what, but we understood that something terrible was happening to us, something incomparable to anything else. Something that had never happened before. We realized that our plight was by no means local, that the Grodno ghetto was not unique but one part of a ghastly whole. If the same thing was happening in Skidel, Luna, Jeziory and Slonim, it was not a coincidence but rather an obvious and carefully crafted system of extermination. The ghettos were being liquidated in sequence. Grodno's turn was only a question of time. We understood this and spoke about it. We made a sober choice, the product of comprehension. We could have chosen differently. Many people chose differently. We chose to understand the atrocity and its satanic nature and to fight against it. Our goal in this war was not victory. We neither thought about nor hoped for victory; we didn't even dare to dream. We knew that we would die at the Germans' hands but devised an explicit doctrine of war to the finish. We were not alone. All the youth movements in all the ghettos drew the same conclusions and made the same choice at almost the same time — even before the joint leadership came together, even before couriers from the movements circulated among the ghettos and unfurled the movement nets of communication, information and aid once again.

Before the war, we in Hashomer Hatzair had been the spearheads of the Zionist pioneering enterprise. We had raised ourselves and others in the doctrine of negation of the exile — the rejection of life and settlement in the Diaspora. We viewed *aliya*, immigration to *Eretz Israel*, as the true Jewish fulfillment, the one that aspires to Zion. Why, if so, had we not dropped everything and fled for our lives, or at least tried to flee eastward into the USSR, where we might find ways to *Eretz Israel*? Why had we not left the ghettos while we still could, and joined the partisans in the forests? Why did we choose to stay?

It was a choice — a knowing, conscious choice — not a necessity. We knew that we would not surmount and defeat the Germans in combat, let alone in the war. We understood clearly that our choice meant our death, sooner or later. Nevertheless, we chose not to turn our backs on our nation, the Jewish masses, but rather to stay with them. In our own eyes, we had been leading the Jewish youth and the nation at large to a new way, hoisting a banner at the head of the Jewish camp — a Zionist and Socialist banner that pointed the way to *Eretz Israel*. The task now was different, we knew. Our role had changed. Our eyes, though focused on *Eretz Israel*, turned to the nation and stayed with it in exile. So long as the ghettos existed, we would be with the nation. We would not abandon it. We would defend it. We would be responsible for it. Only after the ghettos were wiped out would we head for the forests for warfare. We chose to remain in the ghettos because otherwise their populations would have been left defenseless. But we wished to provide the ghettoized Jews with more than defense. We wanted to gather all of them under our umbrella and transform them into rebels and fighters. And we failed.

Today, with the distance of years, time and age, I understand why we failed. Mothers and fathers, children and the elderly, cannot become fighters and rebels. I'm not talking about the physical ability to convert family and parental responsibility into national responsibility. People who had to defend their families could not allow themselves the freedom we assumed for ourselves. People with families simply could not abandon children, toddlers, babies or elderly parents, and join the struggle against the Germans. It was a choice they really did not have. Only we, the young, the offspring of parents who had not yet become parents ourselves, stood at a point in time that allowed us to choose and act as we did. We knew the fate that awaited us and were truly unable to save our families. It was from this impossible position that we chose to go to war, a war we would not win but one that would damage, destroy and impede the enemy to the limits of our strength.

We did not succeed. We could not have succeeded. We were too few. Yong Jews who were unaffiliated with youth movements did not join us en masse. Even at the last moment, when the Germans swept the ghetto's vestigial population into the synagogue, only a few of the young people in the synagogue joined the comrades who burst through the window to escape to the forest.

Much later, when we went over to the Aryan side, to the Białystok ghetto, to the forests and the partisans, we made that war a reality.

The ghetto was under curfew from its first night. From 6 p.m. in the winter and from 8 p.m. in the summer, being outside before morning meant death. The curfew was enforced by Jewish police, who circulated in the streets. We grouped together very quickly. The ghetto area was small; you could cross it on foot in ten minutes. People were not hard to find, and we came together at once. We had no regular meeting place; each time we met, we chose the venue of the next meeting: with Eli at the bakery, with us in our room, at the old Jewish cemetery, or just in the street.

We jelled. Eliahu Tankus, Shaikele Matus, Gedalyahu Browarski, Cyla Szachnes, Mirjam Pupko, Moni Burla and I became an *Aktiv,* an executive leadership of Hashomer Hatzair in the Grodno ghetto. Our first activity targeted children and teens, not only because education was in our blood, but also because nobody was looking out for them amid the disintegration and reshaping of the general frame of life. Nor were we alone in this activity. The same initiatives were taken by other movements in other ghettos. Dror, Hanoar Hazioni, the Communists and the Bund did exactly as we did.

Life was relatively calm during the first half-year. People worked, the *Judenrat* organized, one could leave the ghetto by permit, and children and teens moved about unsupervised. We sensed that we should resume our educational work. The war had been under way for more than two years; we inhabited a world that had lost its bearings. We were mature; we were the movement seniors who had accumulated eight or nine years of baggage. We did our educational work under the auspices of a movement, but the thing we gave the children and adolescents was not food for the road in the face of the lengthy war. Everything that had once been orderly and organized, warm, protective and safe had been shattered and sundered.

We saw the children in the streets. We saw how the imperative of survival had taken over, how street smarts overcame patterns of home and family, education and social values. We saw the pilfering they were forced to commit in order to stay alive or help their families. We watched them smuggle contraband in and out as long as the ghetto remained open, and realized that their actions carried the legitimacy of necessity. We saw the youngsters organize in bands and commit acts of mayhem that escalated into violent harassment. In the ghetto of all places, within the ostensibly self-administering Jewish world, the youth movements could be rebuilt.

We gathered the first children — ten, eleven or twelve years old — off the street. Afterwards, the youngsters organized everything themselves and did a wonderful job of it. They were also more realistic and practical than we. Our years of life and upbringing had instilled conventions, obligations and pangs of conscience within us. The children had grown up in a different reality, and had learned to live and survive in it. We also searched for youngsters from a group called Bnei Midbar (Sons of the Desert), who had joined the movement before the war but had not had a chance to internalize its values.

Four or five groups began to operate, each with a counselor, each on its own. The groups could not be brought together for joint activity; we had nowhere to gather. In the summer, we met in side courtyards or sat next to the cemetery. Later, in the winter, we met at what had been the Yavne School and was now the *Judenrat's* public kitchen. It was a tall building with three stories, a loft and an open-ended rectangle structure opening onto an interior courtyard. The building was vacant after food distribution hours and we received permission to use one of its halls, a small place with long benches — grey, gloomy, Spartan and very cold.

We gathered the very young children in the mornings. They wanted to be with us every day. Twenty children enrolled but some did not attend regularly; they were responsible for taking care of younger siblings while their parents were at work. They bought things, sold things, brought things home and queued for soup. We spoke with them about the Jewish festivals that we were not celebrating, told them about *Eretz Israel* and taught them Hebrew songs. I read to them stories by I.L. Peretz, Sholem Aleichem and Shalom Asch. And I recited Bialik's "In the City of Slaughter." I recounted the pogroms in

Kishinev as the children listened in utter silence. Then Hershele broke the collective reverie; he wanted to ask me something. The other children remained silent, staring at me. "Ask, go right ahead," I said.

"After Kishinev, Bialik wrote. But who will survive after us? I don't think anyone will survive to write...."

The ghetto was still open. Jews were not yet being gathered up for transports; the *Aktionen* had not yet begun. But people were being murdered in the streets and those still alive talked about it at home, on the street, and in the market. Hershele had keen antennas and fail-safe street smarts. He was one of our main sources of news. He was rarely wrong.

Hershele the redhead. The smart kid whom I loved so much. Vibrant, bouncy and amazingly clever. "You've got *shpilkes in tukhes*," I'd tell him: thorns in your rear end. For years I dreamed of having a son like him, with big brown eyes, an enchanting smile, freckles, and hair the color of sizzling copper.

His question caught me off guard. For a moment it hovered in the void of the darkened room. Then it spread, drawing circles of fear and destruction. I'm sure lots of people will survive, I said. Lots and lots. We'll survive, too. But I sensed that my words did not dispel a thing. They offered no response, no comfort, nothing in any way useful.

I must free myself of this sense of terrible despair, I thought then. I must extricate the children and remove them to some other place. I knew as well as Hershele that no one would survive. But you're a senior, I told myself. You do things that children can't. The choice of taking action, like the choice of not thinking about the end, gives you powers that you would like the children to have, too. In the silence that filled the room, I enlisted words, pictures and sights to tell them about *Eretz Israel*: its colors, aromas and flavors, its summer, sand dunes, camels and orange groves. I filled the room with ranks of *halutzim*, Zionist pioneers, working in the fields and pitching tents, and groups of *halutzot*, women pioneers in their embroidered blouses, milking cows in the barn and standing guard at night. I told them about the kibbutzim, the children's homes where only children live — living, eating and studying together. I told them about the youth groups and the first educational institution, established in Mishmar HaEmek, where children from all kibbutzim go to learn. I told them about the sea and the hills, the Galilee, the Sharon and the Negev. I talked incessantly, without pausing. If I were to stop, I feared, the enchantment would fade away and the dream, with its sights, sounds and colors, would vanish. Then I told them the tale of Bonce Shweig, Benjamin the Silent. A poor boy, a very poor boy, he never complained about his wretched life and its burden of hunger, cold and loneliness. When he died and went to heaven, the angels greeted him and said, Bonce, you're a saint, you never blamed God for anything. Therefore, you'll get anything you ask for. He gazed at the angels, contemplated all the world's treasures as they unfolded before his eyes, and said, "I'd like a roll. A roll with butter. A fresh roll with real butter. That's all."

And there, in the silence of the room, you could smell the fresh roll, a warm fragrance that instead of pounding at the nose radiates in soft circles, penetrates the nostrils, makes your eyes water, returns to the cavity of your mouth, and settles on the ridges of the tongue until it becomes a flavor that blends into the fresh butter, which melts like yellow velvet between palate and cheek, the vapors of its fragrance rising through the pharynx and entering the nose from behind until you can't tell the fragrance of life, that of the roll, from the fragrance of pleasure, that of the butter.

Silence. The children aren't looking at me anymore. Some have closed their eyes. Others allowed their eyes to drift into dreams. We spend hours together. We dream together. Then, together, we open the door and exit into the reality of the ghetto.

The children changed over time. The things we discussed, the attention they received and the group togetherness made them stronger. The organized setting, the camaraderie and the relations that we formed gave them strength that other children lacked. All of us considered it a mission. Educating these children was a goal and a task of the highest order. So important was it, and so passionately did we believe in it and in our personal responsibility for the children, that throughout this period I did counseling work in the second ghetto as well. Once a week I marched from our ghetto to Ghetto B and visited them. I organized two groups there: younger children in the morning and older children in the afternoon. By doing this, I also found other movement comrades who had gone to Ghetto B with their families. Before the unrestricted passage between the ghettos was revoked, we managed to bring them to us, to our ghetto. They set out on one-day crossing permits and moved in with us.

After several months of activity, we had become very close to the youngsters and were invited to visit their homes. Winter was approaching and abductions had become daily occurrences. Most abductees were men. The children told us about fathers who had not returned from work, about hunger and desperate attempts to obtain food. In one home I found an ill, exhausted mother in bed, two toddlers on the floor, and my movement's cadets standing in a corner of the room, ashamed. It wasn't just the winter, the wind, the distress and the hunger that made this house cold. The house had become cold and sad because no one was there to provide protection and support.

When I described this visit to the *Aktiv*, we realized that we had to begin mutual-aid activity. We began to visit our cadets' homes systematically, bringing them bread and clothing, shoes and coats. We kept no records but passed information about who needed what by word of mouth. One day as we sat with Shaikele Matus, one of our boys walked in, his shoes torn and all his toes sticking out, exposed to the cold, the snow and the mud. Shaikele leaped to his feet, ran to the other room, and emerged with an intact pair of shoes.

Gedalyahu Browarski with Shaikele Matus, one of the leaders of the resistance

Since they were several sizes too large for the boy, he rounded up some old newspapers and stuffed them into the toes. Now they fit.

The Tankuses lived on the main street of the ghetto, Peretz Street (named for the Jewish author I.L. Peretz) in a tall, spacious two-story house made of light-colored bricks, right on the street. The Tankuses lived upstairs, flour and lumber were stored in the cellar, and the ground floor had a bakery, a confectionary and a storefront. The store had a large, glass door and tall, wide windows. Before the war, in these windows every morning were displays of rolls and loaves of bread, biscuits and salty pastries, enormous opulent cakes and smaller ones for personal consumption, filled with fruit and cream, with wonderful cookies next to them. The store had a long sales counter of dark wood; at its edge stood a huge metal cash register and a stack of brown paper bags. Behind the counter, along the wall, were rows of shelves on which loaves of bread were arrayed. The oven — a huge brick affair — stood in the back room, a heavy black iron door covering its hatch. Across from the oven were large wooden tables and bakers' shovels with very long handles. The workers used them to thrust unbaked loaves deep into the oven and to load baked loaves into large bushel baskets, in which they would be taken to the shop and arranged on the shelves. As long as it remained possible, I stepped into the back room and watched the bakers as they toiled. Even in the ghetto, they wore aprons and bakers' caps. The aprons went all the way down to the feet. One baker, a giant with a huge belly, tied his apron from the front; all the others tied theirs from behind. Although no longer a little girl, I was enchanted by the astonishing dexterity of the bakers as they molded the loaves and carried the shovels, the sight of the flames when the iron door was pulled open, the floury smoke that clung to the clothing and hair, and the aroma of the sizzling logs and the hot bread.

The ghetto version of bread had nothing in common with the prewar variety. It was a grey, hard and bitter substance, produced in long or round loaves that you could cut into 200-gram slices — one day's ration for one person. The Judenrat supplied the flour. Once baked, the bread was hauled away for distribution right away. Nothing was left at the shop for just anyone to buy. Real bread and cakes were also baked in the ghetto, but only for the Germans.

During the ghetto period, the Tankus' house was always open to us. The warmth it offered was generated not only by the oven but also by the entire residence as well as the Tankus family. Mr. Tankus, at the bakery: a good man who never asked us what we were up to, never investigated our choice of his cellar, of all places, as the venue of our meetings and get-togethers. And Mrs. Tankus, a large woman who always wore a skirt down to the floor, her hair gathered behind in a wheel-like bun, greeting us with her face aglow and going about her affairs at home or at the bakery, never inquiring, never inspecting. In those times, parents who did not meddle were very special and important to us. We tried to keep our get-togethers to a minimum. They endangered the lives of everyone involved — those who attended the meetings, those who sheltered them, and the whole household. Eli Tankus had younger siblings and may have had an older brother, but I do not remember them.

During the Soviet tenure, our main meeting place had been my garden. It had the advantage of being safe from prying eyes; it gave us the feeling of a protected zone. In the ghetto, we had nowhere else to go. Only the Tankus' warm cellar provided a refuge where surreptitious encounters could be held. Sometimes, after the Germans ordered some real cakes, the Tankuses trimmed thin slices from the edges and saved them for us, the youngsters of Hashomer Hatzair. We then had bread with cake. We lay the minuscule, transparent slice of cake on a slice of bread that was not much thicker and nibbled carefully. By pushing the cake a little closer to the edge of the slice with each tiny nibble, we set up one final bite of cake and bread together.

In the mornings, we entered the cellar from the street. We never entered together; we came one by one, entered the shop, turned left, and went down the stairs. At night we exited through the back door, where the flour and the logs were brought in. Then we went up the stairs into the courtyard, passed through an opening in the fence, and disappeared into the street — always one at a time and always at measured intervals. The interior of the cellar was packed: benches with sacks of flour on one side and a huge pile of firewood for the oven on the other. A pile of thick logs not yet split stood in the courtyard outside. It was there, in the cellar, that we experienced the few kind moments of our lives in the ghetto — moments of togetherness, intimacy and the ability to sit and talk quietly about anything, ourselves, life and the world. Only there could we express what we really thought about the war, the Germans and the possibility that the war would end some day. We sat on the benches, on the sacks of flour. Some lay down; others propped their legs against the wall. Almost total darkness: daylight penetrated only through the small ventilation hatches, little windows of sorts at street level. At night, we could light a tiny

Eliahu Tankus, head of the resistance

carbide lantern but often chose not to, in order to maintain secrecy. We sat in the dark until our eyes got used to it and learned to see in total blackness.

Our Eliahu. Eli Tankus. *Der geler,* the "redhead." His towering height, his chiseled facial features, the charm of his fraternity and warmth. Ambitious, vigorous, prodigious, boundlessly devoted to comrades and causes. "Boundless" isn't an overstatement. It is a straightforward attempt to define this young man, who never desisted from doing whatever was good and right, daring, courageous and death-defying. A man who never, even for a moment, ceased to be solicitous to those around him — people and friends, family and children. And I am not speaking about the prewar era, when we were all different. I am speaking about the ability to behave that way during the years of horrific distress. How from those depths that everyone inhabited he carried his soul to psychic heights, crossed the limits of hunger, deprivation and fear, and quarried the crystals of the uprising from within himself and us. Our mutual-aid project began with him. The idea of establishing the Hashomer Hatzair underground and going to war in the Grodno ghetto matured inside him.

Nothing was impossible for him. He gathered people together, coordinated them, counseled them and put them to work. And we who adhered to him and marched with him believed that it was really so: that we could do it. That after a long day's work, ending in the dark of night, we could go to the bakery, split logs for the oven, and earn for doing so a bit of bread that we could share with the families of our members whose fathers had been taken away. We came in turns, a few of us each day. I say this about Eli and, perhaps, about us all: friends, comrades and combatants.

The Tankus' house was new. The war had come upon them before they could finish the second-story terrace, where they intended to build their *sukkah* (festival tabernacle). That part of the building had a big hole, a wooden door and three thick cast-iron beams that stuck out toward the street at a perpendicular angle. I won't digress right now to these three metal elements. I won't say anything about the street below them and the alleys that branched from it. I won't conjure the picture of the crowd of people that gathered. I won't express the voices, the words, the terror and the tears. I wish to maintain chronological order as best as my memory permits — to describe with the greatest possible precision the events that evolved into motive force, strength and power.

I walk away from the bakery and the Tankus' house, from the iron elements at the facade of its second story. I leave them behind and move on to the actions that were taken, the events and the outcomes. I'll return to the other things in due course. I can't possibly do otherwise.

Edek Boraks, a member of Hashomer Hatzair and commander of the Białystok ghetto resistance, came to us for a visit. He slipped in and out the same day, but that's all it took to make us different. The sense of connection and belonging and the very presence of someone older than us, someone to whom we could turn, gave us immense relief. Once again we were part of a movement, of something large and wide. Edek said, "What you're doing with the children is a holy labor, but you ought to start thinking about a fighting underground."

Until the ghetto was sealed, every visit from the outside was like an injection of adrenaline and strength coupled with practical ideas for action and organization. The transition from activities for children and youth to warfare came about in stages. We did not disperse the children right away. We contacted members of Dror and the Communists in the ghetto and began to organize. This part of my report is not chronological. I do not remember when and where the meetings took place, how long the meetings lasted, and how long it took until we became a united underground. It did not happen at once; it took time to get accustomed, to adjust to the idea of united warfare, and to carry out the merger.

Our first action as a fighting underground was to prepare the area. Passageways had to be created between courtyards and streets, buildings and alleys. The method was simple: we grouped at a fence, ostensibly engaging in innocent friendly conversation. In the meantime, one of us withdrew a slat or two from the fence. We did no more and didn't do even that all at once, lest someone notice. Two or three weeks later, we returned and pulled out another slat. In this manner we crisscrossed the entire ghetto with secret passageways and escape routes.

Tossia Altmann reported to us about what had happened at Ponary and about Abba Kovner's broadsheet. *Lomir nisht geyn vy shef tsu der shkhiteh —* Let's not go like lambs to the slaughter. Better to perish as free combatants than to live by the graces of murderers! Rise up! Rise up to the last breath!

It was not the first call for an uprising. The preparations had begun previously. We knew about the underground in Vilna and about Warsaw. Edek told us about the underground in Białystok. Now it was our turn. Having no firearms, we began to manufacture "brass knuckles," four soldered metal rings that were mounted on one's four fingers, with serrated pieces of metal atop each ring. Devices of this kind, wielded by people with their fists clenched, could be very significant in hand-to-hand combat. Jewish metalworkers and tinsmiths came aboard and made them for us. They also donated several sharpened metal rods. Our main weapons were these rods and thick wooden poles we collected around the ghetto, as well as the bombs we manufactured by filling light bulbs with sulfuric acid.

We cached our weapons in various places. Each of us stashed away a few accessories for himself, but the large concentrations were stored in agreed-upon places we all knew about: a house that had a courtyard and a little stable made of metal, comrades' houses with lofts, and behind a permanent pile of logs in Eli Tankus' courtyard. These instruments, however, were good for personal defense only; they would not suffice for offense. The main problem was how to acquire real weapons. Grodno was strategically located. In both world wars, enemy armies — Soviet, Germany, Polish — engaged each other there.

The peasants in the vicinity had gathered up weapons and ammunition that the retreating armies had left behind, but were willing to sell them only for gold rings or jewelry. I do not know how Eli Tankus obtained money. None of us knew. We chose to know as little as we could, so that we would have nothing to reveal in the event of capture and interrogation under torture.

One evening in the summer of 1942, we met at Eli's place in the cellar, tensely awaiting his return. He had slipped out of the ghetto into the country-side, we knew. He had gone to look for weapons, we knew. What we did not know is whether he had found any and whether he would come back.

As we waited silently in the cellar, Eli stepped in, carrying a bundle of rags. He set the heap down and removed the rags one by one until a loaf of bread came into sight. Eli sliced the loaf in half and revealed an old black handgun with some bullets next to it in a cloth bag. We passed the gun around. Each of us kissed it and recited the *sheheheyanu* blessing: thank you, almighty God, for allowing us to live until this moment. Passionately we hoped that this sole weapon would be a portent of many more.

I remember clutching that handgun and wrapping my palm around it. Its metal surface was cold and redolent of oil, straw and soil. A few crumbs of gray bread stuck to its short barrel, a dark metal cylinder with a bore of a slightly lighter color, a grayish shade that gleamed in the light admitted by the cellar window. I stroked the gun, moved my fingers across its cylinder, checked the caliber of its muzzle with my index finger, stroking the butt and its etched diagonal stripes, and slipped a finger onto its trigger. I examined the angle of the hammer, the safety catch, and the sharpness of the firing pin. The weapon was full of unfamiliar protuberances and projections; I learned them with my fingers, by physical sensation. Eli lifted the gun and stuffed it back into the loaf of bread, rewrapped it in the tattered rags, and held the parcel on his lap. We dreamed, thought and made plans. It was on that night, when the handgun became a presence in our lives, that we worked out our first real action plan.

Dodik Rozowski of the Hasneh Gdud, who was older than us, had been at the *hachshara* on his way to *Eretz Israel*. When the war broke out, he decided to return, and managed to reach his home in Grodno. An amateur photographer and a talented graphic artist, he placed his photo lab at the disposal of the underground for an incomparably crucial purpose: forgeries. He equipped us with bogus birth certificates, labor permits and transit permits endorsed with rubber stamps that had been either pilfered or manufactured by Dodik himself.

His tools were paper and glue, a brush pencil and quill pens, ink in various colors, and an amazing skill in photography and retouching. It was Dodik's prowess as a forger that allowed us to move safely from Grodno to Białystok as Cyla and I lugged the briefcase that contained the whole lab. That trip, however, had not yet begun; I do not wish to get ahead of myself. Dodik neither joined us on that journey nor followed us. He stayed behind with the comrades in Grodno. But again I stop, trying not to put the retelling of the events before the events themselves.

Outside the ghetto, we had a sole liaison, Eliahu Skowronski, a member of the movement. He had come to Grodno on Polish papers, found work at a print shop that had belonged to a Jewish family, the Majlachowiczes, before the war, and rented a small apartment in town. I don't remember whether he had come from Warsaw or Łódź. Either way, he became our connection with the outside world, someone close and immediate. I was appointed his courier in the ghetto. We met in the courtyards of ghetto houses bordering Dominikanska Street, deciding each time where to meet next. He handed us letters sent from Warsaw, and we provided him with items of clothing and home implements from the ghetto. He asked for gloves, a coat and a cap, so as not to look different from the Poles. The importance of his presence in town transcended the context of our group. A world at war that had no hotels and no friends and relatives on the Aryan side was an impossible place for the liaisons that circulated among the ghettos. Any member of our movement who reached Grodno and could not enter the ghetto that very day needed a place to spend the night. Eliahu's flat was that place.

Long afterwards and in another place, we, too, were on the Aryan side. We were women; it was hard to prove that we were Jewish. Eliahu, however, was male; one needed only to pull down his trousers to disclose his secret. How brave and composed he had to be to set up shop in a strange city, find work, engage in underground activity, and all the time remain vigilant against suspicions and the constant mortal threat. And he survived.

January 1943. Real organizing began with the arrival of Zorach Zilberberg, a member of Hashomer Hatzair and the Białystok ghetto resistance leadership. Free movement in and out of our ghetto had been prohibited by then. Zorach spent almost two weeks with us. With him we began to organize the underground for war. First we formed groups of three or five connected members. Then we added younger people from the Bitsaron Gdud — my Rocheleh, Lonczyk Pinczansky, Chancia Jerzierski and others whose names I do not remember.

On November 1, 1942, the ghetto gates were closed. That very day, the Germans began to liquidate Ghetto B, the nonproductive ghetto. Within three days they had sent its entire population — some 10,000 people — to extermination camps. In our ghetto, the *Aktionen* (extermination deportations) began in the middle of November. By the end of December, some 6,000 Jews of Grodno had been sent from Ghetto A to their death, 2,000 in each *Aktion*. Lists of candidates for transport had been prepared by the *Judenrat*. Anyone who could not afford to ransom himself in cash or valuables stayed on the list. Zorach went to Brawer, chairman of the *Judenrat*, and spoke with him about the ghetto underground and its problems. He demanded that the members of the resistance be left off the transport lists.

Today I think about their meeting: hulking, passionate, stormy Zorach facing Dr. Brawer. Did Brawer sit behind his desk wearing a suit? Did he stand up to shake Zorach's hand? Did his serious, cold and constantly worried demeanor thaw a little? How did Zorach, who had come from another ghetto, another place, address Brawer? Did he request, demand, attempt to persuade or threaten? And what was Brawer thinking during those moments? Did he realize that everyone's fate had been sealed and that it didn't make a difference which lists the underground members appeared on or not? Did he identify in the glint that erupted in Zorach's eyes, and the words that poured out, his own remote youth, his dreams of early manhood, the version of his psyche that would never eventuate? By that time and at that place, did Brawer, too, realize that the *Judenrat* had exhausted its utility? Did Zorach say something that surged, as it were, from the depths of Brawer's own heart? That is, were it not for the circumstances of life and time, would Brawer have been standing with Zorach on the other side of the desk?

I cannot answer any of these questions. I do not know how the conversation unfolded. Brawer promised that the members of the underground would not be placed on the transport lists. However, he attached a condition to this pledge: the resistance must not undertake any combat action until it became clear beyond all doubt that the Germans intended to liquidate the ghetto and its population.

I now return to those iron beams that protruded from the side of the upper-story terrace of the Tankus' house. I really don't have to return to them;

they have been inside me ever since, engaging my thoughts while awake and my dreams at night. The Tankus family home at 33 Peretz Street, the main street of the ghetto. Throughout the ghetto period, the Germans issued edicts by gluing huge broadsheets to building walls. One of them warned that anyone caught attempting to escape from the ghetto would face death — and would be joined by the concierge of the escapee's building. Even so, people continued to fight for their lives. One day, word had it that the Germans had caught the most beautiful woman in the ghetto trying to escape: Miss Prenska, Lena Prenska. For this, a special broadsheet ordering everyone in the ghetto to report and witness the implementation of the penalty was pasted up everywhere.

The Tankus family home. The street in front of it. The second story up. The terrace. The three iron beams. The thick ropes with the nooses at their end. The three wooden gallows. The Jews who massed in the street. A vigil of soldiers, weapons in hand, led Miss Prenska to the front of the house. With her were Moshe Spindler, the concierge, and a young man named Drucker, a refugee who had lived in the house and had not reported Miss Prenska's escape. The three of them stood erect, hands bound, barefoot, tormented, Lena in the middle. The crowd fell silent. The compressed bloc of people parted to make a passageway. Two soldiers led the doomed trio to the gallows. Across from the house, diagonal to Peretz Street, was a small alley, too narrow for carts to pass, wide enough only for pedestrians. I stood there, leaning against a wall of the house on the corner, looking straight at the three pillars that held up the terrace, the iron protuberances, and the ropes that dangled from them. I had to stand in order to see. I forced myself to keep my eyes open and not to lower my gaze even for a moment — so that hatred of the Germans would permeate my being, seep into my bloodstream, and circulate in my arteries. I had to stand there in order to marshal enough enraged power to kill some of them.

The mass of humanity on the street was motionless. People pressed against each other, packed themselves together, touched. Oppressive fear and dread. Silence on the walls of the homes on the street. Silence on the red shingle roofs. Silence in the shuttered windows, their panes glittering with the sunbeams that shoved their way through the clouds.

Wiese, a tall, slender, threatening man, elected to carry out the hanging personally. He approached Miss Prenska. She stood erect. I peered into her eyes and saw that they were open and fixed directly on the crowd and the armed German guards. She stood absolutely still on the platform, neither trembling nor pleading. Even when she lifted her head she was shorter than him. Wiese gripped the noose at the end of the rope with both hands. Lena didn't move. The German's hands draped the noose over her head on either side and dropped it onto her shoulders. I observed his massive back and his hands, now free of the noose, beginning to drop to his sides. He stepped back, and at that moment I saw Lena's visage. She tilted her head forward and lobbed a wad of spit into the man's face. In a split-second of rage I saw the black boot flicker as it kicked at the raised platform on which Lena stood. In that trace, her hands twitched for a moment and her lovely body slumped.

Wiese pulled a white kerchief from his pocket and wiped the spittle off his face. With the wave of a hand, he issued the order to hang the two men. Then he went away, escorted by an armed guard. The street emptied instantly. I stayed where I was, leaning against the wall of the building. Moni Burla grabbed me by the arms, trying to persuade me to go. I nailed myself to the cobblestones of the alley, glued myself to the wall of the house. I'm not going. I'm not leaving this place until I amass enough fury never to regret murdering a German. I stand motionless. I do not notice Moni moving away from me. My eyes are fixed on their slumped heads. Darkness descends on the street, on the house, on the iron beams, and on the little stools where they had stood, that had been tossed aside.

I don't know how long I stood there. When I turned away to go home, my eyes flooded with tears.

The clarity of that moment. The moment when vacillations gave way to resolve: a resolve that evolved literally into a physical sensation. Thus a protective layer formed between me and my soul, something very chilly, very palpable. I was not the person I had been. I had to get revenge.

Streblow, the commander of Ghetto B, was a big man in his uniform. Without the uniform, he was just another guy, nothing special. But he was always in uniform and always went about escorted and armed. He strolled through the ghetto with Wiese or other SS officers. His path was marked with terror and fear: the warning that ripped through the ghetto streets like a bolt of lightning, the slamming of doors as people sequestered themselves in their homes, the emptying of the streets, and the prostrate bodies of people whom he shot to death until he stepped out of the ghetto gate.

Our first operation would be the assassination of this man. Since none of us knew his features well enough to identify him, we contacted a Jewish woman who worked in his home as a domestic and asked her to produce a photograph that showed Streblow's face. In the evening, after work, she brought one. I spent the entire night drawing his facial features on the basis of the photo. Using Dodik's ink and quill pens, I sketched small, fine lines: the forehead, the hair, the cheekbones, the arch of his ears, the angles of his nose and lips, but more than anything else the eyes, eyebrows and eyelashes. And the most important thing: the space between the eyes. I drew more painstakingly there than anywhere else. That's where the bullet would slam in, I was sure. That's what we'd learned: one shot between the eyes.

How young, guileless and inexperienced we were. How unfamiliar we were with a weapon. We had had no training and target practice; we had never practiced engagement and retreat. Two comrades, owning that one handgun, walked down a darkened alley that intersected the street where the gang of murderers was making its way. The comrades went into hiding but made some movement that evoked suspicion. All the flashlights turned in their direction with blinding, unendurable intensity. They were shot even before they could even train the weapon on its target. The Nazi gang walked on, not even realizing that a handgun meant to assassinate Streblow had been there. Nahum Krawicz and Motl Kuperman were the would-be assassins. I was gone by then. Comrades who came to Białystok told me about it.

On Friday, January 15, 1943, rumors about a mass *Aktion* broke out. They spoke about 10,000: ten thousand people. It would be the liquidation of the ghetto. We sat in the bakery cellar, the whole leadership of the Hashomer Hatzair resistance in the Grodno ghetto. Brawer kept his word and told Zorach about the impending *Aktion*. We discussed the possibility of staging an uprising during it. We asked ourselves what options might be reasonable. It was a meeting for decision-making amid a sense of impending disaster. Something very great and terrible was about to happen, and we were so few. Choosing to join the resistance meant being able to kill Germans. When we had first begun to build the underground, we had spoken of a watershed: faith in man. We who believed in man and his good intentions had to study and observe the evil and the Satanism that had risen in our faces. We did not confine this exploration to our internal monologues, each person with him or herself. I remember a few of those talks. We spoke about the need to learn killing. We had to learn how to kill. Everyone who chose to become an underground fighter had to make this very substantive and difficult change in worldview.

The movement had not sent Zorach to us merely to organize the re-sistance. He was also sent in order to try to transfer to the Białystok ghetto the fighters who would survive the uprising. We were plainly too few and our weapons too sparse; meaningful action could take place only where a large group of fighters could come together. The underground leadership in the Białystok ghetto decided that we should all come to them, join the com-rades, and become a large force. That's out of the question, Eliahu said. We will not abandon the Jews of the Grodno ghetto. Zorach agreed with him. So we stayed. The hardest thing for us was to drop the idea of an uprising, the use of firearms, and the possibility of dealing the Germans a severe blow. We were too few and too poorly equipped to do any real fighting. Under the conditions in Grodno, we could only launch an obvious suicide action, for which the en-tire community would pay in the coin of mass deportation. We knew where the trains were heading. Avraham Braude, a Grodno accountant, had been deport-ed in one of the first *Aktionen* but leaped from the train to Treblinka and told us about the extermination. We knew beyond doubt a combat uprising would hasten the liquidation of the ghetto and did not want to be the ones responsible for it.

I do not know when a person makes peace with his impending death. I don't know exactly when it is that he stops hoping, believing, dreaming that something will suddenly change, that some tremendous force will step in and disrupt the course of time and events so that he will be absolved of contem-plating his death and that of his dear ones at a handbreadth's distance and a moment on the clock. Even after we became aware of the extermination opera-tion we hoped that it might be stopped. Maybe the world would stop it. Maybe the few thousand Jews who remained in the ghetto would not be shipped to death. That's why we were so careful; that's why we restrained ourselves. We decided to wait until the last moment. We, I stress. It was a collective decision, even though I was far away when it happened — not in the geographic sense (it was only a one-hour train ride) but in a place where life happened.

My Grodno

I cannot distinguish among the childhood scenes imprinted in me, our Jew-ish lives in those scenes, and the fact that they no longer belong to us and we do not belong to them. We are Jews of our hometown, the community of Grodno.

Grodno: a pretty city. To me, beautiful. A broad river with curves that carve a path between green banks and under bridges, a river that supports steamboats and barges, and sometimes flowing placidly, and sometimes erupting in turmoil or freezing over.

A city of hills that form a pattern of crests and valleys — now you see it, now you don't — and features that come into sight all of a sudden: the royal palace, the ramparts, the turrets of the guardhouse, the ornate stone buildings, large looming churches that sketch silhouettes on a magical skyline. Wide streets paved with great cobblestones, avenues of gorgeous, towering chestnut trees, white blades of blossoms in the spring, giant leaves that burst with dark green and turn into walls in the autumn and shatter when your galoshes tread on them, and clumps of snow that settle from the naked branches to the top of my head as I run up Jagiellonska Street to school.

The forests that established the city's borders were the nature reserves of my childhood and teen years. Lososna and Pyszki and the limestone hills before you get to Pyszki provided an exhaustible supply of shell fossils. What treasures those were.

An ancient city: Grodno dates back to the twelfth century. In the town that I knew, Poles dwelled mainly in neighborhoods far from the center, in unattached houses surrounded with fences and gardens. On the eve of the war, almost half the town's population was Jewish. Five hundred years of Jewish life developed in the old quarter in the city center, a very crowded district where houses touched each other, and at the Shulhof, the opulent Great Synagogue.

Most shops in Grodno were owned by Jews. Due to historical circumstances of residency rights, land purchases and minority occupations, the majority of commerce and most of the economy rested in Jewish hands — in the downtown area on Dominikanska Street and, obviously, around the marketplace. Textiles and clothing, shoes, bakeries and galanterias, smiths, shoemakers, jewelers, house wares, pharmacies, furriers, perfumeries, lumber merchants and metalworkers, retailers and wholesale — all of these were largely Jewish.

Jewish cemeteries — the old one next to the synagogue, another on Grandzicka Street and a third one behind it, across the river. They were all similar in their austerity: no flowers, no trees, just stones. Small and simple, very close to each other, tightly packed. That was for the poor. Elsewhere were large, grand monuments, rich in inscriptions, engraved with gold designs. Those were for the wealthy.

But the Jews of Grodno had a tradition of helping the needy. Clothing was handed down from child to child, and after the last child it went to charity. The community had a *hekdesh,* a religious trust: a public kitchen that fed the unfortunate and the indigent on Shabbat and Jewish festivals. It was located on a street parallel to the railroad tracks, not far from our home. People who lugged pots in the street were never Poles. Those pots did more than shuttle to the bakery on Friday and back home on Shabbat carrying cholent. They also hauled food for assistance and relief; they were lugged a long way. There was a Jewish orphanage on Skidelska Street and a *gemilut hasadim,* a free-loan fund for the needy covered by donations, apart from the Polish government institutions.

A warm community, incomparably organized and supportive. A community that was good to live in. It had a great education system: Tarbut with its kindergarten, elementary school, *gymnasium* and teachers' college, all Zionist and Hebrew-speaking; the Yavne School of the Mizrachi movement, where they taught in Yiddish and Hebrew; *chadarim* and *Talmudei Torah* of Agudath Israel, and the Bund's CYSHO School.

There were Jewish political parties, lots of them — Po'alei Zion and Po'alei Zion Left, General Zionists and, on the other side of the spectrum, the Communists and the Bund. The Jewish National Fund's "blue box" was well in evidence, as were collection boxes for sundry religious institutions and charitable organizations. And youth movements: Hashomer Hatzair and Dror, Bnei Akiva and Freiheit, Betar, the Bund and the Communists. And emissaries from *Eretz Israel* on Zionist and cultural missions — Bialik and Tchernichowski and Jabotinsky — filled large auditoriums with capacity crowds that drank up their words.

It all ended in one stroke, as though it had never been. The accursed war shredded our lives so abruptly. Everything that existed back there, however, is documented in archives, photographs, documents, yellowing letters and people's fading memories.

The Jewish population of Grodno and the vicinity was obliterated step by step. The two ghettos were sealed on November 1, 1942, exactly a year after they were established. On November 3 and November 8, 10,000 Jews from Ghetto B, the nonproductive ghetto, were shipped by train to Treblinka and Kielbasin.

They weren't ten thousand Jews. They were Aunt Rosa and her husband, Yehoshua, and their little children, Yehuditkeh and Avramek. They were Uncle Chaim, his wife Rachel, their two toddler children, and his older children from his first wife, Yenta and Yankele. They were Aunt Ita and her husband, Uncle Iche, and Uncle Yaakov with the children and grandchildren. They were all of the youngsters whom I had counseled twice a week for almost a year. They were the masses of women, men, teenagers and elderly who had constituted my community. They were my friends, teachers, relatives and acquaintances, men of the synagogue and women of the marketplace, shopkeepers and scribes, brides and grooms, fetuses, uncomprehending toddlers, and adults who realized what was happening too late. I have not multiplied them by a hundred but I would have to multiply them by thousands in order to accommodate them all and define and explain what happened.

Those excused from the two transports were moved into our ghetto; the gates of Ghetto B were locked.

It was in Kielbasin, a small town near Grodno, that the Germans set up a concentration camp for Jews from the villages and towns in the vicinity. We knew about Kielbasin because people there had managed to flee to the Grodno ghetto and describe the atrocities.

Karl Rinzler, commandant of Camp Kielbasin, subjected the inmates to lengthy roll calls at the camp square. They lasted from early morning until he ran out of strength to shoot anyone who budged. He weaved in and out of the ranks, from side to side, and from behind, circling with a frightening and threatening slowness, a handgun in his right hand and bullets in his left. No one could stand motionless for hours. People's lives ended with terrible randomness; it depended on where he was looking and whom he saw out of the corner of his lurking eye. Death and murder were his cravings. Jewish girls and women who met his standards of beauty were given evening dresses and delivered to parties that German officers conducted in the camp. There they were forced to dance with one of the men in front of whole assemblage. Then, at some unexpected moment and with no forewarning, Rinzler approached, pulled out his handgun, and shot them in the head.

I don't know whether the moment was really unexpected, whether the dancing took place regularly, or whether Rinzler really singled out the girls and women who danced there. I only try to imagine the terror and the deathly chill that prevailed inside the ballroom dresses that clung to the women's bodies when they were worn. I try to understand how the women's legs did not tremble or their knees fail as they were led to the dance floor. How their dread did not turn into a ghastly shriek that could sunder the cascade of sounds that surged into the circle around the couple in motion.

I try but cannot really manage to understand, except for the hope and the impossible belief — the most appropriate thing to entertain at that place and that moment — that maybe it won't happen to me. The desperate hope that due to my having been chosen I would be privileged to live. I don't really know whether any of those lovely girls and women was privileged to live after that dance. I know about those who were murdered.

Camp Kielbasin was liquidated in January 1943; its surviving inmates were taken to the Grodno ghetto. It was winter: cold, snow, carts with people sprawled in them. Skeletal people: skin and bones, clothing tattered or altogether missing, battered and injured, screaming, crying and calling for help. Unable to sit up in the carts, unable to climb down. Taken to the Great Synagogue and housed there until the next transport.

The trains to Treblinka did not set out from the Grodno station. The Grodno Jews earmarked for death were marched to a railroad station eight or nine kilometers out of town — a long, agonizing, abusive trek that included deliberate humiliation. The attorney Gozanski was forced to sing *Yidl mitn Fidl* (Fiddler on the Roof) all the way, over and over, while wearing a huge clown's hat. The moment he stopped singing, he was struck with a baton until he resumed. Thousands of women and children, men and elderly marched through the cold, the snow and the muck, chased and beaten, falling down and getting up, being shot and dying along the road.

The great *Aktion* took place on January 18, 1943: more than 11,000 Jews were shipped off in one go. The next transport set out on February 12. This was Father's transport to death; he was hauled away from his place of work for the march and the deportation. Afterwards, only a few hundred were left — too small to justify a special transport to an extermination camp. On March 13, 1943, the ghetto was liquidated. The vestiges of the Jews of Grodno were removed to the Białystok ghetto. Among them were my mother and my little sister, Zipporka.

Underground Fighters in the Grodno Ghetto

"You people," Father said, "are too young for the entire Jewish people to join and understand. Your shoulders are too young to bear this responsibility. You don't really understand where you want to take us." In retrospect, I realize with growing clarity that our plans could never have come to pass as we had dreamed.

Our choice was the Great Synagogue, where those who had survived the January *Aktion* were gathered. It was an enormous building. Its arched ceilings, embellished with relief designs of branches and leaves, were supported on towering pillars with capitals. A grand chandelier speckled with a huge number of bulbs dangled from a dome and a Star of David in the middle of the ceiling. A raised platform for the Holy Ark was installed at the eastern wall, and atop it, very high up, a *Shiviti* inscription with God's name rested on a relief that looked like a bunch of little pomegranates. Across from the eastern wall: the women's gallery.

The idea was that the fighting members of the underground would join those at the synagogue. At a prearranged signal, they would create a tumult, open fire on the Germans, break the windows of the building, lead the people through them to safety, and make their own escape as well.

It was such a stunning illusion; we were totally blind. We couldn't fathom what Father had said.

The synagogue windows were very high up. Only behind the Holy Ark did a staircase rise to the windows along the eastern wall. The ledge on the outer side of the synagogue was far above ground level. Who was going to leap to "freedom" from that location? Women with babies in arms? Fathers with two or three children clutching each of their hands? Exhausted old people? How many people would leap out with the fighters? And even if they followed them and survived the jump, how would they escape from the ghetto? How many Poles would not turn them in? How many of the escapees would reach the forest? How many would survive afterward?

The proposed operation derived all its strength from one source: the freedom to choose death. You could choose how you would die. The strong point was that it deprived the Germans of this choice. It would be a victory of spirit over weapons, terror and hatred — exactly as Abba Kovner had defined it: not like lambs to the slaughter, not like the powerless.

Here's what really happened. Zorach, who had remained with us in the Grodno ghetto, made his way to Białystok and described the battle. The fighters joined the few survivors of the last transport, went with them into the synagogue, and created a commotion as they had planned. However, they did not manage to kill even one German. The Germans were prepared and opened fire. Some of the fighters leaped out of the windows and fled. Others remained and were shot inside the synagogue. A few managed to get to Jan, the good Polish peasant in Koropczyce, a village twelve kilometers from Grodno, and camped with him for the night in order to continue to the forest the next day.

I have no one to ask and no one with whom to share and recover memories. None of my fighting comrades in the Grodno ghetto survived. I have no one to discuss it with, no one who was there.

The eleven fighters who escaped from the synagogue reached the home of Jan. There, exhausted, they crept into a barn for a night's sleep amid the piles of straw and hay, in order to move into the forest and join the partisans the next morning.

In the middle of the night, Polish neighbors who had seen them arrive set out against them. They and some Germans whom the peasants had summoned murdered them as they slept.

Farewell Testimonies

Father

Even after the great *Aktion*, forced-labor dispatches continued. Father and Avramele were still working at the Magistrat (City Hall), outside the ghetto, in a huge courtyard filled end to end with warehouses. Their job was to move things around, haul them in and out, arrange them, and load and unload them.

Although Father never inquired about our doings during our stay in the ghetto, I have no doubt that he knew the answer. He was too smart not to understand. But he never said a word; he never interfered. My family accepted what I had become: a member of an underground group preparing to fight the Germans. My knowledge that this was so gave me much relief. Some of my comrades couldn't tell their parents a thing. When I told Father in the summer of 1942 that we were calling off our childcare operation and gearing up for battle, he only asked what would become of the youngsters. I could not involve them in the underground, I replied. They were too young; we had to ready ourselves for warfare. I think he was very proud of me.

When I told Father about Ponary, Slonim and the systematic nature of the extermination of all Jews in the shtetls, he said, "It can't be." "Father," I said, "it's no coincidence. No German would liquidate a ghetto on his own counsel. It's deliberate, something decided upon from high up." Father repeated, "It can't be. Nothing like that has ever happened in history, wiping out an entire nation, and they won't start doing it now." Mother listened in but did not meddle.

During the first *Aktion*, Father suddenly realized what I was talking about. It was a profound and ghastly epiphany, a bolt of lightning that illuminates everything from here to hell. I do not know what Father saw in the abyss this light revealed, what abrupt realization came over him in view of the spectacle that greeted his eyes — eyes that see what's there and eyes that see what they imagine. At the end of the day, he said, "If God can do this to His people, then He isn't my God." At that very moment, he ceased to believe in and pray to God. A horrific shudder transfixed me. I had ceased to believe in God years ago, but I could not stand to watch the rupture, the despair, that seized my father. I knew what religious faith meant to him. At that moment I sensed that Father had been murdered. "Father," I exclaimed, "how can you say such a thing?" He replied, "This is the only conclusion I can reach from a situation in which God is slaughtering His faithful."

Mother said, "*Yudeleh, oy, oy, oy, Yudeleh*, may God not punish you for what you're saying." I said, "If Father says there's no God, then there's no longer anyone who'll punish him."

Father changed. The smile that he had saved for us ebbed. The hope that nestled inside him trickled away. His kindly eyes dulled. He became taciturn and sad. A short time later, after the great *Aktion* — I was no longer at home by then — when Father realized that the end was at hand, that the ghetto and all of its inhabitants would indeed be liquidated, he expressed a wish: that he should not see Mother and the children die. The knowledge that he could not save them, that nothing could be done after everyone was hauled away to certain death, finished him off. He could contemplate his own death, but not the helplessness that gripped him in view of the impending death of Mother and Rocheleh, Zipporka and Avramele. That was the second time Father was murdered, even before they dragged him off to extermination.

Father got his wish. He was taken away from work. One day they rounded up all the older workers and left the younger ones behind. Father did not resist; he did not try to escape, go into hiding, disappear. He joined the transport. It must have eased his agony to have been taken first and to know that Avramele would come home that evening, describe what had happened, and say that Father would not be returning.

Years later, one of Father's co-passengers on the train to Treblinka told me that he had in fact said, "How good it is that I am the first to go; this way I won't witness the death of my wife and children."

Mother

I think about Mother now from the perspective of time, feelings and the strength that I have amassed over the years. By using these devices I can gaze into her eyes with eyes that belong not only to the girl back then, the one who grew up in the war, but also to the adult woman who left, fought, rose up, survived and became a mother.

I gaze into her eyes with my eyes as they are today, but also with those of the girl who had been her daughter. I see her terrible fear, her realization that we were about to die and she could do nothing about it. The fear that filled her was not for herself and her own life but for what would happen to us: the fear of a mother who has committed the terrible failure of no longer being able to protect her children. Accursed be the agent of the immeasurable suffering that became her lot. I do not speak of her physical suffering: the deprivation, the hunger, the poverty, the humiliation, the cold, the dehumanization, the terror. She survived all of these in the firm conviction that she would defeat them. Rather, I speak of the kind of suffering that topples the foundations of the world: the overturning of the natural order of a mother who protects her children, the existential obligation of parents to their children, the product of the essence of parenthood.

Today, as a mother and a grandmother whose age is nearly twice Mother's age during the war, in the ghetto, and at the time she was murdered, I look into her eyes once again and my eyes fill with tears.

I hardly ever cry; after all, one mustn't cry oneself to death. But

I cry for our mother, mother of Avramele and Rocheleh and Zipporka and me, who, in the dying days of the Grodno ghetto and afterwards in the Białystok ghetto, was denied the possibility, the privilege and the ability to be a mother as she had been for us all our lives, as all the other mothers had been.

Avramele
Avramele continued to slave at the warehouses. After Father and the older people were taken away, he was the only Jew still working there. One of the gentiles, who truly loved him, agreed to conceal him for absolutely nothing in return in his house at the edge of town, in a rural neighborhood composed of wooden houses and vegetable patches, fruit trees and storerooms where the firewood for winter and the fodder for the livestock were kept. Avramele shared the news with Mother, said goodbye to our sisters, and set out one day after work. Following this man, he slipped into one of the courtyards, removed the Star of David from his coat, returned to the street as a Polish gentile, and made his way to his house of refuge.

It was winter, February, freezing cold. He spent his days hiding amid the stacks of firewood. At night, as the temperatures plunged far below zero, his benefactor let him sleep in the house.

I do not know how long he stayed in hiding there. When Mother joined me in Białystok, she reported that Avramele was alive and hiding with *goyim* on the outskirts of Grodno.

Long after these events, when I finally returned to Grodno, I set out to find my brother. I located the street, the house, and this good man. He told me what had happened. I believed his account; I had no reason not to.

Several weeks after Avramele went into hiding, the neighbors began to speak about the man as someone who was concealing Jews. Fearing for his life and for Avramele's, he decided to move Avramele to a distant village where one of his friends lived. He escorted him part of the way and then went home. Avramele continued alone. Some Poles whom he encountered along the way identified him as a Jew. They dragged him to the ghetto gate only to find it closed, the ghetto emptied of its Jews, and no Germans around to claim him. So they stabbed and bludgeoned him to death.

What consolation it is that Mother went to her death believing that he was alive, in hiding, surviving.

Bella

After the great *Aktion* of January 18, 1943, the Germans drew in the ghetto boundaries. Only four people remained in the apartment: Mother, Father, Rocheleh and Zipporka. Grandma had passed away and the Epsteins had been transported to extermination. I was in Białystok by then; Sarka had followed me.

When Mother and Zipporka were taken to Białystok along with the vestiges of the Grodno ghetto, they described that *Aktion*. I asked about the grandfather, who was ill and immobile. How had he been away? He couldn't walk, after all. I was sure they had shot him in his bed, but Mother refused to divulge a thing. Bella and Avramele had taken over the space that had been vacated, and Mother and Father prepared a hideout. They still hoped that hiding, evading the searchers, and surviving the death-transport roundup was possible.

The roof continued past the wall of the large room, its beams sloping diagonally from their peak in the middle. At the end of the space that this created, at the point where the beams converged in their last triangle, my parents arranged a place where the family could sit. Whenever a search took place, the four of them went into hiding there. Once, as the police were turning to go away, the Jewish policeman in the search party suggested to his German counterpart, "Do you suppose someone might be hiding up there? It's worth checking." The German fired one round into the wooden wall of the roof. Silence followed.

The fugitives continued to sit there for the rest of the day and then through the night, breathing soundlessly in small drafts that did not shake the air, totally motionless lest the rustle of a leg or the touch of a hand on the boards of the roomlet turn the police in their direction. Who knew whether someone had stayed behind to lie in wait?

As dawn approached, the quiet outside the hideout turned into absolute silence, the kind of silence that lets you hear a person moving about in the room past the door of the hideout, a silence that allows you to sense the presence of danger. All was quiet. Three of them stood up one by one and headed for the door. Only Bella continued to sit motionless. They called her and she did not respond. When they touched her, they felt a gooey moisture.

Bella had been struck between the eyes by that one bullet. She had sat among them all that day and night, dead, and they hadn't noticed. Amid the thick darkness, the compressed fear, and the existential terror, they could not have noticed that her silence, her frozen posture, the silence of wordlessness, were all death.

Liaisons Who Visited the Grodno Ghetto

Irena Adamowicz
A Polish Christian, a Scout, and a wonderful woman. Tall, slender, with delicate facial features, fair hair speckled with grey, gathered behind her neck. Dressed in village fashions: a simple long and dark skirt, a white blouse and heavy, high shoes.

She was, above all, a friend of Hashomer Hatzair since before the war, a close friend of Yosef Kaplan. It was as his liaison that she came. We found it incomprehensible: a non-Jewish Pole who went from ghetto to ghetto in order to keep members of Hashomer Hatzair in touch. One day, she simply showed up and found us. She reached me on the basis of addresses and names that the comrades in the Białystok ghetto had given her. Our entire group went to meet with her in the bakery cellar. She sat there for hours, telling us what was happening outside the fences and beyond the walls: the Warsaw ghetto, the head leadership of the movement, Mordechai Anielewicz, the Białystok ghetto and the movement's organizational efforts there, Abba Kovner and the comrades in Vilna. They were her next stop. She didn't stay the night; she was in a rush to finish her mission.

Irena was a Polish Christian, one of the few, the very few, who made common cause with the Jews. We knew of no one like her. She regarded Hashomer Hatzair as a sibling movement of the Polish Scouts. Due to this perspective and her human principles, she risked her life for Hashomer Hatzair by liaising between the Aryan side and the Warsaw ghetto, and between the Warsaw ghetto and the other ghettos.

Irena Adamowicz: I repeat her name so that it should not be forgotten. Only thus can I thank her and express my appreciation for the heroism of her feats. She was the first who breached the barrier of our ignorance, the first who reconnected us with developments in the outside world, the first who told us that the leadership and the movement still existed and were active. We were no longer alone and cut off from the rest of the universe. Once again we were part of a large, vast movement, part of an endeavor in which the participants had been recruited by force of a different reality.

Edek Boraks

Edek came from Białystok in the spring. What a handsome guy: blue eyes and a huge bush of brushed-back blond hair. He looked just like a gentile. This allowed him to use the trains, move among the ghettos and connect us with each other, the world outside our ghetto and comrades in other ghettos.

He arrived all of a sudden. I don't remember who he visited first and who passed the word on. We met in the cellar of Eli Tankus' bakery. He started by peppering all of us with personal questions. Which members of your family are still alive? What is each of you doing? What are you living on? Only afterwards did he begin to tell us things. A hearty, comradely, amiable and open man — someone whom you thought you had known for years as soon as you met him.

Edek began by giving a general survey of all the ghettos that still existed. Then he told us about Białystok and the resistance — how it was put together, how problematic it was to organize all the Jewish youth movements into one underground entity.

Edek had lots to report and he answered all our questions. We were few in number, very young, and totally cut off from everything beyond the ghetto wall. The sense of being alone had become part of our lives. We were a tiny resistance group that based its operations on education as Hashomer Hatzair understood the term. We offered assistance and relief by following the mutual-aid patterns of the Jewish community, but we were very much on our own. There was no adult leadership to supervise us. Irena and Edek and Tossia and Zorach made the connection, transforming us into one link in a chain of people who were doing something, who were taking action. Suddenly there was someone to talk to, to consult with, to ask.

It was a beautiful sun-drenched day. At times like those, the ghetto looked placid, as though it was not a ghetto and there was no war. They were moments that belonged to other worlds. We strolled in the streets and stepped into the alleys. Edek observed the masses of teens and children. "What's with them?" he asked. "What are you doing about them?" We told him about the children's groups we had formed, the activities, the mutual aid, the second ghetto. We wanted to take him to Ghetto B so that the comrades there could meet him and share with us the experience of elation upon realizing that we were not alone. But you couldn't get a crossing permit in the middle of the day, and Edek left the day he arrived.

Tossia Altmann
The next liaison that visited was Tossia Altmann, a member of the Hashomer Hatzair head leadership in Poland, older than us, and a wonderful friend. She had participated as a counselor in the "executives' *moshava*" in Olegsowki in August 1939. I don't remember where we met in the ghetto but I do remember the embrace, the excitement, the joy, and her cheery smile.

She spent several days with us. We discussed plans for the uprising, how we were getting organized, other ghettos, and common friends. But we soon dropped all those subjects — the uprising, warfare and our lives in that place — and shifted to comradely conversation and shared memories. Then Tossia recovered her charming smile, her glowing eyes, the songs that she hummed, and her inexhaustible optimism.

She described life in the Warsaw ghetto. Not having been ghettoized until November 1941, we had had two years of grace under Soviet occupation. Tossia, who endured almost three years of life in the Warsaw ghetto before we met her, showed us that one could live, get things done, and be active for a longer time than we had thought possible. She told us about an agricultural *hachshara* that still operated in Czestochowa; members of Hashomer Hatzair lived there under German occupation as they had before. She talked about Ponary and brought us Abba Kovner's broadsheet. In fact, she served us as a senior counselor would, bracing us for the worst.

One could climb through the window in our roomlet to the sloping roof of the neighboring building, a structure of strong stone slabs with a gutter running its full length. We lay the pieces of paper and the pencils in the bowl of the gutter so that they would not blow away. We sat the edge of the shingled surface, our legs dangling in the air over the flat roof of another building. Shoulder to shoulder, intimate, we conversed in a whisper above and far from the ghetto streets, the ghetto buildings, the whole ghetto. All around us was silence. It was a place apart, separate from all the rest. For a moment, we were not there: a moment of freedom and absolute happiness. We are elsewhere, in some other space, laughing at the thought of Olegsowki, reminiscing about our camps, our activities, the books, the notebooks.

Then Tossia withdrew from her skirt pocket a creased note bearing an emblem that Hakibbutz Haartzi had chosen for its fifteenth-anniversary fes- tivities. I took the scrap of paper, spread it across one palm, covered it with the other, and pressed my palms together hard in order remove the creases. Even so, I took care not to tear the paper. The sense of the flimsy paper, the connec- tion with the emblem, *Eretz Israel* and the movement managed to penetrate the sealing wall of isolation.

Tossia said, "Make a drawing of the emblem, enlarge it, and circulate it among all the comrades. Set up activities for all the groups about the kibbutz, kibbutzim and the meaning of the festivity. So they should know. So that we'll all celebrate."

She spent the night with me, sleeping on a blanket I unrolled onto on the roomlet floor. In the morning we headed for an outing in the ghetto streets — an easygoing stroll that was actually a fact-finding trip. We were all there: Cyla and Miriam, Eli and Shaikele, Gedalyahu, Moni and I. Tossia spoke about the Warsaw ghetto and noted how different our ghetto was. We had no corpses sprawled in the street, no carts that circulated with loads of dead bodies, and no starving children with distended abdomens roving on their own, because the adults around them were still alive.

"You look the way living people used to look," she said as we walked arm-in-arm down the middle of the street. It was a lovely day, a brilliant- ly sunny day. In the afternoon, lots of people poured into the street. Mass- es of teenagers in the streets were a surprising and impressive sight. "Don't be fooled, don't delude yourselves," Tossia said. "It's the calm before the storm."

We didn't ask her about the duties she had undertaken or about the fear, the dangers, the roads or the railways. Our questions concerned the practicali- ties of survival on the Aryan side: how to foresee obstacles and surmount them in order to make your mission a success.

She left the ghetto as she had entered it. It was she who ignited the flame of uprising in us. It was she who told us about the preparations for the uprising in Warsaw and gave us the tools to contemplate it. Much later, Cyla and I wondered whether Tossia really believed that we could take action and change our reality. I don't think she believed we would affect the progress of the war. But she was immensely determined to do something that would not leave us helpless against the impending events.

Zorach Zilberberg

Zorach was the last liaison who visited the Grodno ghetto. He came during the critical days as the ghetto verged on liquidation. He arrived from Białystok to organize the fighting underground for the last battle. When he saw how weak we were, he decided to move most of the fighters to the Białystok ghetto in order to beef up the forces there.

Zorach reached Białystok from the Vilna *Rikuz* together with Edek, Chaika Grossman, Jandrze Lawiedz and another group of activists in order to organize the resistance activity. He was a young man of average height, dark hair, fair features and pink cheeks — not exactly the Aryan type. Only by dint of his courage and agility did he manage to survive the train rides and the comings and goings from the ghetto. He did not flinch from danger. His sensitive and warm attitude toward people, coupled with his combination of authority and personal intimacy, earned him everyone's affections immediately.

After the Grodno ghetto was liquidated, Zorach returned to Białystok, fought together with the others, and perished in the uprising.

My Notebooks

In the corner of the roof that abutted the window of our apartment in the ghetto, I concealed my treasures, anything I wanted to preserve and remember: the papers Tossia had brought, letters from the main leadership in Warsaw to all the Hashomer Hatzair resistance groups, the note with the emblem of the Hakibbutz Haartzi festivities, and so on.

The war might end some time, I thought. One day, after it was all over, I thought I might return to that place. I never imagined that the ghetto would be destroyed, its wooden houses torched and every last object there obliterated.

Members of the Underground in Grodno

Sadly, I can furnish only a partial list. Some of the names elude my memory.

All the members of the Aktiv, the core leadership of the resistance, belonged to the Carmel Gdud. The underground and its cells, however, also included comrades younger than ourselves, those of my sister Rocheleh's Bitsaron Gdud.

Lonczyk Pinczansky, Chancia Jerzierski, Rocheleh Bielicki, Dodik from Bitsaron and Dodik Rozowski, Meir from Bitsaron, Keyla Cheszes, Miriam Gorbulska, Sarka Szewachowicz, Mirka Stawer, Fanke Lipkies, Bassia Brawer, Mottl Solnicki, Eliahu (Ilia) Jerzierski, Eliahu Tankus, Shaikele Matus, Gedalyahu Browarski, Moni Burla, Miriam Poupko, Cyla Szachnes and Chasia Bielicka.

CHAPTER 6

January 1943–August 1944

I set out the next day, alone. I left behind Chasia Bielicka of Grodno, a member of Hashomer Hatzair, a member of the underground, a Jew. I took only Halina Stasiuk, a Polish Christian girl from the village of Koszewo, not far from Druskienniki.

Friday, January 15, 1943. The ghetto buzzed with rumors about an impending *Aktion*: a huge one, 10,000 people – the liquidation of the ghetto.

That evening, Zorach and the rest of us gathered at Eli Tankus' bakery to make fateful decisions. We resolved not to leave the ghetto to its doom. Only when it was all over, we decided, would the remaining combatants move to the Białystok ghetto and join the comrades and the resistance there. Zorach spoke about the forgery lab: we had to move it to Białystok, into the ghetto. It was crucial for the resistance; it allowed us to turn out fake identities. As long as it existed, we could live like Poles on the Aryan side, move about, find places to live and get jobs. Cyla and I were assigned to deliver the lab to Białystok.

It was almost midnight. Dodik produced bogus birth certificates for us; they did not require photographs. While we waited for the papers, Zorach spoke encouraging and soothing words. We did not want to leave our comrades. We found it hard to set out at so critical a time. We would always be together in life and death, we had thought. We had never imagined the possibility of being separated, and we didn't now, even as Zorach tried to persuade us that it wouldn't last long, that we'd be back within a few days.

Long after that night, Zorach told me that he knew about the *Aktion* for sure. Obviously the lab had to be smuggled out before anything else, he said, because in the impending *Aktion*, or in the next one, the ghetto would be liquidated and everyone would be shipped to death. That night, however, in the cellar, he gave Cyla and me a pep talk: we'd go out, we'd come back and we'd find everything in place. He must have known and sensed that otherwise we wouldn't go.

"Cyla, Chaska," he said, "You have such a great task to perform. You've always wanted to take action, haven't you? Move the lab to Białystok and come back. Here we'll have lots more to do." I couldn't imagine that this was my farewell to Grodno.

We decided to meet at 5 a.m. in order to join the first groups of workers headed for the ghetto gate. Cyla went home. At the time I was working at a Wehrmacht shop that produced handbags for the wives of Wehrmacht and Gestapo officers. I designed the models; the bags themselves were sewn together from scraps of leather from a shoe factory. To move the lab equipment, I needed a handbag. The key to the shop was in my pocket.

It was past midnight: curfew, silence. The building stood behind the bakery. I'll enter and take a handbag, I told myself. Terribly afraid, heart pounding, I crept along the building walls, crossed courtyards, passed through fences in which we had cut openings, stopped occasionally, looked left and right, and listened to the quiet, trying to hear the approaching footsteps of police.

I entered the shop in the gloom and, without turning on any lights, lifted a handbag from a pile of medium-sized specimens. Then I locked the door and returned to the bakery cellar. Dodik was waiting for me with all the lab equipment: little bottles with cork stoppers, large square and round glass bottles, various kinds of ink, quill pens, fine brushes for photo touchups, sponges, blotters, lots of blank documents and a cloth bag with rubber stamps. I stuffed all of these into the handbag and sneaked out through the darkness and the courtyards.

I came home. It was midnight; everyone was asleep. Carefully and quietly I wrapped the bottles in two towels to keep them from breaking or clinking against each other. I wrapped the pens and brushes in paper, one by one,

JANUARY 1943—AUGUST 1944   163

and then swathed them in another towel. Finally, I laid a nightgown, a towel, a blouse, and underwear atop the equipment. Tomorrow, Halina Stasiuk, a girl from Koszewo village near Druskienniki, would be going to Białystok for a doctor's appointment. A one-day journey!

Mother heard me moving about and woke up. I whispered to her, I have to get up before five. I'm going to Białystok. Her sobbing awakened everyone. She was not the crying type. Rocheleh and Zipporka were frightened. "Chasinka," Mother said, "they'll capture you."

"But I have to go," I replied. "I'll be back."

Father was lying in bed and did not make a sound. Mother burst into tears again: "You're our source of support. If they capture you, what will become of us?"

"Mother, they're going to finish off all of us. What does it matter who dies first and who dies later?"

There are words that stay with you all your life. What I'd just told my mother reflected my absolute conviction that I would be executed if I were captured on this trip, and if not on this trip then on the next one, and that none of us would survive the war in any case. So the questions of now or later and who would die first — they or I –really didn't matter. But Mother asked me not to go. She asked me to help the rest of the family go into hiding and survive. I had neither refuge nor hideout to offer. Neither did the resistance. We hadn't considered the possibility of rescue. We knew it didn't exist. But the sense that I was going away and abandoning them to their fate was unbearably difficult.

"Why are you silent?" I asked Father. "Why won't you speak to me?"

"Dead people don't talk," he said. Those were my father's last words to me: dead people don't talk. I have never forgiven myself for the offense I caused him. How could I utter a sentence that treated the living, living people, with such fierce dismissiveness? Had I said, "Father, I received an order from the resistance," he would have understood and accepted it. I reserve no anger for him. For myself I have no forgiveness. Dead people don't talk, Father said, and I walked out.

I met up with Cyla at 4:30. A large group of workers were setting out along the narrow alley leading to the gate at Zamkowa Street. We melted into the group and passed through the gate with them. Before turning onto Mostowa Street, we slipped onto a side street. We removed the Stars of David from our backs and hid them in our coat linings. We would need them to enter the Białystok ghetto.

The morning of January 16, 1943: my twenty-second birthday. Shabbat: a gray dawn, stingingly cold. We headed for the Grodno railroad station on empty sidewalks. I wore my good coat, the blue one that Aunt Rosa had made for me. She'd used the same cloth to make a muffle, a sleeve open at both ends into which you stuff your hands to fend off the cold of winter. It also had a pocket for money and papers. We had a little money from the underground's hard-pressed exchequer. It sufficed for a train ticket. We had no food for the trip and no money to buy any.

We reached the station, an old stone building with wide stairs and a high ceiling. The platform was crowded with women who sat and waited, swathed in scarves and coats, pressing handbags and baskets to their bodies. Cyla waited while I went upstairs to ask when the train to Białystok would be leaving. Cyla had acquired her Polish at the Tarbut Gymnasium; it would immediately betray her for the Jew that she was. I spoke Polish in the Grodno dialect, free of Jewish accents and idioms. My years of study at the Polish school and at ORT had given me this lifesaving skill. We decided that only I would do the talking. I asked about the train and people laughed; no one knew when it would arrive. We would have to do what the other women did: sit and wait.

But I was afraid to loiter at the train station. German gendarmes walked around inspecting people; Poles from Grodno might have recognized me. We decided to head into the street and return to the station every now and then to see if the train had arrived. The station was very close to the public school I had attended, at the intersection of Orzeszkowa and Jagiellonska Streets. Across from train station was a Polish quarter where no Jews lived. Each house was separated from the street by a courtyard and a garden. It was a truly opulent area. We chose to stroll there until the train came. It got colder. We had had nothing to eat or drink. Afternoon came. We walked down several streets in order to avoid attention. Not for a moment did I relax my grip on the handbag. Toward dusk, the station grew dark. It was unlit. Now it was relatively safe to sit with the Polish women. By the time it got really dark, at around 6 p.m., the train arrived. We raced with all the others and hopped aboard one of the cars. The train pulled out. It would be almost an hour's trip to Białystok.

When we got there, we headed for the exit gate amid a crowd of gentile women. As the queue inched forward, I saw German gendarmes on either side stopping each woman carrying a basket. There was no way back; I was too close to the gate. Cyla passed through because she was not carrying a bag; then she disappeared past the station gate.

The women who had bags were led to a small wooden shack for inspection. I was among them. The inspection queue was narrow and long. I slowed to a shuffle so that others could pass me; I wanted to be one of the last. A young gendarme stood at the door to the shack. The women filed in. Three policemen opened and emptied their baskets, revealing butter, cheese, eggs and meat procured on the black market. My mission was over, I was sure. I'd be captured even before I arrived. The queue got shorter and shorter; in another moment my handbag would be opened. With a sudden surge of aplomb, I turned to the young gendarme — I was next to him by then — and said, "Listen, it's late, it'll be curfew soon. What do they want from me?"

He said, "Go over to them in a little while and show them what you've got in the bag. Speculators sell dear."

"Come and see for yourself," I told him. "I don't have any food at all, just clothes. I'm going to a doctor. I didn't even bring food for myself." I pulled apart the straps of the bag a little. He peered in and said, "Tell them."

"I don't really want to lose a moment," I said. "I have a long way to go and it'll be curfew soon. Please tell them that you saw my basket." I pasted an ingratiating look on my face. "Tell them I can go."

He did as told, shouting word for word. The inspectors shouted back, over the heads of the women in the queue: "Alright, go." And he let me go.

Trembling from head to toe, I stepped out of the station and turned right. I remembered the staircase that led to the bridge. Cyla wasn't there.

I didn't know Białystok. Before the Germans came I had been there only once, during the Soviet occupation, for an underground regional conference of Hashomer Hatzair. The night before we set out, Zorach had drawn a map of the path to the ghetto, but we had not been able to take it with us. We memorized the way from the train station. We knew the stairs that led from the station to the bridge, the names of the streets, the church at the top of the hill and the alley where we were to turn left. But Cyla wasn't there.

I went up the stairs. On the top step, peering through the feeble light of the station lanterns, I saw Cyla leaning against the railing in the middle of the bridge, shivering and crying. We embraced. She was sure I hadn't made it, that I was gone, captured and taken away, never to return. Gendarmes pacing back

Cyla Szachnes — a leader of the resistance

and forth across the bridge stopped at her side each time, asking nosy questions. As we embraced, I whispered in her ear that I'd also thought it was all over, that I'd failed, that the lab would not reach the ghetto and the comrades would not be able to take action.

Darkness. Late. We turned to go, following the sketch we had memorized: the bridge over the railroad tracks, the entrance to Tenenbaumstrasse, St. Rocha's Church on the hill to our left. We can't enter the ghetto now, I tell Cyla; we have to find a place for the night.

"Who will let us in?" she asked. "It's dangerous. Let's find a stairwell and wait there until morning." On the other side of Lipowa Street I saw a house with a loft, its windows jutting out from the roof into the street, a small light flickering. I told Cyla, "A hovel like that: I'm sure poor old people live there. Let's go up and tell them we've come from a small village, it's already

curfew, and the Germans have been stopping us for inspections in the street."
We climbed the wooden stairs, knocked on the door and waited with baited
breath.

A young man opened the door. "Who are you looking for?"

"We're not looking for anyone. We've just come by train. It was late
and we're from a little village. We ran into curfew and the Germans are inspecting us all the time. We can't sleep on the platform or sit in the kitchen
until 5, when the curfew is over."

"Be my guest," the man said, turning away to bring us a flimsy blanket.

A baby began to cry in the next room. We lay down on the kitchen floor
and didn't close an eye all night long. Part of it was due to excitement, fear,
hunger and cold. But we also had lots of thinking and planning to do. How
and where would we spend the day? After all, groups of workers didn't enter
the ghetto in the morning; they only left. This meant that until evening we had
to stay outside, in the streets, in the freezing January cold, with nothing to eat
or drink and no way to warm ourselves. Daybreak approached. We stood up
quietly and stepped out of the house without even thanking its inhabitants.
They were the first on the list of the fondly remembered but nameless people
who helped us.

We began to walk. That night in the cellar, before we had set out, Zorach
had given us the address of Bronja: Bronja Winicka, a classmate of mine from
the Gymnasium, a member of Dror, the first girl to go to the Aryan side. It
was Sunday. She might not be working; maybe we could stay with her until
the afternoon. Cyla turned toward Bronja's flat; I continued to walk down the
street.

Few people were circulating there and each stood out badly. Before I
could go far, Cyla came back and said to me as she passed, without stopping,
"Follow me. Don't look back. We have to get out of here. They're following
us." Several lengthy minutes later, she slowed her pace and whispered that
Bronja had told her to disappear the moment she entered her apartment. The
place had been "burned." We couldn't stay there.

We wandered in the streets and alleys, entrances and yards. We crossed
fences and ventured into public gardens. When we finally stopped, we realized
we were lost and no one was tailing us. As we continued to ply the unfamiliar
streets and the alleys not marked in the map of our memory, we wondered how
we would find the ghetto. Since one did not ask for directions to a ghetto, we

asked how to get to the train station. From there we could recreate the map we had memorized.

We were into our second day without food or water, a place to rest, or a corner to stop for a moment. We wore half-height shoes, dresses and high woolen socks upholstered at the knees with several layers of newspaper as paltry insulation against the freezing cold. To warm ourselves a bit, we breathed on our fingers, rubbed our palms together, and stamped the pavement and the muddy snow. We returned to the bridge over the railroad tracks and retraced our steps toward the ghetto. We reached Poleska Street. Then we passed the ghetto gate and paused but did not see any incoming groups. It was Sunday. Few people had gone out to work. The gate was closed. It was already 2 p.m. Reaching the end of our strength, we turned away. Loitering around the gate might have aroused suspicion.

We reached a neighborhood at the edge of the ghetto, a quiet suburb with wooden homes and narrow streets. I said to Cyla, "Maybe we should go to one of the houses and say that we had a doctor's appointment and the train didn't come. Let's say that we've been walking around town since the morning and we're cold. Would you let us warm up a little?"

A simple picket fence, a small creaking gate, an apple tree and a pear tree, both leafless, a closed window and a white lace curtain. We knocked on the door and walked in, finding two elderly women at the kitchen table. We told them our story. One of the women, evidently the landlady, invited us to sit down. Then she stood up and poured tea into glasses: boiling water from a large bronze urn on the stove and then tea extract from a small matching kettle that sat on top of the urn.

The dark amber hue of the extract spread through the water as it descended into the delicate glasses. A wonderful sense of warmth spread from the hands that clutched the glass to the arms and thence to the entire body. The first sip: the first thing that had entered our mouths in almost forty-eight hours. An extraordinary sense of pleasure followed. Then the landlady said, "Stay a little. My daughters will be coming home soon with a few German officers. We're going to have a great time!"

German officers, and I'm holding the handbag! "Thank you," I said. "We'd like to go back to the train station. Our train may have come already. Our parents will be worried." We thanked them for the tea and stepped out. The landlady's neighbor, a sweet grandmotherly type, emaciated and slightly stooped, followed us. "If there's no train for you, you can come back to me," she said, pointing to the house next door and its loft. "My husband and I are the only ones there. My son was in the Polish army and didn't come back. He must have been murdered or killed in battle. Now it's just the two of us. If you don't have a train, come over and rest a little." We thanked her and went on.

Afternoon. It was quite chilly; we walked on and on to warm up, posing as random pedestrians, occasionally approaching the ghetto gate, carrying a leather handbag full of accessories for the manufacture of bogus documents. At around 4 p.m., a large group of women workers marched down the street. Gendarmes guarded the group only at its edges. We slipped in among the marchers and said, "We're Jewish. We want to go in with you."

"Who are you? Where are you from? How did you get here?"

"We'll tell you once we're past the gate!"

I pressed the Star of David to the back of Cyla's coat and she did the same for me. We passed through the gate with the group. It was Sunday; the gendarmes were not checking handbags. Once past the gate, Cyla said, "We're from Grodno. They're liquidating the ghetto. We got away."

The women around us reacted in a frightening way: "Rebels! Spreading panic! It's a lie! Here there aren't any *Aktionen*!"

It was Sunday, January 17, 1943. The first *Aktion* in the Białystok ghetto took place on Friday, February 5.

We quickly stepped away from the group and rushed to Nowy Świat Street, where Hashomer Hatzair had a commune. We stood at the door and called out, "We're from Grodno. Zorach sent us." As the house filled with comrades, Edek said, "Get them something to eat and drink right away. They're freezing. Literally green!"

They gave us drink, food and warmth. We recounted how we had left Grodno, the situation in the ghetto, the train station and the gendarmes, our two days of vagrancy with nothing to eat or drink in the terrible January cold, the one glass of tea, the good grandmotherly woman, and entering the ghetto with the group of workers.

As we told the story, comrades came in and reported that the ghetto was humming with a rumor about girls who had come in to sow panic and foment an uprising. "You'll have to go underground inside the ghetto," Edek said. "Don't go into the street." After we spent the whole afternoon reporting on Grodno, the comrades and preparations for the uprising, they vacated some beds so we could get some sleep. In the protected space of the house, the commune and friends, we slowly thawed and recovered from our hunger, fear and loneliness.

The next day, Edek had news for me: "Chaska, we've decided that you're suitable for the post of liaison. You've proved yourself. Now you have to do it."

"Doing it," meant leaving the ghetto, applying at Gestapo headquarters for a *Personalausweis* — a German ID card — in the name of the Polish woman Halina Stasiuk, looking for an apartment and a job and working for the comrades, the resistance and the Jewish people. But what about Grodno? My friends? And my family?

"There's nothing to go back for," Edek retorted. "You shouldn't go back. We'll bring the combatants here."

"No one has been thrown into the cold water and ordered to swim like we're doing to Chasia," Chaika Grossman said much later. But swim I did. Without knowing the city, without any help, I set out the next morning with a group of workers and again slipped away to a side street. A stranger helped me remove the Star of David from the back of my coat. He also joins that list of good people whose names I do not know and whose faces I do not remember, who momentarily lent me a helping hand.

Gestapo headquarters was on Sienkiewicz Street, a main street not far from the ghetto gate. I entered from the street, went down some stairs, and came to a counter with Gestapo men seated on its other side. I smiled and presented my forged papers. Feigning extreme confidence, I asked whether I would have to wait long. They wrote my name down to have my picture taken and told me matter-of-factly when I should come back.

Returning to the street, I recalled that in addition to all the other dangers, a group of Jewish collaborators was active in Białystok. They circulated in the streets, looking for hiding or escaping Jews whom they could turn in to the Gestapo. The ghetto underground had avenged itself against some of them. I decided to use the time to familiarize myself with the ghetto boundaries. I walked down main streets, blending into the masses in order not to stand out. An individual in a crowd wouldn't be noticed, I thought. The blue coat that my Aunt Rosa had made me, enveloping me like a protective memory of home, slowed the savage pounding of my heart as I left the Gestapo headquarters. Deep in my inner pocket was a dear treasure — the Star of David with its safety pin — removed from the coat that morning as I left the ghetto. With the coat and its matching muffle, I looked just like all the Polish women. All I lacked was a fur collar. My coat had come with a fur collar and lapels but they had been removed when we entered the ghetto. Jews were not allowed to wear fur. Here in Białystok, however, it seemed that I was the only person in the street who had no fur. Everyone noticed the suspicious difference, I was sure.

I explored the streets that encircled the ghetto and studied the buildings, alleys and corners. In the evening, I went back in. As I passed through the gate, my tears burst forth. I was so ashamed. Get used to it, I told myself deep inside. Get used to it and don't get upset, don't cry, be strong.

I had three days to wait until my appointment with the Gestapo to have my picture taken. I spent them at the commune, taking my turn washing dishes, meeting the comrades and resting. Then I went back to the Gestapo, sure that they'd flush me out this time. But all they did was affix a number to my chest, take my picture, hand me a document to sign, and invite me to return a week later. On January 29, 1943, I exited the Gestapo headquarters, leaving my birth certificate behind and clutching a *Personalausweis*. I had difficult mixed feelings: satisfaction for having succeeded but trepidation from the knowledge that from now on I would be alone on the Aryan side — alone to hunt for an apartment, alone to cope with life with a Polish family, alone to find a job with the Germans.

I didn't know the Catholic prayers. I knew only how to cross myself (from head to abdomen, to the right shoulder and then to the left shoulder), to press my palms together (in front, chest high) and to say "amen." I didn't know how truly ignorant I was. Only long afterwards did I discover that my Polish name, Halina, commemorated St. Halina. But which Halina? There were two.

I returned to the ghetto with my *Personalausweis* and told Edek I was prepared to carry out any assignment on the Aryan side, with only one condition: that I must not be excluded from taking part in the uprising. When the liquidation *Aktion* began and the uprising started, I had to be with the combatants in the ghetto. I wanted to fight along with all the others. I wouldn't be the sole survivor after their demise. Edek smiled at me and said, "Very well, I promise!"

Only after it was all over did I realize that Edek never intended to keep his word. His purpose was to make me believe that I would be fighting with everyone and would not be left on my own. He succeeded.

Edek, Cyla, Chaika and I sat down to plan my departure to the Aryan side. We decided that the right thing for me to do was to find work as a domestic servant, a *shiksa*, a simple village girl, anything but a Jew. I should tell the Germans that I had come to town to earn a little money, my comrades said. For Poles, my story should be that I fled from my village because the Germans were inducting all the girls for labor in Germany. Don't stand out in any sense. Your best bet is to be stupid and thickheaded. That way, they won't notice you. So I learned to be unimportant, a dim-witted village girl. I learned not to call attention to myself. I learned not to be.

I set out the next day, alone. I left behind Chasia Bielicka of Grodno, a member of Hashomer Hatzair, a member of the underground, a Jew. I took only Halina Stasiuk, a Polish Christian girl from the village of Koszewo, not far from Druskienniki.

I looked for a place to live. I visited the old grandmotherly woman who had invited Cyla and me in on our first day of vagrancy in the streets, waiting for evening to fall so we could enter the ghetto. I found her on the basis of memory: Zabia Street. We had not realized how close to the ghetto she lived. Her living-room window faced the Jewish cemetery, within the ghetto confines. Before I left the ghetto Cyla said, "She's all alone and she was so eager to have us. Give it a try."

I knocked on the door. She opened it and chirped, "So you're back in Białystok. Great! It's good that you're here. Come in. Have some tea."

"Thank you," I said. "In our village, they're taking the girls to Germany for labor. My family said I should run away to Białystok and work for the Germans there instead of in Germany. This way, I'll be able to visit home now and then. If I go to Germany... who knows? But I have nowhere to live. Could I possibly stay with you? I'll pay rent."

She answered, "I'm so happy to have you here with me, a young girl instead of my son, who's gone. Maybe he'll also come back from the war. But I don't have a bed, just a very narrow sofa, like a bench. If you're willing to sleep on it, be my guest."

I thanked her and said I would return the next day. I spent the night with distant acquaintances across town and left my few belongings with them.

Now I needed to find a job.

The Germans had an *Arbeitsamt* (labor exchange) on Lipowa Street. I went there and signed up for work. Poles worked only for Germans.

"What kind of work are you looking for?" the clerk asked.

"Domestic, servant."

"Herr Luchterhand and his wife from the SS Werkzentrale need a worker. Everyone runs away from that place. Tough people, but it's the only opening we have today. I just wanted you to know."

"I'll try it," I said. "Thank you."

I didn't know that one was allowed to start working at one's volition but needed the employer's approval in order to leave. I found out too late.

Saturday, February 6, 1943. A week after I had left the ghetto, I came back from work and found my landlady, whom I thought of as a *savta* (grandmother), standing at the door waiting for me. She grabbed my arms and said in agitation, "Pani Halinka, don't ask what's happening in the ghetto. Just look through the window. They're shooting and murdering people; they're taking out carts loaded with dead people every day, digging large graves and throwing the people in. Without even writing down their names."

She wept, drying her eyes with her apron. "Look." She took me by the hand and tugged me to the large window. "Look what they're doing to those poor souls. How can you treat people that way?"

Her anguish and sobbing helped me mask my distress. I tried to understand what was going on there. It was all over; I was on my own. I gripped her hand and interrogated her: When did it begin? What did you manage to see? She answered amid sobs that they had begun shooting people that morning and hadn't stopped all day long. The Luchterhands' apartment was far from the ghetto; I had not heard a thing.

In my many months of life outside the ghetto on the Aryan side, I encountered very few Poles who truly felt pain, grief and anguish about the Jews. As long as I lived with her, however, this good *savta* ceaselessly shared her sorrow and agony with me.

I approached the window. It was dark outside and the shooting had ceased. My first thought was to enter the ghetto. However, we had not prepared crossings; that would come much later. I decided to try the next day, by crossing the cemetery after work.

Savta's house bordered a narrow alley. One section of the alley abutted the fence of the Jewish cemetery, inside the ghetto. Two courtyards on the

Polish side connected these in an "L" shape. Both courtyards were very long, running along the fence for about 40 meters. The fence was made of boards fronted with concertina wire.

When I came back from work one day, Savta said it again: they'd been shooting all morning long and taking out dead and wounded people, but in the afternoon the gunfire stopped and the laden carts were no longer moving to the cemetery.

As we sipped tea together, I wondered how I could get out of the house and into the ghetto. Now. I had to go in and find out what was really happening. I stood up, put on my blue coat, and picked up the muffle.

"Where are you going at such an hour?" Savta asked.

"To a friend who works with me. She invited me over." I had reached the door. "Maybe I'll stay with her overnight. Don't worry!"

The streets, the courtyards and the sidewalks were blanketed with snow and the darkness of an early winter evening. I walked into the courtyard that abutted the fence of the ghetto's Jewish cemetery. Not a living soul was in sight. I reached the fence. I withdrew a hand from the muffle so that I could slip it into my coat pocket. That way I would not lose it while leaping over the fence to the other side.

"Halt!" A sharp cry in German split the silence. I froze in my tracks, turned around, and saw a soldier with a rifle trained on me. Without thinking, I jammed the muffle into his threatening hand, rolled up the hems of my coat and dress, squatted, and urinated into the snow before his stunned eyes.

I finished and straightened up. A mighty smack in the face sent me reeling. "I could have killed you," he roared. "I thought you were a Jewess wanting to cross into the ghetto."

"Ghetto? What, there's a ghetto here? I was just looking for a place to do my thing with no one watching!"

I trembled all over from the force of the blow, the fear, the deliverance and my burning cheek, flowing tears and blurred vision. I staggered through twisting alleys and past picket fences. The stench of smoke wafted from white chimneys. Snowflakes settled on my sizzling face, the building roofs and the city as it drowned in darkness. I returned to my apartment at 7:30 p.m., just before curfew. Savta was pleased. "I was already starting to worry," she said.

The next day, I returned from work in the early evening. It was still snowing, still frosty. Pondering again how I could enter the ghetto, I suddenly saw two familiar figures in the corner of the alley: Rocheleh and Chaika. But I had to quell the joy, the delight of the reunion. I had to hug them in a way that would not attract too much attention. And don't let your tears flow!

My beloved soul sister, my Rocheleh, at a place and time of which I dared not dream. "How did you get out? Where did you come here from? What are you doing here? Who sent you? Where are Mother and Zipporka? What about the comrades?"

"They're sending everyone out," Rocheleh related as we walked, Chaika and I at her sides. "Someone is supposed to arrive every day. I came alone by train. They gave me Chaika's address because they didn't know yours. I have to get into the ghetto, to join the combatants."

Chaika walked away; Rocheleh and I continued to my apartment. How would I tell my good Savta that I had suddenly shown up with another tenant?

I decided to tell the truth: she's my sister. They sent her from the village because the Germans wanted to send her, too, to Germany for labor. Our mother asked her to stay with me until the wave of abductions had passed. Then she could go home. Could she possibly stay for a few days? It's my pleasure, the good woman said. But where will she sleep?

"We'll sleep together." I had totally forgotten I was sleeping on a narrow bench. Savta pulled out another blanket and spread it on the floor.

We sat on the narrow sofa, embracing. We hadn't been so close in a long time. Life in the ghetto was so congested that we had always been with members of the family or comrades from the underground. Now, all of a sudden, it was just the two of us. I felt her smooth fair hair brushing my shoulder, the warmth of her body on my embracing hand, her gentle motions, her immense fatigue. The vest I had knit for her in the ghetto descended to her waist. Her palms slowly thawed from the chill. The pace of her breathing slowed a little after her trip from Grodno to Białystok, alone on the train, in the streets of the strange city. My little sister, brave and heroic: her head on my shoulder, her words beginning to slur, her eyes closing, her whole body going limp. I lay her on one blanket, covered her with another, and settled down next to her for a night's sleep.

Early the next morning, I set out for work without awakening my sister. I spent the whole day worrying about her. Maybe someone would notice her strange Polish accent, the one she'd acquired at the Hebrew-speaking Tarbut

Gymnasium. Maybe her fear would rob her of the ability to act. Maybe she'd be affected by the proximity to the ghetto and the things she could see through the window. I raced home from work. The house was empty. Rocheleh was gone.

"Where's my sister?" I asked Savta.

"Oy, Pani Halinka," she replied, "What happened while you were away!"

Jan was a gentile, a poor shoemaker, a good guy and a close neighbor. But he spent most of his time drunk. Whenever that happened, he came over to chat with Savta upstairs or with the neighbor downstairs. That day, he dropped in at my place and saw Rocheleh standing at the window overlooking the ghetto. Through the panes and the lace curtains Rocheleh saw a convoy of Jews being led to the cemetery. Her eyes filled with tears and Jan noticed.

"Why are you crying about the Jews?" he asked. "Maybe you're a Jew yourself?" And he led her to his apartment for dinner.

As I heard Savta telling this story, mentally I was already racing through the darkening streets to Gestapo headquarters in order to liberate my sister. I didn't know how, but I'd find a way, and if I didn't, we'd die together.

"I'm going over to Jan's to get her," I told Savta, forcing myself to look as though nothing terrible had happened.

"What's he meddling for?" I added. "What does he need her for? A young girl like that. I'm going to get her!"

I set out on the run to Jan's apartment. I knocked on the door and pulled it open. It was a spacious place: a foyer, a living room and an adjoining kitchen with a large wooden table. Jan's wife was standing at the stove, frying eggs in a big black metal pan. At the head of the table sat Jan, clutching a large empty bottle of vodka, with Rocheleh next to him.

"Pani Halinka," he calls out hoarsely. "Pani Halinka, come sit down! What, you've come to take your sister? So early? I won't let you take her to the ghetto." He shook his head drunkenly. "I won't let you!"

"Pan Janku," I said, "How can you imagine that I would take my sister to the ghetto?" Then I turned to his wife: "Tell your husband that he shouldn't lose his senses. I know he's drunk but he doesn't have to speak such nonsense. I came here to take her home."

"The two of you aren't going anywhere. Please sit down and have supper here, Pani Halinka and Pani Zosia." He pointed to another chair as his other hand swung over the table drunkenly in an almost perfect pendulum motion until it collided with the empty bottle of vodka, which rolled noisily and crashed to the floor.

I had no choice. To avoid the appearance of escaping, we had to stay there. "Pan Janek," I said to him, "I think you've been drinking too much." Then I joked about the quality of the vodka and described the beverages the village peasants used to make before the war. I tried any topic of conversation that would distract him from the one that pulsed under his inebriation.

The frying pan sat in the middle of the table. Next to it were eggs, grilled *speck* (a slice of pork), a large round loaf of bread and hunks of pork and lard — disgusting, malodorous stuff that stuck in your throat. As I tried to continue talking, I noticed Rocheleh's eyes downcast, trying to mask her fear and dread. We finished eating, thanked Jan for the meal, and set out, clutching each other and trembling from head to toe. Then we went upstairs silently to our apartment.

My good Savta was waiting for us. I had to tell her something. I had to react, make a plan, find a way out. "He's totally drunk," I told her. "He's spouting nonsense. I don't know why. If my sister stays here, he'll come over every day and harass her." I went to work early and was afraid to leave her there alone.

I don't know where my mind invented sundry ideas such as the one that cropped up just then. It had happened before — with the gendarme at the train station, with the soldier at the ghetto fence — and it would happen later. Had I thought it out in advance, made a plan, or drew up a list of right answers and worthy responses to possible and impossible situations, I would surely have faltered at the critical moment. I was not alone in this trait. All my comrades who followed me to the Aryan side had much the same experience.

The ability to survive in the face of the unexpected, to resolve situations in which only a fine line separated life from exposure and death, to maintain inconceivable composure while looking Poles and Germans, civilians and soldiers, in the eye, to get out of predicaments that seem to defy solution. I survived; we survived. Not all of us, not all the time. In due course I will list my courageous sisters and tell some stories of their amazing valor and inconceivable mental fortitude. Now, however, I'm still here, with Rocheleh, in Savta's apartment, asking her for shelter.

"I have a good friend across town," I told her. "They've been remodeling their apartment, repainting the whole place. But they may have finished and my sister can live with them for a few days until she returns to our village. I'll go with her now, because tomorrow when I go to work Jan might come back drunk. Who knows what terrible, nonsensical things he'll tell her?"

With that, we stepped into the evening.

The quietude of a winter evening before curfew: nobody circulated in the frozen streets unless they had to. The quiet was my hope. Since I couldn't hear gunfire from the direction of the ghetto, I thought the day's mayhem may have ended and I could move Rocheleh into the ghetto under cover of darkness. On Sienkiewicz Street, the main street of the city, there was a large vacant lot that bordered the ghetto fence. I decided to try to cross there.

We walked arm in arm. Rocheleh didn't know Białystok. The layout of its sidewalks was foreign to her; so were its alleys unless they appeared on the maps she had memorized. I led the way with purposeful and rhythmic steps. Shortly before the left turn, at the façade of the large building, I slowed down. In front of me, all of a sudden, were many motor vehicles, weapons, glowing flashlights, groaning motors, motorcycles, loud voices barking orders and shouting. The whole lot was full of German soldiers.

I tightened my grip on Rocheleh's arm and continued straight down the street, as if I had not intended to turn anywhere, as if I were oblivious to the whole tumult. Through her coat sleeve I felt her shudder; I tightened my grip to keep her from sinking into the ground, striking the round cobblestones, and calling attention to two simple Polish girls on their way home from work.

We returned to our apartment. Savta was waiting for us. It was night and Rocheleh was afraid — younger than me and unsure about the Polish she spoke. She had had enough of life on the Aryan side: afraid of Jan's drunkenness, afraid that he would return, become sober, and turn her in. And she wanted to be a combatant with the rest of our comrades in the ghetto; she was even willing to part with me for that purpose. "Don't worry," I said. "Stay here one more day. In the evening I'll find a way to get you across. You have to stay and I have to go to work. Don't disappear on me. If something happens, I'll come and rescue you or I'll die together with you. I won't leave you alone, I promise."

Morning. Before 6 a.m. A lengthy trek on foot from my apartment to the Luchterhands'. Rocheleh didn't wake up. I whispered to Savta: "Don't let

Jan come for her. He's no friend of hers. She's scared of him. He drinks vodka, gets drunk and stinks. And she's so young."

"Go," Savta says. "I'll take care of her. I'll take care of her like my daughter!"

So she did. I came back that evening. I walked. You couldn't run in the streets; that would attract attention. In my fear, stress and anxiety, I took the steps three at a time. I reached the door and it didn't budge. It was locked. A moment of panic. What had gone wrong? This door was never locked before curfew. Where was everyone? I knocked on the door. "It's me, Pani Halinka." I heard Savta's feet approaching.

"Where's my sister?" I asked even before the door opened wide. "Is she here?"

"I promised her not to let Jan in, so I locked the door." Then she added, "It's quiet in the ghetto now. Today they didn't take dead people away and there was no shooting."

"That's good," I said. "I feel sorry for them."

I tried to relate to the matter as she did, without overdoing it. I didn't think she would suspect me, but I established inviolable patterns of caution. I decided to wait with Rocheleh for one more day. I wouldn't head out with her that night. If I did, it might arouse suspicion; someone might draw a connection between the silence in the ghetto and her disappearance. Instead, I told Savta that I had spoken with my friend across town. My sister will go to them tomorrow, I said. She'll spend a week with them and then return to her village. Maybe I'll bring her over once more before then.

We set out the next evening. Savta kissed her goodbye. We walked to the courtyard at 63 Sienkiewicz Street, where the ghetto fence loomed. It was too tall to climb. I had to find an opening: a board that could be dislodged so my sister could slip through. There must have been one; someone who needed a secret crossing — members of the resistance, smugglers — must have loosened one of the slats. We moved silently at the base of the fence. My right hand clutched her left hand tightly; my other hand groped carefully, trying to move each slat a little. I had to be cautious not only because of what might happen here, on the Aryan side, but also because of the situation in the ghetto. The ghetto police patrolled the place at night, lurking for Jews coming in, going out, wearing disguises, putting up resistance. Only from smugglers, perhaps, would these policemen accept a bribe or some food return for their lives. And then, at the corner of the next house, bordering the fence, I found an opening.

We stopped moving and embraced soundlessly. Through my tears I listened for the approach of human voices or footsteps. Into her ear I whispered directions to the Hashomer Hatzair commune. It would soon be curfew in the ghetto, too. Then she slipped between the slats of the fence and vanished into the gloom.

Those sobs — sobs of love, concern and intimacy that will be gone in one more moment. Sobbing over the choice that is tearing us apart, over her not staying with me, over her lack of strength to be on the Aryan side. I already miss her; I am already sobbing for the place that she has entered, a place of mortal danger. There's already been an *Aktion* there; maybe there will be another one tomorrow. Who will protect her if I am on the other side of the wall?

I spent the rest of the night tossing sleeplessly on my narrow sofa. Had Rocheleh arrived safely? Had she found the commune? Or had policemen ambushed her in the silence of the night, in the empty streets and delivered her straight to the ghetto police and Gestapo headquarters, doomed and alone? Had she already been shot?

Two days passed before I could slip into the ghetto. I went to the same courtyard on Sienkiewicz Street and used the slat that had been pushed aside in the fence. It was Saturday night. I had a whole night and day to spend in the ghetto, at the Hashomer Hatzair commune, in one bed with Rocheleh. Embracing and sleeping, we tossed and turned over and over together, from side to side in the middle of the night. Then I decided that I, too, would move out of my good Savta's apartment. Rocheleh had gone to the ghetto but Jan might show up, drunk, to harass me and ask questions about the girl who had disappeared so suddenly. His propensity for shouting things outside rendered Savta's apartment unsuitable for underground work. I felt sorry about leaving. Savta had been so good to me. Above all, she was a human being in a place where there were few.

I told her that I regretted having made her tiny apartment such a crowded place. At night, her husband had to step past me whenever he needed to use the conveniences; I felt that it embarrassed him. It discomfited me to cause so much trouble. I'd found a place to live in a separate room with a young family. Savta kissed me and said that her home was always, but always, open to me. If

I ever needed help, a bed for the night, or anything else, I should turn to her as her own daughter would. Don't hesitate to come. With that, I gathered up my few possessions and walked out, never to return. I wanted to come back but I was afraid of a run-in with Jan. The more work I was doing for the resistance, the more I avoided that neighborhood.

Babche, Savta. I don't remember her name and don't know how to re-vive the memory and express my gratitude. She housed me for a full month and asked for nothing in return, trusting me to pay the rent with the first salary I received, as in fact I did. Much later — after the ghetto, after the partisans, after the war — I did not go back. Somehow, in the tumult of anguish and the commotion of victory, she slipped away from the place where I should have remembered her. Her kindness, her sensitivity and the shelter she provided Rocheleh and me while I was staying with her — it all vanished. Today, I think the profusion of events, occurrences and excitements of the summer of 1944 left no room for anything but the realization that we had survived, that I had survived, the only one in my other world who had done so.

I banished her name from my memory shortly after I left her apartment. That way, if I were ever caught, interrogated and tortured, nothing in my con-scious or subconscious mind would remain that might harm her or the other brave partners: my Polish benefactors, members of the resistance and those who helped or cooperated with me. Over the years, I made several attempts to remember Savta's name — and failed. Only Rocheleh and I lived with her; I have no one to ask.

Twenty-three Parkowa Street: new two-story wooden houses, all purged of their Polish tenants so that German officers and bureaucrats could move in. The Luchterhands lived on the ground floor. Mrs. Luchterhand gave me a cheery welcome. She'd gone several weeks without help, she said. Both of them worked for the Werkzentrale SS. Her husband was the superintendent of Polish labor under the occupation.

They're weird, both of them, I decided. She's taller than him and skinny as a scarecrow. She wears simple dark-colored clothes. He's a short man with a scowl on his face. Both are always taciturn; at breakfast, neither makes a sound. Childless. Cold. Bitter. With the passage of so many years, I can't recall how old they were, but back then they seemed downright elderly. They may have been in their mid-forties.

They didn't talk, they gave orders. *"Du machst das."* Do it this way.

Inflexible toward themselves and others. Blunt, insulting. I consoled myself by thinking that they were speaking this way not to me, the Jewish girl, but to their Polish domestic. Every morning began with breakfast at 7 a.m. on the button: an egg cooked to perfection with the help of a timer, along with bread, cheese and coffee. Then, after giving instructions on cleaning and preparing dinner, out they went.

The house was large and plain, dry and empty, with no real personal possessions. It had three rooms: a living room, a bedroom, and a pantry stocked with sausage, eggs, cheese, jam, coffee and chocolate. The kitchen had a coal-fired stove. Every day I brought from the cellar a bucket of coals — shiny black lumps — and a few hunks of wood to get the fire going. I had to polish the wooden floor every morning as if it had never been polished before. I knelt, crouched on all fours, and scoured board after board with woolen rags dipped in wax. The conveniences included a large bathtub that I used to do the laundry, scrubbing it over a washboard with coarse soap. Once a week I pressed the clothing and bedding by spreading it on the kitchen table and running a heavy metal iron over it. The iron was filled with coals that had been kept sizzling on the top of the stove. I finished all the housework by 10 a.m. and then went into the common kitchen.

Across from the house was a large vacant lot with a very long building at its farthest extreme: an office building with a dining hall on its ground floor and behind it a kitchen. Hundreds of German officers and bureaucrats ate lunch there. Every day after 10 a.m., I reported to work at this location with a crowd of Polish girls, and then returned to the Luchterhands until evening.

Physical fortitude was never my forté. At first, I came home after this long day of work and fell asleep straight away. But as had happened while I'd been working in the Grodno ghetto, I grew stronger over time and became capable of much more.

The Luchterhands' kitchen window faced the street, the bathroom window opened onto the kitchen of another apartment, and the rest of the windows looked into the backyard. Later on, when my comrade and friend Lisa Czapnik found work with one of the families, these windows became our rendezvous: her kitchen, my bathroom. Through them we arranged meetings in the cellar jointly owned by all the tenants, a place where coal was stored in one area and vegetables in another. If something had to be moved into the ghetto or if a notice had to be passed among the girls, we discussed it in the cellar. It was such a reasonable place for us to meet; there no one would suspect that we were related in any way or that our encounter had been set up.

In the bedroom, in a little cupboard near the bed, my boss kept handguns and lots of ammunition. In his spare time, Herr Luchterhand amused himself by shooting at birds from the bedroom window or in a nearby park. I decided to steal a few bullets and deliver them to the ghetto resistance. One morning, he greeted me with a raucous tirade: why hadn't I been cleaning the drawer and arranging the bullets? I, the stupid Polish village girl, replied, "I'm scared, it could kill me." Luchterhand burst into laughter. "Look," he said to his wife, "what an imbecile our peasant servant is. She's afraid that a bullet will kill her." He picked up one of the bullets and handed it to me. The great thing about the incident was that it never occurred to him that I would steal bullets....

On several occasions I smuggled bullets into the ghetto. I put them in my coat pocket and walked out. It seemed so simple but in fact it was a conscious choice of life coupled with danger, paired with death. I had come from Grodno, from the ghetto, from a family that had in part already been murdered. These factors, along with the existential space my comrades and my people occupied, truly left me no choice. The education I had received, the examples of my parents and Hashomer Hatzair were so strongly embedded in me that I could not have entertained any other option. Saving my own skin could not be attempted at the expense of possibilities in my place of origin and the place I had chosen to be.

The first time Mr. Luchterhand ordered me to shine his boots, my self-constructed inner defenses felt as though on the verge of collapse. For a moment, I reverted to the person I had been: Chaska, the Jewish girl. They were tall black boots of stiff leather, with leather soles and metal clasps. I grasped them and shuddered. It was like touching the essence of the atrocity: the jackboots of a German SS officer. I cried the whole long way home.

There I rebuilt the defensive ramparts of Halinka, the Polish village girl. In that guise, I thumbed my nose at everyone and everything, including this Luchterhand character, who shouted if I were a little late in the morning after a night in the ghetto, when I couldn't sneak out before the street filled with people; including the slap in the face he administered with sizzling rage when I'd come late one morning because I was returning from the partisans in the forest. I really didn't care. By means of my alternative persona, the fake identity in which I lived, I realized that they treated not only Jews this way but also Poles. Somehow, that made things a little easier. The thing that was really hardest was to put up with their physical presence. I didn't touch their food, even the leftovers on the table after they went away, even a bite-sized piece of bread. Nothing. I was repelled by everything associated with them and their Germanness.

Every morning after the Luchterhands went to work, they left breakfast on the table for me: a glass of tea with a slice of bread. They left just that, no more, and I was not to take anything by myself. I had the feeling that Mrs. Luchterhand marked the exact locations of the sausage, the cheese and the eggs on the shelf, so that she would know if I took any. I didn't touch them; I touched nothing of theirs. One evening after work she stepped into the pantry and came out screaming about the sausage I had eaten. How dare I touch sausage! What gall, to touch it without permission!

"I took nothing," I replied.

"The sausage was out of place," she retorted at the top of her lungs. "You can see it, you can just see, and there's a piece missing, too."

She went into the pantry and emerged with the sausage, which she waved in my face. Just then, her husband came out of the bedroom. "Lucia, what are you shouting about? I'm the one who took it. Not a piece, just a corner, I wanted to taste it…."

I pilfered food from them only once: when Mother and Zipporka were taken to the Białystok ghetto. That afternoon, as I brought the vegetables from the cellar for supper, I placed a few potatoes, one carrot, and an onion on the last step. By the time I came back from work, it was dark. Cautiously I opened the cellar door and stuffed the vegetables into my coat pocket. I didn't take more because I had nowhere to stash it.

In the evening, at home, I dined on a slice of bread and sometimes — when it was handed out with the rations — a piece of fish. I did not know how to cook. When I entered the ghetto, I always told them that I'd eaten. How could I make them share the little they had?

I sometimes joined Missja (the Polish owner of the place where I moved after I left Savta's flat) for a glass of tea or a small bowl of soup. For half a year, however — until Chaika moved in with me and began to cook for both of us — all I had in the evening was bread.

At the end of each month, I was paid a sum of money that covered the rent and a bare living but not a cent more. Throughout my time in Białystok, I wore the same dress, skirt, blouse and half-height shoes that I had worn in the Grodno ghetto. I had no special clothes for work or for Shabbat and festivals. In the German kitchen, there were aprons I could put on in order to protect my clothing as I worked. With the Luchterhands, I didn't dare to touch an apron — because of her, but no less because of me. The very thought of her apron touching my body filled me with revulsion.

They signed my labor permit each month and I took it to the *Arbeitsamt*, the labor exchange, where they imprinted it with a large round ink stamp. It was a permit for life: if caught without it, you were sent to Germany for forced labor.

After passing several months this way, I came down with terrible eczema on my hands. I'd been doing the Luchterhands' laundry with coarse detergent. The evening before, I soaked the laundry in caustic soda powder so it would be easier to wash and require less scrubbing. The soda took a toll on the skin of my palms.

The Polish girls who worked in the kitchen sent me to a doctor, who gave me a salve and ordered me to bandage my hands. I spent several days that way but the condition actually worsened. This earned me my release from the Luchterhands' employ. A German doctor, a Nazi, an SS officer, did me that favor — a favor for me, revenge for them. It didn't happen, however, until I had endured an ordeal of terror that I will describe elsewhere. I worked with them for more than half a year, from late January 1943 until the Białystok ghetto was liquidated that summer.

Lisa and I worked in the kitchen every day from 10:30 on. An enormous kitchen with enormous pots, iron gas jets, coal-fired ovens and lots of benches, stools, working tables and cutting boards. Metal and porcelain bowls, iron frying pans and pots, pitchers, jugs and boxes. All the fruit and vegetables I had forgotten about for the past three-and-a-half years, as well as others I had been eating in measured, rationed doses, arrived in huge bushel baskets and little wicker baskets. Fresh, choice, straight from the fields, orchards and vegetable patches, every day: cauliflower, cabbage, asparagus and potatoes. They cooked lots of cabbage there, and also lots of *speck* and lard, and pudding for dessert at the end of every meal. They also had milk, sour cream, butter, chocolate, vanilla and strawberries.

We ate the leftovers that wouldn't stay fresh for the next day, eating not from the plates but from the pots, pans and molds. The German kitchen manager decided each day what might be doled out to us and placed the Polish chef in charge of distribution. The food was so scant, however, that I never really ate my fill even during that time. True, I did not starve. I had what to eat; it was my salvation. Still, I do not remember having had the sense of true satiation even once.

We worked with a large number of Polish girls and women with families. All were simple and unschooled; they lived in working-class neighborhoods and slums. They had no idea that Lisa and I were colleagues, or that we even knew each other. Even when we spoke with each other, we addressed all of them, slipping into the general conversation that went on as we sat on stools around piles of peeled potatoes, cabbage cutting boards or the large wooden tables.

We had code words for anything that mattered. "Oy," I would say, "I went to see my grandmother yesterday." "My grandmother" was the ghetto. Or "My cousin, the one who lives at the edge of town, got sick." This meant that something unusual had happened. Thus we passed information to each other: my grandmother, my aunt, their children. Our superb Polish accents protected us every day, every moment. Very quickly, however, we realized that various things other than accent were important, too — mannerisms of language and culture, like speaking with your mouth only, not embellishing your words with hand gestures, expressing excitement in a certain way about certain matters, and mentioning the name of Jesus — *oj Jezu* — in every other sentence. And sometimes, to give emphasis or denote something that was especially terrible or amazing, *Jezu Crystu* — the full name of Jesus Christ.

So it went day after day: sitting in the kitchen, peeling vegetables or washing dishes. We cleaned the kitchen implements, the cooking implements and the eating utensils in giant sinks. Mostly, we peeled: potatoes and carrots, onions and garlic, turnips and red beets. The beets made our hands so red that it took two days to get the stains out. We formed a peeling circle, some seated on wooden stools and others on the floor. The peasant women among us were used to this from their village lives. They sang Polish folk songs for hours; we mouthed the syllables as if we knew them. As time passed, we learned the songs.

We liked to hear them gabbing and telling stories and preferred it that way. The younger ones talked about cavaliers and suitors; the older ones, who were married, spoke about husbands and children. Lisa and I listened, looked at each other, and laughed deep inside: What problems they've got! If only we had problems like those....

Sundays and festivals were problematic. We could fool them about Sundays by saying that we were too tired to travel to the village and return so quickly. For Christian festivals, however, there was nothing we could do. Not only did they involve three or four days off but they were strongly family-oriented. How could a young girl spend a festival away from her parents' home?

At first we returned to the ghetto on festival eves and stayed there until the festivals were over; those were our trips "home." Later, when the ghetto was wiped out, we spent festivals with the partisans in the forest or, if for some reason we could not reach the forest, at a house on the path from the town to the forest. The house belonged to a member of the Communist resistance, whose story I will tell in its proper place. I mention her briefly now in order to note that after the ghetto was gone and we really had no family to visit, she chose to be our family – providing us with a home, a cover story for festivals, a hideout, and a source of strength flowing from brave friendship.

I find it hard to reconstruct the exact chronology of those days and weeks. I anchor my memories in events, endeavors and occurrences, and weave associative strands around them, from them, and to them. For certain blocs of time, however, I lack an external indication that would steer me to an exact date and cannot explain what came first and on what day of the week. Sometimes the seasons occur in reverse order and I determine the position of an event in time on the basis of the recollection of a place or something that I saw. Sometimes I mix up sights, sounds and events until I don't know exactly where to locate a given fragment of memory that prompts me to speak.

Seven Świętego Rocha Street. At that house, the first address given me by the *Wohnungsamt*, the German housing office, I lived from the day I left Savta until liberation. Świętego Rocha's Church, named for St. Rocha, sat on a hill in the middle of town at the intersection of Świętego Rocha, Dombrowska and Lipowa Streets. The Germans renamed the last of the streets, a tree-lined boulevard, Tannenbergstrasse.

The courtyard was entered from the street at exactly the place where the church steeple cast a sundial-like shadow that towered over the city at 4 p.m. A side entrance opened onto a spacious courtyard with a house of red bricks at its edge – an elongated two-story building with four entrances. At the last

Missja's house, where Chasia lived under a false Polish identity from February 1943 until August 1944. After the uprising in Białystok, she was joined by Chaika Grossman. Photo of Chasia in front of the house, 2000.

entrance, the one farthest from the street, was an apartment with a room for rent.

It was a working-class quarter with poor families and lots of children. The apartments had large paired windows that peered into the courtyard through lace curtains. Laundry hung on clotheslines strung between posts. A large pear tree, small vegetable gardens and a few ancient oaks filled the rest of the space.

There was only one childless couple. They were the "intelligentsia" of the building. He was a road surveyor whose wife awarded him the title of "Engineer," which gave her a great deal of self-importance. Months after I had moved in, I returned one day with some onions and garlic on a braid of straw.

"You look like a Jewess," she said, "walking along with a clove of garlic in your hand."

"That's interesting," I answered, laughing. "That's exactly what I was thinking all the way from the market...."

The room I rented was in Missja and Tosiek's apartment. I don't remember their family name. Chaika moved in with me after the ghetto was liquidated, but she didn't remember either.

Many names elude me. I cannot break the code by which my memory retains or deletes names of people with whom or near whom we lived, and sometimes by virtue of whom we survived. As the years and the distance pass, more and more sights, sensations, pictures of places, sounds and voices return. The names, however, do not come, and I don't know which drawer in my memory contains the key to that black box.

Missja, Tosiek and their three-year-old son Waldek: a simple family. Missja was young, not much older than me. Tosiek was a security guard at the municipal waterworks. He kept the place in good order and protected it from sabotage. He worked very close to the ghetto, alternating between night and day shifts.

They were eager to rent out their extra room to me because unless they took in a Polish tenant, they knew they would have to accommodate Germans. I was the first to visit. Missja and the boy were at home when I came in the evening after my exertions for the Luchterhands. I sat with Missja until Tosiek came back from work. Then I told them my history: I had come from a village near Grodno, my mother had died several years earlier, my father had remarried, and I had been raised by an aunt. When the Germans began to deport the village girls for labor in Germany, my aunt suggested I move to some other town and try my luck. That's what brought me to Białystok. I had found a job and was living with an acquaintance that had relatives in my village, but his home was small and crowded and I wanted a room of my own. I hadn't given this autobiography any forethought; I made it up as I spoke, using the senses and sensations that had become keener and more focused as my stay on the Aryan side continued. The nonexistent family cell in my village of origin explained why I did not visit them occasionally or for festivals.

The last entrance of the building, where Missja and Tosiek lived, was a narrow and dark aperture. The entrance to their apartment was at the end on the left; on the right side a stairway led to the upper story, where Missja's mother lived. In their apartment, there was a long hallway with conveniences, the kitchen on the left and their bedroom and living room in the back. My room would be the living room. A wall of boards separated it from their room, which they shared with Waldek.

My room had a wooden sofa and a large fireplace along the shared wall, made of bricks and coated with porcelain tiles. Past the fireplace were a dining table, chairs and a narrow closet for clothes. Large windows faced the courtyard.

It was a good apartment with an easy going landlord. It did not have a separate entrance, an important asset for an underground dwelling. Later on, Lisa and Bronja had separate entrances and, to some extent, so did Anja Rod. However, my place was centrally located and its lack of a separate entrance was offset by Tosiek, who was hardly ever at home, and Missja, who was busy with her own affairs.

Missja's affairs were her lovers, a different lover each time. She took no real interest in me, considering me a simple village girl. Every evening when I came home from work and went into the kitchen to fix a glass of tea, she joined me and invited me to sit with her. I accepted the invitation and listened to all of her nonsense. By having the wisdom to listen, I earned her trust. Her lover at the time was my salvation. Not only was she so busy with him that she took no interest in anything else, she also regarded me as an ally and confidant who would not betray her. She needed my help. She arranged her assignations on the basis of Tosiek's shifts. When something went wrong — a change of shift or him returning early from work — I sometimes served as Missja's liaison, riding a bicycle to her rendezvous to tell the waiting man that she couldn't come.

I also used Missja for my purposes. She gave me more than the freedom of a non-inquisitive landlady; when I needed to meet with members of the Polish or Belarusian resistance in locations far from downtown, she gladly lent me her bicycle without really knowing what for. I received her trust and love — I, Halinka Stasiuk, a peasant girl from the village of Koszewo, not far from Druskienniki.

Tosiek liked me for a different reason. I went out alone, at hours when girls no longer circulated in town. I had neither suitors nor male visitors. And I was serious, calm and quiet. These characteristics piqued his suspicions, and as time went by, he became increasingly sure of his intuition.

One of our activities on the Aryan side involved helping Jews in hiding. I tell the following story ahead of its chronological order in order to give an indication of Tosiek and his attitude toward me. A certain Jewish couple was hiding together: a woman under a false Polish identity and forged papers, and her husband, concealed in the flat where she was living. I do not recall how she reached us; these are the sorts of things best forgotten. She asked us to help her husband reach the partisans in the forest because they feared he had been flushed out. The neighbors suspected that there was a hideout in the apartment, she said. Her husband had acquired a handgun and a small bag of bullets as they were leaving the ghetto. That was an advantage: it was easier to join the partisans with weapons and ammunition than without.

We waited for days on end. Liaisons with the partisans were arranged in meetings set up a week or more in advance. One couldn't and was forbidden to walk into the forest without prior consent. We waited for the day of our rendezvous with Marylka Różycka, a liaison and partisan who lived in a forest camp. We asked her to escort the man to the partisans and arranged a meeting. The husband and I reached the meeting place at the appointed time. His wife did not come along; I promised to tell her once we got word from the partisans.

We were at the edge of town, where the path to the forest branched away near the last house. Marylka stepped out of the bushes along the path and together they began to march. I returned to town and made it home before curfew.

Several days later, I found out that the man had been killed. He and his escort fell into an ambush. Marylka managed to get away and reach the forest camp. The man, instead of fleeing with her, opened fire on them with his handgun. They returned fire and struck him. One of the partisans, emerging from the forest the next morning on his way to town, saw his body near the path.

I spent an hour wandering around on Lipowa Street, waiting for the woman to arrive. It was dusk; people had begun to come home from work. I tried to stitch words into one well-crafted sentence that would explain what had happened. How should I tell this woman, who had managed to conceal her beloved husband for two years, that he had been murdered on the way to the forest, en route to what seemed to be the safest hideout possible? There she was, looking me in the face as she approached me from Sienkiewicz Street. And I had not yet found the right words.

He was murdered on the way to the forest, I said, embracing her. We burst into tears together. Her despair was terrible to behold. We couldn't just stand there; we might attract attention. Equally, however, I could not escort her to her apartment without arousing suspicion. We walked up the street toward Świętego Rocha. "Why had I not gone with him?" she cried into her coat. "Why did I stay behind? I might have saved him...."

I shed soundless tears. I could not help her. Curfew was approaching. I hugged her tight, pressed her to me, smoothed her disheveled hair, and wiped away her tears. With that, we parted. I headed home, oblivious to the tears that again flooded my eyes. I turned onto the alley at the entrance to the courtyard, allowing them to drip. The courtyard was empty: everyone was indoors. As I stepped into the flat, Missja leaped at me. "Halinka, what happened to you? Why are you crying?" Tosiek sat at the table, staring at me, saying nothing.

I regained my composure in a split second. Through my tears, I explained, "I saw the trucks with the hostages, they just took them from the prison and they're shooting them outside Białystok in revenge for the murder of a German yesterday. You could hear them screaming up and down the whole street. They're taking our people to execution again...."

Our people: Polish people. The previous day, a German soldier had in fact been murdered in the street. The ghetto had been liquidated by then. The Germans turned against the Poles for vengeance. Missja hugged me and poured me a glass of tea. Tosiek remained at the table, not making a sound. His face had gone cold. He stared at me as I drank the tea and dried my tears. Something about his gaze had changed, I sensed, but I could not put my finger on it. It wasn't frightening; it was just very unfamiliar. When Missja went away to put Waldek to sleep, Tosiek said, "Pani Halinka, I know I'm right even if you don't say a thing. Now I'm sure. You're one of us: the Polish resistance. I've suspected it for a long time, but you never said a word, never disclosed a thing...."

While Missja was gone, he told me about his resistance cell. He was a member of the A.K., the Armia Krajowa, the ultra-nationalist, Fascist Polish underground. There was no doubt about the immense appreciation and absolute trust he placed in me from that evening on.

"Pani Halinka," he said about a week later. "You are extraordinary. You know how to hold your tongue, to leak nothing about your underground. I, in contrast, never stop telling you about ours."

"That's for sure," I said. "You tell me things because you know I won't pass them on...."

Tosiek considered his wife an insipid chatterbox who did not deserve his trust in matters that were really important. He knew she was cheating on him. It wasn't the first time. He loved her and was usually a good and mild-mannered husband. When he became fed up with her cheating, however, he got drunk and became violent. Very violent. Sometimes it ended with the shattering of dishes in the kitchen; sometimes it went much further.

One evening I heard screaming in the kitchen. Tosiek had found Missja reading a book: a stupid novel. A moment later, she shouted, "Halinka! Halinka!"

I rushed to the kitchen and asked, "What happened?"

"Pani Halinka," Tosiek said, "Look what trash she's reading. She was messed up to begin with; now she'll be even worse."

I picked up the book, thumbed through it, and said, "You can read this book, too. It's the story of the life of a couple. You can read it; it's no big deal."

They put Waldek to sleep in various ways. Usually Missja sang songs to him, but whenever he wasn't working the night shift, Tosiek put him to sleep and told him a story. Only a thin wooden board separated their bedroom from mine. I could hear every word clearly, even when they spoke quietly. The nighttime stories Tosiek told little three-year-old Waldek were about concealed Jews whom the Polish underground had flushed out. He told Waldek how the resistance fighters poked out their eyes and beat them up all the way to the ghetto. After the ghetto was wiped out, he related, he had captured a fleeing Jew and turned him over to the Germans with his own hands. I lay in my bed trembling, hardly breathing, as I listened to these tales of terror.

Truth to tell, I knew he was antisemitic. My first evening in their home, as we sat at the kitchen table, he told me about a dog that they had owned before the war: the animal had been trained to bark only at Jews. After the ghetto was wiped out and the Germans allowed people to enter the quarantined zone, Tosiek went in several times and came out with lots of clothes for Missja and Waldek.

After the night he discovered he was right about my membership in a resistance organization, the partisans visited us fearlessly. Weapons and ammunition that had to be moved to the forest were stored in the cupboard of my unlocked room.

Once, however, Tosiek made a remark about Marylka: "Who's your dirty girlfriend?"

Marylka really was very dirty. She came in from the forest after going weeks without a bath, her shoes caked with mud and her hair unkempt. She'd walked all the way from our village, I said, fleeing from the threat of deportation to Germany for labor. Thus we slipped out of that snare.

After the Soviets occupied Lithuania, the *Rikuz*, the umbrella group of Zionist pioneering organizations in Vilna, was dismantled. Some of its members emigrated to *Eretz Israel*, a number remained in the Soviet Union, and others returned to occupied Poland in order to lead the youngsters and the Jews at large. Most were killed in the uprisings they directed in the various ghettos.

Gedalyahu Szajek, Jandrze Labiedž, Riwkele Medajska, Sarah Dobeltow, Chaika Grossman, Zorach Zilberberg and Edek Boraks — head of the Hashomer Hatzair resistance in the Białystok ghetto — all came from the *Rikuz*. Only Chaika remained alive at the end of the war.

In the Białystok ghetto the pioneering movements formed a joint leadership, but there were two separate underground blocs in terms of ideologies. In Bloc A, Hashomer Hatzair merged with the Communists; in Bloc B, Dror, Hashomer Hatzair, Hanoar Hazioni, the Revisionists and part of the Bund came together. Each movement was represented in the united leadership.

Each movement organized its own underground activities, combat groups, five-person cells, smaller units and the transfer of girls to the Aryan side. Eventually the two blocs decided to merge; at this point the movement leaders formed themselves into an *Aktiv*, an executive body headed by Edek Boraks of Hashomer Hatzair, Kawe and Moskowicz of the Communists, and Mordechai Tenenbaum of Dror, who had also returned from the Vilna *Rikuz*. Edek was the commander until captured and sent to his death in the February 1943 *Aktion*. Tenenbaum commanded the Białystok ghetto uprising in August of that year.

The exit of girls to the Aryan side began when the resistance leadership realized that unless we established a network of connections there, we would not only remain isolated from the other ghettos, we would also be unable to acquire weapons, ammunition and medicines, or arrange refuge for those who survived the uprising. Within a few weeks, the girls were on the Aryan side. For the next seven months — January-August 1943 — we were the resistance's liaison with the outside world. We acted in whatever way the resistance needed — by providing medicines, weapons, ammunition or documents, or by communicating with other ghettos. At first, the needs of each movement dictated the actions; later on, the cause served was that of the united fighting organization.

More than seventeen girls went to the Aryan side. Few were sent on active missions. Some spent very short periods of time there. Some returned to the ghetto or were captured and murdered. We don't know whether any of them was captured while crossing between ghettos. At the end of the war, only five of us were still alive:

Bronja Winicka of Grodno — the first to go to the Aryan side, a schoolmate of mine during the Russian occupation, a member of Dror. She worked for two German railroad executives who had left their families behind and she moved into a flat at 66 Warszawska Street, owned by a young Polish woman who was the concubine of a Gestapo man. Afterwards she moved to 43 Mazowiecka Street, where the landlord had a place with a separate entrance. Once she was there, I could knock on her door quietly when I came back from the forest without being afraid of arousing suspicion.

Chaika Grossman of Białystok, a leader of Hashomer Hatzair who was appointed liaison among the ghettos of Vilna, Warsaw and Białystok. She crossed between the ghetto and the Aryan side, and circulated in the cities among members of our movement and all the others. A member of the resistance *Aktiv*, she changed apartments repeatedly to keep the resistance work secure. Her dwellings served as liaison stations for letters, cables and meetings, as well as an overnight shelter for comrades. After the ghetto was liquidated and very few of us were left, she moved in with me — but I do not wish to put the cart before the horse.

I left the ghetto about a month after Bronja did, and was followed by Lisa Czapnik, an old schoolmate of mine. The Czapniks of Grodno — one boy and three sisters. Lisa and Grisha were veteran Communists from before the war. Sarah belonged to Hashomer Hatzair and their sister Bertha was married to Goldberg, my wonderful art teacher. They had one daughter, Alinka. Before the war, Grisha had married Anja Rod. In late 1942, all of them had moved from the Grodno ghetto to the Białystok ghetto on forged papers.

One day, after I'd been with the Luchterhands for a while, a German neighbor who lived in the apartment across the way dropped in. She needed a domestic; might I know someone who was looking for work? Nothing could have been better: working for Germans, as far from the Poles as possible. I don't know, I said, but I'll ask around. Back in the ghetto, they chose Lisa to be the next one to leave. We approached the Luchterhands' neighbor, Marysia Morosowska. "I don't know her," I said. "She's an acquaintance of a friend of mine, looking for work." The German woman was delighted and grateful.

We tried to avoid any appearance of a relationship between us, to give no one the sense that we even knew each other. We were separate, apart, wholly unconnected. The circumstances required it.

Lisa's employer treated her well. She gave requests, not orders; she spoke instead of shouting. Occasionally she remarked that everyone knew how hard it was to work for the Luchterhands: "It isn't terrible," I replied, just in case my words would find their way to the Luchterhands' ears.

Lisa found an apartment in a rural suburb with wooden houses, stone-paved streets, vegetable gardens and fruit trees in the courtyards. The house, 12 Horoszczanska Street, was demarcated by fences shared with the neighboring buildings. Her room was entered from the street; the landlord's flat was entered from the courtyard, the garden and the fruit trees, through a gate that turned onto a side alley branching from the street. On the floor of the room was an opening that led to a cellar almost as large as the room itself.

Later on, after the ghetto, the uprising and the liquidation, the Germans kept a group of Jewish artisans alive, housing them and putting them to work at the Gestapo headquarters. Lisa and I managed to remove one of these workers, Szacman, from the Gestapo's clutches and hide him in the cellar of her dwelling. Later we moved him to the forest, where he joined the partisans and survived the war.

Anja was sent to the Aryan side on behalf of the Communists. Grisha remained in the ghetto. Anja's dark complexion and facial features were sure to betray her. She oxidized her hair with uncompromising care and found work at the Hotel Ritz, the Germans' hotel in Białystok. She was a simple kitchen worker, a vegetable peeler. This, the lowliest of tasks, inferior to all other kitchen jobs, was her salvation.

Anja found housing in a rural suburb that had dirt lanes instead of streets, small, old wooden houses, muddy alleyways, and courtyards with four

Sarka (Sarah) Shewachowicz, member of
the resistance, captured on the Aryan side
of Białystok and murdered

houses, each a room-and-a-half large. The houses all leaned against each other
and tilted sideways. She lived in the farthest room. Whenever we visited her,
we had to pass all the neighbors' windows. These neighbors sat idly all day
long, staring out of their windows to see if anything was happening or if anything had changed. They were gossipy, nosy types who wanted to know who
was visiting Anja.

And there was my Sarka, Sarka Shewachowicz, who had moved from
Grodno after the great *Aktion*, after her paralyzed grandfather was murdered
and her grandmother transported to death. She reached the Białystok ghetto
and was sent to the Aryan side. She was a village girl with curly golden hair
braided in two thick pigtails, blue eyes, and a round, wide face. On Parkowa

Street, where I worked, she found a perfect setup: a job as a domestic for an old German who gave her the servant's quarters.

We fashioned some boards in the loft over her room into a hiding place for sensitive notes, codes and documents. We visited each other often, but only when her landlord and mine were at work so they would not see us, recognize us, and make a connection. We were careful in the extreme. We conversed in the manner of chattering girls who were taking a short break from work, leaning against the picket fence of the house. Sometimes I stayed after work to organize resistance affairs and enjoy a bit of togetherness amid the ghastly loneliness of our lives. Such an encounter had to be arranged in advance. After work, we always met in the street. That was the great advantage of Parkowa Street. Only German officers and bureaucrats lived there; they couldn't tell a faux Pole from the real thing. We strolled down the street, pausing briefly at the garden by the edge of the hill at the end of the street and then retracing our steps. We discussed serious matters only when no one was around. As soon as we approached anyone, we posed as two nondescript Polish girls out for a walk, gabbing and laughing.

We established a norm: anyone who applied to a German office for any necessity had to report it to one of us so that we would know whether and when to start worrying. One day, Sarka went to the *Arbeitsamt*, the labor exchange, and didn't tell me. One morning I visited her place of work, knocked on the door, and received no answer. That was odd. I came back the next day before noon, a time of day when all the Germans were at work. I knocked on the door once: silence. I spun around and walked away. Never again did I approach her room, the building, or even the fence where we used to lean and chatter. My resourcefulness, my heightened senses, caution and alertness, as well as the assumption that somebody was always lurking for us and no one could be trusted — only these saved me.

It was the end of the month and we had to report to the *Arbeitsamt* to have our labor permits stamped. Polish people worked there. They could tell who was faking. The wrong facial expression, a telltale accent, or a question not answered fluently enough would betray you. That's how Sarka, a blonde with wavy hair, was caught. A German couldn't tell that she wasn't Polish. I don't know whether it was the clerks' Polish eyes that singled her out as a Jew and prompted them to hand her over to the Germans, or whether they detected the bogus documents from Druskienniki and Skidel, near Grodno. Too many fake documents had been issued under the stamps from the lab I had smuggled to Białystok and were being flashed by people who left the Białystok ghetto. Gestapo men then interrogated the German for whom Sarka was working, the one who had given her housing. We were spared from certain capture only because he knew none of the girls who worked or lived on Parkowa Street.

Sarka must have been interrogated and tortured. It could not have been otherwise. They could not have refrained from abusing her in an attempt to extract information: Who gave you this document? Who else has papers like these?

From where the immense power that kept her lips sealed? Where in her psyche did she erect her impermeable wall of silence? What embedded in us the notion of total friendship no matter what? The more the years pass, the more certain I am that our years of education in the movement did it. It wasn't only Hashomer Hatzair. Members of Dror, Hanoar Hazioni, the Communists, the Revisionists and the Bund also withstood those places with supreme heroism. In those battles, one didn't counter an armed weapon with a weapon of one's own. It was something much more difficult: the thing you fought was not your captor and oppressor but the horrific pain you experienced. You fought yourself, your life. But none of them faltered, none of them spoke, none of them finked.

The Poles also captured Chanka Lewin at the *Arbeitsamt* when she came to get her labor permit stamped. She was a member of Hashomer Hatzair, daughter of Shayne Patt-Lewin, director of the large ghetto orphanage, and our liaison with the Soviet Communist underground. She had also come on papers from Druskienniki. Right away they handed her to the Germans for arrest and interrogation.

Sarah Dubeltow of Vilna, a member of Hashomer Hatzair and one of those who returned from the Vilna *Rikuz* to the Białystok ghetto and then went to the Aryan side. Blue eyes, blonde hair, fluent Polish, a real *shiksa*. An astonishingly kind person with courage to match, she concealed two young men in the flat she had rented: Chaim Wolberg of Grodno, a member of Dror who had been sent to Białystok; and Chackel Zablodovski, husband of Miriam Grossman, who had fled from the transport in the great *Aktion* of February 1943. Sarah, like all of us, worked for Germans and lived with Poles. Each morning she went to work at the officers' mess next to the railroad station and left her fugitive tenants at home, locking her place from the outside.

Something about her attracted the Polish neighbors' attention and suspi-cion. Maybe she said something in a normal tone of voice instead of a whisper, maybe there were too many footsteps in her apartment, or maybe someone heard voices and sounds that should not have been heard in an empty house during the day. Whatever it was, somebody said something to someone and a Polish woman, a collaborator with the Germans who did not live in that building, visited the Polish landlord in the company of a German officer and asked to rent an apartment. The landlord said that the flat had been let, but the woman insisted and the German broke down the door. The two young men were standing in the doorway. By the time the police came, they had fled down the stairs and into the street. Poles in the street captured Chaim and handed him over to the Germans; Chackel managed to escape and return to the ghetto. No one was left to warn the rest of us not to visit that address again. Today I wonder how Sarah had failed to notice ominous indicators: neighbors peeping through the curtain, cracks in the door for a fraction of a second, no one greeting her with a nod of the head. The darkness that descended on the city.

Maybe it was due to her immense fatigue after a long day's work. May-be it was the trek to her apartment. Then, the ghastly silence when she opens the door. Even before she can figure out what it means, flashlights pounce on her and the frenzied skirmish ends with her capture. The handbag slips out of her hand, she absorbs a torrent of brutal blows, her body falls to the floor, and cold handcuffs are applied to her wrists. Several days later, we found out that she, too, had been taken to prison.

Chancia Jerzierski: *di gele,* the redhead, a member of the Bitsaron Gdud, a comrade of my sister Rocheleh. She was sent from Grodno alone and reached Białystok armed with Chaika's address at 17 Wesola Street. A girl with bangs of fire — a color that only Jews had. Chaika shared an apartment with Chanka Lewin in a separate entrance from the landlord, off the same cor-ridor, their door facing his.

It was afternoon. Chaika was expected any moment and Chancia came by and knocked on the door. The landlord, hearing the pounding, stepped into the hallway and asked who she was looking for. "My cousin from the village," she answered. The landlord considerately invited her to his apartment to wait: "The tenant is at work now," he said. "It's not a good idea to loiter. Have a seat with us."

Chaika came by shortly before dusk, but she was not alone: she was accompanied by two German policemen. She tried to find out where Chanka Lewin had disappeared and thought that Sarah Dubeltow might know something. At the door to Sarah's empty, locked apartment, the neighbor grabbed her and handed her over to the police. In an attempt to convince them that she was not a fugitive Jew but rather a simple Polish girl, she led them to her apartment. The Germans found her act convincing and were about to leave. Just then, the Polish landlord went over and said that the girl's cousin from the village had been waiting with him since the afternoon. The moment she saw Chaika entering with the Germans, Chancia said, "That's not her at all, that's not my cousin, she's not the one I'm looking for, I must have got the address wrong." Chaika stared at her; she ignored her. The policeman asked for her papers and Chancia complied. Druskienniki, he said. A Jew!

"*Ich bin ein Jüdin*," I'm a proud Jewess, Chancia replied, spitting in his face with all her might. He smacked her across the face so hard that she fell to the floor. She stood up slowly, supporting herself with a stool and then a corner of the table, between the Polish husband and wife who were standing at the window. The German policeman wiped the spittle off his face and Chaika's eyes, which had observed the whole incident, didn't betray a thing. Chaika maintained the pace of her breathing so that no one would notice sense the horrific pain, anguish and fury welling up in her.

"Shall we go?" Chancia asked the Germans. Chaika and the Polish neighbor were led away together with her for interrogation. On the way to police headquarters, Chaika managed to persuade one of the Germans that she really was Polish. Thus she was spared.

Seventeen comrades, men and women, fell into the Germans' hands, some due to Druskienniki papers and others because they had been sent from Grodno to the apartment at 17 Wesola Street without knowing it had been burned. Everyone who approached this flat was captured, arrested, interrogated and tortured. To this day I do not know all their names.

Each day after work, we walked to the prison and paced back and forth on the sidewalk across the street, hoping to glimpse one of our comrades looking out the window, hoping they could see us and derive strength from knowing we were there. But the windows remained closed and the panes gleamed like golden mirrors as they reflected the rays of the winter sunset. In only one window, on the fourth floor, the figure of a girl stationed herself each day. We could not wave to her; we could give no indication that we could see her. We could only tilt our heads in her direction, sure that she was one of ours.

Constantly we attempted to extricate our people from the prison, assisted by members of the *Judenrat* and other Jews with connections. Our people refused to buy their freedom by confessing to their actions or divulging details about the resistance. At the end of the winter of 1943, they were taken to the giant pit near Nowosiolki, about ten kilometers out of town. They were shot at the edge of the pit and buried in the mass grave.

Fanka Lipkes of Grodno, a member of our Gdud, went to the Aryan side together with Sarka Shewachowicz. Despite her Jewish face, dark hair and abundant freckles, we thought she could survive on the Aryan side due to the Polish accent she had acquired in school. However, after Sarka Shewachowicz and Sarah Dubeltow, Chanka Lewin and Chancia Jerzierski were captured, she succumbed to the pressure and returned to the ghetto.

Life on the Aryan side was a war you fought every moment for your false identity and the ability to deny, pose and be what you were not. The vigilance you had to maintain in every way and form caused unendurable stress and distress, especially when you had to do it for so long. You had to cross a psychological barrier, a point beyond which your own life had no meaning except as an instrument of war: war against the Germans for the vestiges of your people, for the dignity of their lives and death. Girls from Białystok could not operate on the Aryan side of their own town; the danger of being exposed by Poles who knew them outweighed the advantage of knowing the turf. For us, the girls of Grodno, this risk was almost nonexistent. Almost.

I now get ahead of myself and describe their aftermath and demise before it occurred. I do this in order to keep Riwkele and Jandrze together, to keep them with us for another moment, and not to lose them in the mass of words that accumulates as I recount the lives we lived and the things we did.

Riwkele Medajska and Jandrze Labiedž: a matched pair, friends and lovers. She: small and slender like a little girl, with blonde hair and huge blue eyes; he: tall, clever, very talented, a painter and stage director before the war. Both chose to return from the Vilna *Rikuz* to take part in the movement leadership and resistance in Białystok.

Riwkele was sent to the Aryan side because she looked Polish. Jandrze stayed behind in the ghetto, the place to which we were pledged in body and soul, totally loyal to the cause, the faith and the path. Nothing surpassed these. Love and friendship did not count in the reckoning of the combat resistance.

Jandrze was taken away with Edek and other comrades in the first *Aktion* in February 1943. He leaped out of the train to Treblinka and suffered a smashed hand from a dumdum bullet that railroad guards fired at him. He made his way to a kind and brave peasant who bandaged his wounds, fed him, gave him a place to sleep in the loft of his barn where the livestock feed was stored, and passed on a letter to Riwkele, who by then was living on the Aryan side with one Kopulowa, a childless old woman who loved her like a daughter. Riwkele raced to Chaika and showed her the letter. "We've got to bring him to town."

"Hold on," Chaika cautioned. "We can't put him up in any of the apartments. *Er zet oys vi tsen yidn.* He looks like ten Jews."

Several weeks later, Jandrze entered the ghetto at his own initiative. In August 1943, during the great liquidation *Aktion*, he fought and was killed in the uprising. Riwkele found cleaning work with a German doctor, a Gestapo officer, an expert on racial theory. She lived in Savta's flat until she died. One day I visited her in the middle of work to pass on some information. The doctor was at home and there I was with my bandaged hands due to that terrible eczema. When he asked why my hands were bandaged, I told him I had been working for Herr Luchterhand of the SS Werkzentrale.

"For that cur?" he asked in astonishment.

"Yes. Every day I do their laundry with caustic materials that hurt my hands. I'd like to stop working there but they're not letting me go and I can't leave without their permission."

"I'll give you a sick note for two weeks," he said. "That's all I'm allowed to give at a time. When the two weeks are up, come back and I'll give you another two weeks. We'll do that until he gets rid of you for lack of choice."

He unwrapped my bandages, examined my hands, and rebandaged them. "I'm not a dermatologist," he said. "I'm an expert on racial theory. I can tell a person's race by his eyes. That's really my expertise. That's how I identify Jews."

In a spurt of insane bravery, I asked, "So... what about my eyes?"

He led me to the window, pulled the curtain aside, stared, stroked my cheek and said, "No! Not even close!" and burst out laughing. Riwkele and I joined him in his merriment, sneaking a glance at each other and thinking,

204 CHASIA BORNSTEIN-BIELICKA — ONE OF THE FEW

"One of us is working for him, the other came to visit, and this guy, an expert in racial theory, can't tell…."

My second visit to the interior of a church was for Marysia Medajeska's requiem. Our Riwkele. After the ghetto was liquidated, after Jandrze's death, one evening on the way home from work, in the vacant lot full of debris where the Great Synagogue had stood, Riwkele noticed an elusive figure. She approached him and said, "I'm working with the partisans. If you wish, I'll send you to them." The young man wanted this desperately; he had escaped from the last transport and was ready to go then and there.

"It can't be done that way," Riwkele explained. Meetings like this had to be set up. What's more, he could not go far in his torn shoes. She decided to take the shoes for repair until the meeting with the partisans could be arranged.

So this slight young girl visited the shoemaker with a pair of large, worn-out shoes, plastered with mud. When she came to pick them up after the repair, the shoemaker sent his son to tail her. When he saw where she went and to whom she handed the shoes, the boy called a passing German patrol. The prospective partisan fled and Riwkele raced in the opposite direction. Two soldiers grabbed her and stabbed her in the back. She slipped out of their grip, ran another few meters, and collapsed. They took her to the hospital and began to investigate right away.

Her facial features and fluent Polish fooled her interrogators. "The soldiers scared me so I ran away," she said. She insisted that she knew nothing. She sent them to Savta as a character witness. The old woman came to the hospital and burst into tears. How terribly you're suffering, my little girl. What have they done to you? "It's nothing, Savta," Riwkele replied. "*Jezu Crystu* also suffered before he died, maybe even more than me."

The old woman sat at her bedside for a week as the German interrogators tried to pry information from their victim. The only words Riwkele said were very Christian: Catholic, in fact. There was no way of proving that she wasn't one.

Świętego Rocha, the church that dominated the city. A huge, towering building. Over the steeple, a metal tower and at its extreme a likeness of St. Rocha, his head in the heavens. Lisa, Bronja and I were the only ones among the girls of Savta's acquaintance who were allowed to visit Riwkele. We and Savta's Polish neighbors, that is. We were surprised to see how many neighbors came. They saw the old woman walking to the hospital every day to sit at her bedside. They heard the story of what went on that week and the things the girl said. They were sure she was a Polish girl whom the Germans had murdered.

We sat down in the last row, behind everyone, in order to watch, learn and imitate the congregants' behavior. We genuflected, stood up and sat down, circled the tabernacle, bowed our heads, and opened our mouths wide so that the host could be placed on our tongues. We could not but bid her farewell. Even if we risked exposure by doing so.

Riwkele was buried in the plot of the Polish cemetery reserved for those whose requiems took place at Świętego Rocha's Church. A sublimely brave German Jewish girl laid to rest under a wooden cross and wreaths of daisies.

Fifty-seven years later, I revisited the cemetery where Riwkele, our hero, was buried, in order to place a wreath on her grave. With me were my husband Heini and my three daughters. We searched for her grave at length but failed to find it. We asked the priest in charge of the cemetery for directions and told him the story. He was very moved but explained that if nobody visits a particular grave or takes an interest in the deceased for twenty years, the grave is opened, the remains disinterred, and someone else is buried in his or her place.

Some of the girls with us did not take part in underground activity. They lived on the Aryan side, but could not be active because their looks or dialect were Jewish. One of them was Miriam Grossman, Chaika's sister, who had a telltale Jewish face and dark hair. The Luchterhands' upstairs neighbor came down one day and asked me if I could find a young girl to help them out. She had two young children and needed a live-in domestic. Here was a definite possibility of surviving on the Aryan side: of staying alive.

I conducted some of my encounters with the ghetto and with members of the resistance by visiting, but others took place only by talking through the wall of the latrine in Olla's courtyard. For my next meeting, Chaika waited on the other side of the wall. I'd found a place for someone to work and live, I told her. I gave her the address and told her to send one of the girls there. The girl to be sent should give just any old name as the person who had sent her or should come as a job seeker. Don't mention me. Don't contact me in any way.

The next day, Miriam visited the upstairs neighbor. It was a perfect situation from her standpoint. She had no reason to leave the apartment. The landlady treated her well and the work kept her busy most of the day. Because she was taking care of a child, she was excused from having to work in the officers' mess. That way, she avoided the danger of encountering the Polish women who worked there. And she gave us a special form of assistance: she created our most important crossing into and out of the ghetto at the home of her good friend, Olla.

Mina Kiselstein and her cousin, Mira Kaplan, also hid out on the Aryan side and were not involved in the resistance work — Mina with Schade and Mira with Beneshek. My Rocheleh, after spending several days with me, went into the ghetto to fight along with the comrades because she could not endure the stress of life on the other side. Others were Hanke Zelinska, who lived in the guise of the daughter of our "uncle," Bronisław Burdzinski, and Marylka Różycka, the partisan in the forest of Białystok who liaised between the partisans and the city — a Jewess, a Communist, incomparably courageous.

To protect ourselves if captured, we established an inviolable system of internal communications that determined who knew what about whom and who was allowed to meet with whom. I was not allowed to visit Sarah Dubeltow. Only Chaika, I think, was permitted to do that. Chaika lived with Chanka Lewin and may also have visited Fanka. Chaika did not visit me; we met only in the ghetto. I met with Lisa but I don't remember who else did.

Only Bronja and I were allowed to visit Maryśka (Riwkele) Medajska. Only Lisa and I were allowed to visit Anja. When the number of surviving women activists dwindled to five, only I knew the whereabouts of each of the others and could visit them all. I did not want this responsibility but somebody had to do the job. None of us wanted to know everything. If we were captured, we thought, the less we knew, the better. We feared the tortures that such a situation would bring upon us; we were unsure about how well we could maintain silence and endure the pain. We did not fear for ourselves, our lives. These had been given to us on loan, conditionally, each morning anew, each moment anew. The only reason we wished to live was in order to continue fighting the Germans. That we would die was certain, undoubted. Fear of impending death was not our motive for what we did. We feared for each other, our sisters, the words we could not control. Cyanide was the perfect solution for us.

Our comrades in the ghetto realized that we needed the poison to bolster our confidence that we would not betray or denounce anyone, that we would not cause others to perish. Our own death was expected. We chose it. But the resistance must not stop.

So they wrapped a bit of powder in a paper bag and sewed it into a pocket in our coat lining. It wasn't really sewn there; instead, it was attached so that by pulling on one thread you'd open the pocket and have the bag in your hand. I don't remember whether it was by order of the resistance or due to a recommendation that we passed among each other, but we were not to swallow the toxin the moment we were captured. Only when they were leading us to the prison, the interrogation rooms and the torture dungeons were we to do it.

Several times in my life I was rewarded for not rushing to use the poison. Today I cannot say for sure why I was so privileged at those moments. It may have been my absolute confidence that I could escape the path of death by dint of ten ruptured stitches, or it may have been a conscious decision: as long as there's a chance of returning to the resistance work, there's no reason to hurry up and die.

Hashomer Hatzair had its headquarters on Bielostoczanska Street; the movement commune in the Białystok ghetto was at Częstochowska 15. All members other than those of the leadership lived in a spacious apartment there. This is where I came when I entered the ghetto. Later, too, after Mother and Zipporka reached the Białystok ghetto, I slept at the commune, sharing a bed with my sister Rocheleh. This was my real place of refuge. Here I shed all the masquerades, defenses and Polish affectations. It was a wondrous paradise where I could be myself. I spoke Yiddish, met comrades and shared conversations, general discussions, vacillations and decisions of the *Aktiv*. I was privy to the secrets of weapons and the cache, the manufacture of grenades and firebombs. But in the main, the commune enveloped me in warmth, love and camaraderie.

I felt truly free there. I slept there in absolute serenity, replenishing my strength for what was to come. I arrived on Saturday night after work and stayed until Sunday night or Monday at dawn. This happened mainly during the first period; when only Bronja and I were on the Aryan side we hardly ever met. She worked and lived far from me; I finished work late at night. I was dreadfully lonely. Sometimes I visited the ghetto on urgent business during the week, too. I delivered letters that had arrived from Vilna or Warsaw to the post box I had rented in my false name at the post office on Lipowa Street, or special medicines that one could obtain at certain addresses, as well as people from other resistance groups through whom we could obtain specific information.

There were several ways of entering and exiting the ghetto. One was through the gate; you could join a group of workers coming in or going out. The main ghetto gate was at the end of Jurowiecka Street, on the corner of Sienkiewicz Street. Each time you went in or out, you had to cross Sienkiewicz, a large main street bustling with people. If you timed it right, you could do it exactly when the workers did. Going out with the workers was relatively easy: you joined a group and after you left the ghetto you tore off the Star of David and melted into the nearest alley in the gloom of dawn. Coming in with a group, however, required skills of evasiveness and sleight of hand. You had to worm your way in to the mass of people and press the Star of David to your coat while you walked, within a range of twenty steps. Some of the groups were men only; others were too small to blend into without risking capture by the guards. On Sienkiewicz Street, there were two entrances: one at the corner of a large courtyard and the other closer to Lipowa Street, at the edge of a vacant lot. At both points, you could pass through a towering fence at an opening we had created by dislodging a slat at an angle. It was through this vacant lot that I moved Rocheleh into the ghetto. Another gate was at the edge of Poleska Street, near the railroad station. I used this passage to enter the ghetto with Cyla. Later, we found a much better place: on Bielostoczanska Street, all of which was in the ghetto except for one large courtyard at its terminus, on the other side of the ghetto fence. The courtyard opened onto Poleska Street. Across the street, on the Aryan side, there were no houses. Instead, an earthen embankment carried a railroad track toward the municipal train station. The courtyard had several houses and some shared features: woodsheds, latrines, a well, small vegetable gardens and fruit trees. During the war, Olla and her family had moved into one of the vacated houses.

Olla was Miriam Grossman's friend. She and Miriam had worked together at the telegraph office during the Soviet occupation. Olla's parents were elderly; her father worked for the railroad and her mother kept house. She lived with her parents, her husband Wladek, who worked as a driver at the telegraph office, and their young daughter. Chaika introduced me to them. They knew who we were, where we were going, and where we were coming from. They knew or assumed what our parcels contained, and the meaning of the nocturnal visits to and lengthy stays at the latrine in the courtyard. Obviously they, and we, knew the price they would pay if their collaboration with us were discovered but they didn't say a word. They never let us know that they knew. They hardly ever asked questions. We tried not to overuse this crossing; it was too important to lose.

The ghetto wall was mostly a rampart of boards crowned with concertina wire. In Olla's courtyard, part of the fence was the wall of the latrine. The latrine was a tall, narrow structure with a metal hook to hold the door shut and a low wooden platform with a round hole in the middle, over a pit dug deep into the ground. There was no seat. We pried the nails from one board in the wall and replaced them loosely. The resulting opening was used not for people but for parcels, letters, medicines or, at times of necessity, urgent words.

The courtyard was also advantageous because of the sheds that held firewood for the winter. The sheds were almost three meters high; their sloping roofs faced the ghetto wall at the top and the courtyard at the bottom. It was easy to climb from Olla's side: you hoisted yourself by the handle of the storeroom door, grasped the edge of the roof, and pulled your whole body up. The problem was jumping into the ghetto or climbing from the outer side. You had to do these without the help of friends. They waited on that side and we descended into their outstretched hands as we arrived, or they helped us climb and push us over the fence until they saw us lying on the upper edge of the roof as we left. All entries, exits, movements of contraband and contacts posed mortal danger for all of us from two sides: the Germans on guard and the Polish tattletales.

I reached Olla's house a moment before curfew. Sometimes I couldn't enter the courtyard. The gentile neighbors who sat outside with all-seeing eyes were not the only obstacles; the inhabitants of the courtyard and of the ghetto used the courtyard as a marketplace in smuggled goods, mainly food. If I arrived and found the courtyard full of people, I kept walking down the street to the end and turned slowly to retrace my steps, praying that everyone had gone. Then I went in, sat down in Olla's kitchen, and waited for the courtyard to become quiet.

Olla's kitchen had a long wooden table bracketed with heavy benches, a stove of bricks and iron, and black pots. Olla's mother was a motherly type, always at home — a good, pleasant and talkative woman, dressed in a billowing apron tied from the front, and not inquisitive. Whenever I came, she went out of her way to feed me: a bowl of soup, a slice of bread, a home-baked cookie, a glass of tea. Human warmth that you could feel at once. Warmth we so sorely lacked.

Olla's father was more worried. In fact, he was palpably afraid of, anxious about and angry at the Germans. I have no score to settle with him. Their courage was amazing.

One day at dusk, Chaika and I arrived with a heavy leather case full of machine gun bullets. Our mission was to push it through the opening at the latrine. We had carried the case all the way through town: two girls and a case. Chaika had delivered it in the afternoon after receiving it from Jan, the very same peasant who had sold Eli Tankus the first handgun in Grodno. He had become our main supplier of weapons and also saved many fugitive Jews by hiding them in his home, granary and farm buildings. The case was heavy; the streets swarmed with German soldiers and Polish collaborators on the lookout for disguised Jews. And there we were with the case, clowning around and amusing ourselves alongside the German soldiers — deliberately, so as to avert suspicion. On our way up the street to Olla's house, two gendarmes passed us by. We were afraid to go into the courtyard because it might have called attention to this house. We continued toward the railroad tracks, stashed the case near a large bush, began to cavort as if playing on a lawn, and used our peripheral vision to monitor the gendarmes' movements. As soon as they vanished down the street, we picked up the case and rushed into the courtyard. We set down the case in a corner of the kitchen and walked into the living room with Olla and her mother. Then Olla's father came home. I don't know if he inspected the contents of the case or only noticed it in the corner. He entered the living room and asked, "What's in that package?" Olla jumped: "Daddy, it's OK. Don't worry." But he insisted: "What's in it?" We said nothing. Our trust in Olla was absolute. We trusted her so much. "Daddy," she said tenderly, "Don't ask. There are things you don't ask."

Our other partners were members of non-Jewish resistance organizations: Belarusian, Communist and Polish (the A.L., Armia Ludowa). They were important sources not only of information about Białystok and the vicinity, but also of fresh and reliable news from the front. They helped us access the black market for medicines, materials for the manufacture of grenades, weapons and ammunition, and they concealed the contraband until we could come by to deliver it to the ghetto. I do not know where the money came from.

In our division of labor, as with the burden of information, we compartmental-ized ourselves as best we could. I was the last link in a long chain; I did not want more knowledge than I had. The initial contact with the Communists was made via Chanka Lewin, who used an address in a remote village she obtained from her mother.

We trusted each other immensely. Their lives were also in danger. The only detail we bothered to know or report was where to meet. We didn't know their real names and did not divulge our own. We did not know their exact addresses and did not report ours. We didn't talk about our work; neither did they.

We had a kind of trust we could see in each other's eyes, hear in each other's speech, and test in each other's behavior. As we listened, we examined, pondered and cross-referenced the information we were receiving, analyzing it to determine whether it was possible, reasonable and correct. We developed our own special antennae and thought processes to sense what was true and what was not. Neither they nor we wished to exaggerate or prettify things. On the contrary: everything was bare bones, focused and to the point. Some of our partners were peasants who lived nearby; they knew the turf. This made things easier for us later, when the paths to the forest were "burned" and we had to find alternatives. Resistance matters aside, the main importance of the con-nection was the encounter it created between us and the people who wanted to help us: gentiles who collaborated with Jews. There were too few of them, but just the same they proved the existence of human goodness in a world that had brought its villainy to bear against us.

After Lisa set herself up in the apartment, she smuggled her niece, Alin-ka, daughter of Bertha and Goldberg, out of the ghetto. The girl was six or seven years old, and Lisa's purpose was to save her life. Lisa set out for work every morning and returned in the evening; Alinka stayed behind alone in the apartment. She turned out to be a quiet, smart, vigilant girl who kept herself to herself. Several weeks later, Lisa returned one evening and Alinka was gone. She's with the Gestapo, the neighbors said. Lisa raced across town, burst into my room, and announced, "We're getting her out now!"

The Gestapo headquarters was not far from Świętego Rocha: four blocks down Lipowa Street and left on Sienkiewicz. Lisa stormed in and pounced on everyone there. "You kidnapped my niece," she roared. "How dare you go into people's homes and snatch children?"

Alinka, seated on a wooden bench along the side, joined in when she realized who was making all the fuss. "They said I was a Jew. What do you want from me? They grabbed me and dragged me out all of a sudden. I'm not Jewish at all!"

Finally, in genuine rage, I added, "How dare you frighten a little girl that way? What kind of behavior is this?"

The Germans were stunned. I don't remember what they said and whether they apologized, but the two of us pulled Alinka to her feet and walked out with her in tow, returning to Lisa's apartment without looking back. The next day, Lisa brought Alinka back to the ghetto. The little girl had been so brave, staring down the Gestapo men and insisting all that day that she was not Jewish. Now she was afraid of being kidnapped again from the apartment where she had spent so many hours alone. "Next time they won't believe me," she reasoned with the wisdom of precocious maturity. She returned to her parents in the ghetto and went with them to her death in Treblinka.

It was the middle of March 1943. Winter: still snowstorms, temperatures still below freezing. I entered the ghetto on Saturday night and reached the Hashomer Hatzair commune tired and chilled. Rocheleh leaped at me. "Chaska, come. Mother and Zipporka are here, with Aunt Pesia." We set off at once to 25 Częstochowska, five houses down the street.

We had not seen each other for two months. We almost ran the whole distance, including the stairs and the entrance. I searched for Mother but did not see her. I was looking for someone who could pass for an older sister. Only amid her suffocating embrace and ceaseless tears did I identify my mother in the elderly, white-haired figure I found. We stood there, clutching each other and sobbing. Then we sat down and continued to cry. Zipporka, whom I gathered into our embrace, also said nothing; she merely held me with all her strength. Mother continued to cry and repeat my name, over and over. Then, as her weeping ebbed, words began to break through: "Father was taken away. He never stopped mourning for you."

That sentence stopped my breath. It drove spines of agony into me, leaving me with the stinging physical sense of having been stabbed in the heart. Father had not said goodbye to me. Father, who loved me so and had not even known I had gone that dawn to life and not to death, had performed Jewish bereavement customs for me until he was taken away and sent to his death. That night, Mother's hair had gone white in one stroke.

Mother told me about Bella's death, Avramele's rescue and Father's deportation. Rocheleh had left by then. They had not stood in her way. When only Mother and Zipporka remained and the last *Aktion*, the liquidation of the ghetto of Grodno, began, they survived by hiding in a cellar with other Jews. After the *Aktion* was over, the Germans discovered the survivors and shipped them to the Białystok ghetto. Thus, we had the privilege of being together for almost another half-year. Mother and Zipporka had moved in with my Aunt Pesia Pruczanski, Mother's older sister. Pesia's husband, Koppel, had been deported in one of the first *Aktionen*, leaving behind his wife and their three children, Yossi, Alter and Leahle, plus Leahle's two children, a son of toddler age and a baby daughter. The Pruczanskis had made hosiery before the war. They had had a large apartment, where noisy machines moved endlessly and spun huge rolls of thread that lay atop them but never stood still for a moment. At the edge of each machine, a stocking was steadily woven in an elongated round form. The place was full of hosiery of various lengths. When Mother and Zipporka came, the Pruczanskis received them as if they took it for granted, at a time when nothing was.

From the moment Mother and Zipporka reached the ghetto, they were my first stop on each of my visits. Afterwards, I visited the movement leadership to put things in order and only at the end did I go to the commune to share Rocheleh's bed for the night. Each time I visited the ghetto, I tried to bring them something. After paying my rent, I went to the market and bought them a little krupnik, some barley for their soup, a bit of sugar to pamper Zipporka, and laundry detergent. That was the only kind of soap available. We bathed and shampooed in gritty laundry detergent; real soap was hard to obtain and very expensive in the ghetto.

Each time I came, Mother said, "Chasinka, be careful, be alert, look around you thoroughly to make sure no one's watching when you come in. I don't fear for my own life any more; I'm worried about you."

Mother didn't really know what I was up to. I never told her about it, but with her sagacity and intuition she could not have been far off. Zipporka clung to me with all her strength, hugging me and not letting go. Each time I came in, I found her taking care of Leahle's children, always with one of them in her arms.

Rocheleh visited them almost every day. She took Zipporka to the movement commune so she would meet friends, eavesdrop on their serious discussions, and enjoy their jokes and stories about Hashomer Hatzair and the camps the movement used to have. A girl who had grown into adolescence within ghettos, sixteen years old and so sad: Zipporka, our little sister, my beloved.

When we were together for the last time, we didn't know it . This may have been for the best. I don't know how one can endure a farewell when one knows it's for good. I could not save her. There was nowhere to hide her on the Aryan side. To live there, one needed Polish facial features and hair color — and a personality of steel. Even Rocheleh, who looked Aryan enough, could not endure the horrific stress.

In the first *Aktion* in Białystok (February 1943), Efraim Barasz, chairman of the Białystok ghetto *Judenrat*, refused to excuse Edek and the other Hashomer Hatzair members from the transport. Gedalyahu Szajek, a member of Hashomer Hatzair and the Jewish police, tried to intercede with Barasz, but the latter would have none of it. He insisted on speaking only with Chaika, the Hashomer Hatzair leadership's liaison with the *Judenrat*, but Chaika was busy with resistance affairs on the Aryan side. The comrades turned to Mordechai Tenenbaum, who had Barasz's ear. Something delayed Tenenbaum — we don't know what — so by the time he got in touch with Barasz the transport had gone and nothing useful could have been done about it.

On one of my overnights in the ghetto, several weeks after the *Aktion* and the combatants' removal to death, a fierce debate took place at the Hashomer Hatzair commune on Częstochowska Street: was it right to stay in the ghetto and die as martyrs, it being clear that the warfare would be very brief and largely symbolic, or should the combatants join the partisans in the forest and fight the Germans effectively?

Jandrze, his hands still bandaged, advocated the latter course of action. There was no point in fighting in the ghetto, he said. We should go to the forest, save whomever we can, fight arm-in-arm with the partisans, and, above all, not trust Barasz to tell us when the next *Aktion* was coming. Chaika took the opposite tack: the ghetto must not be left leaderless; the Germans must not be allowed to haul the Jews to death without resistance.

Zorach stood up to speak. I was sitting with Cyla. The whole assemblage listened soundlessly. His calm and sagacity shone through. He understood that the debate was not only one of principle but also a very personal exchange in its arguments and rationales. This was especially evident in the remarks and

accusations that were hurled at Chaika for her absence from the ghetto during the first *Aktion* (she was performing tasks outside the ghetto) and Barasz'
refusal to speak with anyone but her, for which reason Edek and the other
comrades had been sent to death. Zorach tried to stanch the cacophony, rees-
tablish calm and build a bridge between the group that unequivocally favored
remaining and fighting to the end — at any price — and those who saw no point
in death for death's sake, believing it more important to survive and fight on.
Aryeleh Weinstein, the poet, said, "And maybe one of us will also survive to
recount the life and death of Polish Jewry, for the sake of history...."

The decision was made: we would continue to prepare for an uprising in
the ghetto but would also send people out to get the forest ready. Eliahu Warat
and Jakob Makowski were chosen for that task.

On the afternoon of Sunday, August 15, 1943, I set out from Missja and
Tosiek's home to meet with members of the Belarusian resistance. Something
was amiss. Świętego Rocha and Lipowa, broad avenues that ordinarily were
quiet on Sundays, were teeming with Ukrainian and Lithuanian soldiers. It
was easy to distinguish them from Germans because they wore different uniforms.

I heard the noise created by the mass of soldiers: the metal clatter of
rifle barrels against helmets dangling from rucksacks, the monotonous pounding of hobnailed soles and heels on the gray cobblestones in parade step, the
sound of measured commands, the chatter, laughter and cries of encouragement that wafted from the blocs of troops as they moved from the train station
onto Sienkiewicz Street, toward the Gestapo headquarters.

The Sunday serenity had been ruptured. The Poles, on the sidewalks,
looked on, cheering the parade. I stood among them, rooted to my place in the
shade of the green linden trees, realizing in a flash the ghastly significance of
the mammoth military force that was pouring into Białystok.

I walked down Lipowa Street and reached Sienkiewicz, turned, passed
the turn onto Jurowiecka Street, the ghetto gate and the Gestapo headquarters,
and kept going. All the streets were packed with soldiers, trucks and weapons.
The great *Aktion*, the liquidation of the ghetto, was unfolding before my eyes.
The first *Aktionen* in Grodno and Białystok had looked like this, but today the
military forces were much larger.

I had to enter the ghetto and sound the alarm so the comrades would
have time to organize. That way, Edek's promise, given on January 30, 1943,

when I left the ghetto for the Aryan side, would be honored: in the great uprising, you will be fighting with us. I won't surrender my right to fight. I won't survive alone. What use is my life except for this final battle?

Summer: mid-August heat. The sun sets late; light persists until nearly 11 p.m. I cannot go into the ghetto now. It's Sunday and there aren't any groups of workers entering. All the crossings that open onto Sienkiewicz Street are full of soldiers, and Olla's courtyard is packed with food smugglers. I have no choice but to wait until curfew.

I went home. Tosiek was on shift, Missja with her lover, and Waldek with Savta upstairs. The serenity of the place was very good for me. I entered my room and put my things in order. I made sure that everything was there, and that all my documents, permits and authorizations had been stowed in the muffle. I couldn't allow myself to be arrested on the way to this, my last infiltration of the ghetto. I couldn't eat. I gathered up my remaining food — a quarter-loaf of bread, a piece of fish and a little sugar wrapped in brown paper — to deliver to Mother and Zipporka.

Then I lay in bed and mulled the next day's possibilities. To which five-person unit would they annex me? To which post would I be assigned? I had never fired a weapon. I wondered what job they would give me. Time seemed to stand still, but suddenly it was evening. I picked up the muffle, slipped my meager food into my skirt pocket and set out. I put the key under the staircase, in a corner, in the dark. I would no longer need it. I cast a hurried glance at the tops of the tall pines standing darkly against the background of the heavens, gazed at the lace-veiled windows in which the first lights had been turned on, and moved past the clotheslines in the courtyard, under the pear tree. For the last time in my life, I thought, I was seeing the place that had been my home for seven whole months.

I reached Olla's place a few moments before curfew. No one knew I had come. No one was there to help me leap from the storeroom roof onto the hard-packed soil. I jumped anyway. Today I cannot estimate the height of the roof with accuracy. Was it three meters? Four meters? But it was the only way in. I thudded to the ground, bruised. But now there was no time to lose. I ran through the silence, staying close to the building walls, trying to muffle the pounding of my steps on the pavement and avoid the eyes of Jewish police. Breathlessly I reached the apartment where the leadership sat, rushing up the stairs and almost knocking down the door with my momentum.

They were all there: Gedalayhu and Chaika, Zorach and Cyla. I remember the horrified look on their faces. "How did you get in? ... You jumped alone? ... What happened? ..." Still panting from my race up the stairs, I gasped, "The *Aktion* is tomorrow morning! The city is full of Ukrainian and Lithuanian soldiers, lots of trucks all together at the Gestapo headquarters. Tomorrow they're liquidating the ghetto!"

There were no chairs in the room. Cyla stood up, moved toward me, and hugged me. Chaika and Zorach sat on the bed across the room and Gedalyahu stood at the door, on his way out for his shift with the police. Cyla hugged me tight. She didn't let go. Everyone stared at me, at Gedalyahu, at Chaika, and again at me.

"It can't be," Gedalyahu said. "This morning the Germans brought a truckload of skins to the factory that makes shoes for the Wehrmacht. They wouldn't deliver such quantities of goods if they were about to wipe out the ghetto."

The resistance had handed Gedalyahu a difficult, very difficult assignment: to be a member of the Jewish police force that did the *Judenrat*'s and the Germans' bidding. To sit in the eye of the storm. To be a reliable and incomparably important source of information for the resistance.

The city is full of soldiers, I repeated. I described what I had seen as I walked past the Gestapo headquarters to the ghetto wall. It had never been that way. Never had there been so many soldiers, vehicles and trucks in Białystok.

"It can't be," Chaika said. Barasz hadn't told her a thing; he had promised to sound a warning only if something was about to happen. That was his agreement with her as the representative of the resistance: no warfare activity until the last moment. And when the last moment was about to come, he would tip her off.

I sat down. Cyla brought me a glass of tea. No one said a word. My emotions clashed: confidence that I was right and helplessness for having failed to convince anyone. I tried again: "This is the right day for it: Sunday. No one leaves the ghetto for work, no one can see what's happening in town, all the Jews are in the ghetto, no one can escape. It's so suitable for the Germans. And the shipment of skins? This is exactly how they've always deceived us so that we shouldn't suspect anything, we shouldn't be alert, we can't get ready. They did exactly the same thing in Grodno. And Barasz? I don't know. I don't know what to say about Barasz, about the agreement. Look, he didn't keep his word in the first *Aktion*; he refused to release Edek and the comrades from the transport. Maybe he, too, doesn't have any foreknowledge either! Maybe he's also being misled and will be taken by surprise.

I can't figure it out. They don't believe me. They're sure I'm wrong, that I don't understand what my eyes saw. Cyla hugs me with all her might, not letting go. She senses my distress, the stiffness of my body, the incalculable tension, my unwillingness to give up on the possibility of making them understand. Again I begin to list the things I had seen. I've been on the Aryan side for months, I tell them, and my sense of danger has never failed me. It's not only intuition, it's also, literally, the physical sensation of a chill that rises through my body like a strong protective rampart between myself and the world as I cross into the danger zone. Behind that rampart, I think very lucidly, maintain supreme bodily control, see clearly, and understand what's happening in a very, very exacting way, not influenced by fear, anxiety, fleeting memories or a distant facial expression.

Midnight. I failed; they didn't buy it. I had no doubt about how wrong they were and how right I was. Gedalyahu and Chaika had made up their minds. By then it was too late to walk over to Mother and Zipporka. I went to Rocheleh to comfort myself by sleeping in her company. I found her in her bed at the commune: lovely as an angel with her golden hair, round face and placid breathing. I took off my shoes and lay down quietly next to her. She sensed my body, stuck out a hand, hugged me in her sleep, and smiled. I kissed her on the cheek and whispered, "Don't wake up…. We'll talk in the morning."

We didn't make it to morning. At 2 a.m., Gedalyahu sent messengers to report: the ghetto is surrounded!

Frantically rousing the comrades from their slumber. The frenzy of getting organized. Darkness. Fear. Rummaging for clothes and shoes. Two men opened the cache and handed out Molotov cocktails and weapons. Chaska, Rocheleh asked, where are you going to be? I don't know, I answered. I have to go to headquarters to get a weapon and there they'll tell me whom to join. If only they'll put you together with me, she said. Do they know what group you're in? I ask. Yeah! Sure, everyone knows. With that, she ran out the door.

I was so relieved, so happy to be there in the ghetto, so delighted to be with my comrades, to fight together with them, to die with them, not to survive alone. I left my muffle and all the documents on the commune table.

I wouldn't need them any more. I had an astonishing sense of freedom. I was no longer Halina Stasiuk of Koszewo, not far from Druskienniki. I was again Chaska Bielicka, a member of Hashomer Hatzair, a combatant in the ghetto resistance.

One of the comrades showed me the way to headquarters. I went in and waited to be told where to go. Chaika emerged from the second room: "We decided that you have to go out again right away. We need you on the Aryan side. I don't know how long the warfare will last. We may need help with ammunition and medicines, weapons, papers and a place for people to hide. We're preparing for a battle that will last for days. Get ready and organize the girls on the outside."

"I'm not going," I said. "There are enough comrades on the Aryan side. I'm staying to fight."

Chaika went away and came back some time later. "It's an order," she said. "From Mordechai Tenenbaum, commander of the uprising."

I couldn't refuse an order. "But I can't go," I said. "I have no papers." I extended my two empty hands.

"What do you mean, no papers? Where are they?" Chaika asked angrily.

"I knew that if I went out to fight I wouldn't need them any more, so I left them on the table at the commune."

One of the men ran to fetch the muffle. As soon as he returned and handed it to me, we went out. Two men ran with me down the street until Olla's courtyard. One couldn't leave the ghetto by oneself; it took help to climb and cross the concertina wire atop the fence.

It was almost 3 a.m. when I reached Olla's yard: two hours until the end of curfew. I climbed down from the woodshed roof, concentrating so hard that I stopped breathing. One misstep, one loss of balance, and I would topple onto the pile of wood outside the shed. What concerned me wasn't the blow I would sustain but the noise that would awaken the neighbors. I touched the ground opposite the woodshed door. Slowly I turned around, toward the yard. In the space between the buildings I could see past the fence to the hill and the electricity pylons along the railroad track. In the space between the pylons, dark silhouettes moved against the background of the brightening sky. There was no mistaking them: a chain of soldiers spanning my entire field of vision. Sounds and voices in the street on the other side of the fence. People did not walk about during curfew. People who walk use a different cadence. And Poles do not speak German.

There was a well to the left of the gate, between Olla's house and the neighbor's. I took seven paces and crouched behind it. I stayed in that position for the next two hours, ready to spring at any moment. You can spring from a crouch immediately; from a sitting position it takes more time. German soldiers occasionally entered the yard to use the latrine. They passed very close to me and I could smell their perspiration, sense their breathing, hear them opening the metal clasps of their military trousers. They didn't notice me. They didn't hear the wild pounding of the heart, sense the breath of fear, smell the rage and hate that permeated my being.

First light of dawn: almost 5 a.m. Two soldiers ran down the hill toward the courtyard. They must have discovered me when I had risen up to observe them, I was sure. I stood up, withdrew the muffle from the blouse, straightened my skirt a little, and moved to the gate. Across the street, at the foot of the hill, I saw another chain of soldiers. The ghetto was surrounded by three rings of soldiers.

Two sentries at the courtyard gate. "Where to?" one of them barked.

"Zur Arbeit," I answered in German, "To work."

"Where do you work? Your papers!"

"As you wish," I said, withdrawing my work permit from the muffle: Herr Luchterhand, SS Werkzentrale. I was absolutely sure that the name, title and documents would make the necessary impression. They did. And all the way down the street, until I turned away from the ghetto, I was stopped every few meters to be inspected again.

Much later I found out that I was the last person to pass through that crossing alive. Chaika told me that a young man from the ghetto who knew about the crossing tried to escape that day and fell straight into the hands of the Germans who had filled the courtyard. They shot him before he even touched the ground.

5 a.m. The streets far from the ghetto were empty. Few people went to work at such an hour. I walked down Horoszczanska Street, between the tall wooden fences. Rose vines climbed several of the fences; in the light of dawn I could make out their shades of deep pink and gleaming white. And among the leaves of the chestnut trees that lined the street and, spread out like splayed fingers, was the gold of sunrise.

I stood at the door of Apartment 12, Lisa's apartment. A separate entrance. I knocked quietly. Lisa opened up and I fell into her embrace, weeping soundlessly. The walls are thin. No one must hear. "They're liquidating the ghetto," I whispered into her ear. She froze for a moment and then recovered. As she fixed me a glass of tea and got dressed, we decided which of us would inform each of the other girls. Lisa headed for Anja; I visited Bronja and sent her to inform Riwkele Medajska. The four of them had jobs. I was excused; the Gestapo doctor who employed Riwkele had extended my sick note. I hadn't worked in three weeks. We arranged matters so that after work we would all go to the ghetto area and move about in the surrounding streets until we could come together. From Bronja's apartment I turned onto Sienkiewicz Street, corner of Jurowiecka, to the ghetto gate. I was sure I had a simple explanation for my choice of destination. Probably I could not have defended it as a member of the resistance, but I just couldn't help it.

It was after 8 by now. Across from the gate, on the eastern side of Sienkiewicz Street, crowds of Poles had thronged to watch the spectacle. Many did not conceal their glee: at long last the Germans are doing the work for us, wiping out the *żydów*. The gate opened. The first groups marched out of the ghetto toward the railroad station, hastily tied parcels in hand. Children clutched hems of coats, dresses and trousers. Babes in arms. I could not make out faces; almost everyone marched with their heads bent due to pain, fear, humiliation and exhaustion. Violently roused from their sleep, skimpily dressed, shoes tattered after years of war, hunger, poverty and deprivation. Deprived of homes and families. Deprived of the right to move about. Deprived of freedom and liberty. The shadow of death steadily spreading over them.

I opened my eyes so that I should remember. So that I should burn the sight into my memory circuits. I could not help but look. Inevitably my tears blurred the acuity of the spectacle. But I resolved not to allow any detail of the terror and the atrocity elude me.

Then the inhabitants of the orphanage came out. Today I cannot endure the sight. But then, my youth, the strength I had developed and the defensive rampart that encircled my soul — they had taught me to hold the sobbing inside. My tears descended from the throat to the diaphragm, sizzling, burning, halting my breath. But my face betrayed nothing. I was standing amid a crowd of Poles. I began to move. I could not remain in one place too long.

The orphanage children walked past: a mass of young ones in ranks of four, holding hands. A few were carried by the adults who escorted the group. All the rifle bayonets were pointed downwards, at the toddlers' heads. The youngsters marched, a wall of soldiers and weapons on one side and the cheering Polish mob on the other. I thought about the children: What do they know? What do they feel? How do they decode the terror of that morning?

The orphans were gone and the shooting began. Although the two events were unrelated, I remember the sound of it that way. How stupid we had been, I thought, not to have gone in, all of us. After all, none of us would survive and the ghetto was now impermeable due to the mass of soldiers encircling it. All the other ghettos in our area, including the Warsaw ghetto and our comrades who had fought there, had been wiped out. We had no way of knowing what was going on inside. We heard individual gunshots followed by bursts of machinegun fire. Again: a single shot, then more bursts. The individual shots were ours, the bursts German. The combat continued.

Groups continued to exit from the ghetto gate. I tried to identify people in them: Mother and Zipporka, Aunt Pesia and her family, Rocheleh with her head of golden hair, the comrades. A sense of time running out. It was afternoon by now. They had closed the ghetto gate; the Poles begin to disperse. I could not keep standing there without arousing suspicion. I walked up Lipowa Street alone, sad and very lonely. Occasional gunshots and bursts of gunfire from the ghetto. Black smoke and a fiery stench. I turned onto Świętego Rocha Street and stepped through the courtyard entrance. Missja was at home. She greeted me happily: "Halinka, you lost your key. Waldek found it while he was playing under the stairs." She said nothing about what was happening in town. Nothing about the soldiers, the battle, the ghetto, the victims. "That was really lucky," I laughed. "I didn't even notice it falling."

My choice to return to the apartment was the choice to continue fighting. I tumbled onto the sofa and lay there for hours, gazing at the ceiling and seeing in the white plaster the faces of Mother, Zipporka and Rocheleh, whom I had lost without the chance to say goodbye. Someone knocked on the door: "You have a visitor," Missja said. I leaped to my feet and saw Chaika in the kitchen doorway. I allowed myself a split-second of astonishment; Missja was standing between us and I had to respond quickly. After embracing and kissing Chaika, I said loudly, "Halina! How nice it is that you've come. Missja, let me introduce you: This is my cousin from the village. Her name is Halina, too." I turned to Chaika: "Come, I'll make you some tea."

I led her to my room and closed the door. The walls were thin: I mo-
tioned to Chaika: Don't talk. Sit down on the sofa. Chaika was tired, tense and
pallid, her legs scraped from the barbed wire she had crossed. She had washed
off the blood with water from a well in one of the courtyards. She clutched
nothing but a small handbag containing her forged papers.

What do I tell Missja? I have to keep Chaika with me at least for a
few days so she can recover. Missja sat at the kitchen table, reading. "Pani
Missja," I addressed her. "In our village the young girls who've survived are
being taken to Germany. My cousin... I grew up with her. She managed to
escape from the village. She wants to work here in Białystok. Would you let
her live with me?"

"Sure," Missja said. "Why not?"

I returned to my room with two glasses of tea. I had neither drunk nor
eaten since the nighttime emergency wake-up in the ghetto. Chaika must have
been in the same condition. I told her quietly, "I'll set things up with the girls
after work. Come." Missja still sat in the kitchen, reading. "I'm going out to
show her the town," I called to her. "We'll be back in the evening." And out
we went.

We circulated in the streets surrounding the ghetto and turned toward
the demolished Jewish quarter, past the intersection of Sienkiewicz and Lipowa. Lisa, Bronja, Anja and Riwkele had gathered in a vacant lot. I noticed
the eruption of delight in their eyes as they identified us. We sat down — close,
touching, pressed to Chaika.

The Germans had entered the ghetto before dawn, armed with loud-
speakers and broadsheets. The broadsheets, which they pasted to the building
walls, instructed the entire population to report to Jurowiecka Street by 9 a.m.
Each person may bring a small parcel. There are no exceptions and no lists.
The entire ghetto, with its workshops and factories, is to be resettled in Lublin.
Anyone who goes into hiding will be shot.

The resistance was sure that the masses would not comply. However,
most set out at once, parcels in hand, and thronged to the appointed place.
The horde of soldiers that had been brought into the ghetto, the quantities
and power of their weapons, and their deployment defeated all our plans to
wage an organized struggle. The Germans had learned the lessons of the Warsaw ghetto uprising. The combat was brief. An attempt was made to break
away from the crowd of Jews that had gathered, cross the fences and head

for the forest in the belief that the masses would follow them. This failed, too.

We girls, the six of us, sat down on some stones. It was one of the few times I recall that we managed to dissociate ourselves so emphatically from our *faux* existence as Polish women, from our connection with the underground ways of caution. The lot was empty and we would notice anyone who approached, but we were neither cautious nor vigilant. We asked Chaika about our comrades — whom did you meet? What do you know? — and I asked about Rocheleh. Chaika had nothing to report. We sat alone, lost, cut off. Before our eyes, the ghetto was being shipped to death and our comrades were being killed in combat against a superior force, choosing the path of certain death. If any members of our families and any of our comrades were still alive, they were interned behind barbed-wire fences on the exposed lot next to the railroad track. We didn't know how to find the liaison to the partisans. We didn't know how we could be useful. "If only I could find Marylka," Chaika said.

Summer evenings in Poland are very long. Twilight drags on and on. We walked over to the place where the Jews had been concentrated: a large lot across from the freight terminal at the end of Bielostoczanska Street. No shade, fenced in, guards ringing the enclosure at a radius of almost 500 meters from the barbed wire. We meandered among the crowd of curious Poles to find a way to approach, to make out details. We found none. We went back to town — soon it would be curfew — and returned the next morning. Chaika didn't have a job; I had been released with my sick note. The other girls joined in the afternoon. Summer. Hot. Mid-August. Nothing had changed: the fences, the guards, the distance that could not be crossed. The dark mass of people. The mob of Poles looking on. You couldn't make out details. Occasionally a group was led toward the freight cars. Some of its members were sent to the right and others were directed to the left. The heat worsened. *Wasser, Wasser:* water, water. Fragments of screams. Loudspeakers boomed orders and instructions. We circled the compound for three days amid the Polish mob and its hateful, derisive, killing remarks. We stood among them as if it were nothing, keeping our tears to ourselves in an inner sobbing that never ceased.

In all those years, these were my most difficult moments. Mother, Zipporka and Rocheleh were out there on that plot. So were all my friends. I don't know where I marshaled the strength to hold it in, how my legs stood still, how my body resisted my heart's desperate pleading to join them. Inside me was a tremendous urge to race toward the rampart where the sentries over-looked the plot and to be shot, simply to die in the face of the horrible demise of those inside: my mother and my two sisters, Chaika's mother, the comrades who had fought and were captured, and the masses of Jews whom we had not known, but were us.

I'm not sure I can explain the absolute separation of the ghastly physi-cal pain that wells in your psyche, as if your soul is being torn from its un-derpinnings, from the intelligent, detached decision to continue fighting. The battle has not ended. The war has not ended. We had discussed the option of suicide: how to use the cyanide concealed deep in our clothing. But to choose this option was to choose self-indulgence, to evade responsibility. That was not what we had been raised for. We were totally mobilized. The only justifi-cation for our lives within eyeshot of the transport grounds was war against the Germans: the resolve to fight them, to avenge ourselves against them and their accomplices, and to help the partisans. Our connection with the forest. We spoke about it a great deal, Chaika and I at night in our single bed, and with Bronja, Lisa, Anja and Riwkele, during those three days until the entire transport had been sent away, and afterwards as well.

I know nothing about how Mother or my sisters died. I don't know whether they survived the inferno during those three days of August or died of thirst, fallen on the sizzling soil of that vacant lot. Zipporka was definitely with Mother. I hope for their sakes that Rocheleh found them among the thousands who had been massed there. I don't know whether they were packed into one railroad car or separated in the frenzy of the transport to Treblinka. Many days later, when I reached the forest, I encountered the poet Aryeleh Weinstein, a member of the resistance and Hashomer Hatzair. "Lots of people leaped from the train," he said. "Your Rocheleh jumped before I did." For years I dreamed that my door would suddenly open and there she would be. For years I spent sleepless nights fantasizing about the joy of the reunion. I don't know how she died — by the railroad guards' bullets, of an injury sustained when she hit the ground or, perhaps, at the hands of murderous peasants in the villages along the track.

Chaika remained with me. Until then, my supper had been a glass of tea and a slice of bread with or without embellishments. I didn't know how to cook. Chaika was a chef, a champion soup-maker. We lived on my salary, dividing up whatever remained after I paid the rent. Once a week we bought an onion, a few potatoes, or some carrots in the marketplace. By August, however, I was no longer working. My sick note excused me from my job but also deprived me of my wages.

Shortly after I moved into my current apartment, a neighbor dropped by and saw me mending Missja's clothes. "You know how to sew?" She immediately spread the word around the courtyard. Thus, I repaired, designed and made clothing for all the neighbors — all by hand, without a sewing machine. I was paid in cash or food, a crucial supplement in my state of poverty. When Chaika arrived, I taught her how to do the basic stitches. This increased our output, but even that wasn't much.

Our soup was "nail soup." Whenever we ran out of money and the supply of vegetables dwindled, we ate, laughed, and retold the childhood story about the pauper who went from door to door and taught all the matrons to make soup from a nail. You placed the nail in a pot of boiling water and added some salt and pepper, a potato, a quarter head of cabbage, and finally a fistful of noodles. That's how Chaika cooked. But sometimes our soup was only a lonely potato in addition to the nail....

One night, after we'd been sharing the apartment for many months, Chaika and I woke up in a panic. Missja and her mother had broken down the door and squeezed themselves into a corner of the room, trembling and sobbing. Behind them, in the doorway, Tosiek staggered toward them drunkenly, waving a knife.

I couldn't get out of bed. A girl in a nightgown did not reveal herself to a strange man. Instead, I tugged the blanket to my neck and sat up. Chaika remained prostrate, motionless. It was scary: the man was drunk and enraged; he might have killed us all.

"Pan Tosiek," I said. "What are you doing? Did you drink a little? And you've already picked up a knife?"

His physical response was terrifying. Something like a jolt of electricity ran through him. He straightened up for a moment, stopped staggering, and said, "What are you saying, that I've been drinking?" And he turned toward the bed, flashing the knife. The whole thing unfolded like a slow-motion film: Chaika pressed to the wall, I pressed to her, Missja and her mother standing agape, clinging to each other in the corner, and Tosiek's right hand clutching the knife, gathering momentum and swinging backward from his side. Suddenly he spun, swooned and tumbled into the stove with the white porcelain tiles that stood in the corner between the window and the bed. Silence. I shooed Missja and her mother away with a hand gesture. Then I thought about how to calm Tosiek down. "Give me the knife," I said. "Here's a chair. Sit down for a moment and we'll talk. You're tired from work, see? You work so hard. There's nothing terrible about having something to drink, a little is okay...."

I kept talking. I had to sway his thoughts from the knife and Missja. Drunks have short memories. The more I talked, the quieter and calmer he became. Finally, he put down the knife and went to sleep. By that time Missja had gone to her mother's place with her son and that's where they stayed. The mad combination of a member of the Polish ultranationalist resistance who let a room in his home to a member of what he took to be another member of the Polish resistance — a "colleague" — and her cousin, together with a wife who busied herself with dalliances and gave nary a thought to me and what I was up to, allowed me and Chaika to live with them safely. For an entire year, until the thunder of the Soviet artillery batteries surrounding Białystok became audible, Chaika and I lived together, sharing the narrow bed, food and soap, agonies of body and soul, thoughts, schemes and actions: non-stop resistance.

Now I wish to pause for a moment. This isn't really the right juncture in the chronology of events, but for that very reason I want to mention three Poles who stood out from the others. Then I'll describe the year between the summer of 1943 and the summer of 1944. I speak not only about the family surroundings that these three Poles gave us but also, and mainly, their loyalty to us, as well as their absolute willingness to help and assist us. As Jewish women, we were doomed to die whether we took action against the Germans or not. As Poles, they incurred no mortal risk unless they chose to do something such as helping us. Their courage and the uncompromising statement they made by doing what they did were a source of comfort, strength and hope for us — because they returned us, as Jews, to the family of worthy human beings.

The first of the three was Pan Bronisław Borzyński, the *wujek*, the "uncle": a member of the Białystok resistance, a veteran Communist, a Pole, an older man, definitely past the age of fifty. Short, squat, silver-haired, meticulously dressed and very impressive, he was supremely suited to the role. Marylka introduced him to us. He helped us create the appearance of ordinary life in the midst of the war, and prove that we were not strange, other, differ-

Bronisław Borzyński, member of the
Polish resistance

ent, and therefore suspect. He was an "uncle" to all of us. Our landlords never met; each considered himself the "uncle" of his tenant. Pan Borzyński was indeed an "uncle" for me and for Chaika, Lisa, Bronja, Anja and Riwkele. Whenever he visited, Missja summoned us from our room: "Your *wujek* has come; look, he's already here!" But he was much more than a *wujek*. He had a daughter, Hanka Zielinska, the mother of his only grandson. That's how he described her, anyway. In fact, she was a Jewish woman who had been trapped in Białystok while trying to escape to the east with the retreating Soviets in the summer of 1941. As she fled, her convoy was bombarded. When the terror ceased, she found herself badly injured and a little boy whose mother had been killed was at her side. They were inseparable from then on. I don't know how the two of them had made their way to Borzyński — maybe he made his way to them — but he saved their lives by opening his home to them. Since he was always available to us, we reasoned that he was an activist in the resistance, probably the head of an underground cell. Whenever we were in need, he put us in touch with Poles and Soviets, resistance activists or silent partners.

Once a month I had to report to town hall to receive daily ration cards for bread and other necessities. I crossed a spacious hall and went to a long, tall wooden stand at its end, behind which clerks were seated at desks. It was a humdrum thing: I came, queued and received my cards. I couldn't see the clerk who sat there until I stood in front of him, extending my ID card. One day late in that summer, after the ghetto was gone, I approached the stand and stuck out my card. The clerk looked up and I recognized him: my geography teacher from the high school in Grodno during the Russian occupation. I froze, absolutely sure that all was lost. Then a prayer: hold on, don't reveal anything. He's going to turn me in. Don't disclose the horrific fear. On second thought: don't walk away. He's got my ID card. There's nowhere to go and no point in running away without it. He stared at me, glanced at the ID card, and stared again. "Pani Halina," he said to me in a quiet, steady voice, "wait for me outside for a moment. I'll finish up and come out to you" — to hand me over to the Germans, I was sure. I stepped into the corridor that led from the hall to the main exit and leaned against the wall. I couldn't sit down. Instead, I stood stone still. It had been our collective decision that no one should run away until being led to the Gestapo. You never knew what kind serendipity you might encounter. I don't know how long I stood there. From an angle in the doorway I saw his queue getting shorter. Now the last woman moved away from the counter. He stood up: a tall, handsome man with dark hair and rimless eyeglasses. He turned in my direction. I stopped breathing, glued to the wall and wanting to be swallowed up in it. He came over, placed a paternal hand on my shoulder, and said, "I'm on lunch break. Come, let's go out." With that, he led me to the boulevard. A surge of relief raced through my body. I was saved. He did not turn me in, did not denounce me. He was a good and sensitive man, I deduced. But I didn't know then how good he really was.

"I'm so happy to see you," he said. "Could it be that you need help?"

"The most helpful thing you can do is not expose me," I said.

He smiled: "From now on, whenever you come to get rations, come to me, look for me." Then he returned my ID card and handed me a book of ra-

230 CHASIA BORNSTEIN-BIELICKA — ONE OF THE FEW

tion cards twice as thick as the ordinary one. "If there's something I can help you with, don't hesitate to ask. You know where to find me...."

Several weeks later, I took him up on his offer: "I'm alone in town and it's strange that a girl like me has no suitors. We do have a Polish 'uncle' who has adopted us, but he's old. Could you come visit me at the place where I'm living so the landlords will think that you're my boyfriend?"

"Sure," he said. "With pleasure!"

From then on he made it his business to visit every now and then and sit with me and Missja — sometimes Tosiek was there, too — and converse over a glass of tea about Poland and the world. After the conversation, he took me out for a stroll and led me across the courtyard as the inquisitive neighbors looked on. He was of adult age. He made a tremendous impression and, above all, proved that I was Polish.

Not wishing to endanger him, I didn't tell him a thing about resistance affairs. He shared a small flat with his aged mother. When he told her about my bandaged hands, she sent me a salve that she may have bought or prepared — I don't know which — that helped my hands improve at once. For Christmas that year, December 1943, Otto Busse sent him a painting as a gift. Busse, a German, was touched by this amazing Polish man. I don't remember his name. None of my classmates who survived remembers either.

At the end of the war, I returned from the forest but did not visit him again. Today I may have no way of finding him. Too many years have passed, the geographical distance is too great, and that upside-down world is gone.

I retell his story not only because he helped me. I would mention him kindly even if he had merely refrained from denouncing me after recognizing me. The important thing about him, however, was that he was alone, not a member of any resistance group. Even so, he upheld his human image despite the mortal danger. Thus he gave us strength and eased, however, slightly, our ghastly loneliness.

The next-to-last house in the row of buildings on the way to the Supraśl forest was inhabited by a Polish family: a young woman whose husband had been inducted for the war, her bedridden mother and her mute brother. All were active Communists, Party members from before the war. The woman had heard nothing about her husband since he had left, and was convinced that he had been murdered in the army because he was a Communist. They lived in a suburb at the edge of town: a path of compressed soil, *chatki* (little wooden cabins), red brick chimneys, picket fences out front, a bit of land between the fence and the house where vegetables and flowers grew, and some chickens, geese and swine in the back yard. The house had three rooms: a large room that served as a foyer, kitchen and bedroom for the woman's mother and brother, a small living room with a narrow sofa on which I slept when I stayed overnight with them, and a room for herself and her husband. Next to the bed, atop a small chest of drawers, was a photo from their wedding: he, a handsome man who despite his serious demeanor gave off a little smile; and she with dark, smooth hair, a round face, and eyes aglow. The house was poor but very well kept. I remember the lace embroidery, the cushions, the pillows, the white curtains and the flowerpots in the windows.

This woman became my refuge on Christian festivals, when I could not reach the forest or when I had to prove that I had been visiting my family in the village. I celebrated Christmas of 1943 with her. It snowed heavily, I couldn't reach the partisans, and it was a long festival weekend, from Thursday morning until Sunday night. So we spent it together: she, her mute brother, her immobile mother and I. She bought a Christmas tree from peasants who came in from villages in the heart of the forest. She set it up near the fireplace and the two of us decorated it. I helped her cook the festival meal, mainly by peeling vegetables and washing dishes. We held lengthy conversations. She became a true friend. She fixed a few eggs for me and gave me a piece of lard and a small bag of holiday cookies. It was Marylka who had put me in touch with her. As we grew bolder and received more and more orders of equipment from the partisans, her house became more than a convenient and pleasant place to stay; it was now a crucial stopover en route to the forest. Whenever it was dangerous or impossible to move something to the forest by daylight, we brought it to her house and finished the trip after dark. Rifles we had stored inside metal stove chimneys were hidden in the pigsty. A case with bullets and medicines was hidden under a bed. Chemicals, batteries, copper wire and all other commodities were stashed in the space between the stove and the wall or on the roof of the chicken coop. The woman was fearless. Her fury at the Germans and their Polish collaborators had burned away all her fears and hesitancies. We reached her house in broad daylight, carrying parcels, satchels and chimney pipes, and she didn't bat an eye. She never turned us away, never raised her voice, never slammed the door.

As I revisit her now, it seems to me that her name was Irena. Marylka remembers her as Anna. Sergei Berkner, the partisan, remembers her as Bronja Zinmuch, and somebody else remembers her as Bronja Marduch. I regret the inaccuracy of my memory and feel that I've squandered something important. As with others, I return to her in my memory because I didn't do so physically. Today I wonder if it was really impossible to pause in the heat of battle, emerge from the forest and walk to the door of her home in town, and say thank you. It's too late now. We didn't stop, didn't say thank you, and didn't go back. The tumult of war and its aftermath, the joy of victory, vaulted over the abysses of anguish. Afterwards, we fell into the grief and became too deeply and intensively mired in it to re-establish contact with our benefactors.

A Sunday in early September: almost midday. Chaika and I were resting in bed. The bells of Świętego Rocha chimed at 11 a.m., and suddenly Missja appeared at the door to our room. "Halinka, Halinka, come, a German!" Both of us were Halinka. In our division of roles, we agreed that I would be the German speaker. I worked for a German, so it made sense that I could speak it a little. In the hallway stood a tall man in civilian clothing, black hair and Jewish features. Missja wanted me to ask him what he wanted. I stepped toward him and he introduced himself: Herr Busse, looking for an apartment for his Polish worker. This was scary. The Germans could evict people from apartments and hand them over to whomever they wanted.

"There's no room here," I said. "The family lives here with their little boy and I and my cousin live in the second room. There's no more room." I stood still in order to block his progress. He stepped inside anyway. "There's nothing for you to see," I continued. "There are only two rooms here."

"I never saw how Poles live," the visitor said. "I won't throw anyone out of his apartment in order to put up my worker. I'm just curious. How can you suspect me of doing such a thing?" With that, he continued toward the kitchen and the family's room and then reached our room. He found Chaika seated on the sofa and introduced himself courteously: "Herr Otto Busse, your neighbor. I'm living at 5 Świętego Rocha Street. I'm a *Mahlermeister*, a professional painter. Why aren't you at church?"

I put on my underground face and chuckled. "We were too lazy to get up early."

He grinned, bade farewell, and walked away.

I was riveted to my spot, frozen with dread, peril and the thought that we'd have to find another dwelling right away. But before I could ponder all the dire outcomes, Chaika leaped toward me and said, "Halinka, do you know who that was?"

We couldn't really talk with Missja somewhere behind the flimsy wall. Chaika whispered in my ear, "He was known in the ghetto as a rescuer of Jews. He's the Wehrmacht's director of renovations, a civilian working for the German army. He had forty Jewish workers. Bluma, a friend of my sister Miriam, worked for him in his office. He bought food and threw it over the fence to his workers in the ghetto. Maybe you can get a job with him." We decided that I should make the inquiry.

The next afternoon, as I was delivering a parcel, he approached me in the street from the opposite direction. I stopped him and said, "Excuse me, do you remember me? Yesterday you visited us at our apartment. Is it possible that you need a domestic?"

He studied me, remained silent for a moment, and then said, "Come over in the evening, when I'll be at home. Speak with my wife."

Evening: I knocked on Busse's door. He opened it and invited me to join his wife and their fifteen-year-old son for dinner. "Thank you," I said. "I've already eaten. I'd just like to know if you need a domestic."

"Yes I do," his wife said. "You've come at just the right time. Our domestic is about to give birth." We agreed that I would come back the next day.

Busse escorted me to the door and invited me into his office at the foyer for a moment. He sat down at the desk, asked me about my particulars, and jotted them down on a card. Then, out of nowhere, he said, "Here on this chair sat a secretary the likes of whom I never had and never will: Bluma Rosenkranz. A Jewish girl, intelligent, special." As he continued to praise her, I said, "I think I know her name. I went to primary school with her. Even back then she was very outstanding."

Several months after that conversation, by which time I had already disclosed my Jewishness to him, he said, "What you said about Bluma determined your fate. It was the first time I'd heard a Pole put in a good word for a Jew."

He no longer had the forty Jewish employees because they had been transported to death. Now he had forty Polish employees. If I worked in his office, I would have to encounter them at least once a month on payday, and I did not want to meet up with forty Polish workers who might see through my false identity. So I told him that I had only completed primary school and did not know arithmetic. Several weeks later, his wife also asked me to become his secretary. She had taken over for a German secretary whom her husband had dismissed; she hated every minute at the office. Dismally she faced the columns of numbers and the piles of papers. Each time she came into the kitchen and pleaded, "Halinka, would you please try to learn anyway?" And I refused.

One day, Busse came home early and said, "Come, sit here." He placed a page with a column of six numbers in front of me and asked me to try to add them up. I got it wrong. He tried again with five numbers. I got it wrong again. He didn't give up: "I'll teach you." The next morning, and many mornings afterwards, I reported to his office where he had prepared columns of numbers on grid paper. I made sure to get something wrong each time. After accompanying his workers to job sites to give them their tasks, Busse returned to the office in order to see what I'd managed to do. "Are you willing to work in the office?" he asked. He had fired his previous secretary. I refused. Some time later, his wife and son went away on home furlough, taking with them the domestic and her young son. I realized that I had no choice. His need for a secretary was as real as my need for a job. If everything that had been said about him was correct, I knew I should help him. So I accepted. Months later, I discovered that his domestic was a German who had married a Jew. This made their son Jewish by law. When the Nazis threw the Jews into the ghetto, the woman joined her husband and son. After her husband died, however, she decided to escape and made her way to Busse along with the boy. Busse's German secretary suspected them and denounced him for sheltering a Jewish child. That's why he fired her. I don't know how he settled the issue with the Gestapo, but some time later he arranged the joint furlough in Germany. His wife and son went back for the winter; the German woman and her Jewish son were living with Busse's family in Tilsit under the guise of relatives and would do so until the end of the war. Busse's desire to help was boundless, and not only in the material sense. Whenever he had lunch at home, he went to the office to chat a bit. On one such occasion, he described himself as a pacifist, a lover of peace and hater of wars. Another time, he opened his desk drawer and I saw two handguns sitting there. I asked him what a pacifist like him was doing with weapons. "They're for self-defense," he replied.

After I worked with him for some time, I received reports about combatants from the Białystok ghetto living at the labor camp in Majdanek. We decided to go there and bring them to us. Among the candidates for the mission, Lisa — young, intelligent, daring and resourceful — was chosen. The German occupation zones were divided in such a way that one had to cross a border to get there. We were in the area that had been annexed to the Third Reich; Majdanek was in the Generalgouvernement, occupied Polish soil. The crossing required a specific type of transit permit. We decided to ask Busse to help us. He had spoken occasionally about the Jews who had worked for him. He was sure they had been sent to a labor camp. "If only I knew where they were," he said regularly. "I would go and get them out of there."

We made up an awkward cover story for our request. We were not yet willing to be exposed. The less we talked and the less we knew, the better it would be for his welfare and our own protection. So I told Busse that my friend had told me she had a friend, and that this friend had a Jewish lover. The Nazis had sent the lover to Majdanek, to a labor camp. The friend's friend wanted to go there to rescue her lover, but needed a transit pass and a permit to use the train. I wanted to go with her.

"No problem," Busse said, adding a moment later: "Won't she be afraid to travel with a German?"

"I'll ask her," I said.

For more than a week I passed messages between Busse and the friend's friend. We studied him from every possible angle: taking a trip for Jews, risking his life for them, the preparatory meeting. We put up walls and barriers and frustrated every possible contact between ourselves and the young woman: I don't know her, she's just the friend of a friend. However, they had to be introduced and he wanted to do it at our place. One evening after work, Lisa visited us. I called her "Pani Marysia." We did not let on that we knew each other. Busse wrote down all the details appearing on her papers. "It'll take some time," he apologized. "I have to bribe some Gestapo men and find a good excuse for why a Polish girl needs a transit permit into the Generalgouvernement." He began the bribing operation at once. He whitewashed the house and painted the lintels, doors and window shades of a Gestapo commander. From time to time he brought Lisa some form to fill out with her personal details and then had the commander sign them. All the encounters took place in our flat. One evening, the meeting dragged on until curfew. Lisa was unwilling to let Busse escort her. He apologized to us for the bother and pleaded that we let her sleep over that night so that she would not be caught breaking curfew. We agreed only for him, we said. A stranger in wartime is a very dangerous thing, even if she's a girl and the friend of a friend.

On another occasion, Busse stayed behind with us after Lisa left. He spoke with us about philosophy, religion and faith, and related that he was a *Bibelforscher,* a Church dissident. The Church had brought Hitler to power, he said. Then he told us that his brother was in a prison in Tilsit, their hometown in Eastern Prussia, for having posted anti-Nazi broadsheets. It was late by now, after curfew. Busse continued to talk; we listened, replied and listened with another ear, a very sensitive one. Beyond the torrent of his words, he was obviously trying to tell us something. Late at night, after he had gone, I told Chaika, "He suspects something." "I feel it, too," Chaika said. I made up my mind: if the man was risking his life for Jews, I should stop lying to him. If he asks me the next morning at the office why I'm helping Jews, I'll tell him that I have nothing against them. But if he asks me in a way that implies that he suspects my Polishness, I'll tell him the truth.

"You're right," Chaika agreed, "but we're just a link in a chain. You and I will be exposed anyway, but this man is smart: he'll also ask about Lisa." We agreed that I would talk about ourselves only. We don't know Lisa. She's just the friend of a friend.

An autumn morning, clear and cold. The condensation of my breath was still visible and my face was still chilled as I opened the office door. In a departure from his routine, Busse was there, warming himself against the white porcelain tiles of the large stove. A sense of a pierced heart, the chill of death, the terror of discovering that the whole thing had been nothing but a trap. Without saying a word, I sat down with my back to him and began to make work-like motions. I shuffled papers around and put pens and pencils in their place. We were alone; his wife and son were on a winter furlough in Tilsit. I felt his eyes boring into my back, a burning gaze, a trap about to spring. I couldn't work.

"Fraulein Halinka, my girl, I want to ask you a question but I have no intention of offending you. Please don't be offended by the question."

I swiveled at the waist, leaving my legs where they were. "Please ask, Herr Busse," I said in the plainest voice I could muster.

"What motivates you to help rescue Jews?"

The sense of a moment suspended in space. Of the progression of time changing. The pace of my breathing. The tremor that rushed uncontrollably through my body. Movement reduced to a continuum of freeze-frames, so that every bit of movement is preserved, not lost as I stand up from the desk and turn toward the man. And the fear of the psyche as it hears the words that will fill the void of the room in another split second: "Herr Busse... *Weil ich Jüdin bin...* because I'm Jewish."

My memory preserves that moment: a moment of pure kindness in a world filled with nothing but pretense, play-acting and lies. A world reminiscent of a stage we had not chosen, on which we played out our lives as others, as strangers. A world where, whenever something happened, our psyches had to retreat to the place farthest away from what we really felt. A place where we had to laugh, smile, act impudently and throw our lives away. We couldn't cry for real, ache for real or connect with our feelings for real. We were actors in a play that had no intermission, even for a moment, a stage performance with no stages. Non-stop actresses. Sometimes it drove us insane. Whenever we thought we could endure no more, Lisa and I headed out of town and, after passing the last houses, spoke with each other in Yiddish. Then we returned to center-stage, to the show that our lives had become. And now, all of a sudden, the revelation: I said aloud that I'm Jewish. Here, I've established one place on earth where I can be me!

Busse stammered. He couldn't find the words to put an orderly sentence together. "You're a Jew? And Halina, your cousin, she, too?"

Yes," I said, "we're both Jewish."

"And Marysia, too? Your friend's friend?"

"No, she doesn't know who we are. And don't tell her."

Busse remained agitated. "Is your family alive? How are the two of you getting by? How did you survive? Are there other Jews in need of help? Do the Poles in the apartment know who you are?"

A torrent of questions. He couldn't stop. The shock of the discovery left me frozen and somewhat disconnected: "No, Herr Busse, I don't know any other Jews, and how are we living? Well, you've seen it with your own eyes!"

Silence. Early morning. The crackle of wood burning in the fireplace. Through the transparent curtain I see a patch of overcast sky, the crown of a linden tree, the golden leaves of autumn. Busse studied me, noticed my distress, and held his silence. Afterwards, he said quietly, "If you find out about other Jews, if you need any help, come to me. I'll always help!"

And so he did. For almost a full year, until August 1944, he never ceased to be of assistance. At a certain point, he stopped being a mere assistant and instead became a partner and initiator. He gave his fur coat and a pair of gloves to the young men who returned from Majdanek. Whenever my documents needed to be stamped in some German office, he went there in my place in order to reduce the danger of my being exposed. He gave me certificates and permits to help me avoid work and use the railroad. He augmented my salary from his own pocket. Occasionally he gave me food parcels to take home: sausage, smoked fish, oil and eggs, which he was able to buy in military canteens.

Life became more liveable — not only due to his material aid but also, and mainly, because in that location, at the office and in his home, I did not have to make believe, put on a show, lie or play-act. I could be myself.

End of autumn, winter imminent. The partisans in the forest were asking us for more and more: medicines, weapons, landmines, ingredients, ammunition. We decided to disclose this to Busse — to tell him the truth and make him a partner. Chaika found a job with one Arthur Schade, a German, director of Kombinet Textile, a plant that before the war had belonged to the Kiselstein family. The daughter, Mina, was a member of Hashomer Hatzair. Until the ghetto was liquidated, Schade had employed Mr. Kiselstein at the factory. A cool-headed, painstaking and very pensive man. He lived alone; he had left his wife behind in Germany and employed an old Polish woman to run his household. Chaika had a forged labor permit that he had issued her before the uprising, and whenever it was necessary, he renewed his signature with no questions asked. After the ghetto was gone and Chaika could not get by without a real job, she went back to him and he hired her as a nighttime receptionist, so that she would not have to encounter Polish workers who might recognize her and disclose her identity.

Schade was an ideologue, an anti-Nazi who had found his own way to survive. He was in contact with Beneshek and Bola, anti-Nazi Germans like him, and we decided to liaise between him and Busse. Both men were willing to help unreservedly and displayed equal intensities of fear and concern. It took weeks of probing, discussing, negotiating and inspecting until we managed to introduce the two of them. Together they established an underground cell of anti-Fascist Germans.

Whenever Busse had to prepare a house or a building for painting, he took me along to help him measure and keep records. One time we went to Horoszcz, a town not far from Białystok, to prepare a large military hospital that had housed mental patients. While Busse was upstairs in the office, I circulated downstairs among the soldiers — the wounded, the amputees and the blinded. A war hospital. A young guy with crutches approached me, stopped at my side, and stared at me for a few moments. All my senses went taut. I thought about all the familiar possible outcomes — suspicion, accusations, denunciation — but I stood there grinning as if it were nothing, as if it was just a guy going up to a girl. He addressed me in German and began to curse and vilify Hitler. I was too stunned and bewildered to respond. All I could think of saying was something neutral, like, "Aren't you scared? A soldier in uniform: aren't you afraid to talk that way?" He raised his voice. "I was enough of an enemy to sit in Dachau on charges of being a Communist," he said, almost shouting. "But afterwards, when they needed soldiers, I was good enough to be sent to the front in Leningrad. I'm still on crutches and they're sending me back to the front. Tomorrow morning I'm leaving."

I told him, as if in jest, "If you go to the front, you won't need your handgun any more, will you?"

I waited for the roof to fall on my head, for the ground to shake, but nothing happened. "You want a handgun? No problem. I can't give you this one but I promise I'll send you one. Give me your address and I'll send it to you."

He sounded serious but I was cautious. Would he really do it? Might it be a trap? "I can't give you my address," I whispered. "But I'll ask my boss; he's in the office upstairs." When Busse came down, I went over to him and asked. "No problem," he said. "Give him my post office box number."

I spent the next two weeks in terrible fear. Busse went to Königsburg to buy paint; his wife visited the post office every day. A package in my name sent to Busse's address would arouse suspicion. The handgun arrived in the third week. Walter, the soldier with the crutches, had kept his word. Busse fetched the parcel from the post office. I was so happy that I danced in his office, clutching the weapon. Busse concealed it in the office until my next visit to the forest — another risky act that he undertook fearlessly.

Wanda Wasilewska was a Polish writer, the author of *Raduga* (Rainbow), a wonderful story we had read when we were kids. A Communist, she wrote many anti-German resistance posters during the war. The posters had to be printed and Busse, defying ghastly danger, said, "No problem, my office and typewriter are at your disposal."

Night: Busse and his family were away on a home furlough. A large window faced the street. Chaika and I sat and typed. We couldn't do it by day because Poles and Germans entered the office as workers and customers. We stayed over to sleep in his house that night and, when necessary, other nights.

And another night: Chaika and I are getting ready for sleep. Curfew began at 8 p.m.; from then on, only Germans were allowed to move about town. Suddenly someone taps at the window. I go over and see Busse standing there, his face pressed against the pane. I open the window. He extends his palm, revealing a small revolver and a box of ammunition. The next morning, in the office, I was angry at him, the only time during the whole period. "Herr Busse, that was really dangerous," I said. "A German visiting girls and rapping on the window at night."

"I couldn't restrain myself," he said, "I came back from a trip and I bought the gun especially for you. I couldn't wait until morning."

Months after the liquidation, the uprising, the fires, the individual gunshots here and there, and the plunder and dispossession, Chaika and I decided to enter the ghetto. We had to. Left behind at the commune apartment on Częstochowska Street were a typewriter, caches of arms and hand grenades, and a storeroom with Molotov cocktails. We didn't know if any of this had survived, but we decided to look. The ghetto area was fenced and guarded, not against looters but just in case any Jews remained in hiding. One could not enter without a permit. I told Busse that I would like to see the place where I had spent the last night, the apartment where I had slept overnight with my sister. Maybe I'd find something, some vestige that I could keep as a momento. "Give me a few days," he said. "I'll arrange something." And he did.

The entry permit specified, "For the purpose of measuring buildings for renovation." The permit was issued to the *Mahlermeister*, Herr Otto Busse, and an assistant surveyor. We entered the ghetto. Polish laborers were toiling in the building courtyards. Today I tried to reconstruct from fragments of memory the contours of their movements so that I can describe what kind of work they were doing, but all I can see are groups of men circulating in the ghetto courtyards.

Częstochowska Street, the house. "Go upstairs," Busse said. "Take whatever you want and come back fast. I'll stay down here to make sure no one goes up. But try to make it quick so that no one will get suspicious."

I went up the stairs and found the door open. Time stopped. Motion stopped. Table, chairs, objects, pillows and cushions, upholstery feathers and torn fabric in chaotic disarray, and drawers agape. The wall leading to the arms cache had been breached. I stepped inside and groped around. Nothing of what I wanted was there. Silence. People's voices drifted up from the courtyard downstairs. I turned to the second room. The windows had been shattered, their fragments scattered like shards of ice: sharp, transparent, gleaming, crunching and creaking with every footstep. The beds and mattresses seemed to have preserved the forms of the bodies that had used them. And here: the bed that Rocheleh and I had shared. I reached down to touch it and felt moisture and stickiness. My eyes observed a dark stain. It could mean only one thing, nothing but the obvious. The intensity of that realization struck me and toppled me to the floor next to the bed in a faint.

Several days later, Busse told me that he had waited downstairs until he realized that something was amiss. He slapped my face. I refused to wake up. "Halinka, get up, we have to get out of here right now. Halinka!" I opened my eyes; he gripped my arms and helped me stagger to my feet. I looked around. I studied the disheveled room and the clutter of objects — dropped, thrown about, torn, scattered. I stared at the bed. I searched for the bloodstain and saw nothing.

"Halinka, hurry up," Busse insisted. "We have to get out of here." Slowly I recovered, summoning anew the inner gird that made me strong, steady and able. "Just a moment," I said. "There are a few things I want to take." Over Rocheleh's bed was a small wooden shelf. It contained everything she had owned: gloves, a blouse I had sewn and embroidered, and a vest that I had knit for her from old wool. I buried these objects in the bottom of the basket and covered them with my papers and surveying tools. Out we went.

I don't remember leaving the ghetto and having my permits checked. I don't remember walking back to my apartment. Busse clutched my arm and carried my bag the whole way. We made it. Everyone was waiting there. Busse escorted me to our room. The moment the door was shut, I burst into horrific weeping. Chaika clutched me. "Halinka, Halinka. What's happening to you?" I sank onto the bed and lost consciousness. I spent the whole night burning with fever and hallucinating about people and actions. Repeatedly I called out to Rocheleh and Cylka. Chaika tried to stifle the torrent of words with her hand: no one must hear, no one must suspect. She doused rags in cold water and lay them on me. Together with Missja she tried to force-feed me tea from a spoon. Missja also spent the whole night in our room, helping prepare and serve food. I don't remember which was worse, the heat of the fever or the headache. *Boli główka szkolna wymłówka,* a headache is a schoolchild's excuse, Mother used to say. I had never had a headache before, but hammers began to pound at all my innards that night: forehead, nape, skull. As the fever raged all night, I babbled away in Yiddish. "She's speaking German," Chaika told Missja. "She must think she's at the office. I don't understand it either. Let's call Busse." Missja went to fetch him. Busse came right away, listened for a moment, and said something to Missja. In the distress of the moment, Chaika forgot that she didn't speak German and translated for Missja: "He says her boyfriend left her yesterday. She started crying back at the office; that's why he brought her home."

I lay there for almost a week, feverish and hallucinating. Chaika spent the whole time in our room, lest I say something that would give us away. Afterwards, the fever receded and the headaches slackened. I was weak and exhausted, occupying the twilight zone between terrible physical and psychological illness and convalescence. One morning I woke up in panic, sensing clearly that something had happened. Chaika had gone out on her business by then. I got up, dressed and went to the office. Busse's wife was pleased: "You're better?" "No," I said, "but I remembered something important that I left unfinished. Herr Busse might need it, so I came to finish it. Afterwards I'll lie down again."

She left and I moved to the window on my way to the desk. In the corner of my eye I saw Bronja on the sidewalk across the way, retracing her steps as though having deliberately turned around so that I would see her. I went down the back stairs and joined her as she walked. She grasped my hand and placed a key in it. "Run to Anja's flat. There's a bag of bullets and ammunition in her cellar. There was a big break-in at the kitchen of the Ritz Hotel; they took lots of food. The Germans found out about it and they're searching the apartments of all the kitchen workers!"

I walked to Anja's apartment in the rural suburb, quickly pacing over the packed soil, occasionally glancing left, right and behind to make sure no one was following and that no soldiers or police had preceded me. 27 Pi-escynska Street. The courtyard. Neighbors at the window. The last door. I go in. Silence.

I had never done it before. I had to open the trap door to the cellar, po-sitioned in the wooden floor in the middle of the room. Then dangle a chair on the rounded end of a cane and lower it into the cellar. Then lay the cane on the floor, sit on the edge of the hatch, turn around carefully in order to face the inside edge of the hatch and rest my weight on my hands, legs dangling into the darkness of the cellar, and then, with a swift movement, to lower my body and try to place my feet exactly on the middle of the chair. Otherwise, I would surely fall and sustain a genuinely serious blow.

I landed in thick darkness to which my eyes could not adjust. I groped toward the earthen wall. By standing at the wall with my face toward the middle of the cellar, where a little light penetrated from the hatch, I thought I might make out the bag. My legs bumped into the bag; it was in front of me. Now I saw it and picked it up. It was full and surprisingly heavy. I seized the cane with my left hand and the bag with my right. I stood up on the chair, almost losing my balance. With both hands I hoisted the bag to the lip of the hatch and stood on tiptoe, pushing it until it rested safely on the floor of the room. I was alone. No one was there to reach down to me and pull me up. My fingertips touched the inner wooden frame of the hatch. Blood pounded in my forehead. My heart beat crazily. Time was running out.

I cannot explain how I did what I did next. I jumped, grasped the edge of the hatch, my body taut, my arms hoisting the weight of my body onto the wooden floor, legs flailing, and then on all fours, atop the hatch. Once there, I didn't stand up, even to see whether anyone was looking through the window. Instead, I sprawled on the floor and lowered the cane in order to raise the chair — cautiously so that the chair would not bump against any-thing and make a sound. Then I closed the hatch, put the chair back at the desk, smoothed my dress, and picked up the bag with one hand and a jar of jam off the shelf with the other so that I would look as if returning from a shopping trip to the market. I locked the door, crossed the courtyard and stepped through the gate. I brushed against a dark purple wild rose bush and a raspberry bush that climbed the fence. I noticed an almond tree shedding its leaves in the autumn breeze. I strode slowly, as if I had nothing at all in that bag. Four houses away, a group of people approached: three men and a girl.

As they passed me, for a split-second I smiled at Anja, who walked between two policemen and alongside them a soldier. She saw the bag in my hand and knew that we were saved.

Relentless vigilance and an incessant sense of danger. One Sunday, I passed the church next to the Ritz Hotel en route to a mission. Mass ended; the congregation was exiting, pouring onto the sidewalk. As I crossed the ocean of people, I suddenly heard someone behind me call, "Bielicka!" — my Jewish surname. My heart stopped. My thoughts hardened into clarity: I had to do something. Instead of turning around, I took a few more steps and then stooped a bit. Then, protected by the crowd, I evaded the voice and slipped into the church, melting into the kind grayish murk of the sanctuary, the huge, long wooden benches open only at their extremes for comers and goers. The high wooden armrests created a continuum of pickets among which a person could hide. I don't know how long I hunkered among the pews. When I got up to leave a long while later, all was quiet outside. On the other side of the sanctuary, I saw a little door opening onto a side street. I exited through it.

In late 1942, escapees from the ghettos began to move to the forests of Białystok as individuals and in groups. They were Communists, members of *halutzik* (Zionist-pioneering) youth movements, and others who chose to fight the Germans. Some survived the conditions in the forest, the winter, the combat, the tattletale peasants and the hostile Polish partisans of the A.K., the nationalist Armia Krajowa that murdered Jews in the forests of Białystok. Others returned to the ghettos or re-entered the forest, sent by the resistance to prepare bases for combatants who would survive the ghetto uprising.

Here I wish to list and commemorate some of these groups:

1. The Yudita group, established by the partisan Yehudit Nowogrodzka. They lived in the Izowy forest, not far from Trak Napoleon. From the spring of 1943 onward, they were in close contact with the Forois group, which coordinated partisan warfare in the forests of Białystok.
2. A group under Maxim, Moshe Slepak, and Shmuel-Mulia Nisht, a.k.a. Vołodžka. In an engagement with the Germans, several combatants, including Maxim himself, were killed. Despite the damage and losses they inflicted on the Germans, the group disintegrated. Some of its members

joined another group; others returned to the ghetto. A few of the latter re-entered the forest in late winter 1943.

3. The Communist Baumatz group, which set out in February 1943 under the command of Eliasz Baumatz. These partisans established their center in the forests near Supraśl and formed good relations with nearby peasants.

4. The Krinki group, mostly from the town of that name, under the command of Sasha — Jona-Jerzy Sochaczewski — who previously had fought in the forests of Słonim.

5. The Forois (Forward) group. In March 1943, after the first *Aktion* in the Białystok ghetto, a group of resistance members headed into the Supraśl forest to prepare a hideout and a combat infrastructure for comrades who had survived the uprising. The founders of the group were Eliahu Warat, Fjedka (Jacob Makowski of Hashomer Hatzair), Marek Buch and Riwa Wojskowska of the Communists, and Mulia Nisht, who had already been fighting in the forest.

German attacks against the partisans escalated after the ghetto was liquidated in the summer of 1943. The Jewish groups acted jointly. After Chilek Seifman, the machine gunner, and Sasha, commander of the Krinki partisans, were killed in battle, the survivors joined up with Forois. The ghetto was liquidated and its Jewish population deported in the summer of 1943; after that, no one remained in Białystok to help the Jewish partisans except us.

Marylka. Marylka Różycka, known as Michalek in her German documents — a Jewish woman, a combatant, a Communist, a partisan. A woman of Łódź, a proletarian from birth, a Communist from adolescence. From age thirteen she performed factory labor. She pasted Party broadsheets in the streets and was thrown into Kartus-Bereska, an infamous Polish detention camp, for the crime of membership of the Communist Party. She emerged from the camp with a twisted spine and a permanent limp. When the German occupation began, she went to the forest and became a liaison between the forest and the city due to her Polish facial features — blonde (almost white) hair, fair complexion — as well as her courage, resolve and resourcefulness. When reports about the liquidation of the ghetto reached the forest, she came into Białystok to see if any Jews had survived and if she could help. From then on, we liaison girls on the Aryan side were Marylka's comrades. We became one unit, an underground entity that undertook missions, made purchases and obtained and

Marylka Różycka — liaison

pilfered ammunition and weapons, batteries and medicines, copper wire and food for the partisan units fighting in the forest. We never saw her get stopped. Her stamina was stunning. One night, after returning from town to the forest carrying a package of ammunition, it became necessary to send someone back to town. Without a moment's hesitation, Marylka got up and went. "I walked in my sleep," she said after reaching us in the morning, "but I didn't stop." She laughed. Forty kilometers in one night.

    Marylka Różycka — Good-heartedness, glowing demeanor, unbounded devotion to people and ideas, infinite sense of responsibility. One Sunday, she visited us very early in the morning. She knew Lisa and I were supposed to head out to meet with Wanja. She had walked the whole way from the forest just to warn us that the main path had been "burned": Germans had discovered it and set up ambushes. She had come to lead us to a different path. We were in town and Marylka was in the forest. Many times we covered the eighteen-kilometer path to the forest (one way) with her or without her. From her or to her.

Our encounter with Marylka marked the beginning of our connection with the forest. Within a week, we were already in action. Years later, Anja said, "We didn't do much, just what we could and what we were asked to. There wasn't a mission the partisans asked us to do that we didn't do." The end of that summer, the autumn that followed, and the first half of the winter of 1943/44 were difficult for the partisans. The Soviet formations had not yet arrived, and the partisans were low on equipment, weapons and food. Living in the heart of the forest, they moved around regularly to avoid discovery. In the summer, they slept on the ground. In the winter, they lived in *zjemlankis*, deep caves camouflaged with heaps of branches and leaves under a blanket of snow. The partisans cooked only at night, so as not to be revealed by the pillar of smoke. In the summer, they kept their cooking fires concealed from sight; in the winter, they built mud stoves in the middle of the *zjemlanka* and ventilated them with chimneys of metal tubing also camouflaged with branches and leaves.

In the winter, they obtained water for drinking and cooking by hacking chunks of translucent ice from the river. When they couldn't access this source, they filled containers with snow and melted it over the flame. In the summer, they hauled water from springs or rivers in jugs and pails pilfered from the peasants. Many partisans paid for water with their lives. To visit the river, they had to walk for hours and spend much time in hiding, vigilantly making sure that no ambush had been set up. When the containers were filled, they had to be carried all the way back very carefully. The Jewish smith whom we had rescued from the cellar of Świętego Rocha Church and moved to the forest was one of those who perished in the quest for water.

The partisans literally starved that winter. When the cold season began, they returned to the place they had buried one of their horses in the autumn, disinterred the meat that had not yet gone rotten, and survived on it for several weeks. Jewish partisans could not raid villages at night lest the Polish peasants denounce them to the Germans, Ukrainians or members of the A.K. We were their sole suppliers of food. They gave us money with which we visited the villages on Sundays and Christian festivals to buy commodities from the peasants — wheat for bread, barley for porridge, and oil, crucial for anyone who hoped to outlast the winter.

A cobblestone road led to the forest. There were villages on both sides: Grabówka, Borki, Grodniczek, Suraszkowo and Podsupraśl. We studied the villages and the countryside. The road was eighteen to twenty kilometers long, depending on where the rendezvous was set up. In any case, it was a two-way trip except for Sundays and festivals, when we were able to stay in the forest longer. We were careful not to carry parcels in the evenings. Instead, we took them to the house at the end of the road in the afternoon and waited for curfew, or returned to town and continued the trip only when it was time to leave.

We walked to the forest at night, after curfew, when there was no civilian traffic on the road. Thus, any individual or group of people who approached or any vehicle was bad business: army, police or gendarmerie. We always returned at the crack of dawn so we could get to work in town. We walked on the shoulders of the road, avoiding the cobblestones because our footsteps would make noise there. We paused for a second every few minutes, listening for faraway sounds and footsteps. Once we reached the forest proper, we walked faster. There, we had places to hide in case of an unexpected encounter.

One night, I returned alone from the forest under a full moon that spread a bright blanket over the vast plain and its fields of summer wheat. Suddenly I froze. Straight ahead, in front of me, I saw people standing. I dropped to the ground, crawled a short distance back to the edge of the path that ran parallel to the road, and cupped my head in my hands. I heard no voices and no footsteps on the road. I looked up and, some time later, raised my head a little until my eyes attained the elevation at which they encountered the people. The people were motionless. I assumed they were soldiers on patrol who had tired of their task, or maybe a checkpoint of the kind the Germans intermittently set up to thwart food smuggling.

A long time passed. The eastern sky began to glow: the first rays of sun. I looked up again. The figures had not moved. A dog barked. Sensing encroaching danger, I decided to get up and go. I had to report to my job in town and had papers confirming it. I'd be a village woman walking to town. I approached the people. They were motionless, too silent. Then it struck me: all night I had lain next to the road because of sheaves of harvested wheat. They had been stacked together in the form of human beings, wide at the bottom and narrow at the top, clustered in the field.

The machine gun Chaika and Bronja had purchased from Jan, the kind peasant from the village of Koropczyce near Grodno, had to be moved to the forest. First, Bronja smuggled it to Białystok by train. She worked as a domestic for two German locomotive engineers, with whose assistance she boarded the train and moved the weapon, dismantled, to Białystok in an innocuous suitcase. We then delivered the gun from there to the forest in stages, one of us bringing a part or two each time, enduring the considerable weight of the steel parts. We also had to deliver a rifle to the forest. This weapon could not be dismantled and wasn't really short even after we sawed off part of its butt. I don't remember who joined me — Marylka or, perhaps, Lisa — in crossing all of Białystok one Sunday morning as a congregation headed out of church. On our shoulders we carried a metal tube that was supposed to be the chimney of a furnace. Both ends of the tube were plugged with rags and the rifle rested inside. The idea was to haul the tube as far as the house at the edge of the forest, go back there that night, and take the weapon to the forest.

A lovely, almost spring-like Sunday: sunny, a cloudless sky, and streets clear of puddles. Out of nowhere, two gendarmes confronted us in the street behind the market, past the cemetery. They approached and stared at the tube. If I didn't speak, they would.

"What time is it?" I preceded them, turning in their direction. The taller of the gendarmes glanced at his watch and replied. "What, it's already so late? Thank you, they'll be worried about us at home." We walked on without looking back.

We made it. The young woman didn't believe it: "How do you dare walk like that in the middle of the day?"

"It's much more dangerous at night," we replied.

One night, Marylka and I were on our way to the forest carrying two heavy leather briefcases. One of them was the case I had taken from Anja's cellar, full of bullets for the machine gun. I don't remember what was in the other one, but it was so heavy that I expended a tremendous effort to haul it, switching hands from time to time to make the chore easier. Our rendezvous point was next to an abandoned Russian tank in the forest. A birdcall whistle was the agreed-upon signal. We stood next to the tank, whistling away and getting no response. One hour passed and then another. No one showed up.

It was late. I had to go back to work. Marylka stayed behind. She decided to move on to the alternate rendezvous point, a venerable oak tree in the heart of the forest. Since she could not lug both bags, we concealed them in the tangle of ferns and ivy, piling handfuls of dried leaves and pine needles on top. I turned to leave on the path toward the road when a birdcall suddenly pierced the air — our whistle — followed by the figure of Kalman Barkan.

"You're alone? Where's everyone?"

"We've been here for hours," Marylka answered.

Kalman burst into terrible sobbing. "If they haven't come," he managed to filter through his tears, "it means they've all been killed!"

Kalman was older than us: an engineer and a levelheaded man. "They attacked suddenly," he related after his agitation eased slightly. "Germans and Ukrainians. Hilik, the machine gunner, was killed, but I thought the others had survived."

Marylka was the first to recover: "Halinka, you go back to town. Kalman and I will walk to the oak tree."

"Halinka, be careful," Kalman said. "They must still be moving around the forest." They — Germans, Ukrainians and Poles.

I gave no thought to caution. I gave no thought to anything. Through my tears I saw the faces of the comrades from the forest. How would I describe the atrocity back in town? First light: narrow path, towering pines. Blanketed in anguish and remorse, I gave no thought to the path and the sobbing that blurred my vision. I looked up for a moment, and against the backdrop of the brightening sky and a triangle of light breaking through narrow keyholes among the crowns of the pines I made out the figures of two people walking on the path. They were so close I could see the rifle barrels that protruded from behind them. I froze for a split-second. They're not partisans; partisans don't walk in the middle of the path. Should I flee into the forest? No, if I noticed them they must have noticed me. In tears and anger I raced toward them: one Ukrainian, one German. In fluent Polish, weeping and dripping tears, I told the Ukrainian that I'd been with my grandmother in Podsupraśl. "I have to get to work in town. I started out in the dark and got lost. I work for the *Mahlermeister*, Herr Otto Busse. I don't know the way to Białystok." I heaved in agitation and added a few sobs for show. On all my trips to the forest I carried a small pouch with my papers. I always went to my grandmother or returned from a family visit. That was my story.

"What's she saying?" the German asked, studying me again. The Ukrainian translated what I'd said as I produced my papers. The German said, "So take her to the road, show her the way."

"You could have been killed. There are partisans in the forest; you were lucky," the German said. The Ukrainian led me to the edge of the path and escorted me to the road. I was saved.

Reaching Białystok too early that morning to come to Busse, I headed for Bronja. Her apartment had a separate entrance and she had not yet gone to work. I knocked quietly so the neighbors would not hear. I stepped in. The door closed and I erupted in sobbing. Bronja sat me down and brought me a glass of water. I couldn't utter a word. Only sobs and tears were willing to exit. Then I told her about the forest.

We stepped into the morning. Bronja would report to Lisa and Anja. Chaika was working as a night receptionist at Schade's plant and had not come home yet. I would tell her in the afternoon. Marylka came by the next day. Seven of them had been killed there, she said. Peasants had denounced them. The partisans, returning from a sabotage operation against railroad tracks far away, had fallen asleep in their fatigues. Ukrainian, Polish and German companies raided the forest hideout and murdered them as they slept. For weeks we continued to talk about them. For weeks we mourned them.

The Gestapo station at 15 Sienkiewicz Street had a large arsenal. Some of our comrades had worked there during the ghetto period and knew where it was. Now the partisans decided to steal some rifles. We girls did the intelligence work. We circulated for weeks in order to study, memorize and record the changing of guards, as well as the schedules, guard, access and escape routes. We also calculated the time of sunset in order to determine exactly when it would be early enough to leave us with enough darkness before curfew. The weakness of the enemy's arrangements, we found, was the changing of the guard. They didn't do it in the courtyard. Instead, the guard went inside to call or, perhaps, to wake up his successor. The gate would be abandoned for a few minutes.

Evening. We wandered around between Sienkiewicz Street and the alleys leading to the forest, guarding the path. Birdcalls from the forest were the signal here, too. The partisans came. Silently and quickly they went in, emerged with twelve Mausers, and returned to the forest. Among them, I remember Natan Goldstein, who returned to town later on other business.

One day, Marylka showed up on a mission: to blow up the power plant in Krinki, a small town at a large and important railroad junction. To prepare the sabotage charge, she would need a large number of batteries. She and I went on a shopping trip, each equipped with a basket, at a safe distance and a reasonable time apart. To avoid suspicion of having a common purpose, we meandered through the market and bought a few batteries in each place: flat, palm-sized batteries in dark-blue paper wrappers, with copper contact strips on the top. By midday, each of us had a basketful of batteries, a very heavy load. Pleased, we stepped out of the market onto a wide street that turned and climbed a hill at its end. I do not remember the name of the street but I clearly recall that moment. We passed two women in conversation. One of them was carrying baskets from the market but now she set them on the sidewalk, one to her right and one to her left. The other woman had her hands in the pockets of her dark apron. An avenue of chestnut trees stretched to the bend in the road, up on the hill. And in front of us strode a German policeman.

"Halinka, it's bad," Marylka said. "You don't know me. Walk ahead and put some distance between us. Go fast. I'll limp along and stop so that we'll be farther apart." The gendarme passed us. I quickened my pace and suddenly heard a shout: "*Halt Jüdin!*" I kept going and didn't look back. The pounding of his footsteps on the cobblestones. The thud of my heart sinking into my stomach. A gut-splitting rush of agony. He's already caught Marylka. I hear her shouting at him in Polish: Leave me alone; I'm not a Jewess! And he continued to shout at me: "Halt! Stop, Jewess, Stop!" I didn't stop. As though it were nothing at all, I turned around and saw that he had not released Marylka. Instead, he dragged her toward me, roaring, "Yes, you! Stop already, *verfluchte Jüdin,* accursed Jewess!"

"Are you talking to me?" I asked calmly. "I'm not a Jewess! Here are my papers," and I withdrew the pouch from my bag.

One winter night as I walked toward the forest, I had placed my ID card in my coat pocket instead of my handbag. It had rained heavily. The pocket got soaked. Several letters in my name had been blotted out and the round stamp on my photo blurred.

The German shouted at me, "Where did you get that card? Who forged it?"

I answered quietly, "Excuse me, sir, you are offending the Gestapo Office." He did not reply but took Marylka's papers, too.

We were marched to SS headquarters, the policeman up front and us following him with our heavy baskets. It was quite a hike and totally the wrong way from the forest. For a moment we thought about fleeing into the ruins of the Jewish quarter, but right away we decided not to try to escape until the interrogation. He had our papers but we could still try to reason with the interrogator. We arrived: a large building. We followed the policeman up the stairs and passed through the entrance, baskets in hand. The batteries, blanketed with a layer of lingerie and a towel as always, were heavy. Amazingly, they gave us a sense of credibility.

A long, tall counter of brown wood with a duty officer on the other side. The policeman, our papers in hand, stepped to the counter to write down our particulars. Marylka was in shock. Soundlessly she sat down on a bench along the wall, placing her basket on the floor but continuing to grip it. Demonstratively, with forced anger and effrontery that radiated distance and condescension, I leaned against a large door along the wall. Now the duty officer held Marylka's papers. Marylka has a baby. She's been released from work and she has a document confirming this. "So you're not working?" the duty officer turned to her. "You work only at night, slut?!"

"How dare you speak to a mother with a baby that way?" I blurted. To this day I don't know how much of my anger was forced and how much was real.

Marylka remained silent, sitting in suspended animation. Suddenly, the door I leaned against opened and I collided with the huge potbelly of a German officer. He grabbed me to keep me from falling, and as I straightened up I noticed the array of medals and citations on his uniform and the group of young officers behind him, all amused and laughing about the incident. I thanked the officer and he seized my chin, tilted my face upward, and asked, "*Kleine, was machst du hier?*" — Little girl, what are you doing here? — as if we were old friends.

From a corner of my eye I saw the policeman who brought us and I pointed at him: "*Dieser Herr sagt dass ich Jüdin bin.*" He said I'm Jewish.

"Jewish?" the officer with the decorations guffawed. "Step over to the window." He led me to the window and looked into my eyes. In the meantime, the policeman who had arrested us slipped away, off to summon the Polish women from the street, the ones who had denounced us, as witnesses. One of them had identified Marylka as an active Communist during the Soviet occupation.

The officer stared into my eyes and laughed: *"Eine schöne Jüdin."* What a pretty Jewess!

I laughed back. "Herr Chef, I work for Herr Luchterhand of the SS Werkzentrale. If I'm late for work, he'll punish me. Please tell the duty officer to give us our documents back. I must get there on time."

I had not worked for the Luchterhands in weeks but I knew that the sound of their name would save us. "Let them go," he tells the duty officer. "Don't detain them. Right now!"

I thanked him and out we went. On the Gestapo steps we scouted our flanks to make sure no one was around and the policeman wasn't returning with the Polish women. The street was empty. We ducked into side streets and alleys and moved about for a few hours more to be sure we were not being followed. Then we went home. Chaika was pale with shock, sure that we would not be back again. We had been away for so many hours, and she knew that we had gone only to buy batteries in the market.

One Sunday morning, returning at 6 a.m. from a visit to the forest, I found the town deserted. On Sienkiewicz Street, a gendarme stopped me and demanded I.D. Out came the pouch. Out came the document that carried a rain-blurred stamp. I presented it and the gendarme ruled, "Forgery. You're coming with me to the police station!"

I don't know why he left the document in my hand. He must not have considered the possibility that I would run away. It's Sunday, the town is empty, where would I flee? He walked; I followed. He turned left toward the police station; I followed. Just as we began to cross the street, I heard someone call out. The gendarme replied with a whoop of joy and fell into the arms of a colleague.

That was all the time I needed to disappear. We were near the ruins of the Jewish quarter and the Great Synagogue, which had been torched along with the Jews interned inside. I leaped into the ruins and crawled into a crevice between a toppled wall and a pile of broken bricks. The gendarme was too delighted with his encounter to rue the loss of the Jewess who had eluded his clutches. He didn't really bother to search for me. An hour later, I emerged and found the street still empty. I went home by a roundabout route.

One day in late March 1944, as the heavy snow melted and the roads were opened, Sergei Berkner came to town. First he visited Lisa at home, then Anja, and then he set out for several meetings. Afterwards, he came to my flat and, after we talked things over briefly, we went to Schade. Schade, cool, collected, cautious, was agitated from the meeting. When it was over, he gave Sergei a gift: a carbine and some bullets.

Sundays were our days of freedom to move about, of spare time. I am not sure whether one particular Sunday was the first real link in the chain that led us to the Communists, but I remember walking out of town with Lisa that Sunday morning, among the villages, in order to meet Wanja. Walking "among the villages" meant fifteen to twenty kilometers each way. The meetings took place on the main road; we avoided the houses in order to stay clear of any connection that would kindle suspicion. We were supposed to get together at places with landmarks such as pine or birch groves, a little bridge over a brook, or an altar with a towering cross and a likeness of Jesus or Mary stationed at its foot or festooned at its top — really nothing but a lone oak tree in an open field. Village peasants came to such locations with their baskets and, camouflaging our actions as a picnic, we sat, conversed, gave reports and received others. Almost every time we needed new routes to and from the forest, to the group encampment or to the villages, we set out with Wanja Orlow. He was one of the Belarusians who remained in Poland when the Germans occupied the latter country in the summer of 1941, a member of one of the underground cells that had organized and got in touch with the forest, living on the fringe between town and countryside. A master of the turf who knew the forests, the people and the villages, he had an excellent piece of camouflage: his camera. Whenever we saw a group of people approaching or a car moving from afar, Wanja pulled out the camera and we made interesting poses — Lisa in my arms, her feet waving in the air, both of us braiding wreathes from grain stalks and cornflowers, embracing against the background of wheat fields, and laughing at Wanja.

After living in the forest for months, they were used to the conditions, such as no showers or regular conveniences and no laundering or changing of clothes. Lice were their greatest fear. When I stayed over in the forest on cold late autumn or early spring nights, I sat at a tree trunk, hugging myself, shriveled, frozen, not daring to sleep near the partisans. If Lisa or Chaika came with me, we embraced in pairs. The partisans had rough peasant furs, leather on the outside and wool on the inside, an ideal home for lice and fleas. They washed the fur in the partisan way: by digging a deep hole in the ground, burying the fur in it, covering the garment with a thick layer of soil that blocked air and light, and leaving only a small corner of the coat out in the open at ground level, with a tiny opening around it. After a few hours, all the lice and fleas that had been swarming in the fur gathered at the ventilated edge outside the pit. To destroy them, the owner of the garment snipped off that end and tossed it into the fire. By counting the slits on the fringes of a coat, one could tell how many times the coat had been laundered that way. Each time we returned from the forest, we shampooed our hair with kerosene, combed each other out, and made sure not to get infested.

In the spring of 1944, a group of Soviet partisans reached the Supraśl forest after parachuting from heavy aircraft into the Lipiczanski forests and

Nikolaj Wojciechowski, commander of our
partisan brigade

walking from there. They brought lots of equipment: weapons and ammunition, food and medicines. The fringes of my memory retain the likeness of the liaison, a young woman who described having parachuted with all the signal gear. It wasn't an army yet, just companies and battalions sent to conduct relentless guerrilla warfare against the Germans. They joined our partisan groups in the forest.

The Kostjusz Kalinowski brigade, named for a Belarusian hero, belonged to the division of Gen. Kiriczenko ("Kapusta") and was divided into four platoons: Zwiezda (Star), Soviet Belarus, 26th October (referring to the twenty-sixth anniversary of the Bolshevik revolution) and Matrosov, named for another hero. The Forois group russified its name to *Vpjerod*. The platoon commander was Commissar Osipov. Our *Kombrig* (brigade commissar/commander) was Polpodkodnik (Lt.-Col.) Nikolaj Wojciechowski — a serious man, an engineer from Leningrad whose parents had been sent to a Siberian labor camp before the war for alleged treason against Communism. Other partisan formations, we knew, had confiscated the weapons of their Jewish would-be comrades and turned these fighters into camp servants. In many units, antisemitic manifestations were common. Among us, things only got better. The comrades in the forest formed an unlimited partnership with the girls in town. We wanted to introduce Busse and Schade to them. Busse responded enthusiastically; Schade warned against it. Both were concerned about the encounter with the Russians, as they had been when they first met. They needed time to mull it over, vacillate, and decide that the Rubicon of dread, fear and concern could be crossed. When they finally gave their consent, the meeting was set up.

Wojciechowski prepared the forest camp for the commander's inspection with typical strictness. Everyone put in an enormous effort, including in their personal appearance. When Schade and Busse came, the partisans demonstratively set their personal weapons aside.

Lisa and Chaika made the trip with them. When he returned, Busse said, "I was disappointed — for the better. I thought I'd encounter barbaric Russians."

Brigade headquarters established the Białystok Anti-Fascist Committee. Commissar Wojciechowski took charge of the operation on behalf of the partisans. Our Lisa, Lisa Czapnik, was named Chair. The committee members were Anja, Bronja, the *wujek* (Bronisław Burdzinski), Marylka, Chaika and I.

The panel included all anti-German resistance organizations in Białystok: the Polish and the Belarusian, the German cell, and us, the Jewish girls.

Most of our tasks had to do with intelligence. We provided information we gathered about German deployments in and on the edges of town and the locations of caches of weapons and supplies, posts and command centers. We also forwarded information on the movements of ground and air forces we received from the German underground cell. Using gear that the Russians had brought with them, we carried out sabotage operations in town and at nearby strategic facilities.

The mines in use at the time were magnetic: a kilogram of explosives attached to a large chunk of metal. Each time we went to the forest, we came back with several such mines in a basket. Afterwards, for a week or more, we strolled around town after work, each time in a different area, and attached the mines to gasoline stations, fuel depots, locomotives and railroad cars, and facilities around the railroad station and concentrations of military vehicles until our supplies ran out. These were not large-scale operations. The fires they caused were small and bothersome at best, but they were important due to the very fact that they were set — the sense of damage we were inflicting on the Germans by sending sudden flames and billows of smoke into the skies of Białystok.

Schade, as stated, was a cool-headed man. Rifles had been acquired in one of the villages and had to be moved to the partisans. Schade brought us a horse and a cart from his factory, filled the cart with a load of straw, and buried the rifles at the bottom of the heap. Busse and Schade sat on the driver's bench and Lisa positioned herself atop the straw. Next to one of the villages not far from Białystok, a German guard unit stopped them: "Where are you going?!" "To the village, to buy food from the peasants." "And who's that sitting on the straw?" "Our interpreter." "What are you hauling?" Schade grinned, withdrew a packet of good cigarettes from a large satchel, and said, "Come, let's smoke first." The soldiers accepted the offer willingly, gathered around the cart, puffed away, and laughed. Busse then pulled out a carton of cigarettes from his own bag. The soldiers let the party pass.

Some time later, Busse went on home furlough and, to everyone's astonishment, came back with a car. He had noticed that we made our trips to the forest on foot, he explained. He had observed us lugging heavy objects and seeking new paths. So he decided to buy the car to ease our plight. This really did transform our lives – Busse and Schade's assistance, partnership and unlimited willingness to act.

In distant retrospect, I sometimes fail to retrieve memories of actions and events in their full detail. I cannot define the mnemonics that preserve memories or the patterns of forgetfulness. I remember, for example, a German tank passing me, its crew watching me walking along the path with a very heavy bag in hand. They allowed me to hitchhike with them much of the way to Białystok, not imagining what I had in the bag and where I was going. Another memory rises to the surface as if from a dream: walking with Natan Goldstein in Białystok toward a certain house where a Polish family lived. He had come the previous day and slept in our flat. We introduced him to the Polish landlords as a cousin from our village. I recall wooden stairs and an entrance but cannot manage to remember why we had gone there and whom we met. Afterwards, Natek returned to the forest and perished among the other partisans whom the local peasants denounced at night.

I also have a foggy recollection of an evening encounter with a member of the Polish resistance. I don't remember why or where. I dawdled until past curfew and found myself in a wealthy suburb, a place with large, beautiful houses and well-tended gardens. I knocked on someone's door. It was like an old photograph – wooden stairs, a door embedded with ornamented glass elements, and the woman who opened the door, her hair gathered behind her neck. I told her that I had stayed late with a friend, had not been watching the clock, and had run into curfew. "I live on Świętego Rocha Street, it's night now, it's far away, and I'm scared. The German patrols will surely arrest me on the way." They let me in, asked whether I had had dinner with my friend, and whether my parents wouldn't be worried. They let me sleep on a sofa, under a woolen blanket.

In the early spring of 1944, Schade invited Chaika and me to visit him at home. His Polish domestic served dinner and walked away, leaving the three of us alone. Schade stood up, walked over to the windows to make sure they were locked, checked all the doors, and sat down at the table again. For a moment he was silent, gazing at us. Then he said, "I need help. I hid Mina and her cousin Mira in a village with some peasants. The situation on the front is changing and I want to move them to the partisans in the forest." We spent the whole evening weighting the options. We agreed to come back to him with an answer as to the date, place and route. Only after we moved Mina to the forest did she tell us that she had spent the whole evening sitting in the space over our heads, in the attic, not making a sound. Schade had maintained absolute compartmentalization to the very end. I have no doubt that he was absolutely right in doing so.

We spent a whole year with the partisans, coming and going and delivering and hauling and feeling a sense of belonging and intimacy. We visited for festivals and stayed two or three days, set out on operations, participated in ambushes, explored the forest until we knew it well, and learned to plant mines and sabotage railroad tracks. We sat with the partisans on lengthy evenings around bonfires in the forest. When the Soviets came, Wojciechowski gave his partisans special orders about how they should behave when the *dziewoczki,* the girls, were in the forest: an absolute ban on profanity and crude behavior. He treated us as though we were his daughters.

One evening, Lisa and I delivered an important shipment to a provisional camp near the road. The company had set up camp for the night as it prepared to intersect with another company for the purpose of establishing a new camp deep in the forest. Wojciechowski was with the other company that was supposedly on its way. His stand-in with our company was the *politruk,* the political-education officer, a quiet man delicate and sensitive, Kuźmin was one of the most revered partisans of all, a boundlessly courageous Ukrainian and an expert in fieldcraft. A truly fearless warrior, he was the first in blowing up tracks and trains, the first in every operation. Had he lived, he would have amassed the largest collection of citations in the brigade. On each of our visits, he described what he had managed to accomplish since our previous get-together. Sometimes he accompanied his accounts with photos of dead Germans and blown-up and destroyed targets. Afterwards he described his home and family. He withdrew pictures from an inside pocket and said, "Here's my mother, Matulka, Matyushka. Here, close to the heart."

Night. We sat and waited for the second company to arrive. Suddenly the sounds of singing and shouting violated the nocturnal silence. Kuźmin had got drunk. It wasn't the first time. Occasionally he drank himself to inebriation and became a different man. Now his raucous abandon placed the entire company in mortal danger, especially with the encampment so close to the road. Wojciechowski loved the man dearly. Several times he warned him to lay off the booze. When that didn't help, he threatened to kill him the next time, but he adored and appreciated the guy so much that he didn't keep his word. All that evening, the *politruk* tried to remonstrate with him: "Don't drink, don't get drunk. If the Commissar comes, he'll carry out his threat." Kuźmin continued to drink. The second company arrived late that night, Wojciechowski with them. He must have heard Kuźmin's commotion from afar. When he reached us, he didn't say a word to us. Instead, he turned to Kuźmin and said simply, "Step out." Kuźmin turned and stumbled into the forest, followed by Wojciechowski. Wojciechowski didn't have the guts to shoot Kuźmin while looking him in the face. Kuźmin didn't get far. We sat there, glued to the spot, making no sound, knowing what would happen in another moment and already feeling the anguish, the agony and the shriveling of the heart. Then came the gunshot, followed by sudden stillness and the sight of the body crumpling to the ground. Lisa and I shuddered. The partisans fell silent. All heads were bent, all lips sealed. The first to speak was the *politruk*. He tried to explain: "He endangered us all. The Commissar warned him." I couldn't forgive Wojciechowski for the ease with which he pulled the trigger. You don't kill a man that way. A friend. A combatant. They should have bound him whenever he began to drink. We returned to Białystok before daybreak, maintaining silence all the way. For weeks afterwards, Lisa and I talked about it over and over.

The summer of 1944 came. The Red Army advanced; the Germans began to retreat. Division headquarters forwarded a request via our people in the forest: we need accurate information about the German military disposition in Białystok — anti-aircraft weapons, minefields, anti-tank trenches, artillery. Busse brought me a large map of the city and I began to mark it up. Then we girls combed the city for hours in search of anti-aircraft and artillery positions. Schade and Busse augmented this with everything they knew, and members of the Belarusian and Polish resistance provided more. It took weeks, but we drew an accurate map of the German disposition.

The front approached. We had a physical sense of something new taking shape, of change, of an event that steadily made itself clear with the passage of days and, afterwards, fractions of days and even hours. Now we heard the distant rumbles of artillery, watched German families heading west in cars sagging with crates, and encountered German soldiers selling weapons and ammunition to Poles or bartering them for civilian suits in which they could hide. Chaos in the making.

Busse suggested we move into his atelier (art studio). He was worried about what might happen to us among the Poles specifically during these last days. He had lots of room up there; if more people had to be concealed, it would be just the place. The atelier was in the spacious attic of a wooden house on Lipowa Street, separate from his residence and the office. A bunch of us moved there: Chaika, Lisa, Anja, Bronja and I; Łódźia Bodek, wife of the partisan Felek Rosenblum; and other Jews who were hiding in town. We didn't tell Missja and Tosiek a thing. One day, we simply didn't come back.

We'd completed the mapping operation. Everything was sketched out,

Otto Busse — member of the German   Arthur Schade — member of the German
cell of the Białystok resistance   cell of the Białystok resistance

marked and written down. I prepared to leave for the forest in the morning in order to deliver the map and join the partisans in the battle for Białystok. Schade decided not to return to Germany; he would fight with the partisans in the forest. Busse decided to join, too; he sent his wife and son to Tilsit.

Evening. We readied ourselves for the trip. Busse appeared at the atelier. He had changed his mind. "I'm too old, Halinka," he said. "You go fight without me. I don't want to become a burden to you after the war. You know what I've done; the partisans know, too. But everyone else will think that I'm a German and a murderer. You'll always have to protect me. I don't want to entangle you." He reached into his pocket and withdrew a gold ring. "If Bluma comes back alive, give it to her. I've guarded it painstakingly for two whole years: in battles, in war, running borders, in overland marches, in poverty and in frost. I wanted so badly to hand it to Bluma." Here is what became of it: one evening at story time in the children's home, it slipped off my finger and landed under the cupboard. Wanda withdrew the ring, ran away from the house, and sold it for some candy.

When we returned from the forest to Białystok, Arthur Schade returned with us. The NKVD agents neither understood nor believed the German who had served their cause during the war. He was taken to Minsk; Mina Kiselstein stayed at his side. She spent months with him. When the interrogations ended, he was sent to East Germany, where he spent his remaining years in Pössneck, staying in touch with Lisa and Anja throughout.

Yad Vashem recognized Schade as Righteous Among the Nations; The Israeli ambassador in Bonn presented his son the certificate confirming his exploits.

Otto Busse did not go to the forest with us. Taken prisoner by the Soviets, he stated that he had been a member of the anti-Fascist underground in Białystok. They didn't believe him. In 1950, he was liberated in an exchange of prisoners and returned to Tilsit, only to find that his wife and son had been killed in bombardments. He married Erna and spent the rest of his life with her. They had no children.

After the war, Chaika and I searched for Busse ceaselessly. We wrote letters, asked questions, and made other efforts. No one knew a thing. In 1955, the connection was restored by means of the Jewish Agency Relatives Tracing

Otto Busse is honored as Righteous Among the Nations at Yad Vashem, 1970.
Right to left: Aryeh Kubovy, Chairman of Yad Vashem; Chaika Grossman;
Otto Busse; Chasia; Bronja Winicka-Klebanski

Department. It was Busse who had turned to them and found us through their offices.

Busse and Erna moved to Israel and lived for several years at Nes Amim. Later they returned to Germany due to health problems, settled in Dillenburg, and lived on a small pension they received from the Nes Amim movement.

Otto Busse was recognized as Righteous Among the Nations, and planted a tree with his own hands, together with all of the partisans who were living in Israel, on the Avenue of the Righteous at Yad Vashem in Jerusalem.

We headed for the forest at daybreak, Schade posing as a Polish peasant with worn boots and a faded coat, a backpack and a cumbersome bicycle with a burlap potato sack tied to its handlebars. In the sack, Schade had placed a Schmeisser submachine gun and a round magazine. I concealed the map in my case and camouflaged it with Rocheleh's vest, some underwear, a towel and the blue coat — everything I owned.

We walked along the path to the forest. We moved toward the front; opposite us was a convoy of retreating German tanks, military vehicles weaving among them. Occasionally we were stopped for inspection. "This is my uncle. He's a deaf-mute; I do the talking for him."

"You're walking toward the front," the Germans warned us. "They'll kill you. They're Polish murderers."

I replied with a show of fear: "But our family is in the village! They'll be worried if we don't come. All our uncle's young children are at home." Each time, I gave the name of the next village on the way. I didn't swerve from the story even once.

We continued to walk for several hours as the column of tanks retreated in the opposite direction. In midday of all times, with everyone out in the open, exposed and visible, we had nothing to hide. Had we taken the walk at night, we would have been suspected at once. We made it to the forest: a long path, a layer of pine needles, oak leaves, ferns, ivy winding around the tree trunks, cones and acorns crunching underfoot. A tall forest: dense crowns of trees hiding the sun. Dull light, sunbeams drawing diagonals of light. The deeper we went, the more the clatter of the tanks and the sounds of war receded. We reached the rendezvous point — the torched Soviet tank from the summer of 1941 — and sat down to wait for dark.

Dusk. A group of partisans stepped out of the forest. A birdcall intersected our voices. Later that night, the map I had delivered would be sent on to the attacking Soviet forces. I wanted to be the courier who would pass the map through the front lines, but Wojciechowski said, "You have a Grodno accent: you say *heh* instead of *geh*. You'll say 'Hitler' instead of 'Gitler.' The moment they ask you a question, they'll know where you're from. So it would be very dangerous for you, Galinka." A few hours later, two men crossed the lines and the map reached its destination.

Evening in the camp: the silence of the forest was illuminated by the long twilight of summer. We were in waiting mode; no one headed out on operations. Vigilance ruled. Suddenly there was a commotion: a group of people approached. Startled by the unexpected noise, we gathered in the middle of the camp. A group of *vlasowcyws* approached our comrades on guard at the edge of the forest: sixteen Russians and Ukrainians who had collaborated and fought with the Germans. They were turning themselves in hoping to receive clemency. Within a few minutes, the partisans had set up a military tribunal for them. It handed down its verdict — summary execution — and Felek and a few other partisans carried it out.

Two days of stress and uncertainty followed. We remained in the forest camp as the front closed in. The ground trembled all night from the torrent of shells it absorbed. The sky filled with flashing bullets. The tumult continued the next day, intensifying on the second evening. Certain that the Germans had surrounded us, we tore down the camp and sat on the bundles. The relentless cumulative noise, night and day, deafened us until it hurt. Orders were shouted into ears: we were to flee in the direction opposite to the one in which the Germans would raid us. Just flee. Guards were posted around the clock at a radius of about 500 meters from the middle of the camp. We were all at our stations; no one slept. Before dawn, the guards came in on the run, clutching a wooden board they had found nailed to a tree. They showed it to Commissar Osipov, the company commander. He said, "Run over there fast. Put it back where you got it from. It's a directional sign the Red Army scouts left for the force that's following them."

Slowly the Red Army surrounded us, first individually and then in groups of escalating size. I will never forget the elation that accompanied the encounter with them: a sense of relief, salvation and immense delight. The unbelievable had happened. The war was over. It hit us all at once: the war was over! Eyes flooded with tears that no longer reflected incessant weeping. They were just tears that welled up. Through their translucence I saw an enormous oak tree, walked over to it, and sat down at a corner of its trunk, alone, quietly. The war was over. What now?

Throughout the years of the war I had not really thought — we had not really thought — about the moment when it would end. It was so unrealistic. We were totally mobilized for the movement, the resistance, the ghetto, the forest. Suddenly the war was behind us and I had survived. Whom did I still have in the world? Where did Jews still exist? All that remained were the comrades in the forest, the girls on the Aryan side, and a few Jews hiding in town who had not belonged to the resistance. I had no family, no mother, father, Avramele, his wife Bella, Rocheleh or Zipporka. Gone were all the uncles and aunts and their children, my comrades in the Carmel Gdud with whom I had grown up for eight years, the wide circle of friends in the Grodno cell, my comrades-in-arms. If at the beginning of the war people had been asked to predict who would survive, no one would have submitted my candidacy, I least of all. I couldn't understand how, among my entire extended family and the whole glorious Grodno cell, I of all people had survived. I clung to the oak all that evening. The others went wild with joy, firing all their weapons in the air, drinking *samogon* (a form of vodka that peasants made from potatoes), and singing songs.

I always wanted to fire a *polymyot*, a machine gun. When I joined the partisans to lay mines or attack trains, they never let me operate it. I always pleaded with the *polymyotchik*, the machine gunner, "Let me do it once." Now, in the tumult of that night, he suddenly came over and said, "Galinka, come. Now you can fire as much as you want." I grabbed the *polymyot* with both hands. The intensity of my fury, anguish and grief, coupled with the shock of the moment — the end of the accursed war that I had never expected to survive — glued me to the trigger. I couldn't stop. A ghastly rage gripped me inside. The rhythmic automatic fire, the pounding, the body absorbing the blows of the recoil as the round ejected, the assembly shifted back, and the next round clattered into place. Dual strikes: of the metal, the pin and the explosion of the bullets, and of ceaseless sobbing. It was only the intensity of life that got me through that night.

July 27, 1944. In the morning, the Soviet forces headed west. Some of the partisans joined them in order to pursue the Germans and attack their rear all the way to Berlin. We stayed behind with those who could not walk. We spent another night in the forest; the front still fighting ahead of us. A procession of tanks, military vehicles and artillery pieces passed us by. We decamped and, together with Red Army soldiers, entered and liberated Białystok.

I ran to Busse's atelier. The door was open. In the attic, all was silent. No one was there. The girls and the men who had been hiding with them were gone. I didn't believe it. Now of all times. In the last hours. The only girl who had not gone into hiding with us was Miriam, Chaika's sister. I scurried down the stairs and ran to Parkowa Street, intending to visit the houses where we had worked. On one of the street corners, something strange happened. I couldn't digest it for a moment. Signs were posted on all the homes along the street. I stopped and read the nearest one: "Beware, typhus! Danger of epidemic!"

In the panic of the retreat, the girls had joined the last of the resistance members who had posted the signs on every building the quarter. Typhus was a dreaded and a dreadful thing to contract. Few survived it. The ruse kept the Poles away from the abandoned houses. I found our people in Miriam's apartment. By that evening, all the partisans had also gathered on Parkowa. We entered the apartments and found them clear of Germans.

Due to the map I had prepared, the Soviet Army and the partisans occupied Białystok without casualties. The next day, in the spacious yard of the Werkzentrale, they threw a party for us *dziewoczki*, the girls on the Aryan side. It was their way of thanking us for everything we had done for them. My memories of the excitement of that evening have hardly faded: the bottles of booze, the thunderous singing, the huge pot of hot, sizzling tea, and the burn that I sustained when some of that tea spilled on me from the metal cup.

Białystok was a liberated city now. We formed a commune. All the partisans were there. We busied ourselves in particular by testifying to NKVD agents about Schade. They couldn't believe that he was for real. Schade hadn't been able to convince them and we couldn't do it either. They repeatedly investigated his exploits with the partisans and his anti-Fascist credentials. In our spare time, we returned to the ghetto and combed the houses and streets for people who may have returned from places we didn't know about. I didn't go back to the former commune apartment. I avoided all the houses I used to frequent.

We did not properly internalize the meaning of liberation. We had not yet allowed our pain and grief to really sink in. Five girls had spent almost two years underground, one year in active partisan service, and five-and-a-half years at war. Suddenly we could raise our heads. What a contradiction: strolling around town with a mighty sense of triumph, unafraid, not looking behind to see if we were being tailed, surrounded with the partisan company's warmth, love and concern.

One morning, I walked down the middle of Lipowa Street with a group from the partisans. All of us were armed. Suddenly Missja was there, racing toward me, pouncing on me with hugs and kisses. "Halinka, Halinka, *Ja cię kocham*, I love you. I was so worried for you, where did you disappear to?" Then in one stroke she fell silent, staring at the young men around me, flinching backward.

"Missja, I want to tell you something," I said. "And after I say it, I'm not sure you'll love me any more." The boys formed a circle around us and stood still. "Missja," I told her, "I am a Jew and these are my brethren, Jewish partisans."

Her face turned white, almost transparent: the pallor of a person who's scared to death. She stared at me, at the partisans, and at me again, and couldn't get a word out of her mouth. I don't know what she thought about first: my Jewishness versus their antisemitism? Or the fact that she had unknowingly accommodated a Jewish woman in her home for almost two years? Or maybe the death penalty they would have faced had the matter been discovered?

"Missja," I said, "I love you all the same. You were good to me. But I know this is hard for you." Still, she couldn't manage to say a word.

After she left, I told the men about Missja, and Tosiek the antisemite. We vacillated about whether to target him for revenge. I felt bad about what that would do to Missja, who had never said a bad word about Jews. I felt bad about turning her into a lonely widow with a young child. I felt bad about the boy who would be orphaned of his father. "Forget it," I told the men. I never saw her again.

I cannot forgive myself for several things. The more the years pass, the less comprehensible I find them. After the ghetto was gone and there was nowhere to cross into, we stopped visiting Olla and her family. Then our surreptitious movements turned toward the forest. We avoided places we didn't need to visit for the requirements of the resistance. As the front closed in, we were in as much danger as ever. Then, after it was all over — the era of the partisans, the victory over the Germans and the Germans' retreat — I did not return to Olla. We did not return to Olla. I did not remain in Białystok; I rushed back to Grodno. But that wasn't the reason. I try to think: at what moment did we truly begin to understand what had happened to us? Was it when the Germans ran away in defeat? By "what had happened," I do not mean the regaining of freedom, but the loss. Five girls on the Aryan side, each the sole survivor of her family. All our comrades had been killed in the uprising or murdered in *Aktionen*. Not to mention the years of terror and fear, displacement, hunger and ubiquitous, continual death all around us. All these factors may explain why we did not take the opportunity to visit our benefactors again. Deep down and far away, as though detached from the surrounding world, we lived in a steadily expanding bubble of pain, the nature of which became more evident with each passing day.

Anja Rod — liaison

Chaika Grossman — liaison

Bronja Winicka — liaison,
1942, Yad Vashem Photo
Archives, 1618

Chasia Bielicka — liaison

Lisa Czapnik — liaison

Olla and her family, the *wujek*, the geography teacher, Jan and his family, Bronja from the house on the way to the forest, the good "Savta." We never went back to them to say thank you. We couldn't do it. I am not sure the explanation I offer is the right one. But I have no other. All I have is sadness, remorse and the need to apologize to these people, for myself and for the others, for being unable to have acted differently.

About My Comrades

Girls on the Aryan Side

As the years recede, I think more and more about ourselves and our parents. How had we endured those farewells? We weren't alone; there were others like us. Where did we get the tremendous strength to create a total disconnect between the daughter and the member of the combat underground?

No one drafted us; no one sent us. We were drafted and sent by our own inner convictions.

We weren't trying to save our own lives; we did no go into hiding to elude death. We mobilized on behalf of the Jewish people and behaved like inductees committed above all to their war.

Were it not for the role I had chosen, had I not been sent to the Aryan side to establish an outside support system for the ghetto, surely I would not have gone out to save myself. We would not have gone out to save ourselves.

Chaika and Miriam Grossman remained in Białystok. When the war ended, Chaika went to Warsaw and enlisted in movement and public activity. In 1948, she reached Israel and joined Kibbutz Evron. She married Meir Orkin and they had two daughters. She devoted all of her years in Israel to public activity, initially as chair of Matte Asher Regional Council, for years a leading figure in the left-wing Mapam Party, a Member of the Knesset on behalf of this party for several terms, and Deputy Speaker of the Knesset. In 1996, she died in an accident.

Bronja formed a relationship with a partisan parachutist and went away with him. Later on, she made *aliya* and spent the rest of her years working in the Yad Vashem Archives.

Anja, Lisa Czapnik and I returned to Grodno to see if anyone else had survived and returned. Later on, Anja and Lisa moved to the Soviet Union.

Both studied English in Moscow, received professorial appointments, and taught English at the university of Rjazan. They were inseparable throughout the years. In 1990, they immigrated to Israel. Anja did not remarry; she settled in Tel Aviv and recently moved to Beersheba. Lisa and her husband, Julek Mashewicki, live in Beersheba. Their daughter, Ala, died of leukemia at the age of fifteen. Their son Grisha is a professor of mathematics at Ben-Gurion University of the Negev. A terrible tragedy befell Lisa and her family; her grandson Alex Maszewicki was killed in Operation Cast Lead in Gaza in 2009. Due to distance, age and health, we no longer get together as much as we would like, but every evening at 10 p.m. the telephone rings. We talk for hours and fill the gap that way.

Marylka Różycka stayed in Poland and married a Jewish Communist, a high-ranking officer in the Polish army. They had two children. Marylka was killed in a traffic accident in Copot, Poland.

All the Girls on the Aryan Side
1. Bronja Winicka, a.k.a. Jadwiga Skibel — Dror, Grodno
2. Anja Rod, a.k.a. Agatha Kisli — Grodno
3. Lisa Czapnik, a.k.a. Marysia Morozowska — Communists, Grodno
4. Marylka Różycka, a.k.a. Marylka Michalek — Communists, Łódź
5. Chaika Grossman, a.k.a Halina Woronowicz — Hashomer Hatzair, Białystok
6. Chasia Bielicka, a.k.a. Halina Stasiuk — Hashomer Hatzair, Grodno
7. Riwkele Medajska, a.k.a. Marysia Medajska — Hashomer Hatzair, Vilna
8. Chanka Lewin — Hashomer Hatzair, Białystok
9. Chancia "Di Oelle" Jerzierski — Hashomer Hatzair, Grodno
10. Sarka Shewachowicz — Hashomer Hatzair, Grodno
11. Sarah Dobeltow — Hashomer Hatzair, Vilna
12. Rocheleh Bielicka — Hashomer Hatzair, Grodno
13. Fania Lipkies — Hashomer Hatzair, Grodno
14. Miriam Grossman — Hashomer Hatzair, Białystok
15. Mina Kiselstein — Hashomer Hatzair, Białystok, in hiding
16. Mira Kaplan — Hashomer Hatzair, Białystok, in hiding
17. Łódźia Bodek, Lodka Dobrowolska — wife of the partisan Felek Rosenblum
18. Hanka Zelinska and her son, who stayed with the *wujek*

Cyla Szachnes

Cyla and I were very close and good friends. From childhood to adolescence to adulthood we belonged to the same group in the Hashomer Hatzair Carmel Gdud. The three weeks we spent at the "executives' colony" in August 1939, in Olegsowki near Zakopane, along with the trip home amid the terror of the encroaching war, turned us into soul mates and intensified the love and camaraderie we felt for each other.

In the first days of the Soviet occupation, Cyla visited me because she missed me passionately and was concerned for my well-being. She lived across the Niemen River, in the Forstat. When we said goodbye, I made her swear that as soon as she reached the other side of the river, at the Hashomer Hatzair training center in Leib Jaffe's home, she would stop and wave until I waved back. I stood on the bank of the river, among the houses across Podolna Street, until I saw her hand flapping.

How courageous she had to be to take that walk amid the uncertainty of the first days of the occupation, defying the general curfew that had been declared in Grodno. When we entered the Białystok ghetto in January 1943, the resistance leadership decided that Cyla should return to Grodno in order to fetch Zorach, and that I should move to the Aryan side. With her smooth blonde hair, glittering blue eyes and fair complexion, Cyla looked Polish. Though she spoke the language with the Jewish accent of students at Tarbut Gymnasium, she nevertheless returned to Grodno alone so that Zorach would not have to make the trip by himself. A couple was less suspicious than a man alone would be, so she accompanied him back to Białystok.

Until Rocheleh reached the Białystok ghetto, I shared a narrow bed with Cyla whenever I entered the ghetto. I knew that Cyla could not take part in underground activity on the Aryan side; the Poles would immediately have identified her Jewish accent. The only possibility was to find her a job and a place to live with Germans. With her unflappability and audacity, she could use her place of residence as a communication base. Our aim was to place as many people on the Aryan side as possible, to arrange as many available apartments as possible, for the aftermath of the uprising. I don't know what considerations guided the decisions and choices about which girls to send out, but Cyla was not sent.

Poles During the War

I am about to hazard a generalization — a sweeping generalization, as all generalizations are. However, the exceptions were so few that I dare to speak of the rule in the plural.

It was not only as a Jew that I experienced antisemitic hostility. I also lived as a Polish woman and immersed myself in the simple, mundane social fabric of Polishness. Poles really believed that we Jews murdered Christian children in order to use their blood in the baking of Passover matzah. They really believed that Jews were cheats, liars, thieves and carriers of infectious diseases. They imbibed sermons in church and venomous preachings from infancy on. Generations were raised on escalating hatred.

When Missja's Tosiek first met me in their home, the first thing he said was, "Before the war I had a really nice dog: he barked only at Jews!"

The Poles lived under occupation but their schools, hospitals and clinics were open. Peasants came to market. Shoemakers, seamstresses and watchmakers worked; postal and telephone services worked.

The Poles endured rationing and deprivation but they worked and received salaries. Many Poles in Białystok raised swine; some also had chickens. They bought baby pigs and fattened them all year long on leftover food. Afterwards, they slaughtered them for Christmas and ate pork for months. Theirs was an impoverished life, but definitely a viable one. Things were even easier for the villagers. They grew their food. The Germans took some of it but left them with enough to survive. Money could buy anything: beef, butter, eggs, sausage, cheese.

Perhaps I'm talking about the Poles, the Polish resistance organizations, from our vantage point. We Jews were locked up in ghettos, under constant mortal threat, hungry, isolated and almost devoid of ways to communicate, equip ourselves or fight. Notwithstanding their freedom of movement, their communications and their living conditions, relatively few Poles joined resistance groups. We were much more enterprising and active. The Germans attacked Poles only in response to the murder of German soldiers or resistance assaults on military or police facilities. In their daily lives, Poles were not persecuted. Some even maintained friendly relations with Germans. In years of retrospect, however, I think about the duality, the ambivalence, which typified the attitude of most of the population toward the Germans. Yes, they lived under a lengthy occupation that trampled their national pride. When it came to saving Jews, however, I am not speaking about those who held their silence, did not help, or were afraid for their lives and those of their families. I am speaking about denouncers, betrayers and murderers. Those who stood at the ghetto gates, watching the Jews being transported, and rejoiced in their misery. Those who considered us wretched "Jewboys" instead of human beings, and celebrated when they saw the Germans doing the work they considered correct: obliterating, exterminating the Jews.

I don't know if I'm right, but over the years I've been feeling more and more that the Germans were prompted by more than blind chance when they chose to establish the extermination camps on Polish soil: not on German soil, lest it be contaminated with millions of dead Jews; not in Czechoslovakia, Hungary, or any other country. They established the camps in Poland, knowing that the Poles would not object, would not rise up, would not get in the way.

The Poles must have known — if not at first, then some time later — that the Germans were exterminating the Jews. Treblinka, Majdanek and Auschwitz could not have been ignored, if only due to the smoke of the crematoria. Nor could the rest of the camp apparatus have been overlooked, such as the huge numbers of trains that set out full and came back empty. Everyone saw — locomotive engineers, station personnel and the people who lived along the tracks.

I am horrifically angry at the Poles. I seethe, I resent. I am neither willing nor able to forgive them for the way they treated us before and during the war.

CHAPTER 7

Back to Grodno

The first time I returned to my real home, I went alone... Nothing had changed. All the houses were intact. So were the signposts, the fruit trees, the vegetable gardens, the curtains in the windows, the smoke from the chimneys, the voices of children and the flowing Niemen River. Only we weren't there. Podolna Street was Judenrein.

One day in the middle of the night, Lisa and Anja found me sprawling at the door. They had awakened in panic to the thud of my falling body. I had gotten up to use the latrine, I explained, and must have stumbled. Only much later did I tell them that I had a dream about my mother: someone suddenly knocked on my door, and Mother came in. I climbed out of bed and walked toward her. Her face was so close and clear within a circle of light that I wanted to touch it. Mother said, "Chasinka, Chasialeh, *bleyb shteyn,* stand still, *Gey nisht vu ich bin... Du bleyb do Chasinka mayn tayerinke.* Don't walk over to me. Stay where you are, my dear Chasinka."

Never before and never again did I dream about Mother.

In September 1944, we — Anja, Lisa and I — returned to Grodno. We did it by train, just as I had left Grodno, the same route.

A Polish autumn: plains stretching to the horizon; forests of pine and fir, oak trees, rivers, isolated farms scattered among villages. Houses of wood.

277

Cranes' nests abandoned ahead of winter. Geese aloft. Fields of harvested potatoes, dark plum orchards.

A one-hour train ride. I cannot remember what I thought. I don't think
I forgot; I think I simply didn't think about anything. These are the defenses
that the psyche erects around itself when it's going to a place where everything
is lost.

From our standpoint, the journey began at that moment: three sad girls
traveling to a town that had been emptied of its Jews. A group of partisans, including Eva Kraczowska and Josef Makowski, had received a large apartment
on Pocztowa Street. They picked us up the day we arrived. Our partisan comrades Eliahu "Elyosha" Warat, Mulia Nisht and Sergei Berkner, along with
Golda, also came to town.

The few surviving Jews of Grodno had begun to return: Salomon Zhu-
kowski, a Yiddishist, Communist and teacher; Felix Zandman and his uncle
Sender Freydovicz, Fela and Moshe Bielodworski, Josze Wajs and Tanja

From right to left: Felix Zandman, Chasia,
Sender Freydovicz, 1945

Prenska-Kaplan. Some of them found housing with the Freydoviczes, who had been wealthy metal merchants in Grodno before the war. Another arrival was Hershele Chasid, who had leaped off a train to Treblinka. Injured, he had survived by joining the partisans, with whom he saw combat action. He had been our neighbor on Podolna Street and a classmate of my sister's at Tarbut Gymnasium. His sister Naomi, a member of my Gdud, was murdered along with her whole family. Hershele still lives in Grodno.

The entire cadre of commanders from the partisan army in the forests of Białystok settled in Grodno, headed by the divisional commander, Gen. Kapusta, and the *Kombrig*, the brigade commander, Wojciechowski. They deemed us to have been equal partners in the war; as such, now we were worthy of protection like all other partisans, if not more so. Several days later, we received an apartment, ration cards and an arrangement for lunch at the public kitchen. We had the feeling that revenge had been taken. The town had become a charred ruin. Downtown was destroyed: Báthory Square, Mostowa Street, which led to the railroad bridge, and many other buildings. Not only our Jewish Forstat but also Polish streets had been damaged by bombardments and set ablaze.

We visited the ghetto on our first morning back in Grodno. The first stop would be the ruins of what had been my family's apartment, my last home in that life. From Zamkowa Street I turned onto Ciasna Lane. Through the breached ghetto gate I passed the Yavne School, where the *Judenrat* had had its offices. The spacious schoolyard was empty, littered with intermingling shreds of paper, shards of glass and autumn leaves. Down the street I turned left, followed narrow alleys, and came to Krochmalna.

I went up the stairs. The door was wide open. Inside was chaos: bits of furniture, shreds of torn clothing, fragments of shattered dishes, and pieces of paper. I don't know when the place was trashed — during the last *Aktion*, in the looting that followed the liquidation of the ghetto, or some time afterwards — a year-and-a-half, composed of one winter, two springs, two summers, and one autumn.

In the jumble of objects, I found one lonely document: a *Judenausweis*, a German ID card for Jews. It had belonged to Bella, my sister-in-law, Avramele's wife. A few days later, we went from house to house and visited what had been the community institutions, gathering up pictures, documents and any piece of paper that had legible writing on it. Anything, whether we knew the people or not. Thus, I was privileged to find pictures of my brother Avramele with his whole class at the Tarbut Gymnasium.

The first time I returned to my real home, I went alone, taking the whole way on foot, crossing Mostowa Bridge and turning onto Podolna Street under the railroad bridge. The bridge had blocked the great fire that swept the city. Thus, the southern part of the street, including our home, had survived.

Nothing had changed. All the houses were intact. So were the signposts, the fruit trees, the vegetable gardens, the curtains in the windows, the smoke from the chimneys, the voices of children and the flowing Niemen River. Only we weren't there. The parents, siblings, uncles and aunts, the Chasid family, the seamstress and her daughters, Cebulski the shoemaker, the Littman family — the bakers — the Karons, who had lived farther up the street, and the So-kolowskis. Podolna Street was *Judenrein*.

I stepped into the courtyard and passed the gate and the picket fence. The threshold, the garden, the woodshed, the workshop — all were intact. I knocked on the door. I had never done that before. A Polish woman who had lived down the street before the war opened the door a crack: suspicious, fearful, aggressive. All I wanted was to see the house, I said, but she slammed the door shut.

The shock of the thud. The stinging pain. I crossed the courtyard to the Michaeloviches. A moment later I was enveloped in happiness, affection and love. They sat me down, fed me and asked me to tell my story. I told them a little; I didn't really say anything. Then Michaelowa opened her wardrobe and pulled out a large book with a brown cover and old, yellowed pages. "It's yours," she said.

The *ksiazka meldunkova,* the "house book," the courtyard book. Touching it was like touching the living, touching the dead. Every house or court-yard had a book of records. Record keeping was compulsory; you had to write down births and deaths, weddings and funerals, the names of temporary and permanent tenants. The records in this book, all of them, appeared in Father's beautiful penmanship, most in Polish, some in Russian. I recognized only two dates: Avramele's birthday, which fell during Hanukkah, and my own. Suddenly I saw them all again: Father, Mother, Uncle Chaim, Aunt Rosa and all their children, the death of my grandfather, whom I had never known, and of my grandmother, whom I had loved. For a moment I was with all of them. I didn't ask the Michaeloviches whether they had removed anything from the house – the bronze and silver urns, the bedding and the pillows, the furniture and the clothing. The Germans had looted whatever remained in the Jews' homes, they said. Some of the Polish neighbors had got there before them. "I didn't want to take anything of yours," Michaelowa said. "Just this book as a momento, and here, I'm giving it back to you. I kept it the whole year. It sat next to the bed in a pile of textbooks."

The morning I left Grodno for good, I forgot the book in the course of our passionate farewells. Lisa and Anja kept it until it was taken by the NKVD interrogators who came to arrest Anja. Mother had given our fur coats to a Polish neighbor in another courtyard, a widow who had one daughter, for safekeeping. I knocked on the door. "The Germans took everything," she said. As I turned away, the neighbor across the street, Mrs. Narbut, saw me and walked over. "They didn't take the furs," she said. "Those women have been wearing them."

I didn't turn it into a big deal. In retrospect, I've tried to understand my forbearance, my reluctance, my failure to insist on what was rightly mine.

Our apartment: Lisa, Anja and me, at 7 Klasztorna Street, Monastery Street, named for Saint Francis. It was in the center of town, an area that had not been demolished in the war. The Soviets had renamed the street Molodzi-ozna. Our apartment, in a two-story house, was spacious enough to be divided into two small units. You entered from the left side of the building, from the courtyard in the rear, by climbing a narrow staircase.

The apartment immediately became a cultural center. Everyone gathered there every evening, surrogates for the families we no longer had. The Soviet partisans sang, we joined in, and the others eventually learned. How much solace one can gain by singing together, by sharing rhythm, melody and lyrics. We sang about the forest, the snow, the pits, our fellow combatants, our dead brethren. Limitless nostalgia swept us away. We sang about them; we meant ourselves: our parents, sisters, brothers, aunts, uncles, grandparents and lots of children, a whole community, a whole population.

The apartment was unfurnished apart from two beds and a small, rickety closet. Lisa and I shared one bed; Anja used the other. We spent a whole year living that way. Furniture was hard to find. We had nothing to sit on and nothing to eat from. I told the girls, "There are chairs and a table in my house!"

Lisa and I didn't go there by ourselves; we were accompanied by a group of armed partisans. The boys knocked on the door and said, "We've come to take the Bielicki family's table and chairs." The woman, although stunned and deterred by the weapons, stood her ground: "They're not theirs. We replaced everything here." The boys called me over and asked me if I could identify the table and the chairs. I answered in the affirmative. Each boy took a chair, two of them carried the table, and out we went. I don't remember the interior of the Polish house. I didn't turn around. Nothing about it resembled our home. I did not want to get familiar with its other appearance.

Every day we visited the post office on Pocztowa Street to ask if any letters had come for us. One day, a clerk said, "There's lots of mail for Jews. We don't know what to do with it." There were letters from people who had escaped the German occupation by fleeing into the Soviet Union; they wanted to receive news about their families. We decided to take the letters and read and answer them all. We told the correspondents about the ghettos that had existed and the transports to death. We also told them what we didn't know.

That's how a letter from Oka Bolotin, my cousin, my Aunt Ita's daughter who had married a Jewish officer during the Soviet occupation, reached me. They were living in Voroshilov, on the Japanese border. In the envelope she had enclosed a photograph of Vova, her two-year-old son.

For a few weeks, we still nagged the Soviet authorities to allow us to come along with the army. Asserting our rights as partisans, we asked them to enroll us in a parachuting course. The war wasn't over. The victory over Germany had not been completed and we wanted to be partners to the end.

So badly did we want to continue fighting that one day we wrote to Ilya Ehrenburg, a Jewish writer and a confidante of Stalin's. We asked him to ask Stalin to authorize our enrollment in a parachuting course and our enlistment in the combat forces. Ehrenburg wrote back: "You fought, you did what you did, now go to school." Our older comrades, commanders of the partisan battalion, tried to appease us. Enough, they said. You've sacrificed enough. Start living.

I don't know whether we started living, but we received a Soviet government stipend and went to school.

Several days after we returned to Grodno, as we were still circulating in the streets, we had bumped into Valentina Ochanina, the principal of our *gymnasium* during the Soviet occupation. We thought she had gone to Grodno because of her official duties. We were wrong: this special, amazing woman had come to look for her Jewish students, to see who among us had survived and what she could do to help. From the place where we met she led us straight to the office of Vlasov, principal of the Pedagogic Institut, a teachers' college, across from Aliza Orzeszkowa's house.

At first the principal turned us away because we did not have diplomas certifying us as graduates of a *gymnasium*. Then Ochanina walked in, introduced us, and said, "These were my students. I testify about them; my word will be enough."

And it was: three Jewish students among a mass of Poles in a teachers' college opened by the Soviet administration. We didn't study. We attended all the classes but weren't really there. For hours we stared at the teachers and the blackboards but did not see them. Physically we assimilated into the new life; psychologically, however, we went on voyages of memory and sadness, pain and incomprehension, yearnings and anguish.

Rifkind, the partisan and math teacher, and his wife, the English teacher, adopted us. We visited them in the evenings and they made up what we had missed during our musings in the day. The daily walk to town was difficult. We passed the Jewish shops on Dominikanska Street, which remained shut; we passed Kapulski's and Zalucki's wonderful cafés, where we used to split a piece of cake into six pieces. We passed the movie theater, the way to the movement cell, the way home and the way to the forest. Again we saw the Niemen, the flow of its waters, and our reflections in them.

We ate lunch at a *stolovka,* a government cafeteria, in return for ration slips. Its hot soup, thick main dish and bread truly saved us during that long winter. At home, we had only the little food the distribution system provided. Two partisans, the Furie brothers, who had fled from the last *Aktion* in Grodno and had gone into hiding with peasants until they moved to the forests, invited us to join them. During their vacations from studies, they worked in a village for food. We joined them, Anja and Lisa in the fields and I at the home of peasants, making clothes for the whole family. We were paid in food: potatoes, butter, a whole basket of cabbage, eggs and bacon. The peasant drove us home in his laden cart. We spent all our vacations that year, however short, with this village family. When there was no fieldwork to do, Lisa and Anja helped me with my sewing, which was done by hand.

Almost a year after the war, we were still unable to free ourselves totally from the underground mentality. We suspected anyone on the path to the village who didn't look like a peasant. I went everywhere with the small handgun Busse had bought me.

At the teachers' college in Grodno. Foreground, middle: Professor Rifkind, who taught us math. To his right: Chasia; to his left, Lisa. Background, right to left: Rifkind's wife and Anja Rod, 1945

With regular housing in short supply, Red Army officers were billeted with families in town, as had happened in the first Soviet occupation. Misha — Michael Gorczakow, a Jewish officer in the Soviet army who had no connection whatsoever with Judaism — reached the Freydoviczes. Over time, he connected. He asked questions, kept his eyes open, displayed curiosity and became much closer to us. With his rank and status, he helped resolve any difficulty that couldn't be cleared up in civilian ways.

Elyosha, our Eliahu Warat from the partisans, was inducted as an officer in the NKVD and shared some of his food benefits with us. He circulated in the city streets on horseback. Sometimes I joined him and we headed out toward the Forstat and the Lososna forests, where he let me ride alone and experience this other form of freedom.

Late that year, Eliahu went to Białystok on furlough. About a week later, NKVD agents knocked on our door and searched for him in order to arrest him. Several days after their visit, I moved to Białystok. My most urgent task was to find him. I dashed from address to address, combing friends, buildings and people, to warn him not to return to Grodno. Then, crossing the street in front of the Ritz Hotel, I suddenly saw him standing in front of me: a Russian officer in uniform. What a happy encounter it was, what a relief: the dread of death dissipated.

"Elyosha," I said, "don't come back. They're looking for you. Run away!"

Chaika equipped him with civilian clothing. He crossed into Poland and survived. A short time later, the Soviet authorities also began to busy themselves with ideological matters. It was obvious that the war was winding down. The armies had moved off to the west, the Soviets annexed the Grodno area, and the NKVD went into action against the bourgeoisie and the capitalists.

Sender Freydovicz and his nephew, Felix Zandman, had spent the whole war in hiding. At first, the entire family had stayed in a shelter they had built in their large residence. After their hiding place was flushed out due to a denunciation, they fled to their Polish domestic, who lived near the Lososna forests, and she sheltered them in a pit dug into the soil — five people for almost a year-and-a-half, the sole vestiges of their family, Sender without his wife and children and Felix without his parents and siblings. During those months in the pit, Sender made a point of teaching Felix everything that he knew and retained. When our people informed us that Sender was being sought for the crime of being "bourgeois," we concealed him in our apartment. A few days later, Michael Gorczakow smuggled him into Poland.

Due to her function as chair of the central anti-Fascist committee of Białystok District, Lisa was summoned to testify to a special committee about our activities during the war. Several days later, we received certificates confirming our exploits, some of which were written up in detail. All the certificates carried a round stamp, a *kruglaia pieczać,* which was immeasurably more important than a square stamp. For our activities and the map I had delivered, each of us received an *ordien,* a special citation from the high echelon of the Red Army in World War II.

Tanja Prenska-Kaplan was the sister of Lena Prenska, whom Wiese had hanged in the ghetto. Both of them were beautiful. Before the war, Tanja had married Kaplan and given birth to their first-born daughter, Anja. A Polish nanny was brought in from a nearby village to take care of the girl. When the *Aktionen* in the ghetto began, the Kaplans asked the nanny to take two-year-old Anja to her home, and she agreed. Tanja delivered the girl and all her remaining property: clothing, a few utensils and some money. "If I don't get through the war," she instructed the nanny, "bring her up as your daughter."

When Tanja returned at the end of the war and asked for her daughter, the gentile woman refused to return her. She had no children of her own, she explained. Anja had become her daughter and she loved her dearly. It took Tanja weeks to convince the former nanny to surrender the girl. Even afterward, the Polish woman came in from the village every day to visit her. One day, as the two of them were alone for a moment, she abducted Anja and returned to the village. Tanja came to reclaim her; the nanny refused.

Tanja turned to the authorities, who decided to conduct a trial in the village. The nanny apprised Tanja of the expected outcome: "You're not going to get this girl. We baptized her into the Church. The whole village knows she's my daughter. The whole village had decided that if the court rules that she belongs to you and the Jews, we'll kill her. The Jews aren't going to get their hands on a proper Christian girl."

We all knew about the affair. We were few in number, but close and involved. Michael Gorczakow decided to do something about it. On the day of the trial, he drove up in a military truck and we all climbed aboard. "All" meant Tanja, Lisa, Anja, Sender Freydovicz and me, plus all the partisans in Grodno and several armed soldiers whom Gorczakow annexed to the force. The plan: the moment the court rules that the girl belongs to her Jewish mother, we abduct the girl and disappear.

The trial took place in a massive hall that resembled a granary, with huge metal doors, tiny windows and long wooden benches on which the entire population of the village sat, packed together. It was a threatening scene: they were numerous and they carried hatchets they did not even try to conceal. The judge sat at the end of the hall, behind a desk facing the crowd, flanked by army officers. The court was Soviet; so were the rules of jurisprudence and the judge.

We formed a living chain from the entrance and then along the wall to the first bench, which faced the judge. On the bench sat Tanja, the gentile woman with the girl on her lap and another young woman who I cannot identify, although she appears in some photographs that I kept from the time.

The truck was parked at the entrance of the building, its motor running, the driver at the wheel, and several of the armed soldiers guarding the perimeter. Then it happened: the judge ruled that the little girl belonged to her mother. At that moment, one of the partisans snatched the youngster from the Polish woman's arms, somebody else grabbed Tanja Kaplan, and the guards at the entrance opened the doors wide and kept the peasants from leaving.

We formed a protective wall around them and escorted them to the truck on the run. The soldiers covered us with their weapons as we climbed aboard and aimed our rifles at the mob that had begun to gather. After the last soldier clambered up, the driver roared away in mad dash. The group spent the night in an out-of-town hideout; the next morning Gorczakow smuggled them to Białystok.

Pinke Zilberblat, my boyfriend, wrote backwards. In Polish, the slant is supposed to follow the direction of the writing, from left to right. Pinke wrote the opposite way, from right to left. Very peculiar penmanship.

One evening, as we came home with our daily pile of letters, I noticed something about one of the envelopes. There was no mistaking it. I don't know which of my defense mechanisms I employed when I told the girls, "Look, the handwriting is like Pinke's!" I didn't even think it could have been a letter from him. Only when I flipped the envelope over did I see his name and address on the back. It wasn't a personal letter; he had addressed it to any surviving member of the Grodno community. He wanted to know what had become of his family and whether anyone had heard or known anything about them.

Although our war had ended several months earlier, there was still a war. Our existence was physical only. We occupied the world without being connected to the sensations and feelings that a new life would dictate. We were very sad, aching and not really alive. I say this again in order to explain that it was from that psychological location that I answered Pinke. It was a laconic, cold, dispassionate return letter. Apart from sorrow and grief, I don't think I entertained any emotion. I wrote to him as I would a stranger, not the love of my youth for five whole years. Truth to tell, I believed all that time that he was alive and had not been killed while running away. As I walked through the streets of Białystok, it sometimes seemed to me that I saw him in the persona of some blond *sheigetz* who crossed my path or approached me.

Dear Pinke. I was really happy to find out that you're alive because there were rumors that you'd been killed during the German occupation. I was in touch with your parents in the ghetto. I saw how your brother Feivel was murdered in the ghetto. No one in your family survived. I'm alone, too.

Several weeks later, a reply — a lengthy letter — arrived in a thick envelope. Pinke couldn't understand what had gone wrong. How had I answered his letter in such an estranged, reportorial way? Today, I can't understand it either, despite the explanations that I've offered. He asked how I was and what I was doing and told me that he was completing engineering studies and had only to pass the final exams before he'd return to Grodno. I wrote in response that I was studying, too, but that I was planning to go to Elimelech at the first possible opportunity.

Elimelech Hurwitz, our Gdud chief at Hashomer Hatzair, had made *aliya* to Kibbutz Dan before the war. "Elimelech" was the code for saying that I was on my way to Palestine.

Instead of answering this letter, Pinke sent a frantic cable: *Chasinka, don't go before I come. The exams are almost over. We'll go to Elimelech with my engineering diploma.*

I couldn't. I wasn't willing to reunite, probably due to the abyss that the war had opened between us.

I wrote to him: *I'm sorry, Pinke. Can't wait. We'll meet at Elimelech's.*

And a few days after I sent the letter, I went.

Summer of 1945: I'd spent a year in Grodno. The war was over.

When we had left Białystok, Chaika and I agreed that she would inform me if any movement activity started up. Marek Buch of the partisans was appointed to the Soviet repatriation committee in charge of the return of refugees from the USSR to Poland. He was our letter carrier; he held a permit that allowed him to cross the border freely.

After the war, the Soviet-Polish frontier ran halfway between Białystok and Grodno, near Kuznice. Grodno was on the Soviet side, in the area annexed to the USSR. Marek brought a letter from Chaika: she was moving to Warsaw. Many members of the movement were returning from Asian Russia, where they had fled from the war. They were beginning to reorganize Hashomer Hatzair.

For a month I was torn between my love for Lisa and Anja, who had chosen to stay in Communist Soviet Russia, and my life long aspiration of *aliya*.

No one around me believed that I could endure parting from my friends. "The three of you are a 'holy trinity,'" the comrades told us. "You're inseparable."

However, I found no point in living except *aliya*, my childhood dream and my adolescent ambition. Even if I had to walk for ten years, I said, I'd get there. Nothing would stop me. Not even my love for Lisa and Anja.

I spent all of my second life with a terrible internal schism: the ceaseless pain of that farewell. Years later, I still missed them, calling their names at night, speaking with them in night-dreams and daydreams, composing letters in my head, filling pages of real letters that could not be sent across the Iron Curtain.

They were my family; I was theirs. We had no close living soul in the whole world. We were us, and nothing else intruded. Whenever food was scant, each of us told the other that she had already eaten so that they would eat. When one of the partisans gave us a new pair of boots as a present, we took turns wearing them, each persuading the other that they needed them more. Anja had not been a Communist in her youth. An alumna of Tarbut Gymnasium and the teachers' seminary in Grodno, she had managed to study in Vilna before the war. When I decided that the time for *aliya* had come, Anja asked me to talk Lisa into making it a threesome. She was cooking, and as I stood at her side she whispered, "Halinka, talk with Lisa, she'll follow you."

The innocence of youth, the belief in my dreams and those of others. All her life Lisa had dreamed of living in a Communist country. Now that her dream had come true, I could not tear her away from it. I pondered it in terms of myself: how would they try to persuade me? I loved Lisa so. I couldn't do it to her. And Anja, good, grown-up, devoted Anja, decided not to leave her young sister-in-law alone.

If only the three of us had talked it over together.

When we had returned to Grodno, close friends of Anja's family, Polish people, gave her some possessions her mother had placed with them for safekeeping: bedding and tablecloths, a few utensils, some household items, and a diamond ring. She took a few of these things — we used them in our apartment — and left the rest with her family's benefactor.

Now, as I was about to leave, Anja said, "Take the ring. We're in good shape here; our future is assured. But where you're going, there's no telling what'll happen. Maybe you'll need it. Take the ring."

"Your mother's ring? The last thing of your mother's you own?"

I didn't take it.

Michael Gorczakow drove me from Grodno to Białystok. It was against all rules and regulations: a one-person escape operation. He asked me to be ready every morning, not knowing when an opportunity to cross the frontier without suspicion would come his way.

Every evening I arranged my few possessions in my small suitcase. Lisa and Anja insisted that I take the new boots that the partisans had given us because I was heading into a long winter in unknown locales. I stood my ground: I'm on my way to Palestine. It's warm there; I won't need good boots. You'll need them more than I in the approaching Russian winter.

One evening, Gorczakow dropped by and said that we'd be heading out first thing the next morning.

We didn't sleep all that night. The knowledge that we were parting, that I was going and they were staying, was almost inconceivable amidst the logic of our love.

In the bustle of organizing my things at dawn, I couldn't find my old boots. They weren't where I had left them at night. And they weren't anywhere else that I could think of.

"So put on the new boots," Lisa and Anja prodded me. I picked up my suitcase and out we went. At least Anja hadn't asked me to take the ring again.

The three of us sat in the bed of the truck. The two of them accompanied me in the chill of end-of-autumn morning until we were almost at the border. We cuddled silently under the darkness of the tarpaulin.

A short trip delivered us to Kuznice, where I'd have to pass inspection. The others climbed down and cried. I stood up, gripped the metal bars, and sobbed.

When the truck began to move, they shouted at me, "Take care of the skirt, take care of the skirt that you're wearing!" Their silhouettes, erect, embracing and waving on the other side of the steel fence, melted into a blur through the fog of my tears.

Take care of the skirt? What on earth did that mean? I began to think. In the underground, nothing was said unless it meant something. Every word had meaning. Take care of the skirt! I searched the pockets, thinking they might have planted another letter on top of their farewell entries in my notebook. I found nothing.

Białystok. By that night, I was with Chaika and Miriam in an apartment on Parkowa Street, in the building where my former employers, the Luchterhands, had lived. It was late. As I arranged my things for the night, I reached for the buttons of my skirt and suddenly felt a stabbing sensation: something hard at the end of the sash, next to the loop.

What fools, I said aloud, what fools. They had sewn the ring into the skirt because they knew I would refuse to take it. Much later, they also confessed in a letter to me that they had simply concealed my boots so that I would have to wear the new ones.

Before I set out from Białystok to Warsaw, I left the ring with Miriam and asked her to return it to Anja in Grodno by means of Marek Buch. Eventually it was lost or stolen. Either way, it was never found.

CHAPTER 8

June 1945–March 1946

It was my first encounter with somebody I'd known who had sur-
vived the death camps: everything they said dwarfed the hard-
ships I'd gone through during the war. When they stopped talking
and asked what had happened to me, I said, "Nothing. Nothing
happened to me," and from then on I held my silence. For years
after that encounter, I couldn't talk about my life during the war;
I couldn't retell it. After all, how did all the hardships, danger
and fears I'd endured compare with those of the people who'd
lived and died in the concentration and extermination camps?

June 1945

In one of my first days in Łódź, I ran into two sisters in the street, Grodno girls
from the Forstat, members of Hashomer Hatzair: Nyutka, Yehudit Picowski
from Avramele's Gdud, and her sister, Zippora. I didn't recognize them as
they approached me. They wore striped robes. They looked like skin-headed
skeletons. Their abdomens were distended, protruding as if well along in preg-
nancy. Only their eyes remained as they used to be: blue, large, huge. I saw but
didn't understand what I was seeing. "Chaśkie!" Nyutka shouted. She tried to
run toward me but hadn't the strength to do it. I ran toward them, toward their

eyes that gaped like a scream of horrific fear. I don't know how long we stood there, compressed in a whirlpool of weeping and kissing as the street continued to move, until we sat down on the sidewalk.

They told me about the ghetto, the deportation and Auschwitz. They showed me their forearms that carried the tattooed blue numbers. Zippora had contracted typhus, but Nyutka hadn't let her succumb to it. She had dragged her sister from bed to roll call and from roll call to work in the field. Otherwise, Zippora would have been left behind on the bunk and thence taken to the crematoria. Nyutka had fed her her rations of soup, water and bread, and propped her up on the lengthy death march so that she would not be struck, stumble, fall and get shot.

It was my first encounter with somebody I'd known who had survived the death camps. Everything they said dwarfed the hardships I'd gone through during the war. When they stopped talking and asked what had happened to me, I said, "Nothing. Nothing happened to me," and from then on I held my silence.

For years after that encounter, I couldn't talk about my life during the war; I couldn't retell it. After all, how did all the hardships, dangers and fears I'd endured compare with those of the people who'd lived and died in the concentration and extermination camps? If I described something on Holocaust Remembrance Day it was always the lives of children — in the ghetto or at the children's home — never myself. Years later, friends read about us and about me in Chaika's book and protested, "Why didn't you tell?" Today, too, with the benefit of time and accumulated insights, I know there is no comparison. One cannot mention the two memories, of the camps and of my life, in the same breath. I had the privilege of an opportunity to choose my path and put my choice into practice. This was an outcome of the education my parents had given me and my joining Hashomer Hatzair. Even when you choose war — the hard way, the dangerous way, the life-threatening way — you are, after all, making a choice!

I remained in Poland with the entire youth-movement *Aktiv* that had survived the ghettos and the forests, and was joined by movement alumni who had returned from the Soviet interior. I sensed that this was the best place to be, to gather up the vestiges of the youth and the children, to start over, and to build life together with them. After a few days in Białystok, I went on to Warsaw. In fact, I flew — for the first time in my life, in a light aircraft with two other passengers and a pilot. I vomited my head off all the way.

Warsaw: Once, long before the war, I had gone there on an overnight end-of-year sightseeing trip from school. We'd slept on the floor of the Jewish school. Several sights in the lovely city, with its palaces and gardens, had etched themselves into my memory: Nalewki Street in the Jewish quarter, the market and the women peddlers who spoke, shouted and declaimed in a form of Yiddish I barely understood. All the way back on the train we'd mocked their weird Yiddish. When I came home, I sang to Mother like a biscuit-monger in the market: "*Drei beigl a-tsener,* three rolls for ten grush."

Now I made my way with Chaika to 38 Poznańska Street, where we met with comrades from Dror: Zivia Lubetkin and Antek Zukierman, Yitzhak Kopelewicz and Tuvia Boržukowski. They described the Warsaw ghetto uprising and spoke endlessly about Mordechai Anielewicz, Tossia Altmann, Yosef Kaplan and Shmuel Breslav, our Hashomer Hatzair comrades in Warsaw who had fought and fell in the uprising. The idea of unifying the youth movements was born in the course of those days and nights. It was the right and appropriate thing for us to do. Obviously after the war, after the movements had been partners in the Jewish Fighting Organization, the resistance groups and the uprising — an alliance of life and death — Hashomer Hatzair and Dror could not suddenly separate. The decision was to establish joint kibbutzim (communes) and activities in various towns. A kibbutz meant one house where surviving alumni of the movements lived. Their tasks were twofold: to gather other alumni returning from the camps without families and homes, and to reclaim children and teenagers from Polish families that had rescued them, convents that had concealed them and the Soviet Union where they had fled. The goal was to get them all out of Poland. It was impossible to remain there for long. Violent antisemitism was erupting everywhere, in malicious acts of enmity and murder of individual Jews who were returning from the war. Mass pogroms came later.

In Warsaw, a general information center about Polish Jews had been established. Two kinds of lists were posted there: survivors and searchers. They were copies of lists that had been compiled in all the Jewish centers in the various cities. People were trying to trace children, spouses, parents, siblings, relatives and acquaintances; any surviving inhabitant of a town, community or street; relatives abroad; emissaries from Palestine; and members of the Jewish

Brigade. Everyone who could help was mobilized. I went there twice to try to find people until I realized there was no one left to find. I did not inquire about Father, Avramele or Bella; I knew for sure they were dead. But what about Rocheleh, Mother and Zipporka? Might one of them have survived? Years later, I still dreamed of them suddenly showing up at my door. But I never found even one familiar name. No one from my close family, my expanded family, or members of the movement.

In June 1945, I was sent to Łódź with two comrades to establish a

Zalman Zilberfarb,
emissary from Palestine

Shaike Weiner, the first emissary from
Palestine after the war

commune. Communes were established in Warsaw, Kraków, Sosnowiec and Bytom, as well as other towns. We lived on Narutowicza Street, where the Hashomer Hatzair leadership established its headquarters. Later on we were joined by Yehuda Tarmu, Yocheved and Israel Shklar of the "Asians" (Jews who had spent the war in eastern Russia), Rachel Zinger, who had returned from the camps, and Shaike Weiner and Zalman Zilberfarb, emissaries from Palestine. The first counseling seminar for members of all movements took place in Łódź. We established a cadre of counselors so we could start operating. The Komitet house, seat of the Łódź Jewish Committee, gathered all Jews who visited Łódź. Only thus could a Jew survive in Poland. You couldn't return to the smaller towns and villages because the Poles might kill you. The community house had lists of survivors and notes from searchers and seekers. One could also get a bowl of soup and make housing arrangements there. People loitered, milled around and sat down in the street, in the courtyard and on the sidewalk. It was summer; dawn came early and dusk very late. People from the camps arrived in the striped clothing in which they had been liberated. Some found real clothes in relief parcels gathered and sent by American Jewish communities.

It was on that sidewalk that I encountered Zippora and Nyutka, and from there I led them to the adults' commune. After they'd received a bed, food and clothing, they were among the first to immigrate clandestinely to Palestine via Italy with the *Bricha* organization.

We began to round up teenagers in the street and at the Committee building. We could tell who was Jewish among those who approached us, and we invited them to join the kibbutz so they would not be vagrant or wait around all day for a bowl of soup. We wanted to educate them for life in a normal, sane and sound world. We received a house on Południowa Street — a ruined house, missing its windows and doors — and began to assemble the newcomers there.

It wasn't an embrace of Zionism or *aliya* that brought them to us. They came because they couldn't survive any other way. We decided to go over to "productivization." That was our slogan: self-labor and self-support, work as the supreme value in life and education for rural settlement on the way to Palestine.

The first task was to fix up the house. The Jewish Committee gave us a large table, the Joint Distribution Committee provided tools and nails, and demolished buildings along the street furnished us with doors, lintels and shutters. With these materials we repaired the openings in the house. Since windowpanes were very expensive, we boarded up some of the windows. Then, with some sewing machines that we received, we established a workshop in the largest room in the building: sewing lessons for girls on one side, a carpentry and metal shop for boys on the other. Using our meager food rations, we tried to teach the members how to cook. We treated education for independence as a treasured article of faith.

The *Bricha* was established by youth-movement members seeking ways of spiriting Jews out of Poland to ports on the Mediterranean and thence

Chasia in a Russian Red Army blouse, Łódź, 1945

to Palestine. When the Palestine emissaries arrived, they joined and reinforced the organization. The comrades in the *Bricha* knew what I had done during the war. As the young people's commune was being set up and its members receiving care, they occasionally sent me on missions.

In Poznań, a man who worked at a Polish Army print shop collaborated with the *Bricha* by making rubber stamps that could be used to forge personal documents and border-crossing permits. Exploiting my Polish looks, I posed as his girlfriend. Now and then, I visited the print shop and deliberately, demonstratively behaved like a young lover so that everyone would see. Afterwards, we went out and strolled in the courtyard, chatting as any couple would. Before saying goodbye, he handed me a small parcel that I buried deep in my handbag. Then I returned to Łódź by train.

My Red Army uniform and the decoration that adorned it gave me immense power. Once five boys had to move from the Łódź commune to its counterpart in Gdańsk. We knew how dangerous it was to ride the train at night: when trains stopped at small village stations, Poles removed Jews whom they found, robbed them of their scanty possessions, if any, and murdered them. To spare the boys from this fate, I joined them as a chaperone in my blouse and decoration. Few trains were moving then and they did so irregularly. We were traveling at night, enveloped in the darkness of unsettled open spaces. The train was so overcrowded that we could not sit together. Three boys and I occupied one bench; the other two sat on the bench behind us. People filled the aisle. The train stopped: a little station. I stayed close to the boys. Then came sudden shouting: "*To nie prawda.* It's not true. I didn't steal anything!"

Somebody had singled them out as Jews and accused them of theft. I approached and asked firmly, in my army uniform, "*Shto slutzilos*? What's the matter? Why are you picking on them?" The Russian language and the Red Army uniform were emblems of the victors, badges of power and domination. Poles feared the Russians.

"They stole a bag from us," the man said.

"It's a lie," I said. "I'm traveling with them. They didn't steal anything of yours!"

The Poles around him insisted that it was so.

Finally, I said, "We're all going to the station master." Out we went — two Poles, the two boys, and me. While still at the office door, I asked firmly, in Russian, "Who's the manager?"

A man looked up from the desk and said, "Me!"

"Look at these two bandits, these jerks," I said, "picking on children because they're Jewish. I'm traveling with them and I know that they stole nothing. Let them go!"

The Russian language, the uniform and the citation had their effect. "I have to record a complaint," the stationmaster said, almost apologizing. "I can't just let them go."

"Write down your name and your ID number," I replied. "If they lose a hair on their heads, if they don't make it to Gdańsk on the next train, your head…" and I drew my hand across my neck.

"It'll be OK. Don't worry," said the station master, his voice trembling. "May I fix you a glass of tea?"

In the quiet that overtook the room, I heard the clattering of wheels: the train had begun to move. "I've got more children on the train," I hurled at the stationmaster, and ran out.

Each car had an open-end platform surrounded by a metal railing and a door leading to the interior. As I ran, I grasped the railing of one such platform and dangled outside as the train gathered speed. Amid the chill of the metal, the intensity of the wind, and the strength of my grip, my legs found the steps and stood on them. Panting, I groped in the dark for the door handle. My watchband, a momento of home, snapped. The watch fell and was gone.

I stepped into the car. It wasn't the one in which we had been sitting. I began to walk from car to car, calling out the boys' names, making my way among suitcases, parcels and people standing next to their bundles or sitting on them in the narrow aisles. Around me were thick darkness and congestion. Most of the passengers were sleeping. I reached the boys. They had fallen asleep hugging each other, pressed together at the window corner of the wooden bench, frightened by my sudden abandonment, anxious for me and for themselves, not knowing where they would turn when the train stopped. I pushed my way into their midst so that they would sense the warmth of my body between them and the Poles. They were frightened. I hugged them. I stayed awake the rest of the way, guarding their slumber.

We reached Gdańsk at the end of that night. Comrades from the commune were waiting for us on the platform. I asked two of them to stay behind to greet the two boys who had been detained, in case they arrived on the next train. Then the other comrades escorted the three boys and me to the commune apartment. After the boys lay down to sleep on beds that had been prepared for them, I returned to the train station. The missing boys had arrived. The station manager had chased the two Poles out of his office with a tirade of shouting, they said. He had then served the boys some tea, placed them on the next train, and ordered the conductor to promise to treat them like his own children.

Sender Freydovicz, Felix Zandman, Yoshe Wajs and the Bielodworskis, members of the Grodno group, were in Gdańsk at the time. I spent several days with them. How memorable were the scenes of that encounter: the streets and gardens, the statues and fountains. Suddenly I beheld a world that behaved differently, a world replete with affection, love and camaraderie. Afterwards, I went back to Łódź and they emigrated to France.

December 1945. A letter arrived from France: Hashomer Hatzair was preparing its first post-war conference. The circular was signed by Leah Wein-traub and Heini Bornstein.

First visit for the Jewish Brigade soldiers from Palestine, Łódź, December, 1945. Seated, from right: Yehuda Tarmu, Mietek Zilbertal (Zertal), Chasia. Standing, from right: Yehuda Tubin, Chaika Grossman, Pinhas Groner

It was decided to send a three-member delegation from Poland, composed of Israel Shklar, a member of the Central Committee of Polish Jews, Ben (a.k.a. Moshe Meir of the "Asians") and me, representing the ghetto fighters and the partisans. I told Shaike Weiner I would not go. I was daunted by the idea of encountering people who had not gone through the war. It would be a dialogue of the deaf: I wouldn't understand them and they certainly wouldn't understand me!

One morning, as I was at the leadership apartment, I heard knocking at the door. Three Brigade soldiers were there. The left epaulettes of their British uniforms carried the flag of Zion — two purple stripes with a Star of David between them. Soldiers from Palestine, the first I had ever seen. Yehuda Tubin, Mitek Zilbertal and Pinek Groner.

They told us about the British Army and its units from Palestine that had volunteered for war against the Nazis. We had known nothing about this. I told them a little bit about myself. I gave some details and didn't have to explain my emotions; every word in my story stood for the related feelings.

I don't remember the name of the photographer who commemorated that night in the large room of the house at 49 Narutowicza Street. A little sofa stood there. Yehuda sat next to me and nagged me incessantly. Pinek and Mitek sat next to us. They said it was important for me to go, to speak, to say my piece. "I can't," I replied. "I could tell it to you," I said. "You listened like fighters, like couriers. I can't tell others. I won't be able to talk without getting emotional and I'm not prepared to do it in front of people who were not in the war." Yehuda objected. Precisely because I was a member of a movement, a combatant in the resistance and a partisan, it was important for me to go there and say my piece. "It's not for your own sake," he stressed, "but for Mordechai and Tossia, whom you loved, and all the other comrades." Long after midnight, I gave in. I could not stand up to them.

After more than six years of war, all I had left were two skirts, two blouses, a vest I had made from shreds of Missja's old clothing, the boots Lisa and Anja had forced me to take, and the blue coat Aunt Rosa had made for me. The skirts, blouses and coat were bedraggled, crumpled and faded. In Łódź, everyone dressed that way, but I was going to the other Europe, and had to dress up. The Hashomer Hatzair leadership gave Yocheved a little money and the two of us walked to the flea market to hunt for clothing. We found a gray coat and a vest of sorts to provide warmth. I made a dress out of brown

Members of the Hashomer Hatzair head leadership in Łódź. Seated, from right: Yehuda Tarmu, Sonja Winogradow, Israel Shklar (Glazer), Chasia. Standing, from right: Chaim Geller, Zalman Zilberfarb (Livne), Shaike Weiner — the latter two, emissaries from Palestine

woolen fabric, the only fabric we found. With that one dress, the gray coat and the boots, I embarked on a winter tour of Europe. In all the photographs taken during my two-month odyssey, in all the locations — Paris and Fontainebleau, Belgium and the Netherlands, Switzerland, Germany and Czechoslovakia — I appear in the same dress, the same coat and the same boots.

It's almost midnight. I'm ready to go, to head for the train station, wearing the brown dress, the Soviet decoration pinned to my chest in order to make an impression at border control, a small suitcase at the door, the gray coat folded on top of it. A knock on the door. Times were tense. I went to the door in trepidation. In the doorway stood a tall and very handsome Brigadesman. "I've just arrived," he apologized in fluent Polish. "I received your address. May I spend the night here?"

I made him a glass of tea, gave him some of the food that remained, and arranged a bed for him. I set out before daybreak; we did not see each other again. Almost two years after that night, I reached Kibbutz Lehavot Habashan in Israel. One day, I looked around the kibbutz yard and there he was: the Brigadesman, Arieh Dvir. His wife, Gila, had kept the letter he had sent her from Łódź, in which he described having knocked on the door of the leadership apartment at midnight and being greeted, to his astonishment, by a young, willowy partisan girl.

Late December 1945: Poland closed its frontiers. The invitation to the conference entitled us to Polish passports. We set out by train to Czechoslovakia. Rafi Ben-Shalom got us a place on a military flight from Prague to Paris.

January 1, 1946: Paris, 17 Rue de la Victoire, the Hashomer Hatzair cell. The door was locked. Not a living soul around. We did not speak French. We turned to a man who stood in the street. I don't know how we communicated. He understood the words "Hashomer Hatzair" and pointed to the locked door, on which a large placard had been pasted. Then he took the invitation from my hand, read it and said, "Go by train to Fontainebleau!"

Paris after the war: a poor, gray, dilapidated city. It was New Year's Day. We didn't know whether everything was closed for the holiday or due to shortages. At the station, we were told that the last train to Fontainebleau had already left. We would have to get through the night on the little money we had received. We hadn't eaten since Prague.

The experience of my first encounter with Paris may not be very important on the continuum of my story, which had moved on to things other than false identity and losses and had begun to include other matters. In the totality of my memories, however, it glows with a vitality and amusement that are easy to remember even more than fifty years after the events.

One lonely restaurant is open. It's packed. We sit down. The mirrors that decorate the walls reflect twenty Chasias. Couples hug and kiss. Somehow, however, a sense of ghastly sadness reigns. The basket of bread arrives with a French restaurant menu, a lengthy and complicated document with lots of words and frills. We can't understand a thing. At the end of a long string of words, I see "chicken." How simple. We decided to order. The waiter came by and we pointed at that line on the menu. From below, at chair level, I looked up and saw his face become a mask of absolute astonishment. Even so, he walked away soundlessly. We waited. Time dragged on. Our hunger escalated;

we had finished off the bread long ago. I summoned the waiter and asked for something to drink. He spoke nothing but French. I tried my whole vocabulary, saying "water" in English, Russian and Polish. His face showed no signs of comprehension. Out of sheer helplessness, I burst into laughter and showered him with words in Polish: *woda sodowa,* lemonade, *kawas*. His face lit up. He came back a moment later with a pitcher of lemonade. We gulped it down but the food still didn't come. We asked for more bread and the waiter asked for something in return, trying to explain with hand motions. We couldn't figure it out until he came back carrying little bits of stamped paper: ration slips. You couldn't eat in this restaurant without ration slips. But we had already wolfed down the bread without them….

We waited almost an hour. Suddenly we noticed the waiter carrying a huge tray bearing a heap of shellfish. He hoisted it onto his shoulder and approached our table. We could hardly conceal our nausea. We felt like vomiting. We were like three country rubes who didn't know how to behave on their first trip to town. The waiter, taken aback, returned to the kitchen and sent the maître d' to us: "What would you like?" I stood up and wandered among the tables, studying the contents of people's plates, until I settled on fried fish. I pointed at it and extended three fingers: for all of us. Again we had to wait. When the plates came, they had nothing but fish. We didn't receive a side dish of bread. The fish was good, but when the bill came it also included the huge tray of shellfish….

Now our pittance was down to a few coins and still we had nowhere to sleep. Every hotel we entered turned us away, probably due to our sloppy, bare bones, shabby appearance.

I don't even remember what street the hotel was on. I remember only a narrow doorway, a steep staircase, and scary darkness. An old woman came down to us and led us to the second floor: two spacious rooms, old iron beds, a chair, a commode with a bowl, and a pitcher of water. No shower, no conveniences. It was already late at night; we were exhausted and soon would have to get up for the train. We decided to stay, the boys in one room and I in the other, turning off the carbide lamp and lying down to sleep. After a moment of quiet and splaying of limbs, a sensation suddenly struck my entire body that logic refused to believe. A bizarre state, in which the consciousness has already figured out exactly what was happening but refused to forward the information to the exhausted, sleep-starved body and the closed eyes that refused to open. I leaped out of bed. I switched on the lamp and my eyes went dark: the whole bed was brown from the masses of fleas that infested it. The whole thing moved, shifted and rustled. I knocked on the boys' door. No one answered. I pounded on the wall. No one answered. I spent the rest of the night on a chair in the middle of the room, occasionally dozing off for a few moments and waking up again. In the morning, I awakened the boys. They hadn't heard a thing; they had slept the whole night.... with the fleas. They laughed at me: the princess who couldn't sleep with fleas! So what, they said. So we had company in bed! My funny, wonderful comrades.

Fontainebleau, France — the European Council of Hashomer Hatzair after the war. Front row, from right: Mordechai Roseman, Chasia, Binyamin Cohen, Michael Litwak. Second row, from right: Yosef Meir, Israel Shklar, Heini Bornstein, Yitzhak Luzon, Yehuda Wajs, Simha Flapan, 1946

Fontainebleau: the first Hashomer Hatzair convention after the war took place at the summer palace of the kings of France. Much later, we found out that we had obtained the location due to Leah Weintraub's connections with members of the French resistance who now served in the new government. A member of Hashomer Hatzair in France, she had fought during the war, together with her husband, in the ranks of the Maquis, the French Resistance.

In the afternoon, everyone gathered in the dining hall. After the initial bustle, the three of us were seated at one table. I was between Simha Flapan and a young guy with a shock of black hair. Ben and Israel sat across from me. We were very hungry; we hadn't had breakfast and had had nothing the previous day but that bread and fried fish. As food was served, the young man next to me peppered me with questions: about Tossia and Mordechai, Warsaw and the movement. I was dying of hunger and he wouldn't ease up.

I turned to Simha: "Who is this *nudnik*?" I asked in Yiddish, confident that the guy didn't understand a word. Simha said, "This *nudnik* is Heini, a member of the movement from Switzerland, the man who organized the conference across the border. His Swiss citizenship helped him make connections with the Maquis, whom he helped during the war. He coordinated the operations of Hashomer Hatzair in France and Europe during the war. He also sent letters, parcels and South American passports to the main leadership in Poland. By doing that, he enabled people to get out and survive. He even managed to lay hands on a Swiss passport for Tossia, but it came too late to be used."

"So tell him to let me eat first," I said, putting on the most serious facial expression I could muster as Israel and Ben burst out laughing. Afterwards, quietly and away from the center of attention, they told me, "You were *eisen* [iron]," meaning: "You were OK because we were eating, but he didn't leave you alone."

Evening: a wide, long room. The people seated themselves in a circle. I wasn't prepared to speak at that first occasion. I hadn't put together any notes. Just the same, the people there asked to hear us before doing anything else. We were the first survivors from "there" except for Chaika Grossman and Antek Zukierman, who had attended a conference in London at the end of the war. Until Fontainebleau, I had not spoken out. I had not told anyone about my life. I had held everything in. I had not even said a word to good friends who had returned from the Soviet interior, where they had spent the war. The first people with whom I had spoken were the Jewish Brigadesmen who had come to Łódź — Yehuda and Pinek and Mietek. And even to them I hadn't told everything.

I began to speak. I don't know what trembled first, my voice or my body. It was a ghastly feeling to be there while all my comrades weren't, and to be speaking about them and in their names. They were dead; I was alive. I began by mentioning their names. I thought it important to list them all, as though the moment I said them aloud they would be etched into the audience's memory and the loss occasioned by their death would somehow diminish. I spoke about the Warsaw ghetto and the uprising there, and a little about ourselves in Grodno and Białystok. I put our comrades in Warsaw first, not only in recognition of their supreme heroism but also because they had suffered more than we. I had no doubt then, or now, about the possibility of weighing suffering and agonies. They had spent five years under Nazi occupation; we had done so for only three. During our two years under Soviet occupation, we had led relatively good lives, lives of hope. Their lives, in contrast, had led inexorably to death. Their ghetto was more horrific than ours, a venue of starvation, agonies, corpses in the street and rivers of blood. And if under those conditions they had managed to establish so glorious a resistance and launch an uprising within the ramparts of the burning ghetto, then it was about them that I should speak, it was their message that I should give over. Thus, I recounted everything that I knew from Zivia Lubetkin and Antek Zukierman's first, immediate reports — not the accounts that changed with the passage of years — about the decisive roles of Mordechai Anielewicz, Tossia Altmann, Yosef Kaplan and Shmuel Breslav in leading the resistance and the uprising.

Afterwards, I recounted the German occupation and the systematic way in which the Nazis had embittered our lives, used mass humiliation, stripped individuals of their human image, and planned the annihilation down to the last detail. I spoke about how long it had taken us to realize that we would be offered no escape, no kindness, no pity. How every individual, family, community, town and village was trapped and doomed.

I furnished a few details: the deportation order that had given us twelve hours to move to the ghetto, the household effects that had to be packed up, the distance we had to cover, three families in one tiny apartment, the terrible overcrowding with total strangers who suddenly become intimate co-tenants who knew everything about you. Niches that became family dwellings, bathtubs that became beds. People who were kidnapped, people who disappeared, and the ghetto commander who amused himself by shooting at human targets in the street. The hunger, the cold and the forced labor. And perhaps above all, the horrific uncertainty and helplessness. Then I described the resistance groups and the uprising in Białystok.

I didn't tell a lot. I remember the stillness, the silence. I observed the audience. It was very attentive. The people were closely packed and lively. In the inferno of my emotions, I couldn't focus my thoughts and speak with analytic distance. It hurt too badly. I didn't think I could speak. It was too early to revisit the narrative of my private life. I also felt that if I told the whole truth, no one would believe it. Some of the events seemed so impossible to me that I often wondered whether I had really taken part in them.

I didn't close an eye that night. To be precise: whenever I shut my eyes, I heard myself telling the story again and saw an intermingling of those attentive people and scenes from my life. I spent that sleepless night trying to reconstruct what I had said and to phrase what I had not: the things I had remembered and the people I had forgotten.

The people saved all their questions for morning. They asked about Tossia and Yosef Kaplan, about Grodno and Białystok. We spent the whole conference, all those days, surrounded by comrades from all over the world: combatants and members of resistance groups from all over occupied Europe, partisans from the mountains of Slovakia and Tito's formations, activists in the *Bricha*, members of Hashomer Hatzair, and American soldiers and emissaries who had come after the war. Everyone looked after us, surrounded us and tried to shower us with friendship, warmth and love.

My other memory of the Fontainebleau conference has to do with another kind of encounter: not only with comrades from all over — Hungary and Czechoslovakia, Romania, Yugoslavia, France, Belgium, Switzerland, Netherlands and Tunisia, and movement members from the United States who had served in the American armed forces — but also with the world outside of Poland, the other world that had coexisted with the war. We had not known that world: rescue and escape initiatives in Hungary, integration of movement members into Tito's combat formations in Yugoslavia and with the partisans in the mountains of Slovakia, and all the rest. We thought that all of European Jewry had been annihilated as our community had been, that all the peoples around us, not just ours, had experienced ghettos and extermination camps, enmity and hate. The information we received, the stories and reports we heard, evolved into the proud insight that our movement, together with all the other movements, did not disappoint us.

Today, years after the events, in a world that has changed, it sounds like an odd and almost archaic thing to say. However, even more than half a century later, I stand convinced that things were exactly thus: were it not for the education the Zionist youth movements provided and the values their members imbibed from this source, we would not have been the pillar of fire for the Jewish people that we were.

After the conference, Ben, Israel and I were supposed to return to Poland via Czechoslovakia in order to examine escape routes from Poland. My small handgun, Busse's present, was in my possession. I was concerned about being captured at the Czech-Polish border; if I had a weapon, it might make our situation worse. I decided to send the gun to Palestine and reclaim it upon my arrival. I surrendered it to one of the emissaries. Years later, he told me that he had passed it on to a member of his kibbutz who was serving in the Jewish Brigade. The recipient, the emissary continued, claimed he had thrown it into the River Seine in Paris when he had faced random inspection by a police patrol. To this day I don't believe it. A tiny handgun with sixty rounds in a cloth pouch must have been permitted. I rued my inability to get it back.

Our first stop after Fontainebleau was back in Paris. I didn't want to speak before audiences again and made my wishes known. Speaking opened up painful internal wounds. It would be more appropriate, I thought, to occupy myself with the building of life. But my self-discipline, willingness to respond to the call to duty and mobilization for the movement's cause were too strong, and I gave in.

I was on a stage and next to me was Itzhak Grünbaum. Before the war, he had been a delegate to the *Sejm*, the Polish legislature, on behalf of Polish Jewry. His son was a member of Hashomer Hatzair and one of the movement's foremost educators in Poland. He had made *aliya* before the war and became an outstanding leader in the Zionist Movement.

Théâtre du Châtelet: a cavernous hall, packed to the gills. A rally organized for the Jewish community. People sat on chairs, stood in the aisles, lined the walls and crouched on the rugs in the space between the front row and the stage.

I had never done any public speaking before. Eyes and people and silence. I sat down. I don't remember whether I had asked the organizers to let
me do it that way or whether I began by standing and sat only when my emotions surged. I began to tell the story, laconically at first, as though delivering a
chronological report. At a certain point in time in the story, however, a picture
invaded my mind: the members of my movement cell in Grodno, my childhood friends, my friends of adolescence. Every last one of them was there,
their faces flashing before my eyes as I continued to relate something else.
I couldn't reveal my emotions in front of the huge crowd that filled the hall.
But the fissure between the sight of my friends and the things I was saying
widened into an abyss. I choked on my words.

No sooner than I vowed never again to speak in public, the Brigade
people asked us to come and speak to the soldiers. Israel would tell about
Poland after the war and I would describe the war itself. I couldn't refuse a
request from the Brigade. We left France for Belgium and the Netherlands. We
pulled into the station at Lille, where Reuven Dafne (Dunek), a member of the
Brigade and (as I found out later) of Kibbutz Lahavot Habashan, was waiting
for us. We were taken to a Jewish family and issued with uniforms. Reuven led
us to a large truck covered with a tarpaulin and packed with Brigade soldiers.
They seated Israel and me at the front of the bed, next to the cab. At every border crossing, when the truck was stopped for inspection, I prostrated myself
as if sleeping. A border guard climbed aboard and counted the people sitting
there. In the dark of night, amid the crowding and the equipment, it was hard
to determine exactly how many people there were.

We went from camp to camp in Belgium and the Netherlands. At night
we sat and told our stories. We felt not only the connection with Palestine, the
object of my yearnings and dreams since the day I joined the movement, but
also the simple and direct contact with the combatants, the partners. Afterwards, they visited one by one and asked whether I had met or seen any of the
members of their families whose traces had vanished during the war. In the
mornings, they gave us no peace. In a photo album, I arranged pictures from a
grand sightseeing trip they gave us in Amsterdam. You see Israel and me in the
company of our soldier-escorts. I made a very sad attraction: the first combatant who had reached them after the war.

I found Brussels a city of the great outdoors: a lovely place with its
gardens, sculptures, palaces and fountains. Amsterdam, in turn, was a thrilling

With members of the Jewish Brigade from Palestine — Amsterdam, 1946. From right: Mendel Berman, Levi Tzur, Chasia, Israel Shklar, Shlomo Kless, February, 1946

experience in art. I spent hours at the Rembrandt Museum, the Rijksmuseum and in the galleries. Works and artists I had known only from books I had borrowed from the municipal library in Grodno suddenly became real before my eyes. Although the city had endured years of German occupation, Amsterdam was also a very different place for me: canals, boats, old buildings and people wearing wooden shoes. A city that had not been destroyed — so different from the place I had come from.

From Amsterdam we returned to Paris. There we met Vitka Kovner, Abba Kovner's wife, who was waiting for her husband to return from his trip to Palestine, and Shaike Weinberg in Brigade uniform, an emissary from Kibbutz Mesilot. Vitka and I shared one bed at Hotel de la Seine, located on the eponymous street. We talked far into the night. By day, we visited museums and galleries, strolled through the gardens and along the boulevards, absorbing the art, the quiet and the serenity — a slight release from the melancholy of war and memory. We spent hours with Cézanne and Van Gogh, spoke about other things, caressed our psyches with literature and art, and also chattered about nothing.

By the time we reached Paris, a cable from Switzerland was waiting for us: an invitation from Heini Bornstein, organizer of the conference in Fontainebleau. I'm in Geneva, he wrote, offering no further details. Enchanted by the thought of a trip to Switzerland before going back to Poland, we accepted the invitation.

January 16, 1946. Israel and I set out by train, armed with a French laissez-passer that allowed us to cross borders. At the station in Geneva, Heini was waiting for us clutching a copy of the *Grüne Bletl,* the "green newspaper," the nickname of the Jewish paper *Israelitisches Wochenblatt.* The program of our speaking tour in Switzerland filled a full page of the paper. We'd be somewhere else every evening.

We needed money; we had opened many youth communes without sources of funding. Heini knew this and decided to do something about it. We were thrilled by the gesture, the thought and the concern. But mainly we really needed money badly, so we agreed. We traveled together to Basel. Heini put us up in his parents' home, whence we set out and returned each time.

Our first encounter with Swiss Jews took place in a large hall in Basel. The whole community turned out. We recounted, orated and answered questions. The donations were raised afterwards by telephone. In Geneva, the encounter took place at a café. I was a bit pained about the possibility of speaking while people sipped coffee and ate cake. Heini explained that the café had been rented because no hall was available. Refreshments would not be served until I finished speaking. So it was. We spoke in the usual order: First me, then Israel. At the café in Biel, the audience sat at tables. The people were dressed beautifully; their faces serene, like the faces of people whose lives had unfolded in an ordinary way.

I began to speak: about the ghetto, about how systematically the Germans had gone about the labors of liquidation and extermination, about the hunger and the cold, about the insight that led to our decision to rise up. Then, from a corner of my eye, I noticed a waiter approaching one of the tables with an order pad in hand. The whole event soured on me. Pain rippled through my body; air refused to enter my lungs. As my throat suffocated on tears, I said, "I can't go on." And out I went, sobbing.

Heini followed me outside, accompanied by the chairman of the community. Both men apologized. I declined to go back and refused to speak. Indeed, I spoke no more, at least not there, where I had been so badly exposed and anguished. I cried all night long. Heini didn't know how to console me. "Let's interrupt the fundraising tour and head for the mountains," he suggested.

We went to Trevano to visit the Jewish refugee center, where we found children who had survived the inferno of Buchenwald. The next stop was Davos, an alpine town that enveloped us with more mountains, snow and tranquility than one could possibly imagine. From there we continued the tour by train, amidst gorgeous scenery. The last session took place in Zurich, where the large hall was so packed that it seemed the whole community had turned out. Only Israel spoke; I didn't say a word. Afterwards we returned to Basel.

5 Türkheimerstrasse: the Bornstein family home. A Polish family from Łódź. Warm people. Heini's parents had emigrated to Switzerland when they were young. Heini and his sister, Lily, had been born in Switzerland. Heini's father was a passionate Zionist, a follower of Chaim Weizmann, a member of the General Zionist Party and a delegate to Zionist Congresses. His mother opened her heart and home to us, showering us with warmth, concern, fuss and effort.

Every morning, from their window, I saw a street sweeper who reported to work at 8 a.m. on the dot. After several such mornings, I asked Heini, "Does he clean at the same time every day?" Simple things, the daily stuff of life, seemed strange to me. How could one live and do the exact same thing day after day? How had Europe accommodated two worlds that were so different at the same time?! The ghastly catastrophe that had visited us defied all sense. Our years of terror had not made a dent in Switzerland. Here, nothing had changed. As I had struggled for survival on the path to the forest, these people had been sitting in cafés. As my parents were being murdered, they were ordering cake. As the combatants in the uprising were being shot, they were wiping their lips on linen napkins. For the past twenty years, including the years between 1939 and 1946, trains had been departing at 08:01 and 10:04. Here, day after day, people walked to the grocery store and had lunch. Twice a year, at festival time, they bought new clothes for their children. Here, "ordinary life" had continued while we burned in the inferno of hell, as the white-hot steel of malevolence and madness left its horrific imprints on us.

Chasia and Heini on a bridge in Bern, Switzerland, February, 1946

We too, the Jews of Switzerland told me, had ration slips for bread and received meat rations only three times a week. Neither then nor now do I begrudge them personally. But all my life I have suffered a terrible seeping pain: how could people have known and done nothing? In Switzerland, London, the U.S., all over, the world held its silence as we burned to ashes — literally.

Heini was courting me. He lent me a pair of his woolen trousers for an outing in the snow in Davos — the first pants I had ever worn that were not Hashomer Hatzair camp pants. He gave me a bar of Swiss chocolate and a gold watch with an inscription in Hebrew: To Chasia with love, Heini, February 1946.

His warmth melted my ice. He had been active throughout the war; he was not one of those who had done nothing. However, instead of talking about himself he asked about us incessantly: about the war, the Soviets, the second German occupation, the ghetto, our parents, the resistance, the Aryan side, the loneliness and the dangers. His attentiveness won me over.

We had to go. We decided to include Germany in the itinerary: we would stop at the DP camps and meet with members of the communes who had already left Poland. Afterwards, we planned to slip across the Czech-Polish border to get a close look at the border guides and the routes. Much money had been collected. The Jews of Switzerland really did open their hearts and their wallets. Their donations added up to more than 100,000 Swiss francs, the equivalent of some $25,000 back then — an enormous sum by any standards. We would have to get this loot past the borders, the inspections and the guards.

Several memories about Heini have stayed with me throughout our lives together. I was an innocent girl from Poland, the product of a good home and Hashomer Hatzair. The tenth commandment of Hashomer Hatzair, of course, concerns itself with high moral virtue. Heini said, "Let's go into the drugstore for a moment." In we went, the two of us at the counter, and Heini, without showing any signs of confusion, asked the pharmacist for a package of twenty condoms. When I heard him utter those syllables, I thought I'd kill him then and there, with the pharmacist and the customers as witnesses. I blushed as I never had in my life. Sexual relations were off-limits. A caress was an act of audacity, a kiss the ultimate pinnacle. And he had gone with me to the pharmacy and asked for contraceptive devices without a moment's hesitation, and in such a quantity!

As we stepped outside, I tore into him: "How dare you embarrass me! And what do think of yourself, entering a pharmacy with me that way?"

"You don't understand at all," Heini said. "I didn't mean you. I had an idea how to hide the money!"

We entered a perfume shop. He bought a large box containing everything: creams in tubes and in little glass jars, and tabs of soap wrapped in silk paper. We went home and took the thing apart. We separated the metal bottoms of the tubes and removed some of the cream from each tube. We rolled the banknotes into tiny bundles and packed them in the condoms. We slipped the money, wrapped and protected, into the tubes of cream. We folded the bottoms of the tubes back into position. Finally, on the lid of the large wooden box, Heini wrote, "Für Chasia Mein Liebling — to Chasia, my beloved."

We made a point of arriving early at the Zurich train station in order to prepare properly for the trip. Out of nowhere, the son of the chief rabbi of Switzerland, Zvi Taubes, appeared on the platform, clutching a package:

"This is for you!" One evening during our fundraising tour, we — Israel, Heini and I — had been invited to a meal at the rabbi's home. After a fine supper, a lengthy conversation developed. When we bid farewell, the rebbetzin hugged, kissed and blessed me, and the rabbi did the same with the men. Now and then during the tour, I had told Israel how badly I wanted a pair of half-height shoes. Since I had left Grodno, I had worn only those Soviet-issue boots; I did not dare to dip into the money we had gathered for the communes to buy myself a pair of shoes. I opened the package. The fragrance of new leather and the shape of the box left no room for error. Carefully I lifted the white crepe paper that swathed the contents, and after a moment we burst into mighty laughter. In the box lay a pair of gleaming new leather boots. The rabbi and his wife, having seen me wearing the same boots the whole time, were sure that I was really crazy about boots and went out of their way to equip me with another pair for the tour and the Polish winter.

Now we had to board the train: a sad farewell. I'll visit you in Poland, Heini promised. He did visit, but by then I had moved on to the children's home in Salzheim, Germany. A year-and-a-half of waiting, anticipating, correspondence and missing each other would pass until we were reunited in Palestine.

Israel and I hit the road, crossing and running borders. In Czechoslovakia, they arrested us on suspicion of smuggling. They found no cigarettes in our possession and no one suspected the box of cosmetics with the amorous dedication. We crossed into Poland. All the way, I hugged Heini with the box and the woolen trousers he had given me. In late February 1946, we returned to Łódź.

CHAPTER 9

With the Children

January 1943: a three-year-old girl wrapped like an onion in layers of lovely, expensive clothing. Three silk tunics, a pair of shoes, a suit and a little fur coat with a note pinned to it: "Good people, we are doomed to death. Please take in this girl. Her name is Danusia."

I stayed with the children because they allowed me to join them in making the transition to normal life. They were the bridge between my old life, back there, and my new one. "I'm sick of orphanages," thirteen-year-old Rocheleh had said while we were still at 88 Piotrkowska Street. Had she not said that, I'm not sure I would have known exactly what had to be done to transform the orphanage into a real home. We're a home, I told her. We're all brothers and sisters. I'm your big sister. We're a real family.

I don't think she believed me. I sat up that night, pondering what it was that transforms a group of individual children into a family. I tried to study the issue through my own experience: where were all my yearnings directed? In a flash, I understood: my sisters, Avramele, my parents. In a sudden burst of light I saw it clearly: kinship relations are the most important of all. What I should do is have the older children adopt younger siblings. Being a big brother means helping, being there for them, helping them to get dressed in the morning, being charge of the yard and the outing, being the address for all requests. Something like a parent-child relationship would take shape, with

319

the children not only receiving "marching orders" but also expressing wishes and making decisions.

I decided to make them full partners. I couldn't change the grim reality, but feelings could be changed. The feeling I should give them, I realized, is that they are true partners in making decisions about their lives. The children's home needs to have a secretariat, a cultural committee and group discussions. By the next morning, it had all of those.

March 1946: Back to Łódź from the European Tour

The Zionist pioneering youth movements had joined forces to establish an organization called the *Koordynacja* for the Redemption of Jewish Children in Liberated Poland. Its purpose was to round up all Jewish children in Poland, place them in children's homes, and take them to Palestine. The American Jewish Joint Distribution Committee (the "Joint") helped by providing clothing and food. Louis Segal, secretary general of an American-Jewish trade union, was quite wealthy and made a large donation for the children's reclamation.

Shaike Weiner and Zalman Zilberfarb (Livne) waited for me to return from the tour. They considered me a suitable candidate to run the first children's home under the auspices of Hashomer Hatzair. The moment they expressed this to me, I realized that this was my true wish. I knew nothing about working methods and organization. I didn't know that I had just chosen the path that my life would follow during the next year-and-a-half and in all subsequent years.

I moved into the home the day it was inaugurated. For the next eighteen months, the children and I were inseparable — twenty-four hours a day, day and night (sometimes mainly at night), seven days a week, Shabbat and festivals, uninterruptedly.

Exactly a year-and-a-half after I opened the children's home, after Poland and Germany, after France and Haifa and Cyprus, after children's homes and castles and barracks, after escape journeys and breached borders and deportation ships and quarantine camps, I delivered them to safe haven. I do not mean this as a metaphor. I truly delivered them to the place that had become the right haven, the last haven in that journey and the first in their new lives.

88 Piotrkowska Street: a small flat — two tiny bedrooms, a hallway, and a living room that faced the main street. Beds, mattresses, blankets, two small tables and a few chairs. That's how we began. A Jewish woman who was the sole survivor of her family helped me. She did the cooking, the cleaning and some of the childcare.

The first children came from convents and Polish families that had concealed them. Among them were Bashka Klieg and Reuven Finkelstein, a toddler whom Bashka's mother had adopted after his parents died. She dressed him in girl's clothing and migrated with the two children from village to village. Although not yet eleven, Bashka immediately became the smaller children's guardian angel, attentive to their pain and responsive to their distress. Whenever a little one cried, she picked him up and cuddled, caressed and tickled him or her until the tears stopped. And there was six-year-old Zosia Ismach, who came to us under the name "Newiedowska," meaning "unknown," a girl without a name. She had spent most of her life in a convent. She was the only one who arrived with her head shaved and bent. She spoke in a whisper. And there were children from Polish families: Gizia and Marcelek, Shoshana and Tamar and Sabinka.

Then the refugees began to return. The Soviets had opened their border with Poland and allowed all refugees who had found shelter in their interior to go home. Some children who had been placed in wartime orphanages in the USSR were Jewish. All returned by train. Łódź was their second stop on their trip west into the Polish heartland. The trains stopped there for several hours to stock up on food, water and coal.

I began to visit the train station in order to search for Jewish faces. Whenever I found children who seemed Jewish, I turned to them and introduced myself as a Jew. I spoke in Russian, assuming that they had forgotten their Yiddish and might not know Polish. If they responded, I said that I would wait for them at the gate. Amid the commotion at the train, no one noticed the children exiting.

I delivered others to our apartment the same way: Rocheleh Pszesczeleniec and her three younger siblings, Hanan, Riwkele and Zipporka, whom Rocheleh had personally shepherded throughout their years as refugees. Aviva and her brother Yitzhak. Zundel and Michcia and their little brother Reuven. The cousins Eljahu and Abrasza Jakierewicz. And the toddlers Danusia and Miecia Michalska.

They had to be given a ceaselessly warm home, I knew. Only thus could I earn their trust and give them a sense of well-being. I hugged them, caressed them, held them in my arms, and woke up at any hour of night when they needed me. And I smiled. I smiled all the time, even when tears flowed inside me. I made each child feel that I was his or hers alone but also reinforced the sense of family togetherness. Without showing overt signs of pity, I felt the pain of their lives and fate. They inhabited a lonely and sad place where anguish knows no limit, and from where I could extricate them in only one way: by offering unreserved love, unbridled giving and total acceptance.

The sense of well-being had to be visible, I knew. So I made sure to leave a basket with slices of bread on the kitchen table at all times, covered with a napkin to fend off the flies that entered through the screenless windows. Any child who asked for bread was allowed to take some and watch the basket being replenished at once. They didn't eat much. They placed small amounts on their dishes. I never said, "Finish what you've got first and then take more." Having often gone hungry myself, I knew how much security a slice of bread buried under one's mattress can provide. I also talked with them at length about the personal security that would be theirs from now on. "We're going to *Eretz Israel*!" I repeated every evening as I told bedtime stories. "You'll have a homeland and a home that are yours. No one will frighten you there, we won't be mistreated, and we won't be expelled!"

Monday, April 15, 1946 — the eve of Passover. I had asked David Sherman of the *Koordynacja*, a teacher, educator and lover of children, to conduct the Seder for us. He acceded gladly. The children were excited. We busied ourselves decorating the large room ahead of the event. We turned a few pieces of colored paper into flowers and designs that created a homey atmosphere. Suddenly the door flew open. Marysia Fleischer stood there — an amazing and high-minded woman, older than me, the only survivor of her family. Her children and husband, parents, brothers and sisters had all been murdered. After the war, she had begun to gather Jewish children from non-Jewish families and convents. She did it independently. No one asked her; no one sent her. She was driven by a sense of urgency and commitment. Some time later, the *Koordynacja* incorporated her activities into its own. And here she was, standing in our doorway, holding something in a tight grip: a little girl, Irka. "*Fershlis di tir*," she ordered me in Yiddish. "Lock the door. I've brought you a tough case. I've got to run." And she was gone.

Irka remained at the door, standing. "Open it for me. I'm not going to stay with Jews," she sobbed in a heartrending way. I tried to console her: "Tonight's a festival evening. We're all going to sit at the Seder table."

"Tonight," she shouted, tugging on the door handle with all her strength. "Tonight you're eating matzah made from the blood of a Christian child!"

I dragged two chairs to the door. "Sit down," I said quietly. "I want to ask you something."

I sat down; she stayed on her feet. Her posture bespoke refusal: her shoulders hunched and raised slightly, as if to establish a buffer between us.

"Do you remember your parents?" I asked.

"Sure." Her thin lips had turned white from the pressure of her teeth squeezing them.

"Were they Jews?" I continued.

"Yes," she hissed, clamming up again.

"If they come back from the war," I said, "this is the only place they'll look for you: with Jews. And if they don't come back, they surely would have wanted you to be a Jew like them."

"I'm not gonna be a Jew!" Irka screeched. "There was a Jew who left me alone in the forest, in the *Aktion* in Lublin. Daddy was an officer in the Polish army. The Germans murdered him. Mommy and Grandma and I were in a crowd of people that were taken to a train. When we passed by a forest, Mommy decided that we'd run away, the three of us. We ran into the forest and there was a guy with us. The Germans fired, Grandma fell behind, and Mommy said, 'Wait here a minute. I'm going to get Grandma.' And she didn't come back. The guy saw that Mommy was not back there so he left me and ran into the forest. So as I said, a Jew left me alone in the forest." She said no more; her protective rampart, fear and anger, were impregnable.

It was evening by now. Irka still stood at the door. The rest of us, in white shirts, seated ourselves at the Seder table for the first Jewish festival after the war. I kept a chair available for her. The aroma of the food drew her to the table. She hadn't eaten all day. A black-and-white photo taken that evening commemorates her sad face and sealed lips. Some children spoke. The ability to speak denoted the ability to relocate and decipher the initial code of memory cells the youngsters had assimilated during the war years. Other children remained silent, unable to endure the intensity of the pain buried in the memories of their lives; for that reason, they could not remember.

Irka was almost twelve when she was delivered to our door: six years old when the war began. Many days after that Seder, the two of us went for a walk in the street. When I went on errands, I sometimes invited one of the children so that we would have some private time together. A peasant stood on the opposite sidewalk, a clutch of brooms made of sprigs on his back. Irka pressed herself to me, trembling all over, clutching my hand, and said, "Look, Chasia, I made brooms like those in the forest!"

"In the forest? What did you do in the forest?" An eight-year-old girl alone in the forest?!

The story trickled out: an evening in the forest, in which all the legends associated with that place became a scary reality. The thing she feared was not the Germans but the wolf in Little Red Riding Hood. She had spent that night crouching under a huge fern, straining not to breathe. She had lived alone for months, eating raspberries, blackberries and sometimes mushrooms. She slept during the day and stayed awake at night, watching out for the wolf. Sometimes she hoarded handfuls of fruit on the fern leaves and ventured to the path, where she sold the food to passing peasants or bartered it for bread. She spent her first coins on two loaves of bread and a small earthen container with which she could gather more fruit to sell.

Summer was succeeded by a chilly and gray autumn. Sores broke out over her whole body. The fruit ran out. Irka gathered sprigs in the forest and made them into brooms that she sold to the peasants. She got by until winter. It became cold and rainy; soon it would snow. Irka wanted to die. She emerged from the forest, walked to the nearest village, approached the mayor, and said, "The Germans murdered my parents. I don't want to live any more. Please hand me over to the Germans." He could not have mistaken the identity of the person who stood in front of him: a skinny little girl wearing a torn and creased summer dress, covered with pus-infested sores, filthy from months in the forest without bathing, wanting to die. Polish children didn't live alone in the forest. He made a different choice: he took her to a peasant woman who lived in a house apart from the others, asked her to clean the girl's wounds, and promised to pay her for her services. Irka spent several months there. Once she recovered, the woman threw her out. "I'm sick of you," she said. "Let someone else take care of you."

Irka began to circulate among the villages. It was late winter. The nine-year-old found overnight shelter in a goat shed, in a barn among piles of straw and hay, living on handouts from peasants, who gave her a slice of bread or a potato and sent her on her way. At the edge of one village, at the top of the hill, she saw a *chatka*, a wooden shack standing by itself. "Mommy once told me that in one of the villages, at the edge of the village at the top of the hill, lived an old, good *savta* [grandma]," she said. "I knocked on the door and walked in. A big room. Over on one side there was a fireplace with a fire going. On the other side there was a big bed with a huge cushion covering it. When I got a little closer, I saw a woman lying there. She raised her head: she was this old *savta* kind of person, just like Mommy said. I was sure that she was the one that Mommy meant. She asked me who I was looking for and I said I was looking for work. 'You were sent from heaven,' the *savta* said. 'I'm ill and the cows have to be taken to pasture.'"

Irka kept talking. The torrent of her story wouldn't stop. The sprig-brooms had touched the expanses of memory that had been sealed behind her inner ramparts. So boldly had they broken through, so firmly had they exposed the memories, that the crack in the ramparts grew wider and wider as the words fought to exit, to describe the dread, the abandonment, the helplessness, the cold and hunger, the loneliness and fear, the sobbing and death.

Irka closed her eyes: "Savta gave me *skulę chleba*, bread that you break off pieces with your hand and dip into milk. I tore some off, dipped it and ate, and tore some more off and dipped it again, until I couldn't do it any more. Then she gave me a big, soft cushion, and didn't wake me up until it was almost noon, when the cows were hungry. They had to be taken to pasture. And I went out."

But then the good woman fell ill and died. Her son came over and threw Irka out of the house. From then on, Irka migrated among the families and worked as a domestic. The last family was devoutly Catholic and very antisemitic. They were the ones who had taught her to hate the Jews. They were the ones who had delivered her to the Jewish Committee at the end of the war. The Committee had paid a great deal of money to redeem her.

After two weeks in our first location, we moved the children's home to an apartment at 18 Narutowicza Street. Adam Chanachowicz was in charge of routine administration of the home. A serious and straightforward man who loved children, he took care of everything: equipment, food and maintenance. The place had two large bedrooms, a kitchen, a spacious living room and two roomlets. I needed a quiet corner of my own, a place where I could sit privately with a child. This was a very crucial necessity at moments of sudden weeping, anger, pain, yearnings or quarrels. The flat on Piotrkowska Street had had no such place. In the new locality, I installed a bed and a small cupboard in one of the roomlets. There was no space for anything else.

At night, when the children fell asleep, I wrote down the day's events. I filled two notebooks at that home. When new children arrived, I recorded their particulars and anything they could tell me about their families and where they had lived before. I added follow-up notes of my own, including vacillations and difficulties. I was especially careful to do this for children who had come from convents or Polish families. I felt that I had to write in order to produce knowledge and establish a basis for memory. In the torrent of surrounding events, after all, things might be forgotten. In that case, the memory, too, would have to be rebuilt.

Easter eve. Everyone was in bed; I was alone in the roomlet, the notebook open on my desk. Amid the silence, I began to write. Suddenly I thought I heard weeping. I stood up quietly and tiptoed so as not to wake anyone up. The girls' room: a chamber filled with beds from end to end and only a narrow aisle in the middle. In the middle of the surface of beds, Wanda was kneeling, her palms pressed together in the manner of Christian prayer. All the young convent girls were seated around her, sobbing.

"What happened? Who hit who?" I didn't really have to ask. I had no doubt what the crying was about, but I wanted them to tell me.

"Jesus won't forgive us," they wailed. "It's Easter today and we're with the Jews. We're not praying, we're not going to church, and there's not even one cross on the wall!"

"Jesus is a master of mercy and forgiveness," I said as the lachrymose outpouring crescendoed. "He knows you're not at fault for anything."

But the girls were terribly afraid: living with Jews, without a prayer-book, without beads and without a crucifix. They cried and cried, their eyes repeatedly searching for the Christ-figure on the wall. The transition from a strict, rigid life that left no room for free will, wishes or requests was hard for them. They still feared the punishment that surely awaited them for living among Jews, failing to observe the religious precepts and refraining from prayer.

Whenever I spoke with the convent children, I could almost see the grim-visaged mother superior or martinet nun haranguing them about reward and punishment. I imagined myself experiencing the fear of a young child who cringes under the burden of sin and awaits in dread the punishment to come.

I tried to connect with them through the instruments of warmth, embrace and protection against everything that was difficult, bad or threatening. I sat down among them. Speaking quietly, I tried to explain that there are times in life that are watersheds between worlds. They had to distinguish between the time of the war and the present time, between having to repudiate their Jewishness in order to survive and being entitled to reclaim their Jewishness as free human beings. I tried to draw a very clear line between the ghastly loneliness of false identity and membership in a large family of children who have no parents but have siblings, a home and a whole people.

I don't know what had the stronger effect: the late hour and their exhaustion after the emotional turmoil, or my quiet lecture, which may have touched lost memories like a kindly caress. Either way, they all fell asleep.

Whenever children from a convent or Polish families came in, the group suffered a shock and had to be restabilized, as if after an earthquake. For the first few days, we kept the door locked even during the day so the new arrivals would not run away, and I devoted myself to them totally. Some of these children did try to escape in order to return to their rescuers. We spent hours searching for them in the streets, the parks and the train station. I assigned this task to the older children. They always managed to find them, talk them out of leaving, and bring them back, with one exception: Waldek. From the day he was brought to us, he refused to move away from the door. He stood there for hours, motionless, waiting for a moment of distraction. He escaped twice and was brought back, but the third time he was gone for good. That's how badly he missed the Polish family that had rescued him. This handsome, bright kid returned to his rescuers; the *Koordynacja* people were unable to find him.

The older girls always mobilized to help the younger ones at moments of crisis, when the abyss between Judaism and Christianity was exposed. Ruthka was the first who leaped out of her bed to perform this task that Easter eve. Ruthka took pride in her Jewishness, speaking Yiddish because it was a Jewish language even though she was fluent in Polish. Strong, determined, clever and funny, she had come from a truly different place. From my standpoint, her story began in the early summer of 1939. *Halutzim* (Zionist pioneers) from

Palestine were going for a visit to Lithuania. Parents, brothers, sisters and extended families were awaiting their arrival.

Night in the Kovno ghetto: a girl being carried by her mother to the ghetto fence. On the other side stood her father. Her mother hugged her tight and said, "I'll come later. Go with Daddy. I'll come." She crossed the barbed-wire fence into the arms of her father, who led her down the city streets in the dark, eluding soldiers and gendarmes, and then on dirt roads through the fields to the village.

All the way, he drummed the message into her head: "You are Rudzika. But every night when you're in bed, remember: 'I am Ruthka, Ruthka Alpern.' You'll survive and when the war's over you'll know who you really are." Late that night, they came to a house and opened the door. A woman served her a cup of hot milk and her father kissed her and put her to sleep. When she woke up the next morning, she saw a different family and her father wasn't there any more. She stayed with the other family until the end of the war, as their child.

The Lithuanian woman with whom she was living surrendered her to the Jewish Committee, which placed her in the children's home in Vilna. That is where she learned Yiddish. She reached us via a group of children who had been repatriated from the Soviet Union.

Despite all the problems, it was easier to deal with children of strong faith than with those who had ceased to believe. One could reverse the polarity of a child's faith and refer it to a different object. It didn't always work, but it was easier for a believer to believe in something extra than for a nonbeliever to take on a belief. Children who had lost their faith had a sadder and more difficult experience. I refer to those who had spent time with the forest partisan battalions, "Asians" who had returned from Eastern Russia, youngsters who had been raised for years in a tough, hostile and threatening environment in which all rules were observed in the breach, and cynics who were sure that they'd already seen and known everything and could teach me a thing or two about life. "Chasia," they would say, "you don't get it at all." Difficult and lengthy efforts were needed to teach them again that they could trust people, that there is another way of life, that limits are meant for protection and not violation.

The oldest children were Ala, Samek, Romek, Rocheleh, Joske and Mottele. They were thirteen. They immediately formed a group that provided leadership, assistance and, above all, a striving for Palestine. Together with some of the younger children, they wanted to return to Judaism at once and learn Hebrew. They displayed an uncommon responsibility and total devotion to action. They were more than helpful elders; they were also my closest friends. With them I could share agonies and fears and speak about pain and anguish. Together we engaged the Polish kids in a stone-throwing battle in a public park. Together we set out at night to find children who had run away because they wanted to be elsewhere.

There were lots of us. Our apartment, originally meant for one family, now accommodated seventy-three children. At night, their mattresses were spread across the living-room floor. The mattresses touched each other and most were occupied by two children. There was always a queue at the conveniences and a row of buckets for the younger ones. By day, the mattresses were piled up in the bedrooms and the living room became a dining and activity room. Showers were taken in three-day cycles, twenty children each day. Meals were served in shifts. To keep life organized and orderly, the children were divided into two groups, old and young. The oldest were thirteen, the younger ones seven to ten.

Morning: reveille. The younger ones had big brothers or sisters who helped them get dressed, tie their shoes and wash their faces. Then came calisthenics, breakfast and, for the older ones, an hour of study. Until a Tarbut school opened up, I taught them myself every morning. The little Hebrew I knew sufficed to acquaint them with the alphabet and help write a few words and sentences. The younger ones played in the bedrooms among the beds. Afterwards, we all went out for a walk. The nearest public park was across the busy street, plied not only by horses and cars but also by an electric streetcar that rode on rails in the center of town. I didn't let the youngsters go alone, not only due to the traffic in the street but also because of the mortal danger: any outing to the park was accompanied by provocations by Polish children and teenagers.

I spent my mornings with the younger children. In the afternoon, when the older ones came back from school, we played circle games together. This was a quiet time for the older kids, in which they enjoyed something of a sense of home. They received a little free time of their own, corresponded with relatives who had been traced after the war, and produced a wall newspaper that Ruthka painstakingly edited every week — a children's newspaper in Polish, Russian and Yiddish. And some kept diaries.

In the evenings, I told stories: about *Eretz Israel* and the kibbutz, children's homes where youngsters were brought up together, the Jewish National Fund and the planting of trees, the forest at Mishmar HaEmek, the *halutzim* and the laborers, the Galilee and the Negev. The kids took turns acting out personal fantasies of *aliya*: how they arrived, whom they met, how the children in Palestine welcomed them. We all needed something real to dream about.

Sabinka, white and pale as plaster, peered from the hideout she had found in the closet behind the staircase. She had been bought from the gentile woman who had brought her to the Jewish Committee. For days on end she lay in bed, gaping at the ceiling, clutching the crucifix around her neck. I sat for hours at her side, talking to her and trying to get her to talk. Nothing helped. During the afternoon activity, as I told a story or taught Hebrew songs, she tried to stop the action by pounding on the wall. One morning, in the midst of a shopping exhibition, I saw a box of crayons for sale. Something struck me; I don't know how or why. I bought the crayons, threw in a pad of drawing paper, and placed them before Sabinka. Her eyes lit up. She took the pad and the crayons and clutched them to her heart. From that day on, she drew incessantly. Later, she also wrote.

One morning, after the older kids had left for school and I was with the younger ones in the living room, I heard a knock on the door and got up to open it. There stood a man from the *Koordynacja* and a little girl. I don't know what struck me first: her eyes, her halo of curls, her enchanting beauty or her stunning resemblance to Yehuditkeh, my Aunt Rosa's daughter. With infinite caution, lest the charm fade away, I pulled up a chair and sat down close to her. She was Danusia, born at the beginning of the war. A kind Pole had found her sleeping alone on a bench in a train from Warsaw to Częstochowa.

January 1943: a three-year-old girl wrapped like an onion in layers of lovely, expensive clothing. Three silk tunics, a pair of shoes, a suit and a little fur coat with a note pinned to it: "Good people, we are doomed to death. Please take in this girl. Her name is Danusia."

A good-hearted Pole removed her from the train and placed her with the Kowalczuk family in Częstochowa. Afterwards she was placed in a convent; we didn't know when or why this happened or for how long she had lived with the nuns. She came to us wearing a crucifix on a chain. However, she adjusted to her new setting at once. She was the youngest of them all. The older children loved to treat her like a little sister. For me, she was a memory of everything I had lost.

Here I wish to report a few things that belong at the end of the story. I feel the need to close a circle before its boundaries are breached. A circle — as a metaphor for the linear time in which we go about our lives, a circle as a metaphor for the encounters that recur at different junctures on the straight path of our lives, in which we connect with women, men, places, sensations and feelings, and with whose strands the fabric of our lives is woven.

In the blink of an eye Danusia became an artifact of my former life as well as the foundation of my second. I listened to her breathing through my own lungs. I breathed her dreams through the curls of her hair that rested on the pillow. I smelled the tranquility and serenity that wafted from the pores of her skin between the folds of the blanket. Months later, when it became clear that no one was coming to claim her and there was no way of tracing any member of her family, I asked Leibl Sarid, the kibbutznik from Yagur and the Mapai Party emissary who headed the *Koordynacja*, to let me adopt her. He refused. To this day I don't know why. If I ask him, I'm not sure he'll remember.

I retain an inner collection of questions and puzzlements that does not contract even as my life goes on. They carry an implicit element of "if only" that may be unanswerable. And the answers to some of the questions — if they ever emerge clearly from the chains of connections, associations and understandings — cannot add to or subtract from anything in the events and demarches that have occurred in my life and the lives of others.

We were together, Danusia and I, for almost an entire year. When I set out for Palestine with the older children, she stayed behind at the children's home with the younger ones, waiting for legal *aliya*. Despite my love for her, or maybe because of it, I could not insist that she undertake that voyage with me, a voyage replete with uncertainty, dangers, border-running, lengthy waiting at stops on the way and sailing on roiling seas amid destroyers and other vessels of war. In the continuum of life, happenings and events I lost her for forty years. When I gathered all those children of mine for a first get-together, I searched for her. I asked and investigated, linked and composed words, memories, fragments of information and things said by people who had heard or seen or imagined that they remembered. A week before the gathering, I found her. After the fact, it was one of those impossible coincidences of life. During most of the lost years, she had been living fourteen kilometers from me, at the end of the road that branches southward from my home, at the foothills of the Golan Heights, on Kibbutz Gadot.

Ours was not the only children's home. Others opened later on. All the counselors in these homes were survivors of the war. Zvi Erez, David Sherman and Haim Liss were superb counselors and outstanding people. All of us, however, were very much alone in the task of education and caregiving. We received no assistance or guidance — medical, psychological, educational — of any kind as we tackled the process of restoring these children to sound life. Our main instructors were our gut feelings and cumulative experience in life: life during the war and the life that had preceded it.

I derived my insights on working with the children from four sources: the patterns of my life, my parents' home, Hashomer Hatzair and my wartime experiences. No one knew how to tell us how to behave. No one could possibly know how to care for children who had survived camps, convents and nomadic lives among villages. Children who had lost parents, siblings, homes and families. Children who for years had had to repudiate their identities, live a lie — a fraud — and harbor deathly fear lest their identity be discovered. Children who for years had suffered from hunger and freezing cold. Children who had herded cows and tended geese and horses. Little girls who had been concealed in bordellos, cupboards, walls behind cupboards and pits that had been excavated under floors of homes, barns or granaries. Children who had not been allowed to speak all day long and had had no one to speak to for weeks if not months.

We were able to touch their psyches and connect with them. We had taken the same ghastly journey. We had been older than them when the war broke out, old enough to have assimilated the notions of home, family and normal life. The longer we lived, the less meaningful the ten-year difference was. It did, however, create a significant difference between a complete, normal and happy childhood and the lives of children who had been deprived of their childhood.

They hid slices of bread under their mattresses. I never touched those slices; I merely replenished the supply in the basket each time so it would be available day and night. When the children wet their beds, I did not air out the sheets in public view; instead, I changed them quickly and surreptitiously when the children were away. It was clear to me that one should not confront the children or hurt their morale. That one should use infinite caution in steering them toward proper behavior and manners of life. I didn't tear down crucifixes. I didn't forbid Christian worship. The processes of change were animated, intrinsically, by the power and necessities of life.

We spent three months at the children's home in Łódź. The enmity around us escalated. Antisemitic acts by Poles became daily fare. Mortal danger surged. Clearly we had to get the children out as quickly as possible. In Germany, the triumphant Allies had established camps for DPs — Displaced Persons — in order to accommodate masses of Jewish refugees from all over Europe until they could make *aliya* without restriction or emigrate to Western countries. The borders of Poland were drawn and sealed. We would need special exit visas. Plainly, masses of Jews would not be receiving them. The *Bricha* people, alumni of the youth movements, emissaries from Palestine, older Jewish volunteers and many dozens of local inhabitants smuggled out the *She'erit Hapleta* — the surviving remnants — from the sealed and guarded frontiers of Europe in all possible ways: hikes through forests, over mountain ranges and along distant passes, sailing down rivers and across lakes in fishing vessels, in the beds of trucks covered with tarpaulins, and by train. Always in the dark, always surreptitiously, on nights when the moon and the stars weren't out. Secretly and furtively they wove and unfurled a network of liaisons, places and people that led all Jews who wished to reach Palestine to their destination.

Taking groups of young children on mountain roads and across Austria and Czechoslovakia seemed dangerous to all of us. Therefore, we waited. Whenever a route by train opened up, the children were sent out first. They and their adult escorts gathered at Stettin, disguised as families returning to Germany after the war. Four children's homes were evacuated from Łódź. Ours were the first that had been set up and the first to set out. We told the children nothing. The *Bricha* people operated in our vicinity and the children did not know who they were. Only in the evening, twelve hours before departure, did we tell the children they were about to leave. This left them enough time to stuff their few belongings into knapsacks but not enough time to divulge the scheme to anyone else. After supper, I assembled them in the living room. The children sat close together, some on tables, others on the parquet floor, the younger ones on the laps of the "elders." I began to describe the camps in Germany, the way to Palestine, the journey that would begin the next morning.

Before I finished, Polcia burst into tears. The others maintained silence for another split-second. The older ones, who understood the meaning of this news for her, remained silent. The younger ones, not knowing what she was crying about, merely sensed her distress and joined her. Polcia was a twelve-year-old who had ridden out the war in a hiding place she had shared with her grandmother. Of their large extended family, only the two of them had survived. When we opened the children's home, the grandmother came to me and said, "I'm too old to start traveling. Take her with you to Palestine."

Our orders were unequivocal: no one was to leave the children's home for any destination other than the train station. We were concerned that someone might say something, someone might infer the final destination from the way they said goodbye. We handed out knapsacks and the children began to pack all their belongings: photos (if any), a change of clothing, and little souvenirs from their outings to the park: dried leaves, an acorn, a pretty stone. The older ones helped the younger ones and then did their own packing. Anything they didn't stow, I took with me. I refused to abandon any item of the sparse property they had accumulated. After all, this was the beginning of their new life! My large knapsack had enough room. Besides, I didn't have much of my own to pack — the brown dress, two skirts and the photos from postwar Grodno and the tour in Europe.

After the others went to bed, I quietly approached Polcia. She lay in a fetal position, tucked into herself, a small body, elbows touching knees. She had placed her head under the pillow, covered herself with the blanket, and trembled with sobbing. I crouched at her side, slipped a probing hand under the pillow, and stroked her hair. Beyond anything else, I knew, she needed to be touched, to feel a warm hand clutching her curls and caressing her forehead in an attempt to provide a bit of solace. My fingers touched her cheek and her wet eyelashes. I tried to quell a small amount of her horrific anguish at the thought of parting with her grandmother forever and entering a world of absolute orphanhood and immeasurable loneliness. Just then I decided to do it. I unrolled the blanket a bit, moved the pillow aside, pulled the mass of curls aside to reveal an ear, and whispered, "Come. We're going to Grandma!"

I asked the older children to lock the door behind us. One of them should wait there until we returned, I continued, and the others should watch over the children in the bedrooms. If anyone asked about me, they should say I had gone out on some urgent errand. I totally trusted the sextet of older children. They understood, cooperated and displayed total responsibility.

Out we went. I heard the key turn in the lock and the latch click into place. Hand in hand we walked quickly down the darkening streets and climbed the steps to the small loft. We tapped quietly on the door so that the neighbors would not hear, and stepped in.

What strength, courage and heroism this woman marshaled in order to embrace the little girl without shuddering, without revealing the bone-penetrating pain, and to say, "Go, my little girl, my dear Polcia. I'll follow you later…." The mind-boggling horror of it. And she continued — "I'm so happy that you're going" — just to give her strength and vitality.

We returned to the children's home. The youngsters had not really gone to sleep. They were tense and agitated, frightened, nostalgic and anxious about the trip. They had had a home for three months and were already being uprooted. I hugged Polcia all that night. She wept uninterruptedly until some time before dawn, when sheer exhaustion and helplessness forced her to sleep. When I awakened her, she picked up her knapsack, placed her few belongings and a photo of her grandmother in it, and marched to the train with one of the first groups.

After she had fallen asleep, I went to my room. Today I cannot hold myself to judgment over decisions I made and orders I obeyed almost sixty years ago. The conditions and times were different then. I do continue to ask myself whether those were the right and most appropriate decisions. My puzzlement, however, stems from the distance of years and different understandings and considerations that adulthood and motherhood placed inside me. I cannot say I would have behaved differently today. To say that, I would have to ignore the whole chronological order, abandon historical thinking and understanding, and disregard the conditions that existed then.

I sat down to divide the children into groups for departure: ten children per group and one of the older children in charge. Buried in my desk drawer were the notebooks in which I had carefully recorded every collective or personal event at the children's home. After I finished listing the groups, I wrote a little about that evening, what the children were feeling, how I had presented the event to come, and the weeping. Suddenly ,someone tapped on my door. Hella Michalska-Slucka wanted to come in. Her eyes were red.

Two of the children who had been delivered to the home on Piotrkows-

336 CHASIA BORNSTEIN-BIELICKA — ONE OF THE FEW

ka Street were sisters, Danusia and Miecia. Both were toddlers, one aged three and the other four. We knew nothing about their family. A few weeks after their arrival, a young woman knocked on the door. She was lovely, hardly grown from girlhood herself. Blue eyes, golden hair. She introduced herself as Hella Michalska and asked to have a word with me. "They sent me from the *Koordynacja*," she said. "They said I could come to work with you, if you agree. I'm the mother of Danusia and Miecia. I was afraid they wouldn't be allowed in the children's home if it were known they weren't orphans."

She made all the cleaning chores in the home her own. She gave all the children tender, loving and warm care, as if they were her own, never uttering a harsh word and never shouting. She was always helpful. "How does she care for all of them with equal measures of calm, quiet, pleasantness and love?" I wondered. "How does she treat them all as her own?" Not only didn't she favor her daughters, but she also gave all the children exactly what she gave them.

Now Hella sat at the edge of the bed, rolling a wet, creased handkerchief in her fingers and pouring her heart out. "All this evening I sat up and thought: they won't let me leave Poland with you. I'd find a way to cross the border if I were alone, but the girls are too young for a hike in the mountains. I decided that the right thing is for them to go with you and I'll come later. But they're so little. How can I send them on the trip alone? Who will take care of them? You've got so many children on your hands!"

She spread her arms wide in a gesture of helplessness, her right hand gripping the handkerchief and the fingers of her left hand splayed. Again her tears flowed, clear and transparent. A heart-rending sigh escaped from inside her in the intensity of her anguish. Through my own tears, I said, "I'm taking them. They will be my children."

I made many decisions on the spur of a moment, following intuition, without pausing to apply systematic judgment, driven by the sense of urgency that wells up when lives are at stake. Had I taken the time to think it through, I might have wondered at that moment how much personal attention I could really give to two girls of such tender age while traveling with seventy children. But I didn't think it through, and Hella went out to sit with the girls during the time that remained. As I circulated among the rooms before dawn I saw her there, between the two of them, her hands on their heads as they slept.

Breakfast: the younger children sat at the tables, already wearing their coats and knapsacks; the older ones stood along the walls. The tension was so thick that the air itself hardened. The children were withdrawn and silent. I had to ease the tension a bit. "Each of you is going to say farewell to Poland aloud," I announced. "Each of you will think of someone or something that you want to say goodbye to: a person, a special tree, a flower." The tension did not slacken, but the things they said filled the void of the large room with some kind of emotion and allowed small talk to flow amid the pain and sadness of parting and the fear of the unknown.

I recited the list of groups and the names of the older children who would be in charge of each group: Joske, Romek, Ala and Samek, Rocheleh, Shmulik and Motke. Silence. The sound of knocking at the door: the *Koordynacja* people walked in. Each group of children was joined by an adult who would escort them as far as the railroad station. The station was far away; it would be a long walk. I would go out with the last group.

The first group left; the next followed fifteen minutes later. The purpose of the time interval was to conceal the fact that this was a guided operation, that something was happening, that so many children were marching to a train: seventy children in seven groups. There would be an interval of two hours between the first and the last. Everyone was very quiet. Occasionally I tried to break the tension a little by telling them something I must have told them many times before. Then one of the escorts suddenly returned along with Miriam, a girl from the Betar movement.

"Chasia," he said, "Leibl sent me to tell you that you're not going. Instead, you're staying in Łódź to open up a new children's home. I've brought your replacement, Miriam Parsikowicz. She's going with the children!"

She's going with the children? How could such a fateful decision be made out of nowhere, at the last moment? Betar hadn't even joined the *Koordynacja*. I sent the last group with Miriam and the escort and ran to Shaike Weiner, who was at headquarters down the street, at 49 Narutowicza.

"It can't be," I said, panting from my headlong dash. "Such a thing can't be done to the children. After all they've gone through, we managed to steady them a bit. Now of all times, as they're going on this dangerous voyage, you're taking me away from them and sending them with a stranger who doesn't know them and whom they don't know?"

I wasn't thinking of myself at those moments. My concern was for the children. Miriam didn't know their names, let alone anything about them.

Where had this stupid idea come from? Suddenly I turned off the torrent of words. Suddenly I understood. Suddenly the whole thing became clear.

A few weeks before, it had been May Day. After supper, the whole ensemble at the children's home had gathered in the living room and sat down in circles, the older ones on the periphery and the little ones in the middle. I told them about this holiday and then taught them a May Day song in Hebrew:

> Flame, rise up oh flame, rise up oh flame.
> With the hammer shall we pound all day, pound all day.
> Flame — as you are, so are we, as you are, so are we, our flag is red....

Leibl and Sarah Nishmit walked in as we sang. Without waiting for us to finish the song, Leibl tore into me as the children looked on: "You're teaching them proletariat songs? You're training them for Hashomer Hatzair? Our organization represents all the movements!"

I burst into laughter. "Leibl," I said. "Do you really think I'm telling these little urchins about Hashomer Hatzair? After everything they've gone through in their lives, would I talk with them about Hashomer Hatzair?"

Leibl's concern was that I would steer the whole group to Hashomer Hatzair and that, contrary to decisions, they would refuse to part with me in Palestine and the kibbutz movement would "win" them all. Therefore, they decided to separate me from the group by leaving me behind in Poland and sending them on with new people. Shaike figured it out right away. "Don't worry," he said. "You'll join them tomorrow at the latest. I'll make sure they don't go on from Stettin station before you reach them." With that, he headed for *Koordynacja* headquarters.

I walked to the train station. 'I'll come tomorrow," I told the older children. "Until I arrive, you're in charge of the whole group." I didn't explain what had happened but I'm sure they understood. Shaike came to the station a short time after me with the accompaniment of another comrade. "He's going with them. Don't worry; he'll take care of them until you arrive." I boarded the train. All the younger children had already seated themselves on the benches; the older ones sat among them. Hella was sitting between Miecia and Danusia. When I entered the car, she stood up and told her daughters, "I'm going to buy you some more candy for the trip." Then she disappeared into the mass of people on the platform.

Samek and Romek took charge of the girls and their knapsack. Alone on the train. The girls sitting on the boys' knees or on the knapsack. The station master blew his whistle. That meant the train was about to depart. There would be two more warnings like that. I told the girls and the younger children that I was going to get something and would return soon. The train moved.

I felt terrible about having lied to them. I had told the truth all my life but just then, on the train, I couldn't. It was small consolation that I would rejoin them next day again and explain. I returned to the empty apartment. Silence, eerie silence. The children were gone; only our cook and a man I didn't know were there, cleaning the apartment. I moved from bed to bed, making sure nothing had been forgotten, waiting tensely for Shaike to return. If the *Koordynacja* wouldn't send me, I decided, I would go by myself. Even if I wouldn't be the children's counselor, at least I would be at their side.

I hadn't had a chance to reflect on the significance of the trip, the departure from Poland. I had not said goodbye to the comrades at the commune and Hashomer Hatzair headquarters in Łódź. I had not said goodbye to my dead family and comrades. It took me more than fifty years to find a way to return for a proper farewell voyage.

I don't remember the identity of the young man who Shaike sent with the children. Together with Yaakov Erner, the Hashomer Hatzair member in charge at the Stettin station, Shaike made sure they wouldn't keep going into Germany without me. The next day, I arrived on the first train out of Łódź. In the exhilaration of the departure and related events, I had left my two notebooks behind in the desk drawer. By the time I realized that they were missing, I had already crossed the border. Thus, I asked the members who had returned to Łódź on the *Bricha* route to look for them: maybe they were lying somewhere in the apartment. I had written the children's entire lives in them: all their hardships and their adjustment difficulties. But no one found them.

Stettin, a Polish border town. The route had been padded with lots of bribes for officials in charge and field personnel. Yaakov Erner was waiting for me at the station. The city was in ruins. The entire group that had left the train was housed in a demolished building. I stood on the stairs, the children sat on them. The moment they saw me, they raced toward me, entangling each other and falling in a mesh of legs — tired and dirty, bits of straw in their clothing and hair, laughter and tears intermingling. The building was empty — no furniture, appliances or anything else. For the next three nights, we slept on straw bedding that had been strewn in the rooms. People from the Joint Distribution Committee gave us food. And we prepared to cross the border.

The crossing into Germany was undertaken as part of the repatriation. The officials at the border station had been paid a lot of money to overlook what anyone could see, but we had to prepare for surprise inspections by people who might not have been in on the secret.

We didn't know the adults with us on the trip. A few of them were real families. For the rest, we had to put children and adults together in the form of families until we could cross into Germany. I began to do the work: two children per family. I tried to match men with women and both of them with children so that they would look like real families. The two little ones, Danusia and Miecia, stayed with me.

Stettin railroad station. We were on our way to Lübek, Germany. Yaakov Erner approached me and said, "Chasia, there's a knapsack I'd like you to take along. It's got all the adults' property: dollars, gold and jewelry. You're traveling with two little kids; I'm sure they won't inspect you at the border crossing." Always obeisant, I didn't even think about refusing. I wasn't even concerned about what would happen if I of all people were singled out to be searched. That's how it ought to be, I believed.

The train pulled into the station. Yaakov said, "Don't worry. I'll keep the train waiting. Walk over to the grove of pines behind the station, as if you're looking for a place for the girls to relieve themselves. There you'll see two men guarding a knapsack that's resting against a tree. When you come back, you'll have the knapsack on your back...."

It was a simple pack, not very big but surprisingly heavy, stuffed with clothing in which everything was buried. We boarded the train. I sat between the girls, the knapsack on the floor and my right leg threaded through its straps to hold it down. The train lurched into motion. Suddenly, the refugees with us began to shift incessantly, jostling each other and staring at me. Finally one of them marshaled his courage and spoke in a demanding tone: "Hand over the stuff now!"

I knew what the treasure in the knapsack meant to them. It was everything they owned. I explained what my orders had been: to divide up the valuables only after we crossed the border. I swore that I wouldn't abscond with the money and wouldn't leap from the train. They would be searched, I warned, and would have their belongings confiscated. I would not be searched.

The absolute distrust I observed in these people was one of the psychological blows the war had caused. I don't know why they left me alone. Had I really convinced them, or was it my determination not to surrender the knapsack at that moment? But as soon as the Polish border guards left the train and we rumbled slowly into Germany, my wagon filled up with people who had deposited all their belongings with Yaakov Erner. They wanted their things and wanted them now. I turned over the little girls to Romek and Samek, who moved with them to another bench. Then I opened the knapsack, removed the list Yaakov had placed there, and began to divide up its contents on its basis. To my good fortune, nothing was missing.

It took days and days to reach Lübek. The train stopped at the first border station. We were all forced to get off and were separated — women and girls from men and boys. We were led to two barracks next to the station and ordered to undress completely. Then German women in gray smocks sprayed us with DDT. The American occupation authorities were so scared of epidemics they had decided to use blanket prevention. It happened over and over, at every station until Lübek. The worst was one night when we stopped at a station whose name I don't even know. All the children were asleep and had to be awakened for the debarkation and spraying process. The disinfection was performed to the accompaniment of the heartrending weeping of children who had been torn from slumber. We lowered them on the metal steps in our arms, crouched at their side to undress them and re-dress them, and finally hoisted them back into the wagon. Those moments came with a ghastly feeling, not to mention the vile odor and taste of the powdered chemical spray. One had to know how to seal parts of one's heart and soul to endure such a trip.

The *Bricha* people in Lübek led us into a synagogue, a ruined, violated building with no windows or doors. That night, the children still slept with their "families" on a layer of straw.

In the morning, people from the JDC (Joint) distributed food. I sat with Miecia and the two Danusias, the younger and the older. As they began to eat, two of the younger children rushed over and said, "Chasia, we're hungry." It had happened several times during the trip. Their "families" weren't giving them their proper share of food. I approached the offenders and peppered them with entreaties and complaints, but they kept doing it. Some lavished attention on "their" children; others treated them with total disregard. At that time, in the synagogue in Lübek, I seated the deprived children with the younger girls and gave them some of the rations we had received. Then I went over to the *Bricha* people at the other end of the hall.

About an hour later, the far corner of the hall was clean and covered with fresh straw and all the children slept together. We would not be separated again, I promised them. We endured a second night on the floor and the straw in the synagogue in Lübek, with no regular latrines or showers and without a quiet corner.

After supper, one of the girls cut her hand and I bandaged it by the light of a kerosene lantern that hung on the wall over our corner. The children were quiet and melancholy, exhausted by the trip. They needed a little happiness, I decided. I still clutched the pair of scissors I had used to cut the bandage. "You know where these scissors came from?" I asked. "I took them when I left my home in Grodno. These scissors cut the fabric for the yellow patches in the ghetto and they made clothing in Białystok so I could buy bread. My whole journey during the war went via these scissors."

I don't know how long it took me to tell the scissors story. It must have been several hours. The story ended when the last of the children fell asleep. To this day, almost sixty years after that night, they still remember my scissors story.

After a few more days and train stations and overnight lodgings on straw-covered floors in ruined synagogues, we reached Salzheim, next to Frankfurt am Main.

Of all the periods, homes and camps, Salzheim was the finest. We were separate from the large DP camp, outside the town, and free from having to look at Germans. We were housed in an enormous building that had served as a school or barracks of an army base.

All of a sudden, freedom. Out of nowhere, a home and a yard, grass and trees, rows of sycamores and poplars, a swimming pool and a large dining hall in a separate building in the yard.

A long corridor bisected the top floor of the building, with little rooms to its sides and showers at its end. Each room housed two or three children and offered each a bed and a small cupboard. The cellar, an enormous place as long and wide as the building itself, served the children as a wonderland for play, hidden treasures and inventions.

The commune of the Mapai Party's Noham movement, populated with refugees waiting their turn for *aliya*, occupied the first floor. By the time we reached Salzheim, the emissaries of the other movements knew the story of the song I had taught on May Day. It could mean only one thing, they figured: I was brainwashing the kids into joining Hashomer Hatzair. By then, the Palestine emissaries had adopted party factionalism as the guideline in all matters. Distribution of supplies, going on outings, and leaving for good were all determined by political quotas. By that standard, I had done a terrible thing.

We had reached Salzheim in the evening, exhausted, filthy and hungry. The Noham commune people urged me to rest up and offered to take care of the children. I don't know if it was due to the attempt to oust me from the counselor corps shortly before we left Łódź or my immense fatigue, but I imagined in their offer a veiled attempt to usurp my place. I refused.

So I was alone with seventy children divided into two age groups: 7–10 and 11–13. We divided up the rooms so as to pair the younger children with the older ones. All were very tired and didn't take more than a few minutes to fall asleep. Rocheleh and Ala put the little girls to sleep in my bed and I went from room to room to make sure everything was all right.

I returned to my room, unpacked my knapsack, opened the window, leaned against the wall, and stared into the dark. Silence. The fragrance of fields. I inhaled the nighttime air. I was seized with a rush of calm, the sort that melts your bones from sheer pleasure. Facing the open window and the crisp air, I had a thought: now we have really left Poland. The mortal danger has passed. How odd: Germany, of all places, had become the safe haven. But it would not be so for long. Palestine seemed closer than ever.

I approached the bed in order to shift the girls a little so they would not fall out. I placed my hands between Miecia's tiny body and the sheet and stiffened in shock. Miecia was burning with fever, her clothes drenched in sweat. Sensing the touch of my cold hands, she woke up and burst into tears. I carried her to the shower room, washed her feverish face, seated her on the bed, withdrew my clean undershirt from my knapsack, moistened it, and laid it on her forehead. Then I pulled over a chair and sat down next to her. Within a few minutes, Danusia, who had been sleeping next to Miecia, woke up crying mightily. She writhed in pain until I reached out to pick her up. Then a stream of vomit erupted over the blanket, Miecia, her clothes and me.

I spent the rest of the night with them, bathing, changing bedding, repeatedly moistening and cooling off my one undershirt and placing it on their heads, stroking them, and making them drink a little water. I had never felt as helpless as I had that night. I had no nurse or doctor to summon, no medicine to offer. I had never really cared for a sick young child before.

I seethed at myself. How irresponsible I had been, setting out alone with seventy children. I was afraid the girls would die by morning. After all, children who had such high fevers died, didn't they? And how would I look Hella in the eye when she came to reclaim her daughters? All that night, my eyes seesawed between the girls and the window, checking the sky for signs of brightening. That would mean morning, when one could summon help. When the first sunbeams touched the windowpane, I awakened Miriam and asked her to go to the large camp to fetch a doctor.

After that night, I began to understand things I had not thought about before. The main epiphany concerned the difference between being a counselor in a movement that offers "activities" that end with the children going home to Mommy and Daddy, and the journey of the type I had undertaken with seventy children. In the latter type of voyage, you never cease, even for a moment, to be responsible for their lives, welfare and health. I also learned the difference between being responsible only for myself and accepting responsibility for such a large group of children. I became truly angry: at myself and also at the *Koordynacja* people. They were older than me and knew that I was only twenty-five. Nevertheless, they had sent me on this trip alone, with no escorts, doctor or nurse, without a first-aid kit, and with no one to call in an emergency.

Wherever we stayed, I felt an urgent need to give these children a home. I didn't know how long we would be staying in Salzheim, but on the first morning I gathered the children after breakfast for a talk. "From this moment on, we're at home. There's a daily routine, personal responsibility, activities, studies, decorating the home and committees." And that's how it was. Precisely because I don't have the personality to be a guard, a policewoman or an enforcer of orders, perhaps, I felt I had to provide the little ones with mechanisms of organization and order for sound, independent life.

Then we elected committees, chaired by the older children: a secretariat in charge of social concerns, a cultural committee to prepare parties, a decorations committee to spruce up the house, a labor committee to make sure the rooms and the yard were clean and to establish duty rotations for the dining room, and a newspaper committee that would produce a weekly wall newspaper. All members carried equal weight in making decisions. I provided guidance and counsel but wholeheartedly accepted decisions that clashed with my views.

We settled into a regular routine from the first week. After breakfast and table cleaning, I taught arithmetic and a little Hebrew. Afterwards, I read stories in Polish and Yiddish and engaged the children in conversation about what they had just heard. When there were neither lessons nor general activities, the children were free to play. They played everywhere: in the yard, in the cellar, in the rooms, at the pool and on the lawn. Ten children from elsewhere joined the group.

My first organizational tool was the morning roll call. Everybody had to wake up, get organized, make the beds and clean the room by roll-call time. After roll call came calisthenics, followed immediately by breakfast. The children still remember me for the shrieking of my whistle. There was no other way to make sure everyone would hear the summons to roll call and breakfast. We didn't have the dining room to ourselves; the members of the commune also ate there. To make sure the children would eat in the first shift, I had to make sure they got there on time.

Whenever we visited town, we also set out in order, in ranks of three. A narrow road and a scattered crowd of children were a sure recipe for disaster, even if traffic on the road was light. Midday and evening roll calls were needed to make sure that all eighty children were really there. The older boys and girls were in charge of these roll calls. Miriam the counselor, my only assistant, had reunited with a brother and sister somewhere on the way from Poland and suggested they join us and take charge of the food and the money. Having no other counselors, I agreed. My aptitude, after all, leaned toward working with children and not making arrangements. Very quickly I discovered how wrong I was. They were a strange couple, corrupt and deceitful, especially where money and morals were concerned. They mustn't be allowed to stay in the company of the children, I realized. I sent them away.

Several weeks passed. A family named Teitelbaum reached the camp and asked to admit their daughter, Halinka, to the group so that she would make *aliya* with us. They came and stayed. Halinka joined the older group. Her father, Aharon, formerly a professor of mathematics, began to teach the children right away. Her mother, Rachel, volunteered for kitchen duty and became a mother to all of us, cooking, caregiving and showing concern. Both of them radiated calm, warmth and pleasantness, and became not only close friends but also part of the staff. Some time later, I asked for a counselor who would teach the children song and dance. The candidate sent to us, Ruthka Kleinman, bonded with the children so strongly that she decided to move in with us and work with them. The burden was no longer mine alone.

The biggest surprise of all was a group of Jewish soldiers who served in the American army and were based nearby. When they found out about the children's home, they dropped by for a visit. I'm not sure who was more excited, them or us, but that was when the chocolate experience of the trip was born. Postwar Poland had plenty of food for people who had money. The shops and markets were full of produce and victuals of all kinds — fruit and vegetables, sausage and beef, cheese and bread, cakes and sweets. But we had no money to buy them.

Friday night: we gathered in the large room, excitedly anticipating the encounter. The Jewish soldiers came in, each carrying a cardboard box. They didn't even wait a moment for the excitement to quiet down and the joy of the encounter to slacken. They fanned out among the tables, opened their boxes, and withdrew their contents: chocolate bars. The children knew about chocolate, although I'm not sure any of them really remembered what it tasted or looked like. I remembered its flavor and had had some during my travels in France, Belgium and Switzerland. Still, I was also stunned for a moment. The bars in each box were thick, really gigantic. The children burst into laughter and shouting and then began to sing and dance between the tables with the chocolate in their hands. The soldiers' eyes brimmed as they watched them. They kissed and hugged the little ones, tossed them in the air, and laughed amid their tears. After that episode, they visited whenever they were free, always bringing chocolate, lots of chocolate. We amassed a warehouse of chocolate.

Chocolate was valuable currency. Children earned it by letting themselves be photographed, bartered it for other sweets, or used it to buy bric-a-brac they wanted. For the great party where they would be issued with Scout ties, we equipped them all with white shirts made from fabric acquired in coin of chocolate. We used chocolate to buy warm blankets that we fashioned into trousers and battle dresses — winter clothing for all the children.

We began to write up a list of commandments for life, to draw a new map of right and wrong, what one could and could not do. We held a series of talks in which the children agreed on rules of personal and group behavior.

Morning roll call, Salzheim, Germany

The Geulim group parades at Salzheim

The decisions were adopted by democratic vote. My vote was equal to any other. No more.

We named the group Geulim, Hebrew for "the redeemed," redeemed from the land of death to the land of the living, from Poland to *Eretz Israel*. I made a flag and the children embroidered it. Sabinka presided over the work.

The most important thing was to inject content into their lives, something that would make up for the missing years and establish an appropriate basis for the years to come. The routine we established centered on study and activities that imparted values. The words "Hashomer Hatzair" weren't mentioned at all. Instead, we spoke about the Scouts, a politically nonaligned youth movement.

In the general DP camp at Salzheim, the members of the movements had formed *aliya* communes. Shalom Chowalski, a partisan and chairman of the Pioneer Partisan Soldiers Oganization, visited every Friday night for our *Kabbalat Shabbat* service and taught the children Hebrew songs. Ruthka helped them produce a play for the evening, in which we celebrated their having become Scouts.

Of all feelings, emotions and gestures, the most meaningful tools in working with the children were touching, hugging and warmth. With these, one could begin to fill something of the vacuum, to instill in each child's inner reservoir the memory of sensations of tenderness, pleasantness and solace. We hardly spoke about their lives in the war in the group setting. I thought it more appropriate for the group to look ahead and tackle the future. When we spoke face-to-face, however, they told their stories and I probed and tried to capture as much as possible. Some children told their stories whenever they remembered them, others rarely said anything, and still others did not speak at all. For hours, in my room, I tried to extract words from the convent girls, those who had been so powerfully educated in obedience and silence that they couldn't say a thing about their prewar families. Issues related to crucifixes and Christian worship became less blatant even though some of the girls persisted with them for some time, until they stashed them with their other souvenirs.

Some of the children decided to take on Hebrew names. The name-change ceremony we held for them, in which they tossed bits of paper with their old names into a huge bonfire at the yard in Salzheim, was part of the rebirth process we tried to induce. I must note that despite everything they had undergone, almost all the children kept their original Jewish or Polish names and have done so to this day.

Hella, mother of Miecia and Danusia, arrived almost five months after us. We all enveloped the little girls in warmth and love. When they called me Mommy, I corrected them — "It's Chasia" — but they stood their ground. They had forgotten their mother. But that didn't bother Hella, that amazing woman, at all. Very slowly they re-bonded with her. She employed infinite patience. Even when they called both of us Mommy, she smiled and told them, "You're lucky. You have two mothers." Right away she threw herself into caring for all the children, as if she and her own daughters had not been apart so long. To enable her to live with her daughters, I vacated my room and moved into the counselors' room, sharing it with Ruthka Kleinman and Miriam Persikowicz.

Having taken total responsibility for the children, I had no time for myself. Therefore, I did not ask for a furlough in order to attend the Zionist Congress in Basel, held in December 1946, and to get together with Heini, who had sent me an official invitation. For this reason, too, I didn't visit friends. They visited me at the children's home, first in Łódź and afterwards in Salzheim.

During all that time I left the children only twice and only once by choice. The first occasion was when Meir Ya'ari, a Hashomer Hatzair leader in Poland, head of the movement in Palestine, and a member of Kibbutz Merhavia, visited Germany. All members of the movement on German soil convened in Munich in his honor, and I, a Hashomer Hatzair girl from Grodno who had taken part in the movement's last seminar in Poland in the summer of 1939, and had operated and fought on the movement's behalf in the ghettos of Grodno and Białystok, felt I should be there. It would be a one-day trip. The very thought of encountering comrades and emissaries from Palestine left me ecstatic and exhilarated.

It was indeed: hundreds of Hashomer Hatzair members, all in white shirts, stood for roll call. After so much killing and death, there was no mistaking it: the movement was alive and well!

I returned to the children that night.

Once that was over, everyone came down with mumps. It didn't happen all at once; it took a few days, like dominos tipping slowly. A doctor came over from the general DP camp and said, "There's no point in quarantining the patients. Everyone's going to catch it anyway, so it's best that they do it in one go." All the caregiving duties were ours to perform. We went from bed to bed, taking temperatures, administering fluids, changing sheets, bringing food, pampering, hugging, boosting morale. Children who recovered helped care for those who had not. Everyone was very weak. It took weeks to get over it.

The children made something special out of that mumps epidemic. Once they'd recovered a little and no longer felt ill and weak, they began to write *fueilletons*, funny sketches and dialogues, all on the theme of mumps.

Just as the last of the kids climbed out of bed, I fell ill. I couldn't really afford the luxury of taking to bed. I directed the morning calisthenics through the window; the children stood in the yard downstairs and I guided them through the motions and called out instructions. I spent a few hours awake in order to be with them at their activities and then went back to bed. The sense that it wasn't too bad, that one could get over it, gave everyone strength and turned the mumps, like other experiences, into the memory of a something we shared.

We spent the spring and summer of 1946 in Salzheim — five months of open spaces and fields, sun, brightness and long avenues. Hours of games and talks. Pillow fights and reading, lots and lots of time to get to know each other, make friends and recuperate. Almost happiness, almost freedom.

Then came a decision to concentrate all the children's homes in Dornstadt, the former base of a squadron of the Luftwaffe, the German air force. I don't know why that decision was made. It happened in October 1946, at the beginning of winter. It was already rainy and cold; soon there would be snow. They put us in an enormous hangar coated with camouflage paint. Inside we found a chilly, dark and dirty dining hall and gloomy, unheated rooms. What's more, the camp was fenced in.

Truth to tell, I did know why the decision was made. The *Koordynacja* wished to gather all the children in one place so it could set up a regular central school for youngsters from all over. I knew right away it wasn't the right thing to do. They settled us on the outskirts of a German city, behind camp fences. Every venture beyond them meant encountering Germans, a difficult and unnecessary proposition that required a special exit permit. The people in charge were from UNRRA, the United Nations Relief and Rehabilitation Administration. But I was disciplined. The children balked at leaving Salzheim but I said that instructions had to be followed. The moment we entered that camp, I regretted it, but I realized there was no choice.

The first thing they did was separate the younger children from the older ones by taking them to a separate children's home in a different building. They had caregivers and counselors. But the farewell was hard for both sides; they visited us and I visited them every day. The *Koordynacja* then attached older children from Sala Druker's group to ours. They had also spent the whole spring and summer of 1946 in a children's home — located in an enchanted castle — and they, too, suffered from the transition.

The youngsters had no winter coats; they owned only the short battle dresses we had made from the proceeds of the bartered chocolate in Salzheim. The coal-fired heat was inadequate against the cold. The dining hall was hundreds of meters from the bedrooms, on the other side of exposed airfield runways. The children suffered from having to trek through wind, cold and snow to and from their meals. Sometimes we hauled trays of food along the same path, but by the time we arrived the food was wet and cold. The kitchen was filthy, the sanitary conditions ghastly. Dysentery was just a matter of time. It took the children weeks to recover from it.

From the first week I took a strict approach to the maintenance of orderly life. I suggested to the children that we crowd into the bedrooms in order to leave one large room vacant for activities. It would be our clubhouse, where we could talk, play games and do homework. I don't remember who presented me with photos of Herzl and Bialik, but they were the first to be pinned up on the wall, next to the paper decorations the youngsters made, the bulletin board, the wall newspaper and the weekly schedule. Later they added a picture of Trumpeldor, under which I inscribed, "It's good to die for our country." Then I hung it up next to the photo of Herzl, with an inscription "If you will it, it is no dream."

I invited all the counselors at the camp for a getting-organized session at our place. There we decided on joint educational endeavors, drew up a program and reached agreement on the principles of the school. Some 450 children had been gathered in Dornstadt. Emissaries from Palestine came to teach. Anda Amir-Finkerfeld, Michael Deshe and Ruth Alon became close friends of mine. They lived in a building across from the camp. Sometimes, on rare occasions, I visited them briefly.

Some time later, my children began to complain they were being called names such as *Shomrakim* and were being told that I was destroying their Jewishness and leading them to Hashomer Hatzair. There were counselors, I knew, who were undermining my efforts, engaging in defamation, and spreading lies and fictions. Others, however, were wonderful comrades and partners, including Sala Druker-Frankfurt, who had become a very good friend of mine; Zvi Erez of Dror; Yones Guler and Avramek Zelig of Hanaor Hatzioni; Haim Liss, and David Sherman.

"There's nothing to gain by fighting all kinds of names and words," I told the children. "We have a home, a clubhouse and a truly good life. People can talk and make fun as they wish. They're just jealous." It really didn't matter. We'd just ignore it. But it wasn't easy. The atmosphere around us became turgid and the children suffered from the personal hostility of one of the Betar counselors. The main accusation was that my youngsters were luring youngsters from all the other groups in order to strengthen Hashomer Hatzair. Above all, the children continued to rue the loss of Salzheim and its open spaces, home-like quarters, independence and freedom.

The Hashomer Hatzair issue resurfaced in full painful fury when David Ben-Gurion visited Germany. At Camp Dornstadt, there was a group of Hashomer Hatzair children that existed outside the *Koordynacja* framework. Raya Oppenheim, my good friend, was their counselor. The youngsters in that group made welcome signs. We all put on white shirts and lined up at a festive roll call in the great man's honor. The *Koordynacja* children stood on two sides of the open-ended rectangle; the external Hashomer Hatzair group lined up on the third. Renia Sowinska, one of my girls, presented Ben-Gurion with a wreath of flowers. Ben-Gurion then approached the *Koordynacja* children, stopped in front of each one, and exchanged a word or two. When he reached the edge of the other side, he asked, "And who are these children?" "They are Hashomer Hatzair children," Leibl said, and Ben-Gurion, the human being and the towering leader, spun and walked away.

The children were stunned. Raya's eyes filled with tears of insult and rage. I was sure that he had made a mistake, had not understood. He couldn't have meant it, could he? To this day, even though the sting of the insult has passed, I can neither forget nor forgive him for that offense.

We treated Germany and Germans with utter avoidance, although living on German soil and surrounded by Germans, I refused to see or relate to them. Even years later, my mind still hasn't come to a point that would allow me to cope with their presence.

The years of war, the length of my trips to the forest and the weight of the cargoes I had hauled, almost a year of working with children without a moment of free time or relaxation for body and soul, and my state of continual mobilization, commitment and responsibility evidently combined to bring on exhaustion. One morning I fainted, and the two Jewish doctors in the camp issued unequivocal orders: ten days of rest and recuperation in a convalescent home. That was my second separation from the children.

I went to a hotel in the mountains: magical scenery of snow, pine and fir forests, and clear skies all around. I allowed the hues of white, dark green and bright purple to envelop me. But the hotel staff was German and I was beside myself with revulsion, disgust and loathing. I lay in bed with a stinging physical sensation, flinching from the German hands that spread the sheets, unfurled the blanket cover, and fluffed the pillow, not to speak of those who did the cooking and served the food. My contact with them was much more immediate and terrible here than anywhere else. How I missed the children; how disconnected I felt. From the moment I arrived, I counted the days until I could leave. I did realize that I owed myself and the children the rest, recuperation and convalescence the place was providing. The older children surprised me by paying a visit. We spent hours outside together, chatting, playing in the snow and strolling. The pictures taken at that encounter commemorate some very happy people. I returned a few days later.

From day one, I organized life as though we would be there forever. I avoided anything that would give evidence of transience, impermanence and the sense of being a refugee. Whenever the children asked when we would be leaving, I quelled their jitters by giving one pat answer: we are here and aren't going anywhere. The moment I know, I'll tell you too, I promised. A person cannot live in continual uncertainty and without a permanent daily and weekly routine. I tried to establish small anchors for the children so we would not be truly displaced persons.

Winter ended and gave way to a hesitant spring that melted the layers of snow. The raising of anchors was already in the air. I wanted to give each child something to remember me by, something very personal. From here, I thought, our lives would relocate to Palestine and be very different. I went to a photographer in Dornstadt and asked him to print up eighty small copies of my picture. For nights I sat awake and wrote each child a personal dedication.

Sunday, March 10, 1947, Purim Eve. Moshe Unger of Hanoar Hatzioni visited me that morning. "I have two things to tell you," he said. "First, we're leaving tonight, only the older ones. The trip is illegal and too dangerous for the younger ones and the toddlers. If you get caught, they might take you to Mauritius or Cyprus. The little ones will wait and make *aliya* legally, with 'certificates,' with the approval of the British. The second thing is your appointment by the Koordynacja to be in charge of the trip. They've decided that you're the right person. From now until the moment of arrival in Palestine, you're responsible for all the children, all the counselors and all the organizing. If you're deported to Cyprus, your appointment will remain in effect until the deportation is over."

Sometimes you feel something that comes not from the heart but from the gut. "I'm not leaving the little brothers and sisters here," I said quietly. "There'll be no more goodbyes!"

"But Chasia, the conditions are tough. They'll follow us; don't worry."

"No one's going to separate little children from their older brothers any more. The only little ones we'll leave behind are those who don't have siblings. That's ok, that's correct, but we won't leave siblings behind. Either we all go or we all stay."

I had no doubt that the children would understand this, but I owed it to Moshe that he should understand, too.

I told him about Rocheleh and her younger sisters and Binyamin's little brother. He listened and then went off to *Koordynacja* headquarters. I don't know who he spoke with, who he consulted and who he listened to, but before midday he came back with an affirmative answer: "The young siblings will go with you, but don't tell them because they might disclose it inadvertently to the other children. Only at night, when the little kids go to sleep, bring them together in your room until the moment they board the trucks."

I was relieved. I breathed freely again. Now all that remained was the necessity of overcoming the parting from the little ones without really parting from them. The trip would be difficult and dangerous and it made sense to leave them behind. The fact that I knew this made my lot easier. I visited Rocheleh and Binyamin. I told them that we'd be leaving that night and explained the arrangement with the younger siblings. Together we rounded up the whole group for a meeting in the living room. I told the children that we'd be leaving that night, that they mustn't tell anyone, and that they would be packing small knapsacks. That's all we would be allowed to take. The joy of departure was diluted by sadness about parting with friends in other groups, as well as the younger children. Then came some indecision about what to take and which of their meager belongings — things they had received or swapped for the American chocolate, photographs and souvenirs — they would have to leave behind.

I walked to the young children's dormitory. I asked the caregiver to pack their knapsacks but not to tell them anything and to put them to sleep as usual. We would lead them to the truck at night, straight from their beds.

Among my possessions were a small radio and a suitcase I had received as a gift. I relinquished them without indecision. But what about the album that contained a year's worth of accumulated photos of the children and our activities? What about my trove of documents and testimonies from the war years — Bella's German ID card (the *Judenausweis*), my partisan certificate and the Soviet decoration? What about the diplomas and certifications I had earned during my year of studies in Grodno after the war? And what about the notebooks from the children's home?

I asked Anda and Michael what to do. "Bring it all to me," Michael said. "And if the children have things that are very important to them and are afraid of losing them, gather them up too and bring them to me." In Palestine, almost half a year after that night, Michael Deshe handed me a package. It contained everything, down to the last souvenir the children had surrendered to him. Not a thing was missing.

The children packed up their paltry clothing and a few objects and souvenirs. Then they tidied up the house; it would be used for another group and we considered it a matter of educational value to have them ready the house for their successors. The place churned and buzzed like a beehive. As time passed, happiness and excitement surged and drove away the melancholy of farewell.

Sunset. We waited for dark. Someone knocked on the door. A sudden silence: the excited commotion stopped at once. The children shouldered their knapsacks soundlessly and went into the yard.

We moved toward the column of trucks as an inseparable bloc. In absolute silence the children clambered up the iron ladder. Benches lined the sides of the bed. Those who couldn't find room there sat down on the floor. I walked with Rocheleh and Binyamin to the younger children's dormitory to bring the little brothers and sisters. Darkness. I tapped on the door. It opened at once. Three knapsacks lay in the doorway. Binyamin walked to the bed of his brother, Reuven. Rocheleh and I moved toward the beds of her little sisters, Riwkele and Zippora. Whispering, we awakened them, dressed them in coats, hoisted their knapsacks, picked them up and walked out in silence.

I moved from group to group, from counselor to counselor. More than 200 children were leaving, plus counselors and escorts, and I was responsible for them all. I wasn't alone this time. People from the *Bricha*, the Hagana and the Jewish Brigade were doing things, taking action, being in charge. I found much strength in the sense of partnership and the responsibility of playing an active role in the escape. It surmounted the hardships of the job and gave me a source of inner fortitude.

Sala Druker-Frankfurt, counselor

I made sure all the groups had boarded the trucks and the counselors had counted the youngsters at least twice. I compared lists, added up numbers, confirmed we were ready and returned to my children. Everyone was seated, with adults along the tailgate at the end of each bench. The *Bricha* people tugged on the tarpaulin, threaded its straps through the metal loops, and fastened them tightly. I calmed the children so they would not be scared. The trip was illegal but all the border guards had been heavily bribed to let us through without inspection. The only reason for the gag order was our concern that one of the guards might have been replaced and his stand-in wasn't in on the secret.

The trucks moved. We didn't see the gate of Camp Dornstadt as we passed through; we didn't see the city as we crossed it — the lights in the houses, the streetlamps, intersections and bridges, the other cars on the road. We only heard noises, sounds and tones that were different each time. When we reached the road heading south, I could tell by the changing fragrance when we were crossing open fields and when we moved through forests. The young children pressed themselves to me, expecting to be hugged. Everyone maintained silence, introspective and crowded, a compressed mass of children, knapsacks and coats. We drove for hours; I don't remember how many.

Somewhere between Ulm and the French border, the convoy stopped at the edge of a forest. In the silence and the dark, we awakened the sleeping children. One by one they climbed down the short metal ladder. The cold and crisp nighttime air struck us like a sudden slap in the face, stinging our lungs after the warmth and congestion of the truck. We moved around a little, stretching bodies that had been folded for hours, spreading hands, straightening legs. Instead of the regular conveniences we did not have, I sent the boys to the right of the road and the girls to the left. I wanted no one to enter the darkened forest. We stopped again a short distance before the border crossing. Someone from the *Bricha* climbed aboard the truck and said, "Don't be afraid. If they stop us at the border for inspection, it will be for just a moment. Maybe they'll turn a flashlight on you. Pretend to be sleeping."

We crossed France in broad daylight and drove southwest until by dusk we reached Sète, a town on a hill with a castle and groves of pines, overlooking an enchanting blue bay and a small fishing port opening onto the Mediterranean. It was the only place we did not unpack our things and I did not even try to make a home. Obviously we'd be spending only a few days here.

All the *Bricha* people blanketed themselves in secrecy and doggedly maintained silence. They disclosed nothing even to us counselors. The children didn't believe that we didn't know. After all, I always knew everything. So how could it be that now, at the most meaningful place and time of all, I wouldn't share information? It doesn't matter much, I told them. Obviously we're on the way to Palestine. Our trip would be long in time and distance. Not knowing exactly how long wouldn't change a thing. We passed the time. Each morning we re-packed our few nighttime things in order to be ready to go. People from the Palyam (the Hagana navy) taught us how to behave at sea. The children wanted to be allowed to choose whom they'd sleep next to on the ship.

After a week, I began to think that I might have been wrong and that we'd be languishing here, too, for months. Maybe I should reorganize life along the lines of a regular children's home, I thought. But the chasm between thought and execution was too wide to bridge. I couldn't convince the other counselors to come along. The stress, the expectations and the certainty that we wouldn't really stay here for long — after all, we might be discovered if we stayed — deprived us of the ability to set up a real home and resume educational activity. We, like the children, were mired in a state of ignorance, uncertainty and desperate craving to be aboard a vessel that would not only deliver us to Palestine but also remove us, physically, from European soil.

Sunday, March 31, 1947: Anja Lichten's birthday. She was thirteen. Anja was one of Sala's girls who had joined us in Dornstadt. She had beautiful blue eyes and golden curly hair. When her father, Michael Lichten, had realized that the Kolomija ghetto was about to be liquidated, he had contacted an acquaintance — a Jewish woman living on the Aryan side under a Polish identity — with a request: "Take my daughter so she won't die with us." Anja easily passed for a Polish girl not only in appearance but also in the way she used the Polish language. The woman agreed and took her to Warsaw, where she had a small apartment in a faraway suburb. When difficulties arose, she passed the girl on to a Christian family. Thus Anja went from hand to hand and place to place. When the war ended, her last rescuers delivered her to Sala's children's home. I decided to celebrate her birthday that evening in order to alleviate a little of the stress and expectations, and ease the difficulty of not knowing. I went with the children into the grove of trees next to the building in order to gather pinecones and branches for decorations and a bonfire. The children collected mushrooms and roasted them over the flame. In the middle of the party, people came in and announced, "We're leaving tonight!" The children didn't believe it. They thought it was an April Fool's joke and were loath to budge from the bonfire.

April 1, 1947: after midnight, we walked down to the bay. A dark, moonless night, the end of the Jewish month of Adar. We strode silently, hearing only the crashing waves, the breathing of the person behind, the clatter of stones dislodged under the weight of trampling feet. And the nighttime air: crisp and cold, stinging noses and throats with a mixture of salt spray, the stench of dead fish, nets that had dried in the sun, and vapors of burnt fuel and machine oil. A long stringy column of children and adults, a difficult path for young children with knapsacks on their backs. They trusted me totally, accepting as self-evident the stress, fear, anxiety and burden they carried on that trek. I moved among them, touching them, smiling, whispering messages of encouragement. At the end of the slope, a huge dark object in the sea suddenly came into sight: a ship, an outline of smokestacks, masts and chains against the background of the sky.

A little wooden bridge, demarcated by an iron railing, led from the wharf into the belly of the vessel. The children crossed. I counted to make sure that all were present: children, counselors and escorts. No one was missing. Now we were in the hold of the ship. Total surprise: a huge void, darkness illuminated here and there with kerosene lanterns, and towering rows of wooden bunks filling the whole place. There were shelves, too. Each was almost 1.80 meters long but the space between the tiers did not exceed 60 centimeters. I enjoyed the way the children responded: by laughing and joking. They enlisted their sense of humor right away so we could get organized. We lay down on the bunks in sardine fashion: head to toe, toe to head. Each person received 40 centimeters of shelf space. That's where they had to place their gear; there was nowhere else to put it. Sometimes they rested their heads on the pillows and sometimes the edge of their feet. The children arranged themselves as they chose, but it took us until midday to complete the jigsaw puzzle of people and knapsacks. The ship sailed; we were in its guts. In the huge maze of bunks that had been specially installed to accommodate masses of clandestine immigrants, it had not been possible to leave space to move about freely. Everything had been measured with strict precision, and maximum room to sleep had been the highest priority.

My memory does not preserve the fourteen days of the voyage in calendar sequence. In the commotion of getting organized, the excitement and the stress, a number of details got lost, some because they weren't important and others because they were too numerous to remember. I can't really separate the portion of my memory that reflects things that I saw from the portion that represents emotions, tones, sounds, odors and feelings. Sometimes my recollection of a word projects the image of a place or a person on a mental screen. Sometimes the recollection of something I saw retrieves sounds and voices. And sometimes a bit of a smell or a flickering movement reconstructs physical and psychological sensations.

I can't say at what time of day we descended into the bowels of the ship, how long we stayed there, and when we set sail. The children lay on the bunks, pressed together. The motions of the vessel scrambled our senses, made our heads spin and added to the vile feeling. The air was dense and bothersome, a jumble of odors that got thicker and thicker over time. The mass of people emitted embarrassing mixtures of odors that persisted after years of hunger and had spread into long-unlaundered clothing. The bodily heat generated by hundreds of men and women, children and elderly in close quarters made its contribution to the whirlpool of odors, as did the stench of the latrine pails that became more concentrated, pungent and acrid as the hours passed, and the escalating sourness of the aroma of vomit.

Toward evening, we were ordered up to the deck. I don't know what struck me more — the crisp air, the sensation of being in open sea or the soft light of sunset. And there was a stunning sight that I had never beheld before: the concavity of the sea, the vault of the firmament, the intersection of both of these on the horizon, the resulting full circle, and the colors of the rim of the sun in the mirror of the sea. An enchanting spectacle indeed: neither on solid ground nor in the air. Your body rocks to and fro and it's beyond your responsibility and control. Its motions are dictated by the incessant heaving of the Mediterranean waves. I sensed the height of the vessel over the waterline and observed the masts over the deck. I had grown up next to a river that thronged with barges, but never next to a sea and ships!

We were a crowd of people. For the first time I noticed how many we were. The children needed supervision; otherwise they might run to the railing, slip or get lost in the congested crowd. They had to be kept in sight all the time.

Suddenly, silence: the silence of a crowd that had stopped crowding. It didn't happen all at once; instead it was like a wave that moved from the middle of a circle to its periphery. I don't remember anyone speaking or issuing an order. But from the midst of the bloc of people, there erupted a hushed, hesitant singing that a moment later surged and swept us all: Hatikva.

I say "singing" but I mean prayer, strength, trembling and weeping. As though all the insults had blown away, the memory of death was repressed, and the uncertainty, displacement, refugeeship, bereavement, orphanhood, aches, concerns and fears — those we had known and those we were expecting — all disappeared. At that exact moment we became a free people advancing toward its homeland, its home, the hopes of its new lives.

We spent fourteen whole days on that vessel. For the first few days we were allowed to go up to the deck only in the dark and never by day. At night, everyone stayed on deck until it was time to sleep. We made that time as late as we could in order to maximize the respite and the open space, to avoid the dense air below, and to avoid bumping against someone else's body every time we moved. The nights were difficult, sleep easily disturbed. Whenever someone moved, everyone sleeping in the same row moved as well. Now and then, when we were truly in open waters, far from land, other ships and strangers' eyes, we were allowed to go up on deck during the day, too.

How strange: during our days at the castle in Sète, I had given no thought to the beauty of the place, the splendor of the serenity created by the combined spectacle blue sea and green pines, through the translucent sky glimmering in purple light. Only afterwards, during the weeks at sea, did I revisit them and unlock the secret of their enchantment in my rare moments alone.

They were long, difficult days, not for me but for the children. I was upset about the meager food they received and more so by the rationing of water for drinking only. There wasn't a corner where you could step away from the crowd for a moment. "Look at the old people and the babies, the pregnant women, the sick," I told the children, "everyone who's having a harder time than we are." Off Crete, the sea became turbulent. We were gripped with helplessness as the ship rocked, our bodies thudding against the bunks and rolling from side to side, overcome by nausea and incessant vomiting. We were one united mass, the children and I. If we still lacked a degree of cohesiveness, fraternity and team spirit, that voyage filled the gap. The children's steadfastness under the harsh conditions, the mutual assistance at moments of crisis or exhausting marine storms, the sense of personal commitment that gained acuity in those moments of vulnerability — to support, help, give care — had their effect!

And there was my responsibility for all groups of children and teenagers aboard the vessel, my relations with the Palyam people, concern for proper conduct of life in transit, assuring food and drink and completing all preparations ahead of the encounter with the British destroyers.

The closer we got to the shores of Palestine, the more prepared we were. I alerted the children to the possibility of a struggle. Some of the *ma'apilim* (clandestine immigrants) were issued with rubber batons, and cans of food and crates of bottles were hoisted onto the deck. These would be our weapons. We were ordered to stay below and soak lots of rags in boric acid to protect ourselves against teargas.

Night. All was quiet; the voyage was nearing its end. Inexplicably we hoped to make it to shore even though we knew full well that it was very hard to cross the Mediterranean without being discovered. We knew that the ship was cruising toward the coast at Tel Aviv and that it was supposed to run itself aground at full speed. This would make it impossible to tow the vessel to Haifa port and give us a chance to make it to shore before the British arrived.

So we were all below deck, the children on the bunks and I circulating among them, quieting them, calming them down, making sure that everyone had wet rags handy. Tense quiet. The older children wanted to join the adult *ma'apilim*, who had been trained over the past few days how to fight, where to stand watch and what to do to keep the British soldiers from boarding. I tried to convince them that combat was a grown-up matter. I was anxious for my children, concerned they might be injured in the mayhem that would break out on deck and by the teargas that would certainly be used.

Suddenly the ship's horn blasted an alarm. A destroyer was closing in. All hands on deck! At the top of the staircase, out of the darkness, a glow of luminescence erupted with pounding intensity. It was the powerful searchlight. The children raced to the location where the canned food and crates of bottles had been placed. Several *ma'apilim* and crewmen unveiled enormous placards carrying the inscription *Theodor Herzl* in Hebrew and suspended them on either side of the vessel. Others unfurled and waved protest signs for the soldiers to see: *Did you join the fleet in order to persecute widows and*

orphans? The Germans destroyed our families and homes. Don't destroy us! You are our hope!
     A young guy, very tall and very handsome, clambered to the top of the tallest mast. It was Muka Limon, attractive and impressive, the commander of the ship. Climbing the rickety mast was a dangerous task and he reserved it for himself alone. He tied a sheet of fabric to a rope that dangled from the top of the mast. A moment later, the rope was tugged. It hoisted a flag that flapped in the nighttime breeze. The searchlights exposed its dimensions and features: a white background, two blue stripes, and a Star of David in the middle! The strains of Hatikva burst from the throats of the crowd of heads that tilted upward, gazing at the marvel of the flag that had unfurled before their eyes. It was a totally revolutionary moment: a clandestine immigration vessel, trying to posture as a merchantman and keep everyone below deck who had no business there, had, in one stroke, become a demonstration of reproach and outcry.
     Almost 10 p.m. To the east, the lights of Tel Aviv. The closer we got, the larger and brighter they became, evolving into glowing beads and a splendorous halo that spanned the dark sky. From the loudspeaker of the destroyer came a cry in English, German and Hebrew: "This is a British warship. You are about to enter the territorial waters of Palestine. If you do not surrender, we will board your ship and lead you to Haifa." The masses of people aboard the *Theodor Herzl* answered with the Palmach hymn and Hatikva.
     Then a pitched battle took shape and lasted into the night. I'm not speaking about the cans of food, potatoes and bottles that hundreds of fighting *ma'apilim* hurled, the teargas bombs and the grayish-black cloud that blanketed the deck, the enormous jets of water the destroyers sprayed or the beams of light the searchlights projected onto the sides of the vessel, the deck and the masts, turning the spectacle into an enormous blazing hallucination. I am talking about the gunfire, the three young *ma'apilim* who were killed in the battle, the others who were wounded and the surrender that took place only when there was no choice.
     When the shooting began, I led the children into the bowels of the ship. Affected by the vapors of the gas, we fled to the shreds of fabric and the bandages soaked on boric acid we had prepared to ease the foreseen stinging of eyes and bloating of lips. Several older children remained on deck until the end of the battle; I feared for their lives. Three hours later, it was over. We re-

turned to the deck, the children surrounding me at the railing, still stunned and agitated by the battle that had been quelled and the sense of lost opportunity.

At the end of the night, the metal cable had been repeatedly tied and snapped, and the *Theodor Herzl* was tethered to the destroyer and towed to Haifa Port, escorted by six ships of the fleet.

We stood on the deck all that time, facing the coast, watching the Carmel range loom from the sea in the morning mist, the white houses on its slopes, the contours of the bay, the mountains of Galilee in the distance. The Hagana and Palyam people had vanished. Fifty years after that dawn, we discovered that they had gone into hiding in the huge water tanks under the prow of the vessel so as not to be captured, not to be deported, and to set out once again.

Before the tussle began, I knew we would not defeat the British in battle but said nothing. The children were sure we would succeed, we had to succeed. I was very anxious for them. It pained me to know that again they would be nomadic, that they would be living in camps, and that they still would have no home.

We remained on the deck, a sad, sobbing, seething, wounded mass of people. Stronger than anything else, perhaps, was the sense of stinging insult over our helplessness against the military force, the arrogance and the heartlessness. After having come so far as to see our coast and homeland, we were being deported to camps in Cyprus.

The commotion of debarkation: utter disorder and disorganization as we crossed from the *Theodor Herzl* to the deportation ship. Only two rows of armed soldiers were stationed there. About half of the *ma'apilim* were transferred that day; the others were deported the next. We were ordered to leave all belongings aboard the *Theodor Herzl;* they promised us we would receive them in Cyprus. I told the children not to get separated and to stay together all the time. They were responsible for themselves, just as the young people and the counselors would be responsible for themselves. I made sure they were all there and the counselors were sticking with their charges and had counted them all. A huge metal gangway was towed to the ship and attached to it with metal hooks. Someone barked an order: to the exit! British soldiers stood on either side, making sure no one leapt into the water, prodding passengers to debark, and shoving them rudely. I was the last off; first I made sure that all 500 children on the ship had left. I counted my children one by one amidst the frenzy of the debarkation, the mass of people and the other youngsters.

I don't remember details of what happened on shore. The children told me there was a huge demonstration against the deportation. A crowd of people who had heard about the nighttime battle gathered behind the fences of the port area to protest.

We were led into large buildings that may have been customs houses. At the entrance I reached, a British soldier asked me to surrender my suitcase — an old, worn-out cloth satchel that contained all the lists of names, the photos I had gathered from the children before we had set out for sea, my notebooks and the children's diaries. I refused. The soldier insisted and tried to yank the satchel from my hand by force. The children rushed over to defend me, stepped between me and the soldier, and created a mob effect that could not be breached in the turmoil at the entrance. As I saw the surprised look on the soldier's face, one of the boys who had gathered to protect me fired a wad of spit that landed next to the button of his shirt pocket and formed a stain. My guts contracted in dread; I was very afraid that the soldier would respond with anger if not gunfire. But he stared and held his silence. I couldn't read his thoughts but despite my anger, sense of offense and helplessness, I managed to thank him silently for his forbearance. That's how I passed through the entrance.

We exited out to the deportation ships from the other side of the building. The sight of the four British corvettes immersed us in a sense of total failure. After a night and a day of fighting, surrender and deportation without food, water or sleep, we all fell silent. No one said a word. To be precise, we said a few words, enough to decide on a hunger strike. We sat for six hours, refusing to touch the water and food the British served us. Then came a sense of immeasurable sorrow as we stood on the deck of the corvette, our backs to the sea and our faces contemplating the landscapes of our country as they retreated into the distance until they faded on the eastern horizon. Some of the children fell asleep in exhaustion; others rested their heads on me. The togetherness was nice.

We reached the port of Famagusta, Cyprus. In the background, we heard orders on loudspeakers, loud cries of sailors and bustling activity on the piers. We waited on deck. Our pier filled with open-bed army trucks. As the vehicles delivered us to our camp, Cypriots lined both sides of the roads, waving and calling out things I didn't understand. Given the insights of our experience, we immediately associated them with cursing, invective and *Schadenfreude*.

Only afterwards did we understand they were saluting us, congratulating us, praying for our well-being.

Camp 65, a camp for children and teenagers: tall barbed-wire fences, locked gates, wooden British watchtowers, long buildings with rounded edges made of rolled metal sheets. Twenty beds and a door per building. The children were dispersed in four buildings. One of the barracks had a corner demarcated by a wooden partition — a place for a narrow bed. This would be my room for the next six months. All the equipment we left behind on the *Theodor Herzl* caught up with us. Nothing was missing.

The reception given us by emissaries from Palestine who had settled in the camps eased the pain of detention and the shock of the surrender. They worked as JDC personnel and joined us immediately. Hanoch Rinot (Reinhold) of Youth Aliyah directed our camp, which we called *Kfar Hanoar,* the Youth Village. Moni Langerman-Alon, Dov Zakin, Yehoshua Leibner and emissaries from the other movements served us as a protective rampart and a handy and proper infrastructure for the immediate construction of an educational array. After three days, I asked for a place to set up a clubhouse. By the end of the first week, we had half a building for a clubhouse, materials for crafts and decorations and an organized daily routine. We took our meals in the general camp dining hall, did our laundry by hand from metal spigots, brought water from the distribution point in jerrycans, used public showers whenever there was water, and listened to news from *Eretz Israel*, which was broadcast on the one radio in the camp over a public-address system composed of loudspeakers mounted on tall wooden pylons between the buildings.

As I review the details of our lives in that camp, I suspect that my account is inaccurate. My laconic rendition conveys a somewhat Spartan sense about the place and its ambiance, as if it weren't all that bad. That would be a mistake and a misrepresentation. I ought to phrase it differently: not from the softening distance of years and prisms, but rather as things felt back there and then.

It was hot. The Mediterranean sun of April was followed by the suns of May, June, July and August. The metal buildings sizzled; so did the dunes in the camp and the tents. There wasn't a scrap of shade except that created by the buildings themselves. There were neither trees nor bushes. We saw the sea through the fences but were never allowed, even once, to visit it during that lengthy summer. No one left the camp except to the infirmary next door.

Drinking water was rationed. People had to wait in lengthy and exhausting queues, armed with empty cans of food or metal vessels. The water didn't flow; it squirted and dripped slowly. One had to marshal one's patience and sagacity to respond to this with humor and not hapless rage. Each metal vessel was named for one of the *ha'apala* ships, in accordance with its size. Large containers were *Knesset Israel,* medium ones *Theodor Herzl* and little ones *She'ar Yashuv.*

The huge shower buildings were equipped with metal pipes perforated at regular intervals. Water dripped through the holes; it never really flowed. You never knew when there would be water or how long it would last. In the best case, it lasted only a few hours. If you weren't on your toes, you wouldn't have time to run over and take a shower. Sometimes the water stopped while we were still lathered up. Sometimes seawater was pumped through the pipe, causing itching and sores. The worst of all, perhaps, was the latrine building, a lengthy shack with an open interior lined with a wooden bench of sorts in which fifty or sixty holes had been cut. You sat down over the holes. There was no partition between the holes. You could never forget the humiliation that accompanied the most private thing a person does. You could never forget the nakedness, the sounds, the odors, the physical ailments, the stomachaches. We all experienced them, and there were pregnant women, adolescents, old women and little girls among us. I held it in for days in order to avoid the place. When that option expired, I waited for the latest hours of night. That wasn't always possible. What anger, fury, helplessness and insult were engraved in us then!

It was a difficult camp, a camp that doused its inhabitants in physical and psychological abuse — not only by depriving them of physical freedom but also by depriving them, due to those existential conditions, of the legitimate rights owed to them as members of human society. Everything related to the simplest human practices of daily life — food, water, shower and hygiene — was accompanied by humiliation. It was this place that made me realize that the children must be offered a different world, one that would make the physical conditions less important in our lives and take us far, far away from there.

The school set up immediately upon our arrival was one part of that other world; the clubhouse the other. Non-stop activities were devised: handicrafts to decorate the clubhouse and hours of *Eretz Israel* songs and stories, talks and games. Lots of collective activities and individualized activities, too.

I don't recall exactly where the story of the new settlements came from. I don't remember what triggered it. Had one of the emissaries from Palestine told the children about it, or was it a report that had been broadcast over the public-address system? Either way, it gave me an idea: the dunes in our camp must resemble those of the Negev. So let's establish a kibbutz. Let's conquer the Negev.

All the committees and functions that had existed and operated at the children's home continued. I presented my idea to the secretariat of the group. They responded enthusiastically, divided up the duties and informed all the others in a group talk. With that, the preparations began. The tent and the flag were my responsibilities. I turned to Yehoshua Leibner, an emissary from Palestine on behalf of JDC, and he furnished all the supplies I requested: a prefab tent and materials for the flag, which I sewed together with the children. I don't know where he obtained the stakes and ropes, the mast, the shovels and the hammers. When everything was ready, we reverted to our original procedure: I woke them up in the middle of the night and out we went.

The Geulim group "conquers the Negev" and establishes a kibbutz at Youth
Camp 65, Cyprus, 1947

The children lugged the gear and their personal knapsacks. They chose the location where we would settle: the farthest point from the buildings inside the camp fences, facing the base of the British watch post. It was dark. The lights along the barbed-wire fence projected cones of murky light onto the sand between the posts. The children were excited. We'd walked only a short distance but it was far enough to put us elsewhere.

We reached the chosen spot. By daybreak, the tent had to be standing, the flag fluttering at the top of the mast, and the circumferential fence completed. How I remember the bustle of the work, the joy of the action and the enthusiasm that swept everyone away: erecting the tent, stretching its flaps, digging a hole for the flagpole, the festive hoisting of the flag, stringing the rope for the compound fence, constructing and building the wooden gate. We labored and toiled, sang, encouraged each other to keep going and occasionally stole a glance at the British guard at his post.

By dawn, our "kibbutz in the Negev" was up and running. Some of the children assumed guard positions along the fences, at the flagpole and at the gate. The others sat with me around the campfire. We sang songs, spoke, told stories and recounted the night's experiences. In the morning, the rumor spread like wildfire through our camp and the other camps: Chasia's children had established a kibbutz in the Negev! An incessant parade of visitors and guests ensued and continued throughout our days at the location: children and teens, emissaries and counselors from our camp and ordinary people from Camp 68, which was linked to our "kibbutz" by a bridge over the fence. I kept up all our regular activities at the kibbutz. The children left for school in the morning and returned afterward. We walked to the dining room from the kibbutz and returned afterward.

At night, we played steal-the-flag and raid-the-camp. I taught the children all the scouting games I knew and afterwards we went to sleep in the tent or on the sand around it. Only the guards walked about vigilantly until morning. For almost two weeks we sustained our kibbutz in the sands of Cyprus. Then we returned to the metal barracks.

I prepared for two years in Cyprus until our turn for *aliya* would come — a lengthy spell that would really be an in-between time, a seam on which we would be stranded for no choice, but still, a sheltered enclave where the reality of *Eretz Israel* would prevail. It was just the right time and the right place to retell our life stories so they would endure and avoid the oblivion and the corrosive chasms of time. I wanted to gather the children's life stories and publish them in the form of a pamphlet. The children embraced the idea eagerly and elected an editorial board to take charge of the venture. However, we needed help: paper, writing implements and various services — translation into Hebrew from Polish and Yiddish, typing, mimeograph and binding. I turned to Dov Zakin. His response was totally favorable and the children began to write.

I suggested that they choose the topics: their prewar lives, their lives during the war, our journey, the children's home or a fictitious story. "Anything goes. Everything will be accepted," I promised. However enthusiastic they were, it was difficult. I had asked them to embark on a lengthy voyage into the psyche. They did not know where to begin. Not everyone experienced it with the same intensity. Some could not really dig into themselves. It was the first time they tried to recount their lives during the war. For most, the story was a continuum of shreds of memory. Some forewent the pain and exposure and wrote about the trip from Germany to France, the voyage at sea or the battle against the British. Some described landscapes and places. Some refused to write at all. We don't know how to write, they said, and have nothing to tell. "You can write about anything," I explained. "There's no 'correct' or 'incorrect,' no 'good' or 'bad.' Every story is correct and important."

They wrote for hours, in the afternoon in the clubhouse, on my bed as a hideout, and in their beds before falling asleep. Several wanted me to listen to or read their works. In the main, however, it was a process they worked through with each other: consulting, showing, questioning and passing the written pages around.

One evening as I was at my corner in the shack, Rochele approached me clutching some rolled-up pieces of paper and asked me if she could read them to me. I invited her to sit down on the bed. Quietly she began to read about home, the beginning of the war and the family's escape to the east. The subdued nature of her rendition swallowed her tears and masked the trembling of her voice, as if whispering somehow diminished the intensity of her pain. I sat next to her, my eyes fixated on her hands as they clutched the pages and lay them on the bed one by one as she finished reading them. I observed her penmanship: straight and precise lines drawn in black, the innocuous writing of a girl who had not written anything since second grade.

She recounted her mother's death and her younger sisters, whom she had vowed to take care of and had been taken from her and placed in an orphanage. Suddenly the white pages slipped from her hands and fluttered to the floor like snowflakes. Immediately she followed them, falling unconscious with a thud. Frightened, I emptied the large jerrycan next to my bed onto her prostrate body. Then I crouched next to her on the concrete floor, slapped her cheeks, and cried, "Rochele, Rochele, get up, get up!" She burst into tears. I hugged and caressed her and tried to offer consolation, ease her anguish and restore her peace of mind.

We had spent a whole year together and she had never said a word. Now that she had begun to reveal the course of her life aloud, her agony had pummeled her with immense, unendurable force. I laid her down in my bed. "If you don't want, you don't have to put it in the pamphlet," I promised. "I want you to read it to the end," she said. I read. It's important for this to appear in the pamphlet, I said; it's important for everyone to know how she had cared for her younger siblings throughout the war years. She assented.

When I handed the material to Dov, I made him promise not to smooth the rough edges of the stories. Stick to the truth and the atmosphere, preserve the nuances, don't try to prettify things, I implored. Keep them exactly as the children had written them. We labored over the pamphlet for weeks, writing, translating, editing, typing and illustrating. From the psychological standpoint, it was the best thing we could have done. I had no other tools and had not been trained in psychological care. But no one knew more about the topic than we did. The process was evident in the children: it was like the opening and draining of an infected wound, an expurgation of harmful things they had ingested. It gave them a little relief. Many years after Cyprus and the pamphlet, I reflected on it: how right it had been to have done this writing then. Otherwise, the children would not have spoken out, would not have told their stories, would not have been asked.

There in Cyprus, it seemed that the counselors of the other *Koordynacja* groups had finished their work. They took administrative responsibility for the children but offered nothing else, such as regular educational activity. Only our group continued to meet; only it had a clubhouse, a regular daily routine after school and a sense of an expanded family. Children from the other groups visited us at the clubhouse. It was hard for me to observe them in their imposed inaction, but I was not allowed to involve them in what we were doing. The various parties and movements that made up the *Koordynacja* had drawn up clear agreements that ruled this out.

I approached Moni Alon, head of the youth village, a sensitive, attentive man who took an interest in everything. I told him about the children in the other groups who were visiting our clubhouse and whom, for reasons of loyalty, I was barring from our activities so that I should not be accused of abducting them. If the other counselors offered educational activity, I noted, the children would stay in their own groups and would leave ours alone.

Hans Beit, director of Youth Aliyah, came to Cyprus for a visit, and Moni invited me for a personal talk with him. I described our journey from Poland and the *Koordynacja* agreements that forbade the transfer of children from group to group. Each group had a counselor from a youth movement or political party, I said, but only our group was doing anything. The other counselors had already gone to Palestine as far as their thinking was concerned. They were conducting no educational activity with their children and, for this reason, had ceased to be *Koordynacja* people de facto. It wasn't my intention to rip the *Koordynacja* apart, I assured him, but I could no longer tolerate the educational neglect that surrounded me.

Hans Beit and his associate, Hanoch Rinot, listened quietly, asked a few questions, and went out to tour the camp. They circulated among the children, conversed with them, walked among the shacks and visited our clubhouse. In the evening, they called a meeting for all the counselors and announced their decision: every child should be allowed to join the counselor of his or her choice. A placement process followed. Together with Moni Alon, they interviewed and conversed with all the *Koordynacja* children one by one. Many older children in the other groups expressed the wish to join us. Hans Beit found this intriguing and asked them why. They found our activity enchanting and attractive, they replied.

The workload was enormous: day and night, hardly a break, lots of bureaucracy and educational activity including individualized talks and attention. All youth movement members that viewed kibbutz life as the goal gathered and waited their turn to be liberated for *aliya*. Hashomer Hatzair chose Avraham to join me as a counselor. All the members of the Hashomer Hatzair *hachsharah* in the camp adopted us, visiting us to offer help and support. Suddenly we felt, especially the children, that we were not alone, that we were not isolated, that we had a really large family. However, the flow of life together came with no few difficulties in feelings, relations, activities, cooperation, successes and disappointments. There was also anger, anxiety frustration, moments of helplessness, agonies, weeping and even violence. At a certain stage, however, organized settings and proper patterns of life and behavior jelled and a sense of confidence developed that we — I and others who joined to offer assistance and counseling — would always be there. Only then did it become possible to address the individuals' distress, and mobilize them as a group for educational endeavors that demanded much personal psychological fortitude.

Then, all of a sudden, our Cyprus episode ended. In August 1947, we were told we'd be leaving. The British were upping by one hundred each month the special quota of "certificates" (Palestine entrance visas) for children. A group of Hashomer Hatzair youth slightly older than my children that had been deported to Cyprus before us forfeited its turn for *aliya* on our behalf. That was a very high-minded act on their part; it meant that they would stay behind in the camp for another unknown number of months, until Hashomer Hatzair's turn came around again in the rotation of youth movements for the one hundred children's visas.

The British refused to allow the counselors to join; they authorized the *aliya* of the children only. The following compromise was attained: the counselors would travel with the children as far as the camp at Atlit. The children would be released and we would wait until we could join the quota under which those on our ship would be allowed to make *aliya* — as if we would be remaining in Cyprus all that time. Members of Hashomer Hatzair visited me the day we reached Atlit. It was obvious that the children would be leaving and that I would be staying behind in the camp. I asked the visitors to provide them with two things: a special counselor who would understand their minds, and admission to a well-established kibbutz so they would have good living conditions. Shlomo Yitzhaki, in charge of the youth groups for Hakibbutz Haartzi, replied a week later with the names of two kibbutzim willing to take them in — Merhavia, where new houses had been built for a youth group that had not yet found a counselor, and Gan Shmuel, where houses had not yet been built but a counselor, Benio Grünbaum, had been recruited.

It was a no-brainer. I decided at once in favor of Gan Shmuel and Grünbaum, an educator and psychologist, a member of the Hashomer Hatzair vanguard in Poland whose articles were basic materials in our educational work. We were privileged, I felt. Yair Lifshitz of Gan Shmuel was serving in Atlit as a member of the Jewish supernumerary police force set up by the British. When he heard about my choice, he asked if he could tell the children a little about the kibbutz. He spent a whole evening with us, and the children hung onto his every word. He described the orchards and the field crops, the citrus and canned-food factory, the vegetable garden, the working members, the large numbers of children, the cows that had names, the horses and the mules. The children were enraptured. For the rest of their stay in the camp, they clung to him.

Two days after our arrival in Atlit, Raya Oppenheim gave birth to a boy, Yair. We thought it would happen in Cyprus, but she promised to do it in *Eretz Israel*, and so she did. The camp situated its infirmary in a little shack. It was August and the whole place sizzled. I raced about among Raya, the baby and the children. Raya was consumed with fever; she couldn't get out of bed and lay there weak, spent and very thirsty. I visited Yair at the infants' home in the camp and found him covered with a red rash. I drew a little lukewarm water from the porcelain sink, bathed him and wrapped him in a dry sheet. After Raya's fever ebbed a little, she asked to nurse him but couldn't. "I'm so thirsty," she whispered to me. I walked to the mess and found several people working there who had been *ma'apilim* and had come there with us. "I need some milk for a comrade who's given birth," I explained, and came away with one cupful. I headed back carefully so as not to spill a drop, gripping the cup with both hands and rejoicing in having obtained it. At the entrance to the infirmary shack, the head nurse, a strict, cold Jewish woman, confronted me: "Where are you going?"

"To Raya Oppenheim."

"What's in the cup?"

"A little milk that I got for her."

What happened then, the rage and insult of it, still hurts me. Never before and never since have I dared to tell anyone what I told her when she grabbed the cup from my hands and poured the milk down the drain. Stunned, seething and above all helpless, I hurled the following in her face: "You're behaving like a Kapo in the camps." In tears I went to Raya and quenched her thirst with lukewarm tap water.

The children spent almost two weeks at Atlit, living in an elongated wooden barracks with a metal roof and rows of iron beds lining its sides. They had lights out and roll call every night. The British came through and counted the children in their beds on the basis of their feet. There was a queue for food, a queue for the shower and a queue for the latrine. By then, however, the physical conditions were no longer really important. We were in *Eretz Israel* now. They entertained a ceaseless flow of visitors from all over the country: members of the movement, friends and Jewish Agency people came. The children exulted — the voyage was over!

The farewell morning came. I escorted the children to the gate. Only there, as the gate creaked open and revealed the huge truck that had come for them, did they suddenly grasp the meaning of our separation. They were going; I was staying. An eruption of weeping, shouting, crying and hugging ensued. Shlomo Yitzhaki, in an article he wrote about the Atlit camp, described that moment as the "children's uprising." I silenced the children and eased their emotional turmoil. It isn't so bad, I told them. We've made it to *Eretz Israel*. I'll join you in another few days or weeks. "Write to me every day," I requested. "Tell me about your kibbutz. Don't worry about me. Raya's staying with me." They boarded the truck.

After they disappeared around a bend in the road, I walked back to the barracks and sprawled on the bed, choking on tears in the sudden silence and emptiness. I had been with them for a year-and-a-half, save my few days in the mountain sanatorium. I wasn't worried about them now; I knew they were going to a wonderful place. But it was sudden, as though my whole life had been taken from me. I wasn't concerned about being separated for years, but I did think that we'd be apart for a long, long time.

Letters, literally bundles of letters, began to arrive at once. Yair, the supernumerary policeman, delivered them and delivered the replies. Everyone wrote, every day. They'd been accommodated in a citrus-packing house hurriedly partitioned into two large rooms. Around them were citrus and fruit orchards, a swimming pool and a dining hall, a shared shower and mosquitoes. They began to do farm work right away, as if fulfilling all the dreams I had inculcated in them about *Eretz Israel* and the home we would have. I read their letters with a delight that persisted for hours afterward. The feeling that I had acted correctly, that I had made appropriate choices for them, filled me with serenity.

Suddenly I had time on my hands, lots of time. For the first time in my adult life, I had no job. Repeatedly I visited the groups of older children, conversed with the counselors, made a little dress and handbag for Sheike

Weiner's baby daughter from some fabric I'd obtained, and embroidered everything using a special needlepoint pattern. I answered the children's letters, spent time with Raya and baby Yair, and entertained lots of comrades who had come from all over the country to visit. One of them was Nessia Resnik-Orlov, who had made *aliya* before me with a group of children and had settled at Kibbutz Amir in the Galilee. Others were Meir Talmi, Judeks (secretary of Hakibbutz Haartzi), and friends from Grodno who had made *aliya* before the war and heard that I had arrived. They were not allowed to enter the camp. Instead, they stood at the fence. Nessia cried, kissed me, stroked my face through the chain links, and slipped me a fountain pen and some cookies. I'm so sad that you're there and I'm here, on the outside, she said. "It's okay," I replied. "It really isn't so bad, and after all, I'm already here in *Eretz Israel*."

Throughout my voyage with the children, I had become very close to the comrades who surrounded me. Some were making *aliya*; others had come from *Eretz Israel* and were returning at the end of their mission. Each one passed me to his or her successors like a baton in a relay race. They had created a network of communication, support and security that never ceased to exist. Therefore, everyone knew that Heini was waiting for me. They also knew that I had reached Atlit, and they gave Heini the news.

I hadn't seen him since the March 1946 tour in Europe; since then, we had only corresponded. In June 1946, while on an assignment in Poland, he reached Łódź a week after I had left with the children for Germany. In December 1946, during my stay in Dornstadt, he sent me an invitation and a train ticket to the Twelfth Zionist Congress in Basel. I was elected to be representative in the Polish delegation. However, I was unable to leave the children and did not go. Between January and April 1947, Heini was active in Paris in organizing the *Bricha*. His Swiss passport enabled him to sign purchase contracts for the clandestine-immigration vessels. During my stay in Sète, Ehud Avriel made a wonderful human gesture: he sent Heini with a car and driver from Paris to meet me after we'd been apart for a year. One of the *Bricha* people in Marseilles arrived with an announcement for me: Heini was on his way, he wanted me to wait for him, and together we would make *aliya* using his official certificate. "Aliya D," they called it. "We'll meet in Palestine," I wrote on a piece of paper that I placed in the messenger's hand, "I'm not leaving the children." Heini reached the port of Sète two hours after I'd sailed. Two days after we reached Atlit, the children burst into the barracks, running and shouting: "Chasia, Chasia, Heini's coming! Heini's coming!"

Before the war, back in Switzerland, Heini had gone to an agricultural school to train himself for life as a kibbutznik, a worker and a *halutz* (Zionist pioneer). His settlement group joined the founders of Kibbutz Gat in the Negev and he worked in the vegetable patch. It was late August 1947. The whole commune had one telephone. The world moved at a different pace back then. When people went out to the fields, they were inaccessible for hours on end. To handle emergencies, the kibbutz installed a public-address system and stationed a giant loudspeaker on top of the water tower. Shortly before noon, the speaker boomed: Heini Bornstein, there's a notice for you from Merhavia. Go to the secretary's office!

A personal notice from Merhavia, where Hakibbutz Haartzi was headquartered, could be sent only if war had broken out. Nothing less portentous justified this action. Whatever it was, it was so exceptional that they arranged a car and driver to deliver Heini to Atlit.

Suddenly, after almost two years of letters, yearnings and uncommon patience, there he was, facing me on the other side of the fence. The children crowded around me; a clutch of other visitors thronged around him. For the first time in my life, perhaps, I truly ignored everything around me and focused on the touching of fingers through the metal mesh and the sensation of lips kissing.

Sunday, September 14, 1947: the eve of Rosh Hashanah. I have never searched for signs in times of the year, special days or peculiarly numbered days. My education, my upbringing and the wisdom of realism I have acquired in life do not allow me to entertain delusions. Things happen because of people's choices, actions and intentions.

Yair dropped in from Gan Shmuel with a bundle of letters and New Year's cards from the children. The youngsters described the preparations for the festival, the festooned kibbutz, the arrangements in the dining hall, the autumn (so different from what they remembered in Poland and Germany!), and things they missed. After breakfast, I returned to the barracks to answer the letters. An armed supernumerary policeman walked in and introduced himself: "I'm Shmuel Neugrischen of Kibbutz Ma'anit. I have come to take you to a hospital in Haifa for tests. Something about your heart."

"Who sent you?"

He disregarded my question. "Bring everything with you. There's no telling how long the tests will take."

Suddenly I had a feeling inside: I'm hearing things even if they're not said.

Inspection on the way out of the camp: Shmuel showed them a letter signed by a doctor and they let me pass. A pickup truck waited outside the gate. I climbed into the cab; Shmuel seated himself in the back. The open window admitted the hot breeze of end-of-summer. Odors that took me a long time to learn to inhale without trembling: green pines, dry soil, thistles, boulders. The road twisted in the foothills, now almost touching them and then retreating. The sea extended to the limit of my vision. Very blue. White light, yellow sun, black road. I closed and opened my eyes and closed them again, wondering which of the sights, smells and sounds to choose from, to which I should let myself become addicted the next moment. Now, at the outskirts of Haifa, a checkpoint: another inspection by British soldiers. The suspense struck me in stomach and throttled my breathing. Fear, dread — the appearance of the checkpoint reminded me of other checkpoints in my life — until the perfunctory wave of a hand said that I could keep going. Relief.

Haifa in midday. Independence Street, the port. Shmuel invited me to lunch at a huge workers' kitchen on the second floor of a building next to the port. My first meal in *Eretz Israel* and I don't remember what I had. Then the central bus terminal: congestion, noise, soot and smoke. We made our way to the bus amidst a mass of Arabs, Jews and Christians, women, men and babies, swerving among peddlers' stalls laden with beverages, sweets and piles of fruit that looked like mountains to me. People called out, shouted, in a jumble of Arabic, Hebrew, Yiddish and English. The bus with its wooden benches, heavy glass windows and metal railings, and the horn that cleared the way. We drove for hours and passed lots of stops. People got on and off carrying suitcases, briefcases, parcels wrapped in cloth, sacks, tins of kerosene and wooden crates. Some of the women wore fragrant embroidered dresses. Some of the men wore turbans drenched in the odor of smoke. Others wore jackets and hats and gave off a faint aroma of naphtha. In the passing scenery, all the smells merged into one.

We arrived. Shmuel and I got off the bus at the entrance to Kibbutz Gan Shmuel. It was almost evening. In the gentle twilight illumination I observed a long road lined with citrus orchards and hedges of acacia and prickly pear and cypress — the golden bulbous fruit of the acacia with its sweet fragrance, the orange fruit of the prickly pear, and the towering cypresses lining the road.

Sunday, September 14, 1947, the eve of Rosh Hashanah. The yard at Gan Shmuel was empty; everyone had gone to the dining hall. Shmuel ushered me in. The festival scene startled me: long tables, white tablecloths and tableware, a profusion of flowers, and lots and lots of people, all in white shirts. The smell of washed bodies and shampooed heads. Brilliant light. I don't know who noticed who first, the children or me, but shouts of joy broke out at once, joined by the patter of running feet, tremendous exuberance and laughter, and limitless clutching and grasping.

I spent two months with them in Gan Shmuel in order to ease their acculturation and alleviate the pain of separation. I spent hours in conversation — with the children, Benio Grünbaum, Tova Tenenbaum the caregiver and members of the kibbutz. I made the children Hashomer Hatzair shirts out of navy blue fabric and slept in the packing house. Throughout that time, I braced myself for the farewell. May my heart not crack, not break. May I be able to embark on my new life. I won't tell the whole story of their acculturation and their lives and aftermath at Gan Shmuel. That's the beginning of another chapter, another book.

The Redeemed

The question of whether we had acted justly in searching for and gathering the children never arose in regard to those who had been liberated from the camps, the partisan children of the forests, the village nomads and the repatriates from the Soviet Union.

In the past few years, however, the question has begun to come up in the context of children who had been reclaimed from non-Jewish families and convents: was it right to uproot children of such tender age, who had been so traumatized and hurled about, from what had become their home, their island of stability in the tempest of those days?

I do not believe the question was posed that way in the spring of 1946. The war was over. Polish Jewry was no more. Jewish children were not seen in the streets. Returning survivors were at risk of dying in pogroms, murders and assaults by antisemitic Poles. We gathered the children because we felt that mortal danger would await them if they remained in Poland. We removed them from Poland because we wished to return them to the bosom of their people even before we knew whether their own families had survived and would come to claim them. We kept them because it seemed unacceptable to allow the few remnants of Polish Jewry to assimilate into Christianity and the Polish nation, which had been accomplices in the Jews' extermination.

Most of the Polish families that had adopted Jewish children or concealed them in their homes risked their lives by doing so. Some provided the youngsters with warm and loving homes. But we approached the matter from a different point of departure: our world had fallen asunder and we considered ourselves the first who would revitalize it. Such were our insights, our choices and our decisions.

Over the years, I have occasionally revisited the question in my encounters with the children. Without exception, they do not believe it would have been right to leave them in Poland with their non-Jewish families. We registered all the children with the Komitet, the Jewish committee in Łódź, so that if their families returned and searched, they would know where to find them. Indeed, a few parents came back alive and reclaimed their children. The people who directed us to the convents and Polish families were relatives, acquaintances or neighbors who had seen the children being handed over or had heard about it. On the basis of that information, we set out to reclaim them.

I don't know whether the children dreamed about the moment when the door of their new family's home would suddenly open and their parents or some other member of their real family would be standing there. I think they entertained such a dream because I did, too. All my life, there has existed in me the expectation of a miracle, of a door that would open, of immeasurable elation. After years, when it became certain that had my parents not been murdered they would have succumbed to old age, I still find myself for split-seconds expecting the door to open and Avramele, Rocheleh or Zipporka to be standing in its frame.

The Children

Marcel Fuchs, aged 6
Reuven Finkelstein, aged 10

Batya Klieg, aged 11
Shoshana Bajman, aged 10
Yoram (Arnold?) Bankier, aged 4
Tamara Friedman, aged 9
Wanda Golembiowska, aged 13
Stefcia (Miriam) Morgenstern, aged 11
Gizia Mebel, aged 6.5
Miecia Michalska, aged 4
Danusia Michalska, aged 5
Sabina Neuberg, aged 13
Lala Ismach (Zosia Newiedowska), aged 7
Shura (Yehoshua) Sturm
Gala (Guta) Sturm
Edek (Aharon) Szuflita, aged 7
Buzio (Benyamin-Jumek) Schwarc, aged 9
Szymek (Szyman) Schwarc, aged 6
Bronja Sosnowska (Sfira) Nagur), aged 9
Waldek-Wladimir (Zeev) Toren, aged 8
Irka Zilberstein, aged 12
Eliabieta Dabinska, aged 8
Fela (Felicia) Rosenberg, aged 11
Ala Rosenberg, aged 14
Julian Rabinowicz, aged 6
Adam Hirszhorn, aged 4
Romek Rosenberg, aged 13
Krysia Medaj (Rachela Kahan), aged 6
Danusia Warszaska, aged 7
Herzl Piereplotczyk, aged 11
Josef Piereplotczyk, aged 8
Tova Piereplotczyk, aged 13
Emanuel Bodniew, aged 8
Zundel (Binyamin) Sadek, aged 13
Miriam Sadek, aged 12
Reuven Sadek, aged 6
Eliahu Jakierewicz, aged 11
Abrasza (Avraham) Jakierewicz, aged 13

Rachel Pszesczeleniec, aged 13
Hanan Pszesczeleniec, aged 12
Riva (Riwkele) Pszesczeleniec, aged 8
Feigele (Zippora) Pszesczeleniec, aged 7
Haviva Ostra, aged 13
Yitzhak Ostra, aged 12
Rina Goldschmit, aged 11
Mordechai Nowak, aged 11
Rosalia (Shoshankeh) Nowak, aged 12
Boris Nowak
Renia Sowinska, aged 12
Yitzhak Sowinski, aged 9 (?)
Genia (Chaya) Orlik, aged 8
Ruthka (Ruth) Alpern, aged 10
Chaim Kaplan, aged 10
Staszek Jwaszczenko, aged 9 (?)
Lusia (Leah) Krupnik
Joske (Josef) Alterwein, aged 13
Shmulik (Shmuel) Krol-Keren, aged 13
Morduch Pozniak, aged 11
Eliahu Pozniak, aged 10
Chasia Pozniak, aged 9
Jenta Pozniak, aged 6
Polcia (Margalit) Szliwinska, aged 12
Leah Weizer, aged 10
Mendel Cohen, aged 14
Rachela Cohen, aged 13
Haviva Cohen, aged 11
Sima Wachs, aged 17
Samuel (Samek) Kestenbaum, aged 14
Yitzhak Saporznikow, aged 11
Rafael Resniker, aged 16
Helenka (Nehama) Teitelbaum, aged 11
Moniek Rosenberg, aged 9
Mordechai (Mottke) Nordman, aged 14
Yaakov Nordman, aged 13

Tova Nordman, aged 13
Eliahu Kaplan
Dov Kaplan
Rina Goldberg

Sala Druker's Children
Stefcia Grosman
Fredzia Studen, aged 9
Anja Lichter, aged 11
Lusia Herzler
Celina Mamet
Marysia Teitelbaum
Leike Slavik
Cyla Rosenblitt

Children Who Joined in Cyprus
Hella Bajder
Szlomo Bajder
Rivka Brodner
Lena Genzel

Joined in Atlit
Dziubek (Shmuel) Rothbard, aged 14

EPILOGUE

I was about to part with the first chapter in my life and cross the threshold to my second. I had to close off some things and open some others. To say goodbye.

I couldn't stay at Gan Shmuel. I had to go. I had become a mother and a sister, a counselor and an educator to the children. Whenever I was around, their hearts and minds had no room for anyone else. From my own standpoint, too, I could not establish a family of my own if they were next door. They had become my family — my siblings and my children — and I needed mental room to build a home of my own and fulfill the dream I had entertained since I was a girl in the Grodno cell of Hashomer Hatzair — to establish a new kibbutz in the Negev or the Galilee.

I spent two months at Gan Shmuel. Heini visited me; I didn't venture out. Only after I parted from the children did I free myself to visit friends, travel around, meet people and start getting to know the country. Before anything else, I took a trip to Gat, Heini's kibbutz. I had never seen a desert before. We had spoken so much about the Negev; it had been the symbol of all our years in the movement. Only now, maybe, did I begin to understand what the Negev was: a long trip through hardly changing scenery — plains, gentle hills, endless yellow and brown dunes, and then, all of a sudden, a kibbutz, a green kibbutz in the heart of the wasteland, like a mirage, a miracle.

The comrades at Gat greeted me with an outpouring of joy, comradeship and warmth. One thing I found immensely attractive was the group of

385

women officials: treasurer, kibbutz secretary, coordinator of the vegetable garden. True equality.

But I wanted to establish a new kibbutz, to be part of an act of genesis, and not to come to a table already set. From my standpoint, Gat was a veteran kibbutz. It already had houses, a dining hall and farm buildings. For so many years I had dreamed about the kibbutz I would establish. I couldn't relinquish my dream.

Sheike and Hannah Weiner invited me to their kibbutz, Ein Hashofet. I spent almost two straight days sleeping in the roomlet that they gave me, intoxicated by the fragrance of the pines, the silence, the birdsong and the sense of total tranquility. For the first time in almost eight years, I had no job of any kind, no affiliation with any organized setting, no commitment to anything. I was so tired and so badly in need of rest. After two days, Hannah couldn't take the suspense: had something happened to me? So she woke me up. That very evening, a group of comrades from the movement in Poland met with me: Sheike and Hannah, Yehoshua Leibner and Luba and Yitzhak Ben-Horin. I sat with them for hours, telling stories, asking questions, conversing.

Heini came, too. The kibbutz members tried to talk us into joining them. I almost agreed. The people, the camaraderie, the forests, the pines, the green before my eyes — I was sorely attracted to them all. However, I wanted to build a kibbutz from the ground up. Then I visited the comrades at Beit Zera. Yehuda Tubin and Zalman and Sonia Winogradow wanted me to stay, but the heat was terrible: the Jordan Valley air sizzled even at night. It was too hard for me.

Miriam Wiszniewski and Yehudit Dworecki had been members of my movement Gdud. Their families had been affluent and could afford to buy them "certificates" and pay for their trip to Palestine. Thus, they had made *aliya* in 1938 under the Youth Aliyah program and enrolled in the agricultural school at Ben Shemen. Both had siblings and relatives who had come before them. Miriam was a close friend. Together we sat in her house and reviewed the list of things she had been asked to bring: bedding, towels, clothing, blankets — an *oyssteuer,* a dowry for *Eretz Israel.*

The autumn of 1947 lasted into the winter. Everything about that season was totally different from the pattern that had been implanted in me: the direction of the wind, the intensity of the light, the leaves that did not turn yellow and fall to the earth, the flocks of birds that arrived and stayed, the fragrance of the soil, the colors of the flowers, the travel of the clouds. Miriam was a member of Kibbutz Lehavot Habashan, a little spot in the Upper Galilee at the base of the Golan Heights. It was cut off from everything; it had no road, no paved path, and no regular transportation. Passengers went as far as Kibbutz Amir and stopped there for the night. In the dark, they signaled in Morse code with a flashlight, and in the morning the kibbutz members would pick them up by sending a tractor or a team of mules across the fields.

Kuka and Tovia Hacohen, members of the movement in Poland who had been repatriated among the "Asians," welcomed me at Amir as though I were a long-lost sister. They cleared their bed for me, served food and drink, signaled in Morse code to Lehavot Habashan, and spoke angrily about the long trip I had taken on unsafe roads, especially a young woman alone. In the morning, David Azolai of Lehavot Habashan came from the kibbutz on mule-back to deliver me to my destination.

I had not ridden on horseback since postwar Grodno. The sight of the mule suddenly reminded me of that beloved activity. "Would you let me ride the mule?" I asked. David acceded and he walked in front of me, gripping the halter.

A lovely day, a gentle autumn sun. From my perch on the mule's back I peered through the translucent blue mist that fell almost to the edge of the valley. I wore the white dress with miniature flowers I had received as a present from Ala's aunt in Dornstadt. Throughout my travels I had not worn it until now. A summer dress was not useful in the German winter. Here, however, in the lengthy summer/autumn, the sense of freedom germinating inside me, it was just the right thing to wear.

The fierce winter rains had not yet fallen. I rode along Wadi Kali, its banks lined with stands of reeds. The water flowed weakly and the compressed trail that crossed it turned into a sludge punctuated by puddles. The mud was in no way extreme, but it was enough to make the mule slip and lose her balance.

I can still picture it as though it were a slow-motion film. The mule skids, her front right leg buckling. She falls on her side, her large body striking the trickle of water. I'm hurled to the ground, the mud and the mucky sediment of vegetation. It was so absurd that I burst into laughter as I tried to wring out the hem of my dress and cleanse it of the grime, branches and leaves that clung to it. I walked the rest of the way, the mule and David at my side. I made it to

Lehavot Habashan drenched, disheveled and spattered with mud. So did the dress.

Miriam was waiting at the gate. The joy of the reunion, the melancholy of the pain, and the sobbing over everything: her parents who had stayed behind in Grodno, her sisters and her extended family, none of whom had survived. I don't know how long we stood there that way, hugging and crying. Afterwards, we turned and walked to a tent. Miriam gave me some dry clothing and laundered mine with cold water and a large brick of soap, grinding the whiteness of the dress into a cylindrical pail in order to remove the mud stains.

An exposed hill at the northeastern slopes of the Huleh Valley. A group of tents surrounded by barbed wire. Black basalt stones. An ancient oak. The tomb of a sheikh. A plum tree, laden with fruit. Stands of dry ferula. Snakes and scorpions. Mid day heat; nighttime chill. Netting against malaria-bearing mosquitoes. Flocks of goats, an Arab village. A wadi. The Golan Heights across the way.

I never thought I'd have a new home to replace the one I'd lost. I believed I could never really start over from scratch. Then, as if I hadn't gone through the chaos, I found my old enthusiasm returning. Suddenly I dreamed again, as if a profound belief had budded inside me that this was the right place to start over.

Heini and I established our home at Kibbutz Lehavot Habashan in the winter of 1947. The mothers and children had gone to the temporary Kibbutz-camp in Karkur; childless girls and young men lived in tents at the location on the hill where the kibbutz would be built. We all worked at clearing the fields of basalt stones and boulders, setting up the farm, performing guard duty, building and planting trees.

We were given a family tent. That was just fine; for years I had dreamed of living this way in the early years. We spent the entire War of Independence at Lehavot Habashan. I was in charge of first aid. Since no one around had medical training, I took care of the casualties — those who survived their injuries and those who did not.

In March 1949, as we awaited the birth of Yehudit, our first-born, I joined the women at the collective in Karkur. In June 1949, everyone returned to Lehavot Habashan. I worked with immigrant youth in the vegetable garden, and opened the first kindergarten at the immigrants' transit camp in Kiryat

Chasia and Heini. Background: the first buildings of Kibbutz Lehavot Habashan, their future home, 1948

Shmona. Our second and third daughters, Raheli and Dorit, were born. Twice Hashomer Hatzair sent us on missions, to South Africa and to France. Our housing improved: from the tent to a shack, and from the shack to a real house. We endured all of Israel's wars at the foothills of the Golan Heights. Lehavot Habashan is a living, breathing kibbutz, perched on its verdant hill. The girls are married; we have eleven grandchildren and six great-grandchildren for the time being.

I went to work at Tel Hai Regional College in 1967 and spent the next twenty years producing and teaching ceramics, heading the ceramics department for some of that time. When it came time to retire, I went home and have ever since been designing and making children's and women's clothing at the kibbutz sewing shop, using the techniques I had learned seventy years ago at ORT in Grodno.